Lecture Notes in Computer Science   12796

More information about this subseries at http://www.springer.com/series/7409

Gavriel Salvendy · June Wei (Eds.)

Design, Operation and Evaluation of Mobile Communications

Second International Conference, MOBILE 2021
Held as Part of the 23rd HCI International Conference, HCII 2021
Virtual Event, July 24–29, 2021
Proceedings

 Springer

Editors
Gavriel Salvendy
University of Central Florida
Orlando, FL, USA

June Wei
College of Business
University of West Florida
Pensacola, FL, USA

ISSN 0302-9743 ISSN 1611-3349 (electronic)
Lecture Notes in Computer Science
ISBN 978-3-030-77024-2 ISBN 978-3-030-77025-9 (eBook)
https://doi.org/10.1007/978-3-030-77025-9

LNCS Sublibrary: SL3 – Information Systems and Applications, incl. Internet/Web, and HCI

This Springer imprint is published by the registered company Springer Nature Switzerland AG
The registered company address is: Gewerbestrasse 11, 6330 Cham, Switzerland

Foreword

Human-Computer Interaction (HCI) is acquiring an ever-increasing scientific and industrial importance, and having more impact on people's everyday life, as an ever-growing number of human activities are progressively moving from the physical to the digital world. This process, which has been ongoing for some time now, has been dramatically accelerated by the COVID-19 pandemic. The HCI International (HCII) conference series, held yearly, aims to respond to the compelling need to advance the exchange of knowledge and research and development efforts on the human aspects of design and use of computing systems.

The 23rd International Conference on Human-Computer Interaction, HCI International 2021 (HCII 2021), was planned to be held at the Washington Hilton Hotel, Washington DC, USA, during July 24–29, 2021. Due to the COVID-19 pandemic and with everyone's health and safety in mind, HCII 2021 was organized and run as a virtual conference. It incorporated the 21 thematic areas and affiliated conferences listed on the following page.

A total of 5222 individuals from academia, research institutes, industry, and governmental agencies from 81 countries submitted contributions, and 1276 papers and 241 posters were included in the proceedings to appear just before the start of the conference. The contributions thoroughly cover the entire field of HCI, addressing major advances in knowledge and effective use of computers in a variety of application areas. These papers provide academics, researchers, engineers, scientists, practitioners, and students with state-of-the-art information on the most recent advances in HCI. The volumes constituting the set of proceedings to appear before the start of the conference are listed in the following pages.

The HCI International (HCII) conference also offers the option of 'Late Breaking Work' which applies both for papers and posters, and the corresponding volume(s) of the proceedings will appear after the conference. Full papers will be included in the 'HCII 2021 - Late Breaking Papers' volumes of the proceedings to be published in the Springer LNCS series, while 'Poster Extended Abstracts' will be included as short research papers in the 'HCII 2021 - Late Breaking Posters' volumes to be published in the Springer CCIS series.

The present volume contains papers submitted and presented in the context of the 2nd International Conference on Design, Operation and Evaluation of Mobile Communications (MOBILE 2021), an affiliated conference to HCII 2021. I would like to thank the Co-chairs, Gavriel Salvendy and June Wei, for their invaluable contribution to its organization and the preparation of the proceedings, as well as the members of the Program Board for their contributions and support. This year, the MOBILE affiliated conference has focused on topics related to the design, development, and evaluation of mobile interaction systems, as well as the user experience, acceptance and impact of mobile communications.

I would also like to thank the Program Board Chairs and the members of the Program Boards of all thematic areas and affiliated conferences for their contribution towards the highest scientific quality and overall success of the HCI International 2021 conference.

This conference would not have been possible without the continuous and unwavering support and advice of Gavriel Salvendy, founder, General Chair Emeritus, and Scientific Advisor. For his outstanding efforts, I would like to express my appreciation to Abbas Moallem, Communications Chair and Editor of HCI International News.

July 2021   Constantine Stephanidis

HCI International 2021 Thematic Areas and Affiliated Conferences

Thematic Areas

- HCI: Human-Computer Interaction
- HIMI: Human Interface and the Management of Information

Affiliated Conferences

- EPCE: 18th International Conference on Engineering Psychology and Cognitive Ergonomics
- UAHCI: 15th International Conference on Universal Access in Human-Computer Interaction
- VAMR: 13th International Conference on Virtual, Augmented and Mixed Reality
- CCD: 13th International Conference on Cross-Cultural Design
- SCSM: 13th International Conference on Social Computing and Social Media
- AC: 15th International Conference on Augmented Cognition
- DHM: 12th International Conference on Digital Human Modeling and Applications in Health, Safety, Ergonomics and Risk Management
- DUXU: 10th International Conference on Design, User Experience, and Usability
- DAPI: 9th International Conference on Distributed, Ambient and Pervasive Interactions
- HCIBGO: 8th International Conference on HCI in Business, Government and Organizations
- LCT: 8th International Conference on Learning and Collaboration Technologies
- ITAP: 7th International Conference on Human Aspects of IT for the Aged Population
- HCI-CPT: 3rd International Conference on HCI for Cybersecurity, Privacy and Trust
- HCI-Games: 3rd International Conference on HCI in Games
- MobiTAS: 3rd International Conference on HCI in Mobility, Transport and Automotive Systems
- AIS: 3rd International Conference on Adaptive Instructional Systems
- C&C: 9th International Conference on Culture and Computing
- MOBILE: 2nd International Conference on Design, Operation and Evaluation of Mobile Communications
- AI-HCI: 2nd International Conference on Artificial Intelligence in HCI

List of Conference Proceedings Volumes Appearing Before the Conference

1. LNCS 12762, Human-Computer Interaction: Theory, Methods and Tools (Part I), edited by Masaaki Kurosu
2. LNCS 12763, Human-Computer Interaction: Interaction Techniques and Novel Applications (Part II), edited by Masaaki Kurosu
3. LNCS 12764, Human-Computer Interaction: Design and User Experience Case Studies (Part III), edited by Masaaki Kurosu
4. LNCS 12765, Human Interface and the Management of Information: Information Presentation and Visualization (Part I), edited by Sakae Yamamoto and Hirohiko Mori
5. LNCS 12766, Human Interface and the Management of Information: Information-rich and Intelligent Environments (Part II), edited by Sakae Yamamoto and Hirohiko Mori
6. LNAI 12767, Engineering Psychology and Cognitive Ergonomics, edited by Don Harris and Wen-Chin Li
7. LNCS 12768, Universal Access in Human-Computer Interaction: Design Methods and User Experience (Part I), edited by Margherita Antona and Constantine Stephanidis
8. LNCS 12769, Universal Access in Human-Computer Interaction: Access to Media, Learning and Assistive Environments (Part II), edited by Margherita Antona and Constantine Stephanidis
9. LNCS 12770, Virtual, Augmented and Mixed Reality, edited by Jessie Y. C. Chen and Gino Fragomeni
10. LNCS 12771, Cross-Cultural Design: Experience and Product Design Across Cultures (Part I), edited by P. L. Patrick Rau
11. LNCS 12772, Cross-Cultural Design: Applications in Arts, Learning, Well-being, and Social Development (Part II), edited by P. L. Patrick Rau
12. LNCS 12773, Cross-Cultural Design: Applications in Cultural Heritage, Tourism, Autonomous Vehicles, and Intelligent Agents (Part III), edited by P. L. Patrick Rau
13. LNCS 12774, Social Computing and Social Media: Experience Design and Social Network Analysis (Part I), edited by Gabriele Meiselwitz
14. LNCS 12775, Social Computing and Social Media: Applications in Marketing, Learning, and Health (Part II), edited by Gabriele Meiselwitz
15. LNAI 12776, Augmented Cognition, edited by Dylan D. Schmorrow and Cali M. Fidopiastis
16. LNCS 12777, Digital Human Modeling and Applications in Health, Safety, Ergonomics and Risk Management: Human Body, Motion and Behavior (Part I), edited by Vincent G. Duffy
17. LNCS 12778, Digital Human Modeling and Applications in Health, Safety, Ergonomics and Risk Management: AI, Product and Service (Part II), edited by Vincent G. Duffy

38. CCIS 1420, HCI International 2021 Posters - Part II, edited by Constantine Stephanidis, Margherita Antona, and Stavroula Ntoa
39. CCIS 1421, HCI International 2021 Posters - Part III, edited by Constantine Stephanidis, Margherita Antona, and Stavroula Ntoa

http://2021.hci.international/proceedings

2nd International Conference on Design, Operation and Evaluation of Mobile Communications (MOBILE 2021)

Program Board Chairs: **Gavriel Salvendy**, *University of Central Florida, USA* **and June Wei**, *University of West Florida, USA*

- Štefan Bojnec, Slovakia
- Su Mon Chit, Malaysia
- Dhanapal Durai Dominic, Malaysia
- Zhongwei Gu, China
- Dedi Inan, Indonesia
- P. S. JosephNg, Malaysia
- Mitsuru Kodama, Japan
- Kai Koong, USA
- Taowen Le, USA
- Caihong Liu, China
- Manlu Liu, USA
- Andy Lu, USA
- Alok Mishra, Turkey
- Kongkiti Phusavat, Thailand
- Bharat S. Rawal Kshatriya, USA
- Omair Shafiq, Canada
- Sharon Mirella Wakhu, Kenya
- Fuhong Wang, China
- Jiaqin Yang, USA
- Shuiqing Yang, China
- Lifan Yang, China
- Peiyan Zhou, China

The full list with the Program Board Chairs and the members of the Program Boards of all thematic areas and affiliated conferences is available online at:

http://www.hci.international/board-members-2021.php

HCI International 2022

The 24th International Conference on Human-Computer Interaction, HCI International 2022, will be held jointly with the affiliated conferences at the Gothia Towers Hotel and Swedish Exhibition & Congress Centre, Gothenburg, Sweden, June 26 – July 1, 2022. It will cover a broad spectrum of themes related to Human-Computer Interaction, including theoretical issues, methods, tools, processes, and case studies in HCI design, as well as novel interaction techniques, interfaces, and applications. The proceedings will be published by Springer. More information will be available on the conference website: http://2022.hci.international/:

General Chair
Prof. Constantine Stephanidis
University of Crete and ICS-FORTH
Heraklion, Crete, Greece
Email: general_chair@hcii2022.org

http://2022.hci.international/

Contents

User Experience, Acceptance and Impact of Mobile Communications

Designing, Developing and Evaluating Mobile Interaction Systems

Design of Customer Satisfaction Evaluation System Based on Big Data

Long Cheng, Jing Cao, and Zhongwei Gu[✉]

Shanghai Dianji University, Pudong, Shanghai, China

Abstract. The traditional customer satisfaction evaluation adopts the method of questionnaire survey, small data samples are subjective, which can not truly reflect the level of customer satisfaction. Using big data analysis technology, combined with questionnaire statistical analysis, is a useful attempt. On the basis of previous research results, this paper innovates and integrates, designs a set of customer satisfaction evaluation and management system based on big data, gives the technical architecture and function map of the system, and describes the big data mining analysis method. In the follow-up research, the system will be more in-depth research and application development.

Keywords: Customer satisfaction · CSE · Big data

1 Introduction

Customers are the most scarce resources of enterprises. How to improve customer satisfaction and loyalty has become the focus of enterprises. The premise of improving customer satisfaction is to measure customer satisfaction, so as to take targeted measures to improve customer satisfaction [1].

At present, many researches on customer satisfaction are carried out by using customer satisfaction measurement model, questionnaire and other methods. When measuring customer satisfaction, the respondents may have subjective feelings, which leads to the distortion of the questionnaire and can not correctly reflect the customer satisfaction. Moreover, the number of questionnaire samples collected by the questionnaire method is relatively small, and there will be a certain lack of persuasion and credibility. In addition, with more and more factors affecting customer satisfaction, the customer satisfaction measurement model cannot fully adapt to the needs of the current enterprises. So as to meet the requirements of rapid and efficient measurement of customer satisfaction, customer satisfaction evaluation and management system based on big data came into being.

This study aims to build a customer satisfaction evaluation and management system based on big data. This system can be used in online retail platform, telecommunications industry, power industry, mobile communication field, employee satisfaction, government public opinion supervision and other scenarios. The system tests and evaluates the real satisfaction level of customers by analyzing the business data of customer center,

© Springer Nature Switzerland AG 2021
G. Salvendy and J. Wei (Eds.): HCII 2021, LNCS 12796, pp. 3–10, 2021.
https://doi.org/10.1007/978-3-030-77025-9_1

external product comment crawler data and data collected by some hardware devices. In this way, the enterprise can provide better products and services according to the current situation of customer satisfaction. Meanwhile, it is also conducive to the enterprise to strengthen the continuous innovation of its own products, so as to better improve customer satisfaction and loyalty.

2   Literature Review

2.1   Review of Foreign Literature

The word customer satisfaction is translated into English as customer satisfaction, which was introduced into the field of customer satisfaction marketing by American scholar cordozo in 1965. His research found that high customer satisfaction will increase the probability of customers buying again [2]. Westbrook Robert A (1980) and Oliver (1980) believed that after consumption, customers would compare their pre-purchase psychological expectations of products or services with their actual feelings after purchase. If the products or services did not meet their pre-purchase psychological expectations, customers would be dissatisfied; otherwise, they would be satisfied [3, 4]. According to Churchill and Supreme (1982), customer satisfaction is a cognitive state produced by buyers comparing the return of expected results with input costs [5]. Bolton and drew (1991) believe that customer satisfaction is obtained by comparing the measured expectation of the product or service with the actual perception after purchase, and it will further affect the service quality [6]. Most of the above researches on customer satisfaction are from a qualitative perspective to study the relationship between various variables.

On the basis of qualitative research, some foreign scholars began quantitative research. In the research of customer satisfaction model, Sweden conducted the first customer satisfaction test in the world. In 1989, Sweden adopted a national satisfaction survey tool (SCSB) [1]. After that, the theoretical results of this study were summarized by Professor Fornell of the University of Michigan, and the earliest customer satisfaction index model was proposed, as shown in Fig. 1.

Fig. 1. Sweden Customer Satisfaction Barometer(SCSB)[7]

Professor Fornell (1996) established the American ACSI model based on the SCSB model, as shown in Fig. 2. Different from SCSB model, this model adds the variable of perceived quality to analyze whether customers' purchasing behavior is driven by price or quality. On the basis of inheriting the basic structure of ACSI model, European quality organization and European Commission have made two modifications. On the one hand, the variable of corporate image is added to expand the application range of the satisfaction index model, so that the satisfaction index can be applied to different enterprises, industries and even countries for comparison [8].

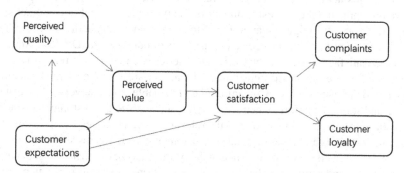

Fig. 2. American Customer Satisfaction Index (ACSI) [7]

2.2 Domestic Literature Review

The study of customer satisfaction in China started relatively late, which may be greatly related to the level of economic development in China. In the past decade, many scholars have studied the theory of customer satisfaction, and these studies are also fruitful. Since 1998, Chinese experts have introduced the theory of customer satisfaction evaluation, and also carried out the construction of service quality evaluation index system model in practice. The main research status is as follows

Yongqing Wang and Haoren Yan (2000) draw lessons from the theoretical research of customer satisfaction abroad and build the customer satisfaction evaluation system, which has a strong practical value [9]. Yu Liu (2001) proposed the comprehensive application of customer satisfaction evaluation system for general industries on the basis of SCSB model. His research mainly focuses on the evaluation method of customer satisfaction [10]. Meihua Zhou (2004) constructed the index system of customer loyalty and established the customer loyalty evaluation model [11]. Xiangyang Liu (2005) analyzed the relationship between quality investment and marketing decisions from the perspective of customer profitability and customer satisfaction [12]. Xiangcui Wang (2006) constructed the evaluation index tree model of customer satisfaction of port logistics system [13].

Although these studies in China have made some achievements, they are not perfect, and need the continuous efforts of a large number of scholars and experts. Only when the theoretical knowledge is applied to some enterprises, can the two complement each other. In this way, our country's customer satisfaction research can get vigorous development. At present, in terms of customer satisfaction, because the method has a certain representativeness in the world, it is relatively perfect, so this method has also been widely used in China.

2.3 Summary of Research at Home and Abroad

Comprehensive domestic and foreign research review can be found that foreign research on customer satisfaction started earlier, the research scope is wide, the research problems are more in-depth, and the earliest summary of the theoretical model of customer satisfaction, the theory of foreign research, for us to do customer satisfaction research has a good reference significance, can be used as the basis of our research. Domestic research on customer satisfaction started relatively late, the research content is relatively small, but because these researches on customer satisfaction are based on China's national conditions, so the results are very meaningful and valuable, and also very worthy of our reference and study. Therefore, when we research and analyze the customer satisfaction of domestic enterprises, we must refer to the relevant foreign theories and index models, and refer to the results and cases of domestic customer satisfaction research. Only in this way can we combine theory with practice to study and analyze the customer satisfaction of the enterprise, and truly study the customer satisfaction of our enterprises in place, so as to find out the true customer satisfaction According to the characteristics of Chinese customers and domestic companies, it puts forward targeted measures to maximize the company's customer satisfaction and make the research content and results convincing and credible.

In addition to the above findings, we also found that whether domestic or foreign literature, most of the literature is about the measurement of customer satisfaction and satisfaction model research, there is no research based on big data customer satisfaction evaluation management system. This article starts the first study of customer satisfaction evaluation and management system based on big data.

3 System Design

3.1 Technical Framework

The system is based on cloud computing +Hadoop big data platform, which is grouped into six levels, namely platform management, data analysis layer, programming model layer, data storage layer, file storage layer and data integration layer. The back end of application layer adopts Linux (Windows) + Apache (Nginx) + MySQL + J2EE + PHP; the clients support app, miniprogram, H5 (Fig. 3).

3.2 Function Map

This system has four main functions, which are data collection, satisfaction evaluation, satisfaction promotion and system management (Fig. 4).

The data collection function mainly completes the data collection of traditional online questionnaire survey system, customer service business data collection from call center, external data collection based on crawler technology and related data collection based

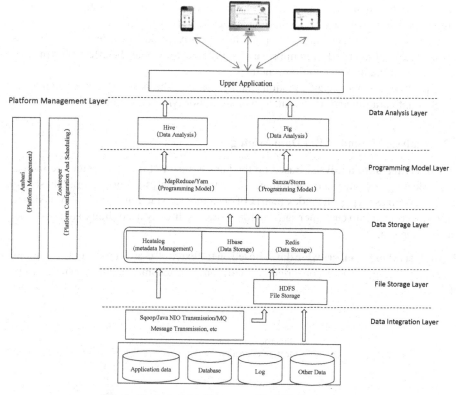

Fig. 3. Technical Architecture of B-CSE System [14]

Fig. 4. Function Map of B-CSE

on intelligent hardware devices. This function module is the data base of customer satisfaction evaluation.

Satisfaction evaluation function is the core of the system, in addition to using the traditional questionnaire statistical analysis to evaluate satisfaction, the most core function of this system is to use big data mining analysis to evaluate satisfaction. It includes the establishment of customer satisfaction evaluation score based on business type by analyzing business data and business type of call center; the establishment of customer satisfaction score mapping conversion matrix by text mining and web mining through external crawler data; and the collection and analysis of customer satisfaction index based on intelligent hardware, such as wearable watch/Bracelet Points.

Satisfaction enhancement function module, mainly based on the results of satisfaction evaluation, targeted design improvement scheme, as well as the effect tracking and monitoring of the implementation scheme.

The system management function mainly includes the basic data management of system configuration and operation, as well as authority/user/role management.

3.3 Analysis Method of Big Data Mining

1. Call center data analysis. Based on the business data of the call center, the indicators reflecting customer satisfaction are extracted for analysis. For example, based on different business types, the index matrix of customer satisfaction score is designed, and then transformed into customer satisfaction score. Or directly according to the customer satisfaction score.

2. Analysis of external crawler data. Based on the external crawler data for text mining, web page mining, and then converted into a response to customer satisfaction index value (Fig. 5).

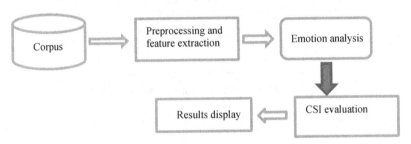

Fig. 5. Big Data Mining Flow Chart [15]

The figure shows a schedule of the text data mining based on external crawler data when the system implements customer satisfaction evaluation. The first step is to screen the existing corpus, through which the problems that need to be solved can be clearly defined. Then the data preprocessing and feature extraction, including checking the integrity and consistency of the data, filling the missing domain, deleting invalid data, after the above procedures, according to the system settings for intelligent feature extraction, the next step is to process the data for sentiment analysis, after sentiment analysis, the system will analyze the group characteristics according to the classified data, and finally the group characteristics will be extracted The results are displayed, including the results of emotion analysis and theme analysis.

3. Hardware acquisition data analysis. Based on the active data collected by intelligent hardware devices or the log of device usage, the big data analysis is carried out, and the index factors that indirectly reflect or affect customer satisfaction are extracted for customer satisfaction evaluation and analysis.

4 Conclusions

Based on the research on customer satisfaction at home and abroad, this paper summarizes and considers the existing literature, puts forward the idea of customer satisfaction evaluation and management system based on big data, and describes the system's technical framework, functional mapping, and big data mining analysis methods. Both from the current economic development situation and market demand, customer satisfaction measurement system based on the big data application prospects are very broad, modern society needs a customer satisfaction measurement based on large data management system, the system's efficiency, convenience and other features to meet the needs of enterprises, reduce the cost of enterprise.

Build a customer satisfaction measurement management system based on big data can greatly reduce the cost of measuring customer satisfaction, and can measure customer satisfaction quickly and efficiently.

Through the construction of customer satisfaction evaluation system, customer satisfaction evaluation will be more systematic, systematic and complete. In addition, the system can be used in multiple scenarios and has strong scalability.

The research of customer satisfaction measurement management system based on big data makes up for the previous blank in this field, creates a new research field, and provides a research reference for future scholars.

References

1. Wang, X.: Customer satisfaction analysis of Fuji Xerox. Huazhong Agricultural University (2013)
2. Cardozo, R.M.: An experimental study of consumer, expectation and satisfaction. J. Mark. Res. **2**, 244–249 (1965)
3. Westbrook, R.A.: Intrapersonal affective influences on consumer satisfaction with products. J. Consum. Res. **7**, 49–54 (1980)
4. Oliver, R.L.: A cognitive model of the antecedents and consequences of satisfaction decisions. J. Market. Res. **17**, 460–469 (1980)
5. Churchill, G.A., Suprenant, C.: An investigation into the detaninants of custaner satisfaction. J. Market. Res. **19**, 491–504 (1982)
6. Bolton, R.N., Drew, J.H.: A multistage model of customers assessments service quality and of value. J. Consum. Res. **17**, 375–384 (1991)
7. Zhou, Q.: Research on customer satisfaction model system and application of telecom enterprises. Beijing University of Posts and telecommunications (2007)
8. Wang, M.: Research on online retail customer satisfaction from the perspective of big data. China University of Geosciences (Beijing) (2020)
9. Wang, Y., Yan, H.: Evaluation of customer satisfaction. Econ. Manage. **08**, 36–38 (2000)
10. Sun, C.: Research on the application of internet of things in smart home. Comput. Program. Skills Maint. **09**, 134–135 + 138 (2020)
11. Zhou, M.: Measurement of customer loyalty and its empirical research. Sci. Technol. Guide **12**, 48–52 (2004)
12. Liu, X.: Nonlinear and trap analysis of "satisfaction profit" chain. Shangxun, Bus. Econ. **05**, 66–68 (2005)
13. Wang, X.: Research on customer satisfaction of port logistics enterprises. Sci. Nd Technol. Econ. Market **12**, 202 (2006)

14. Borthakur, D.: Hadoop distributed file system: Architecture and design [EB/OL]. Apache Software Foundation. http://hadoop.apache.org/docs/r1.0.4/cn/hdfs_design.html
15. Zhu, L., Zou, W.: Research on the construction of big data platform of tourist satisfaction based on Hadoop. Inf. Recording Mater. (7) (2020)

The Evaluation Framework for Wearable Devices Service Quality Based on SERVQUAL Model

Youxiang Cui, Haibo Tang[✉], and Zhongwei Gu

Shanghai Dianji University, Pudong, Shanghai, China

Abstract. Service quality is increasingly recognized as being of key strategic value by organizations in both the wearable devices manufacturing and service sector. With the development of wearable devices technology, how to improve service quality becomes hot topic for wearable devices providers. This paper studies on the service quality of wearable devices based on the SERVQUAL model and establishes the assessment system to explore the factors influencing wearable devices service quality.

Keywords: Wearable device · Service quality evaluation model · SERVQUAL model

1 Introduction

Wearable Technology refers to items of clothing or accessories further improved by using electronics, intended for information or entertainment purposes. This type of technology is usually attached to the body and can be used to monitor information about users and their surroundings. Wearable Technology is different from mobile phones and is designed to be imperceptible for everyday use [1].

During the past few decades, wearable devices service quality has become a major area of attention by practitioners, managers and researchers owing to its strong impact on financial performance, costs, user satisfaction, customer loyalty and profitability. As a result, there has been continued research on wearable devices definitions, modeling, measurements, data collection procedures, data analyses etc.

With the rapid development of information technology and big data, the rising pace of the emerging industry of wearable devices is also accelerating, and further driving the growth of its service applications [2]. Service application as a direct contact with users of the channel, the level of service quality directly affects the satisfaction of the application. As the core concept of modern quality management, customer satisfaction has become a key factor for organizations to gain competitive advantage and ensure sustainable and stable development [3, 4]. At present, the market penetration of service applications of wearable devices is getting higher and higher. Naturally, users' overall satisfaction and service quality will directly affect consumers' purchase sentiment, and even indirectly affect the overall loss of customers. Therefore, it is of great practical

© Springer Nature Switzerland AG 2021
G. Salvendy and J. Wei (Eds.): HCII 2021, LNCS 12796, pp. 11–18, 2021.
https://doi.org/10.1007/978-3-030-77025-9_2

significance to study the application satisfaction of wearable device service [1]. On the basis of related theories, this paper constructs the satisfaction index model. From the perspective of user satisfaction evaluation of service applications of wearable devices, a set of theory and method of satisfaction evaluation of service applications of wearable devices is established according to the characteristics of service applications of wearable devices [5].

2   Literature Review

Quality models emerged in the late 1970s, as a result of numerous studies proposing concepts, operationalizations and systematization for quality services. Already the subjectivity present in the perception of quality is being incorporate through different approaches and their consequences [6].

2.1   Wearable Devices Service Quality Evaluation System of China Mobile

China Mobile Test Center forms the final service quality evaluation system with more than 20 communication manufacturers in the industry chain. as shown in Fig. 1.

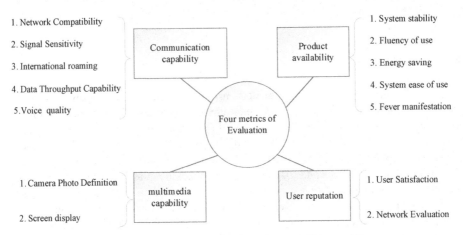

Fig. 1. Service quality evaluation system of China mobile

Based on the research of service perception and service expectation, the metrics of Evaluation can be concluded into four categories: product availability, user reputation, communication capability and multimedia capability.

Product availability (PA): The probability that an item will operate satisfactorily at a given point in time when used under stated conditions in an ideal support environment. It excludes time for waiting or downtime, and preventive maintenance downtime [7].

(PA1) System stability [8]: A system is said to be stable, if its output is under control. Otherwise, it is said to be unstable. A stable system produces a bounded output for a given bounded input.

(PA2) Fluency of use: the quality or state of being fluent for use.

(PA3) Energy saving: the effort made to reduce the consumption of energy by using less of an energy service. This can be achieved either by using energy more efficiently (using less energy for a constant service) or by reducing the amount of service used (for example, by driving less).

(PA4) System easy to use: takes less time to accomplish a particular task or easier to learn—operation can be learned by observing the object.

(PA5) Fever manifestation: Fever detection easy.

User reputation (UP): allow users to rate each other in online communities in order to build trust through reputation.

(UP1) User satisfaction: the opinion of the user about a specific wearable device's application.

(UP2) Network evaluation: a systematic online survey of determining the value/worth of a wearable device.

Communication capability (CC): is the fundamental Communicate capability within the network.

(CC1) Network capability: intent to achieve enhanced satisfaction through the better use of wearable devices towards the goal of "right information, right place, right time – and not too much".

(CC2) Signal sensitivity: is the minimum magnitude of input signal required to produce a specified output signal having a specified signal-to-noise ratio, or other specified criteria.

(CC3) International roaming: have mutual roaming agreements that basically allow you to use their wireless network when traveling abroad. Generally you do not need to do anything.

(CC4) Data throughput capability: is the valuable information for assessing network performance which tells you how much data was transferred from a source at any given time and how much data could theoretically be transferred from a source at any given time.

(CC5) Voice quality: full digital technology instead of the existing analog technology will be adopted to improve clarity in both the clear and encrypted modes of operation [9].

Multimedia capability (MC): new capability can be included in the online multimedia content.

(MC1) Camera Photo definition: the image size as the number of pixels it contains, typically as 'width × height'.

(MC2) Screen display: an image superimposed on a screen picture, commonly used by wearable devices.

2.2 SERVQUAL Model

As a multi-dimensional research instrument, SERVQUAL is designed to capture user expectations and perceptions of a service along the five dimensions that are believed to represent service quality [10].

Five dimensions of SERVQUAL Model were [11];

1. Tangibility: the appearance of physical facilities, equipment, personnel and communication materials
2. Reliability: ability to perform the promised service dependably and accurately.
3. Responsiveness: willingness to help customers and provide prompt service.
4. Assurance: the knowledge and courtesy of employees and their ability to convey trust and confidence.
5. Empathy: caring individualized attention the firm provides to its customers.

SERVQUAL Dimensions/Items

Tangibles (TA)

TA1 have up-to-date equipment.

TA2 Physical facilities are virtually appealing.

TA3 Employees are well dressed and appear neat.

TA4 Physical environment is clean.

Reliability (RL)

RL1 When they promise to do something by a certain time, they do it.

RL2 When customer has a problem, they should show sincere interest in solving the problem.

RL3 perform the service right the first time.

RL4 provide their services at the time they promise to do so.

RL5 keep their records accurately.

Responsiveness (RN)

RN1 make information easily obtainable by customers.

RN2 give prompt services to customers.

RN3 always willing to help customers.

RN4 never too busy to respond to customers' requests.

Assurance (AS)

AS1 The behavior of employees instill confidence in customers.

AS2 Customers feel safe in their transactions with the employees.

AS3 Employees are polite to customers.

AS4 Employees have knowledge to answer customers' questions.

Empathy (EM)

EM1 give customers individual attention.

EM2 Operating hours is convenient to customers.

EM3 Employees give customers personal service.

EM4 have their customers' interest at heart.

EM5 Employees understand the specific needs of their customers.

3   Evaluation Framework Based on SERVQUAL Model

Wearable devices service quality has become a significant differentiator and the most powerful competitive weapon that all wearable devices producer seeks to possess [12]. For a wearable devices producer to gain competitive advantage in terms of service quality, it must use technology to gather information on market demand and exchange information between wearable devices producer for the purpose of enhancing service quality [13].

Measuring the quality of a wearable devices service can be a very difficult exercise [14]. Unlike product, a service can have numerous intangibles or qualitative specifications. SERVQUAL is the best known and most used scale measuring service quality in a wide variety of service environments. The customers' service quality evaluation is part

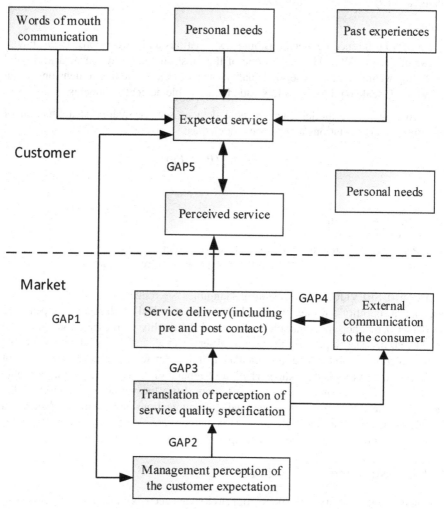

Fig. 2. Five quality gaps of service quality evaluation

of the SERVQUAL analysis, understanding how wearable devices processes contribute to this evaluation is the key to providing consumer driven quality assessment. Thus, the model is based on the notion of minimizing the five quality gaps [15] as shown in Fig. 2.

These gaps include the:

(GAP1) Difference between consumer expectations and wearable devices perceptions of consumer expectations;

(GAP2) Difference between wearable devices perceptions of consumer expectations and service quality specifications;

(GAP3) Difference between service quality specifications and the service actually delivered;

(GAP4) Difference between wearable devices service delivery and what is communicated about the service to customers;

and

(GAP5) Difference between customer expectations and perceptions. Even though the use of the SERVQUAL scale is one of the most efficient ways of measuring and controlling wearable devices service quality, the research on the five dimensions of the SERVQUAL scale on the consumers' side for wearable devices is nonexistent.

According to the model, the wearable devices service quality is a function of perception and expectations and can be modeled as:

$$SQ = \sum_{j=1}^{k} (P_{ij} - E_{ij})$$

where:

SQ = overall service quality;
k = number of attributes.
Pij = Performance perception of stimulus i with respect to attribute j.
Eij = Service quality expectation for attribute j that is the relevant norm for stimulus i.

The first SERVQUAL dimension of "tangibles" is reflected in the categories for "product availability". Rather than looking at the physical facilities and appearance of contact personnel, the wearable devices and the quality of presentation should be considered. In order to perform the promised service, the "reliability" dimension, the " communication capability and multimedia capability" of wearable devices in terms of the promised services is examined. The " user reputation " also requires the wearable devices to provide clear usage to the customers. With the variety of material on the wearable devices in terms of informational, communications and commercial sites and the virtual nature of online business it is sometimes more difficult to determine the purpose of a purely wearable devices company than a traditional business storefront [6].

4   Discussion and Conclusions

To conclude, the mobility of the population, as a social need, is one of the most important factors to the development.

Wearable devices service quality is determined by the value that the wearable devices service brings to both the wearable devices service provider and its customers [16], but service value is not measured in most wearable devices service organizations today. We describe the wearable devices service quality measurement framework and the evaluation of the framework in the wearable devices service industry. The paper focuses on the universal framework the proposed wearable devices service quality measurement framework in industry as well as the importance and feasibility of measuring and interlinking various wearable devices service quality aspects. An important finding is that although most respondents recognize the importance of wearable devices service value, very few providers measure the value of their wearable device's services. The findings also support the importance of taking a systemic approach to wearable devices service measurement. Various service areas are inter-linked: wearable devices service stability impacts on customer satisfaction, and process performance affects wearable devices service stability.

Further research should be carried out in order to investigate the understanding of the concepts of wearable devices service quality and customer satisfaction, how they are measured because they are very important for wearable devices organizations in terms of profitability and growth. A similar study could be conducted with a larger sample size analysis so that results could be generalized to a larger population. Similar study is recommended to other areas including the impact of poor support to the quality evaluation, the impact of regulatory policies to quality evaluation and the impact of quality evaluation strategies to the user satisfaction levels.

References

1. Segura Anaya, L.H., Alsadoon, A., Costadopoulos, N., Prasad, P.W.C.: Ethical implications of user perceptions of wearable devices. Sci. Eng. Ethics **24**(1), 1–28 (2018). https://doi.org/10.1007/s11948-017-9872-8
2. Bhushan, D., Agrawal, R.: Security challenges for designing wearable and IoT solutions. In: Balas, Valentina E., Solanki, V.K., Kumar, R., Ahad, Md.A.R. (eds.) A Handbook of Internet of Things in Biomedical and Cyber Physical System. ISRL, vol. 165, pp. 109–138. Springer, Cham (2020). https://doi.org/10.1007/978-3-030-23983-1_5
3. Khakurel, J., Porras, J., Melkas, H., Fu, B.: A comprehensive framework of usability issues related to the wearable devices. In: Paiva, S., Paul, S. (eds.) Convergence of ICT and Smart Devices for Emerging Applications. EICC, pp. 21–66. Springer, Cham (2020). https://doi.org/10.1007/978-3-030-41368-2_2
4. Seth, N., Deshmukh, S.G., Vrat, P.: Service quality models: a review. Int. J. Q. Reliab. Manage. **22**(9), 913–949 (2005). https://doi.org/10.1108/02656710510625211
5. La Rotta, D., Usuga, O.C., Clavijo, V.: Perceived service quality factors in online higher education. Learn. Environ. Res. **23**(2), 251–267 (2020). https://doi.org/10.1007/s10984-019-09299-6
6. Pena, M.M., Silva, E.M.S.D., Tronchin, D.M.R., Melleiro, M.M.: The use of the quality model of Parasuraman, Zeithaml and Berry in health services. Rev. Esc. Enferm. Usp. **47**(5), 1227–1232 (2013). https://doi.org/10.1590/S0080-623420130000500030
7. Glossary of Defense Acquisition Acronyms and Terms .Department of Defense. Archived from the original on 13 April 2014. Retrieved 10 April 2014.: Glossary of Defense Acquisition Acronyms and Terms. Department of Defense. Archived from the original on 13 April 2014. Accessed 10 Apr 2014

8. Los', G.A.: Stability, asymptotic and exponential stability of a linear differential system. Ukr. Math. J+ **30**(1), 80–83 (1978). https://doi.org/10.1007/bf01130637

9. CAPITAL WORKS RESERVE FUND HEAD 708 - CAPITAL SUBVENTIONS AND MAJOR SYSTEMS AND EQUIPMENT Hong Kong Police Force New Subhead "Replacement of the Radio System of the Operations Wing of the Hong Kong Police Force"

10. Parasuraman, A, Ziethaml, V., Berry, L.L., SERVQUAL: a multiple- item scale for measuring consumer perceptions of service quality. J. Retail. **62**(1), 12–40 (1985)

11. Munthiu, M., Velicu, B.C., Tuţă, M., Zara, A.I.: Service quality evaluation models determined by online consumer perception and satisfaction. Procedia – Soc. Behav. Sci. **109**, 1303–1308 (2014). https://doi.org/10.1016/j.sbspro.2013.12.629

12. Gao, S., Zhang, X., Peng, S.: Understanding the adoption of smart wearable devices to assist healthcare in China. In: Dwivedi, Y.K., et al. (eds.) I3E 2016. LNCS, vol. 9844, pp. 280–291. Springer, Cham (2016). https://doi.org/10.1007/978-3-319-45234-0_26

13. Degerli, M., Ozkan Yildirim, S.: Identifying critical success factors for wearable medical devices: a comprehensive exploration. Univ. Access Inf. (2020). https://doi.org/10.1007/s10209-020-00763-2

14. Brentari, E., Di Battista, T., Crocetta, C., Simonetti, B.: New challenges for services quality evaluation. Qual. Quant. **53**(5), 2273 (2019). https://doi.org/10.1007/s11135-019-00890-w

15. Jureta, I.J., Herssens, C., Faulkner, S.: A comprehensive quality model for service-oriented systems. Software Qual. J. **17**(1), 65–98 (2009). https://doi.org/10.1007/s11219-008-9059-2

16. Aleksy, M., Rissanen, M.J.: Utilizing wearable computing in industrial service applications. J. Amb. Intell. Hum. Comp. **5**(4), 443–454 (2014). https://doi.org/10.1007/s12652-012-0114-2

Customer Satisfaction Evaluation Method Based on Big Data

Zhongwei Gu[1], Youxiang Cui[1(✉)], Haibo Tang[1], and Xiao Liu[2]

[1] Shanghai Dianji University, Pudong, Shanghai, China
[2] Xiamen University of Technology, Xiamen, Fujian, China
`xliu@xmut.edu.cn`

Abstract. The traditional data of satisfaction evaluation comes from questionnaire survey, however, the accuracy and objectivity need to be strengthened, the practical application value is limited. The output of the research is usually the result of satisfaction evaluation, but the deep reasons of low customer satisfaction are not deeply explored. The purpose of this study is to propose a new customer satisfaction evaluation method system based on big data. According to different data collection methods, three evaluation methods are proposed, namely business big data evaluation, crawler big data evaluation, hardware big data evaluation and so on, to test and evaluate the real customer satisfaction level. These methods are helpful for enterprises to strengthen innovation, so as to improve customer satisfaction and loyalty.

Keywords: Satisfaction evaluation · Big data · Text mining · Emotion analysis

1 Introduction

Traditional customer satisfaction research mainly includes customer satisfaction model research and model application research. In the aspect of satisfaction evaluation, there are five kinds of commonly used evaluation models [1]. (1) The Quadrant Model (2) Analytic Hierarchy Process Model (3) Customer Satisfaction Index Model, including ACSI, ECSI, CCSI, etc. (4) Service Quality Model (5) Carnot Model. In the specific quantitative evaluation algorithm, there are mainly Network Analytic Hierarchy Process, Fuzzy Integral Method, Fuzzy Entropy, BP Neural Network and so on [2].The data of satisfaction evaluation usually comes from questionnaire survey, however the accuracy and objectivity need to be strengthened, the practical application value is limited. The output of the research is usually the result of satisfaction evaluation, but the deep reasons of low customer satisfaction are not deeply explored. With more and more factors affecting customer satisfaction, customer satisfaction measurement model can not fully meet

G. Salvendy and J. Wei (Eds.): HCII 2021, LNCS 12796, pp. 19–26, 2021.
https://doi.org/10.1007/978-3-030-77025-9_3

the needs of enterprises. In order to meet the requirements of rapid and efficient measurement of customer satisfaction, customer satisfaction measurement method based on big data came into being.

The purpose of this study is to propose a new customer satisfaction evaluation method system based on big data. The system can be used in online retail platform, telecom industry, power industry, mobile communication, exhibition service industry and other fields. The system tests and evaluates the real satisfaction level of customers by analyzing the business data of customer service center, external product comment crawler data and hardware equipment collection data. In this way, enterprises can provide better products and services according to the current situation of customer satisfaction, and also help enterprises to strengthen the continuous innovation of their products, so as to better improve customer satisfaction and loyalty.

2   Customer Satisfaction Evaluation Methods Based on Big Data

There are many factors affecting customer satisfaction. Big data evaluation and analysis method helps to find some objective factors and explore the deep-seated reasons. At the same time, big data analysis technology itself has certain difficulty and complexity. According to the organization scope, it can be divided into internal business big data evaluation and external intelligence big data evaluation; According to the time dimension, it can be divided into historical big data evaluation and current big data evaluation; According to the different data collection methods, it can be divided into business big data evaluation, crawler big data evaluation, hardware big data evaluation, etc. This paper mainly discusses the big data evaluation method of customer satisfaction according to the way of data collection.

2.1   Based on Business Big Data Evaluation

Business data related to customer satisfaction covers a wide range, but customer service center is undoubtedly the most direct channel to contact customers, and its business data can often directly reflect the level of customer satisfaction. Therefore, this paper takes customer service center as an example to discuss customer satisfaction evaluation based on business big data.

The business types of customer service center include user complaints, user consultation, user direct evaluation, and after-sales maintenance. Therefore, based on the business data of the customer service center, it is a very effective way to extract indicators reflecting customer satisfaction for analysis. The following table gives the classification of customer satisfaction evaluation methods of customer service center.

Table 1. Satisfaction evaluation method based on big data of customer service center [2]

Business type	Satisfaction tendency	Customer comments	Business process	Evaluation method
Praise Recommendation	Very high	Very Satisfied Satisfied Basically Satisfied Dissatisfied Very Dissatisfied ...	Telephone Recording Problem Recording Treatment Measures Customer Feedback ...	Type Scoring Customer Scoring
Complaints Report	Very low			Type Scoring Customer Scoring
Suggestion Feedback	Middle			Type Scoring Customer Scoring
Return Refund	low			Type Scoring Customer Scoring
Application Registration	Not sure			Customer Scoring Text Mining Speech Mining
Business Consulting	Not sure			Customer Scoring Text Mining Speech Mining
After-Sales Maintenance	Not sure			Customer Scoring Text Mining Speech Mining

According to the above Table 1, we can see that there are three ways to evaluate and analyze the satisfaction of big data in customer service center: first, judge whether it can be scored according to the type of business. For example, the praise type can be considered as the performance of high satisfaction, so it can give a high satisfaction score. For complaints, if the user is very dissatisfied, it can give a very low satisfaction score according to this type. However, if it is business consultation, registration application, after-sales maintenance type, it is often difficult to judge whether the user is satisfied or not, then it needs to be judged according to the customer's comments. Customer service center will usually let users evaluate the service before the end of the service. If the users give the comments, they can get the score of satisfaction; if they don't get the comments, they need to further carry out data mining in the customer service process. Generally, text mining is based on text records. For example, text mining is based on customer feedback problem records, processing measures, user corpus, etc. Key feature thesaurus is extracted and word segmentation is carried out to get keywords, which are mapped and matched with customer satisfaction evaluation rules to indirectly get customer satisfaction score. The process of text mining can refer to Fig. 1.

In addition, based on speech recognition artificial intelligence technology, it can also carry out intelligent speech recognition on the customer call recordings of customer service center, extract key features, evaluate customer satisfaction, or convert the recording into text for text mining.

2.2 Evaluation Based on Crawler Big Data

Crawler big data mainly refers to the use of crawler technology to collect and capture the evaluation data of the enterprise's related products and services from e-commerce

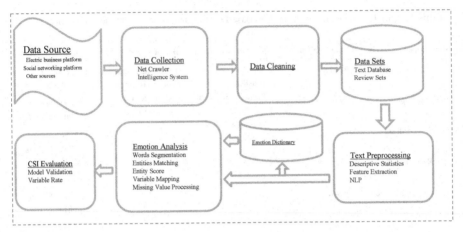

Fig. 1. Customer satisfaction evaluation process based on crawler big data [3]

platform, microblog, wechat and other social platforms and other channels. Through the
crawler technology, text mining and web page mining can be carried out based on the
external crawler data of the enterprise, and then converted into the index value reflecting
customer satisfaction [4].

Figure 1 is the flow chart of text data mining based on external crawler data when the
system implements customer satisfaction evaluation. The data sources are mainly from
the big data of product reviews published by e-commerce platforms such as Taobao, JD
and social platforms such as microblog and wechat. After cleaning the data collected by
crawler technology, we can get the text database or review sets to be processed; After
data preprocessing, combined with the third-party emotion dictionary, we can expand it
into a domain dictionary, and then use emotion analysis technology to process the text
big data, such as words segmentation, entity matching, entity scoring, variable mapping
and missing value processing, finally we can get the measure value of each variable in
the customer satisfaction model.

Peter D. proposed the application of semantic bias for the first time in the
classification of unsupervised comments [5].

Yang and Mai found that negative reviews had a greater impact on sales volume than
positive reviews, and the overall quality of a product could be measured by the number
of reviews [6].

Mudambi and Schuff took commodity reviews on Amazon as the research object.
Through analysis, they found that the polarity of comments and the number of words in
comments had a significant impact on the usefulness of online reviews [7].

Wang and Liu used web crawler technology to capture customer reviews of iPhone
5S from an online store of Taobao, and based on MOA theory, studied the impact of
consumer reviews on product performance from multiple perspectives [8]. There are
great differences between Chinese and English in terms of word formation, pause, etc.
Therefore, the research on customer satisfaction based on network reviews in Chinese
field is different from that in English field.

Li, Zhang, Chen et al. collected more than 7,000 online customer reviews of clothing products from Taobao, identified content elements from Nvivo 8.0, obtained the relationship between content elements of reviews and customer satisfaction through multiple regression analysis, and extracted the factors affecting customer satisfaction [9].

Geng took tourism blogs as the research object, analyzed their word segmentation and emotional tendency, constructed an evaluation system of tourist satisfaction in Hainan, and measured the tourist satisfaction index in Hainan by using fuzzy comprehensive evaluation method, factor analysis method and IPA analysis method [10].

Niu extracted keywords from online shoppers' comments on goods through text mining, constructed an indicator system of online shoppers' satisfaction with these keywords, and then analyzed some characteristics of customers' attention and usage through word frequency statistics [11].

Xu and Lan to comment on user data such as word segmentation, word frequency statistics and build related word library, then uses the simple quantitative seed word and target word similarity algorithm, the similarity between the emotional analysis, and evaluation target point of view of the word in a sentence tendentiousness, point polarity laid a good foundation for quantitative user [12].

2.3 Based on Hardware Big Data Evaluation

In the era of Internet of Things, more and more devices are connected to the cloud. Especially with the development of Artificial Intelligent Internet of Things technology, hardware terminal has become one of the main sources of big data collection. Therefore, it is also a feasible scheme to carry out big data analysis based on the data collected by intelligent hardware devices or device usage log, extract the index factors that indirectly reflect or affect customer satisfaction, and conduct customer satisfaction evaluation and analysis, just like the above text mining. But this is not the only way for hardware big data to participate in the improvement of user satisfaction. We can also improve product experience, improve product performance and reduce user complaints based on hardware big data. For example, using the operation feedback of end users to improve the user experience of mobile phone UI design; or using system crash, stuck and other data to optimize the memory management mechanism and improve the performance of software and hardware products, etc. Figure 2 shows the process of customer satisfaction evaluation and improvement based on hardware big data.

At present, this technology is not mature. At the same time, the data collection of hardware terminal is also facing the challenges of privacy security and policy supervision. Under the premise of user authorization, enterprises need to carefully record the data of equipment operation and use it legally to improve customer satisfaction.

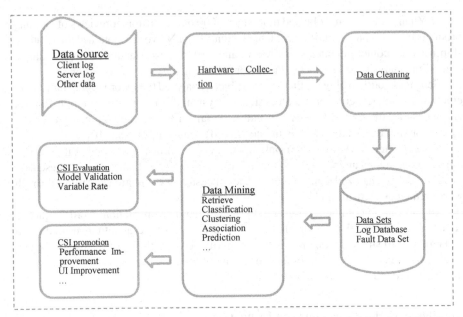

Fig. 2. Customer satisfaction evaluation and improvement process based on Hardware Big Data

3 Discussion and Conclusion

The research method based on big data technology opens a new way of thinking for traditional satisfaction measurement, overcomes the limitation of traditional questionnaire survey method using small data sampling, and lays a theoretical foundation for establishing a more scientific customer satisfaction measurement system. In the next step, our research will focus on the improvement of the big data mining algorithm, the innovation of the evaluation model, the development of the satisfaction evaluation system platform based on big data, and the industrial application research. Therefore, it has good value in both theory and practice and is worth further exploration and research.

There is no doubt that the application of big data technology in the field of customer satisfaction evaluation is a trend. However, the customer satisfaction evaluation method system based on big data is still in the exploratory stage, and many technologies are not mature or difficult to implement. In the process of practical application, we can build a customer satisfaction evaluation management system based on big data, analyze the collected data, and use Python language to dig out the deep reasons for low customer satisfaction, so as to guide enterprise customer service and further improve the quality of enterprise products and services.

Funding. This work was supported by the National Social Science Fund of China under No. 16CGL021.

References

1. Zhu, C.: Hadoop Distributed File System: Architecture and Design [EB/OL], https://Www.Jianshu.Com/P/E5cf2e95bd4e
2. Zhixin, L., Xu, H., Jiaxiang, W., et al.: Power customer satisfaction analysis based on 95598 big data. Power Big Data **21**(230(08)), 25–30 (2018)
3. Linqi, Z., Wei, Z.: Research on the construction of big data platform of tourist satisfaction based on Hadoop. Inf. Record. Mater. **7** (2020)
4. Lei, Y.: Research on customer satisfaction of unstructured text data from the perspective of big data. Capital University of economics and trade (2017)
5. Turney, P.D.: Thumbs up or thumbs down? Semantic orientation applied to unsupervised classification of reviews. In: Proceedings of the Association of Computational Linguistics (ACL 2002), pp. 417–424 (2002)
6. Yang, J., Mai, E.P.: Experiential goods with network externalities effects: an empirical study of online rating system. J. Bus. Res. **63**(9), 1050–1057 (2010)
7. Mudambi, S., Schuff, D.: What makes a helpful online review? A study of customer reviews on Amazon.com. MIS Q. **34**(1), 185–200 (2010)
8. Wang, B., Liu, M.: Research on the influence mechanism of online consumer comments based on text analysis. Wealth Emerg. Transfer **4**, 41–48 (2014)
9. Li, J., Zhang, X., Chen, W., et al.: The factors of customer reviews of C2C e-commerce apparel products and their impact on satisfaction. Chinese J. Manag. **02**, 261–266 (2014)
10. Geng, M.: Research on Tourist Satisfaction Evaluation of Tourism Destination Based on Tourism Blog. Hainan University (2010)
11. Niu, L., You, L.: Construction and analysis of online shopping customer satisfaction index system based on commodity reviews. Netizens World **Z2**, 23–36 (2013)
12. Xu, L., Lan, D., Zhang, J., et al.: Product review orientation analysis based on sentiment computing and text mining. J. Guangdong Inst. Petrochemical Technol. **26**(1), 35–39 (2016)
13. Wang, X.: Customer satisfaction analysis of Fuji Xerox. Huazhong Agricultural University (2013)
14. Cardozo, R.M.: An experimental study of consumer, expectation and satisfaction. J. Mark. Res. **2**, 244–249 (1965)
15. Westbrook, R.A.: Intrapersonal affective influences on consumer satisfaction with products. J. Consum. Res. 49–54 (1980)
16. Oliver, R.L.: A cognitive model of the antecedents and consequences of satisfaction decisions. J. Mark. Res. 460–469 (1980)
17. Churchill, G.A., Suprenant, C.: An investigation into the determinants of customer satisfaction. J. Mark. Res. 491–504 (1982)
18. Bolton, R.N., Drew, J.H.: A multistage model of customers assessments service quality and of value. J. Consum. Res. 375–384 (1991)
19. Zhou, Q.: Research on customer satisfaction model system and application of telecom enterprises. Beijing University of Posts and telecommunications (2007)
20. Wang, M.: Research on online retail customer satisfaction from the perspective of big data. China University of Geosciences (Beijing) (2020)
21. Wang, Y., Yan, H.: Evaluation of customer satisfaction. Econ. Manag. **08**, 36–38 (2000)
22. Liu, Yu., Ge, X.: Customer satisfaction index and its structure. Res. Quant. Econ. Technol. Econ. **10**, 70–73 (2001)
23. Zhou, M.: Measurement of customer loyalty and its empirical research. Sci. Technol. Guide **12**, 48–52 (2004)
24. Liu, X.: Nonlinear and trap analysis of "satisfaction profit" chain. Shangxun Bus. Econ. **05**, 66–68 (2005)

25. Wang, X.: Research on customer satisfaction of port logistics enterprises. Sci. Technol. Econ. Market **12**, 202 (2006)
26. Borthakur, D.: Hadoop distributed file system: Architecture and design [EB/OL]. Apache Software Foundation, http://hadoop.apache.org/docs/r1.0.4/cn/hdfs_design.html
27. Zhu, L., Zou, W.: Research on the construction of big data platform of tourist satisfaction based on Hadoop. Inf. Record. Mater. **7** (2020)
28. Wang, M.: Research on online retail customer satisfaction from the perspective of big data. China University of Geosciences (2020)
29. Cheng, L.: Application of big data in customer satisfaction evaluation mechanism. Consum. Electron. **20**, 145–146 (2014)
30. Haoxiong, Y., Wen, W.: Research on customer satisfaction evaluation system of third party logistics enterprises. Manag. Rev. **27**(001), 181 (2015)
31. Fengping, S.: Research on customer satisfaction model. Jinan University (2005)
32. Yong, Li.: Customer satisfaction index model and its evaluation method. China University of mining and technology (2008)
33. Qun, J.: Research on customer satisfaction based on big data modeling network. Electron. Technol. Softw. Eng. **190**(20), 209–210 (2020)
34. Zhenwei, Z.: Analysis of customer satisfaction based on product reviews – Taking JD mobile phone evaluation data as an example (2017)

Investigation of Information Requirements for Smartwatch-Based Evacuation Support System

Tomoko Izumi[1]([⊠]), Fumiya Takarai[1], Takayoshi Kitamura[1], and Yoshio Nakatani[2]

[1] Graduate School of Information Science and Engineering, Ritsumeikan University, Kusatsu, Shiga 525-8557, Japan
izumi-t@fc.ritsumei.ac.jp
[2] Ritsumeikan Trust, Nakagyo, Kyoto, Japan

Abstract. Mobile computers are becoming rapidly miniaturized and widespread in the form of smartwatches. During a disaster, people are expected to wear and use smartwatches to evacuate from their current locations to a safe place. However, the small size of the screen of a smartwatch is a problem when used to guide an evacuation. The end goal of this study is to develop a smartwatch-based evacuation guidance system, and this paper describes the potential of smartwatches for guiding an evacuation using limited information provided on a small screen. In other words, we investigated what type of information on the smartwatch can be used to realize a safe and effective evacuation. As the minimum necessary information, we focused only on the directions from the current location to the evacuation site and any danger zones. In this paper, we present the results of an experiment conducted to verify the evacuation behaviors of the participants using our prototype system. The results show that the proposed system can guide the participants to the evacuation site. In addition, we show that while the two pieces of information presented are the necessary minimum, additional information regarding danger zones is also required.

Keywords: Evacuation support · Smartwatch · Information design

1 Introduction

1.1 Background and Motivation

To minimize the damage caused by a disaster, it is critical that victims evacuate to safety as soon as possible after the disaster occurs. In particular, "self-help" is emphasized, and it is important that victims take actions to save themselves in a disaster situation. However, people are generally not used to evacuations, and therefore evacuation guidance systems can be of significant help.

Mobile computers are becoming rapidly miniaturized and widespread in the form of smartwatches. Owing to this trend, an increasing number of people are expected to wear smartwatches to evacuate during a disaster. Because mobile devices are portable,

G. Salvendy and J. Wei (Eds.): HCII 2021, LNCS 12796, pp. 27–37, 2021.
https://doi.org/10.1007/978-3-030-77025-9_4

they can provide adaptive guidance using the location information of the evacuees and can assist in guiding the evacuees from their current locations to a safe place.

However, the small size of the screen is a problem when using smartwatches to guide an evacuation. Currently, popular smart watches are becoming smaller, with displays of approximately 1.5 in. or less. Therefore, to provide a visible interface to users, it is important to present only limited information and to present it in a suitable way for such small screens. Thus, several studies have been conducted on navigation systems for smart watches [1–3]. These studies have attempted to reduce the amount of information presented, such as using a deformed map or directional information only, instead of presenting all detailed information. The results show that the systems can guide users to destinations even if the provided information is reduced.

However, these studies target navigation under a normal situation and provide information such as a user's current location, destination, and desired route. By contrast, in a disaster situation, it is necessary to provide not only such information, but also information on dangers to be avoided during an evacuation, such as collapsed houses, damaged roads, and fires. That is, the information to be provided to users in a disaster is different from that under a normal situation. Thus, the information to be presented on a smartwatch for support of an appropriate evacuation needs to be discussed.

1.2 Our Contributions

Therefore, in this study, we investigate a method of displaying information on smartwatches to support an evacuation from a current location to an evacuation site in a disaster situation. We assume that the evacuees are in an area where they are familiar with and know the shelter facilities. In a disaster, evacuees need to take adaptive actions while confirming the surrounding situation. Therefore, we consider a system that supports them to avoid losing their direction while allowing them to make decisions about their route selection.

Existing evacuation support systems use electronic maps, but as pointed out in a study by Kono et al. [1], electronic maps can be difficult to read when displayed on a smartwatch. To present an understanding of the screen size of a smartwatch, we do not use electronic maps, and investigate the minimum amount of information required for evacuees to move to the evacuation site and avoid any danger zones.

As the minimum necessary information, in this study, we focus on directions from a current location to an evacuation site and potential danger zones. Specifically, for the direction of an evacuation site, an arrow indicating the direction is shown in the center of the screen, and for a direction of a dangerous zone, the direction in which the zone exists is shown along the edge of the screen.

In this paper, we present the results of the experiment to verify the evacuation behaviors of the participants seeing the two types of information above. The results show that the proposed system can guide the participants to the evacuation site. However, this approach is insufficient for allowing the participants to avoid a danger zone in a specific condition. We also show that while the two pieces of information presented are the minimum necessary information, additional information about danger zones is also required.

2 Related Studies

2.1 Navigation Using a Smartwatch

Considering the small screen sizes and the limited interaction capacities of smartwatches, some studies have proposed interfaces specific to the devices. In particular, there are studies on navigation interfaces that guide the user. In [4], a user-centered design of a smartwatch interface is investigated. Specifically, the authors proposed an interface combining a map view with the directional view. In this interface, the map view provides an overview of the surrounding environment and route, and the directional view provides instructions for a turning corner. Owing to the problem of poor visibility when detailed information is displayed on a limited screen, there have been proposals to reduce the amount of information presented. Kono et al. [1] proposed a method to generate and display a deformed map based on landmarks, instead of displaying a detailed map. They considered that smartwatches have difficulty using a zoom in and out function, and thus it is necessary to display a deformed map with good visibility. By contrast, navigation using the vibrations of a smartwatch has also been proposed [5]. In this study, flexible strolling is provided using vibrations to indicate the direction of a target.

Some studies have applied navigation with limited information to sightseeing. Wada et al. [2] and Kitamura et al. [3] proposed a method to guide users only in the directions from the current location to sightseeing areas. In these studies, their goals are giving flexibility of action based on the consideration that the purpose of tourism is not all about arriving at the destination, but also about enjoying strolls around the area.

However, there have been no studies on the desirable information design of smartwatches to support evacuation behavior in a disaster. Yasui et al. [6] focused on children who are unable to read maps and proposed a guidance system using smartphone vibrations. As a situation in which this system will be used, they mention a case where a child must evacuate alone in a disaster. However, they only used the vibration function and did not consider presenting information on a screen or using a smartwatch.

2.2 Support for Evacuation Activities

Research has been conducted on supporting evacuation behavior by displaying expected affected areas. Fukada et al. [7] proposed an evacuation support system using hazard maps for a tsunami evacuation. With this system, tsunami hazard maps are stored in advance on a tablet PC for offline use. The map shows the current location and movement path of an evacuee, evacuation sites, and inundation height when evacuating. In [8], a system for evacuation guidance is also proposed to provide early disaster warning to evacuees. The system determines the probable disaster-affected area by using a ray-casting algorithm based on the current location, and if a user is in the area, then the system notifies it.

There are also studies that show danger zones in real time. Ishii et al. [9] proposed a system that provides real-time information and assists in an evacuation to the outside of a building by installing a device in the rooms to identify dangerous situations and the user's location. By using these data from the devices, a route search algorithm can provide a safe route to avoid danger zones.

3 Minimum Required Information

3.1 Investigation of Information to Be Provided

In this section, we consider information that should be presented by smartwatches to assist evacuees in moving from their current locations to the evacuation site during a disaster. Because evacuees need to take adaptive actions under a disaster situation, we consider supporting them to avoid losing their direction while allowing them to make decisions about their route selection. Please note that we assume evacuees are in a familiar area and know the facilities and locations of the evacuation sites. Under such a situation, it is easy to walk to a shelter under normal conditions. During disaster conditions, however, fires or impassable roads might be present. We consider supporting evacuees to avoid such danger areas and move to evacuation sites.

As mentioned above, we should consider the small screen size of the smartwatch. Because the provided information needs to be reduced, we investigate the minimum information required for evacuation actions. Because electronic maps are difficult to read on a smartwatch, they are not displayed. In the previous studies on evacuation behavior support [7–9], dangerous places to be avoided during evacuation are presented to users. To support an evacuation, it is essential to present information on roads and danger zones that are difficult to pass through, and the presentation of such information is provided in this study. However, because we do not use electronic maps, the exact locations of the roads and zones cannot be pointed out on a map. Since the importance is that a user does not approach or pass through the danger zones, we present only the directions to the nearby danger zones from the user's current location. Moreover, if the user approaches a danger zone, the smartwatch will vibrate to alert the user. If only danger zones are shown, evacuees will move to avoid those areas and may lose the direction of a shelter. Therefore, the direction to the evacuation site is indicated by arrows.

To realize this system, a function to detect and notify danger zones in real time is necessary. However, because our goal is to clarify the minimum information to be provided to users during evacuation actions, the realization of these functions is beyond the scope of this research.

3.2 Details of Providing Information

We developed on Android Studio 3.5.1, using Java as the language. The smartwatch we used was a CASIO WSDF20-RG PRO TREK Smart with Android Wear 2.0 OS and a 1.32-in. color TFT LCD display (320 × 300 pixel resolution).

The information presented on the smartwatch screen is the direction from the current location to an evacuation site and danger zones. Figure 1 shows an example of the smartwatch screen of our prototype system. The direction from the current location to an evacuation site is indicated by the blue arrow at the center of the screen. The directions from the current location to potential danger zones are shown by red cloud symbols displayed along the edge of the screen. In Fig. 1, it is shown that there are dangerous zones in the direction from the current location to the evacuation site, to the left front, and to the right rear.

Fig. 1. An example of the smartwatch screen of our system

In the prototype system, when a user approaches a dangerous zone within a radius of 100 m, the information (i.e., red cloud) about the zone is displayed on the screen, and the smartwatch vibrates for 2 s as a notification. Although there are various types of danger zones, such as fires, collapsed buildings, and cracked ground, the information is presented in the same way regardless of the type of danger. If the distance to the danger zone is within 100 m, the information regarding the zone continues to be shown on the screen. When the user moves and the distance to the danger zone is greater than 100 m, the information disappears from the screen and the smartwatch vibrates for 2 s as a notification.

4 Verification Experiment

This experiment verifies whether an evacuation to a shelter is possible by presenting only the directional information to the shelter and the danger zones. In addition, we aim to investigate whether the provided information is necessary for the evacuation and whether there is any other necessary information by having the participants actually take evacuation actions using the prototype system.

4.1 Experiment Outline

The experiment was conducted at the Biwako Kusatsu Campus of Ritsumeikan University because the participants were familiar with the area and the campus is quite large. Because there are several buildings on campus, and there are several paths between the buildings, the participants could choose the path to reach the destination.

The participants were asked to move from the starting point to the goal point as an evacuation site on campus, referring to the information on the smartwatch equipped with the prototype system. Several dangerous locations were set up in advance on the campus, and when the participant approached each location within 100 m, the direction of the location was displayed on the smartwatch. However, although the information on dangerous locations was shown on the smartwatch, the experiment was conducted under normal conditions, and thus all the participants could not confirm the actual damage to buildings or roads.

During the experiment, we recorded the evacuation behavior and route selection of each participant. After arriving at the goal point, we interviewed the participants and asked them to talk about the factors of their route selection in chronological order. They were also asked whether the information presented was necessary and whether they needed any other information.

4.2 Setting of Dangerous Locations

The locations of the start and goal points and dangerous locations set up on the campus are shown in Fig. 2. The starting point of this experiment is a point on the south side of the campus, and the goal point, assumed as an evacuation site, is on the north side. The movement time between these two points takes approximately 10 min at the walking speed of an average adult.

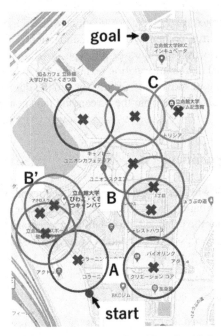

Fig. 2. Experimental area (Map data ©2021 Google) (Color figure online)

In this experiment, we set up 11 danger locations, as shown in Fig. 2, with red cross marks. The circle around the mark represents a radius of 100 m. When the participant enters this area, the corresponding information is displayed on the smartwatch. These locations were set by considering the patterns of the three situations. As the first pattern, a dangerous location was along the path that the participant tried to follow. These locations are indicated by red circles. The second pattern shown by the blue circles is one in which there were multiple dangerous locations in a particular direction. In this case, the information of these multiple locations was displayed on the smartwatch simultaneously. The final pattern, which is indicated by the green circles, dangerous locations were located on both sides of the road.

4.3 Participants

The participants were 10 fourth-year students (5 males and 5 females) studying at Biwako Kusatsu Campus of Ritsumeikan University, and the experiment was conducted sometime between December 2019 and January 2020. We described a scenario in which a major disaster with the magnitude of the great earthquake had occurred, and that the student needed to evacuate to a shelter on campus. Moreover, we explained that there were dangerous locations in many different areas, and that information about them was available on their smartwatch. All participants were informed and agreed that the experiment would be a disaster-related experiment, that the experimenter would take video from behind while moving, that the experiment could be stopped at any time, and that the results would be published with no personal information.

4.4 Results

First, we show whether an evacuation to the evacuation site is possible by presenting only the directional information to the site and the dangerous zones. All 10 participants arrived at the goal point. The average travel time in this experiment was 11 min and 34 s, with a maximum of 13 min and 59 s and a minimum of 8 min and 32 s.

For the three patterns of the dangerous zones described in Sect. 4.2, the results of the participants behavior are shown. We focus on three areas, A, B, and C, as shown in Fig. 2. Table 1 shows the number of participants in each area who went straight in the direction of the dangerous location and the number of participants who took a detour. Figure 3 shows two examples of the experimental evacuation behaviors. Participant i moved to avoid all dangerous locations. By contrast, participant vi moved through relatively dangerous locations.

In area A, in which there was a dangerous location in front of the path, six of the participants went east to avoid the location (similar to participant i in Fig. 3), whereas four of them went straight ahead in a northern direction (similar to participant vi in Fig. 3). Those who went straight ahead stated that they decided that the road to the east had buildings and the road was too narrow. Of those who detoured, four decided to avoid the dangerous locations, and two were heading east toward the main road. In area B, in which the multiple locations are shown as dangerous, half of the participants avoided them (similar to participant i in Fig. 3). Even those who went straight ahead, however, stated that they were careful to pass between the cloud marks displayed (e.g., participant vi in Fig. 3). It is considered that they moved straight because they knew it would bring them closer to the goal point. In addition, those who went straight north from area A approached area B', but all of them moved to avoid B' (one example is the behavior of participant vi shown in Fig. 3). In area C, in which there are dangerous locations on both sides of the road, all except one of the participants went straight north through the danger zones. As the reason for this, it is also considered that they knew that the goal was straight ahead to the north. Based on these facts, because each participant made different decisions regarding their route selection, we can see that the participants made their own decisions and moved based on the given information. However, simply pointing out the direction of a dangerous location is insufficient for the participants to avoid it, particularly in the case of paths directly connected to the evacuation site. As one reason for this, there was no actual damage in this experiment, and thus the participants could not confirm the damage and did not feel threatened. As in area B', however, unless there was a direct path to the shelter, the participants acted to avoid the dangerous locations.

Table 1. Number of participants who went straight or who detoured in each area

	Go through	Detour
Area A	4	6
Area B	5	5
Area C	9	1

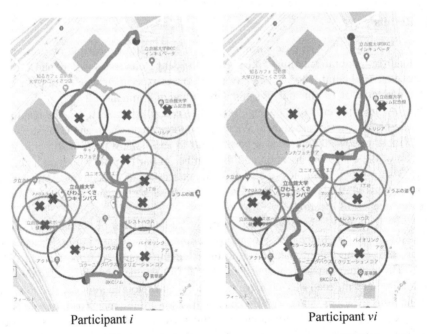

Participant *i*   Participant *vi*

Fig. 3. Examples of experimental evacuation behaviors (Map data ©2021 Google)

Table 2 shows the information considered necessary and unnecessary for the proto-type system obtained from the results of interviews with each participant. The alphabetic characters indicate the common responses among some of the experiment participants, and are listed in alphabetical order according to the number of respondents. The items for each participant in Table 2 are listed in the order in which they were stated. The number of respondents with the same answer is summarized in Table 3.

As a result of the interviews, many participants suggested that more detailed information on dangerous locations is needed, such as the distance, type, and degree of damage. In particular, 7 out of 10 participants pointed out the distance to the danger location. The participants would want to understand the location of the damage by distance and choose their actions depending on the degree of damage. That is, it is necessary to consider whether it is actually possible to pass through the point. As for the straight distance to the shelter, more than half of the participants answered that it was necessary. Even if they know the location of the shelter, it is considered that many of them would like to know the distance to the shelter. However, two of the participants listed the direction to the shelter as being unnecessary information. Therefore, it is possible that in a familiar place, more evacuees would want to know the distance rather than the direction to the shelter. As for the information considered unnecessary, because 8 out of the 10 participants answered "None," the information provided in this experiment was evaluated to be necessary.

Table 2. Answers for the interviews about required and unnecessary information

	Required information	Unnecessary information
i	(a) Straight distances to the dangerous locations (b) A straight distance to the shelter - different types of vibrations when approaching or leaving the dangerous locations	None
ii	(e) Degrees of danger at the dangerous locations - information about locations of food and disaster prevention goods supply (directions and straight distances)	None
iii	(a) Straight distances to the dangerous locations	(f) Direction to the shelter
iv	(a) Straight distances to the dangerous locations (b) Straight distance to the shelter	None
v	(a) Straight distances to the dangerous locations (d) Safe routes (on an electronic map) (c) Types of damages at the dangerous locations (d) Map of people distribution	None

(*continued*)

Table 2. (*continued*)

	Required information	Unnecessary information
vi	(c) Types of damages at the dangerous locations - Name of the landmark building (b) A distance of route to the shelter	None
vii	(a) Straight distances to the dangerous locations. - Notification of dead end in the direction (c) Types of damages at the dangerous locations - Information on people in need of rescue	(f) Direction to the shelter - Vibrations when leaving the dangerous locations
viii	(d) An electronic map (b) A distance of route to the shelter	None
ix	(e) Degrees of danger at the dangerous locations (a) Straight distances to the dangerous locations (c) Types of damages at the dangerous locations (b) A straight distance to the shelter	None
x	(a) Straight distances to the dangerous locations (b) A straight distance to the shelter (d) An electronic map (d) A current location on an electronic map	None

Table 3. Numbers of respondents with the same required information

Required information	Number of respondents
(a) Straight distances to the dangerous locations	7
(b) A straight distance or a distance of route to the shelter	6
(c) Types of damages at the dangerous locations	3
(d) An electronic map	3
(e) Degrees of danger at the dangerous locations	2

5 Conclusions

In this study, we investigated the smartwatch interface for route planning support for evacuation to a safe location during a disaster. We proposed a smartwatch application that indicates the directions to an evacuation site and various danger zones and conducted a practical evaluation experiment. The results showed that the participants made their own decisions and moved adaptively based on the given information. However, this approach is insufficient for allowing the participants to avoid a danger zone, particularly in the case of roads directly connected to the shelter. In addition, many of the participants stated that the information about the two directions were necessary. The necessary information to be provided additionally was the type and degree of danger and the straight distance to the evacuation shelter.

Our future tasks are to investigate how to display the additional information to be provided and to verify the effectiveness of the system. As another opinion in this experiment, the direction to the evacuation shelter was thought to be unnecessary. Thus, we will consider a method for determining the priorities of the information to be presented according to the surrounding situation and the specific user.

Acknowledgements. This work was supported in part by KAKENHI no. 18H03483 and no. 20K11911.

References

1. Kono, K., Nitta, T., Ishikawa, K., Yanagisawa, M., Togawa, N.: Comprehensive deformed map generation for wristwatch-type wearable devices based on landmark-based partitioning. In: Proceedings on IEEE 5th Global Conference on Consumer Electronics (2016)
2. Wada, T., et al.: Yuru-Navi: a flexible navigation system for a sightseeing using a device like a watch. Proc. IPSJ Interact. **2011**, 661–664 (2011). (in Japanese)
3. Kitamura, T., Gang, Yu., Izumi, T., Nakatani, Y.: Proposal of the onion watch application for enjoying a stroll. In: Meiselwitz, G. (ed.) HCII 2020. LNCS, vol. 12195, pp. 559–568. Springer, Cham (2020). https://doi.org/10.1007/978-3-030-49576-3_41
4. Perebner, M., Huang, H., Gartner, G.: Applying user-centered design for smartwatch-based pedestrian navigation system. J. Location Based Serv. **13**(3), 213–237 (2019)
5. Dobbelstein, D., Henzler, P., Rukzio, E.: Unconstrained pedestrian navigation based on vibro-tactile feedback around the wristband of a smartwatch. In: Proceedings of the 2016 CHI Conference Extended Abstracts on Human Factors in Computing Systems, pp. 2439–2445 (2016)
6. Yasui, T., Kitamura, T., Izumi, T., Nakatani, Y.: Evaluation of a vibration-based route indication for children who are not familiar with maps. In: Proceedings of the IEEE 8th Global Conference on Consumer Electronics (GCCE 2019), pp. 40–44 (2019)
7. Fukada, H., Hashimoto, Y., Akabuchi, A., Oki, M., Okuno, Y.: Proposal of tsunami evacuation support system using a tablet PC. In: Proceedings of the IPSJ, Multimedia, Distributed, Cooperative, and Mobile Symposium, pp. 1938–1944 (2013). (in Japanese)
8. Rahman, K.M., Alam, T., Chowdhury, M.: Location based early disaster warning and evacuation system on mobile phones using OpenStreetMap. In: Proceedings of the 2012 IEEE Conference on Open Systems, pp. 1–6 (2012)
9. Inoue, Y., Sashima, A., Ikeda, T., Kurumatani, K.: Indoor emergency evacuation service on autonomous navigation system using mobile phone. In: Proceedings of the Second International Symposium on Universal Communication, pp. 79–85 (2008)

Application of Improved DTW Algorithm in Smart Home Industry

Wen Jiang, Yiling Zhao, and Zhongwei Gu(✉)

Shanghai Dianji University, Pudong, Shanghai, China

Abstract. Based on the mobile era, with the rapid development of the Internet of Things and artificial intelligence technology, human-computer interaction based on intelligent voice has become one of the main stream in people's daily life. Taking the intelligent voice interaction technology as a clue, this article first elaborates the practical application of intelligent voice human-computer interaction in smart homes and other daily life fields. After analyzing this, it is found that even intelligent voice has greatly facilitated people Daily life, but there are still shortcomings, that is, the machine cannot efficiently and accurately recognize the language commands given by people, and there is a voice recognition barrier. Secondly, we learned about the DTW algorithm by reading related books and literature, and found that it solves the problem of template matching with different pronunciation lengths, but the recognition efficiency and accuracy are not high, so we propose improvements based on the original intelligent voice interaction technology. The method is to improve the local path restriction and improve the efficiency of the DTW algorithm. The purpose is to make the machine more intelligent, improve its ability to recognize and understand text and language, and achieve barrier-free communication between humans and machines. The research method can provide a feasible reference for the improvement of intelligent voice interaction technology. The advantage is that it not only promotes the development of intelligent voice human-computer interaction, but also ensures that people can have a more intelligent and convenient life.

Keywords: Smart home · DTW algorithm · Intelligent voice interaction technology

1 Research Background and Significance

With the development of science and technology in the times, China has made great breakthroughs in the fields of computer, Internet of Things and artificial intelligence, and people's quality of life and conditions have been improved by leaps and bounds, but also brought great convenience to our daily life. At this point, our living habits and intelligent systems are closely related, the basic needs of life are gradually closer to intelligence, and even slowly developed dependence on this.

As intelligence gradually surrounds our lives, the smart home industry has also begun to rise to become a popular industry in modern society, such as Xiaomi, for example, Xiaomi launched smart home, such as smart speakers, smart lights, smart doorbells and

© Springer Nature Switzerland AG 2021
G. Salvendy and J. Wei (Eds.): HCII 2021, LNCS 12796, pp. 38–44, 2021.
https://doi.org/10.1007/978-3-030-77025-9_5

other smart home appliances have become the needs of life. Smart home to the home as a unit, through the Internet of Things technology [1], wireless communication technology, automatic control technology, cloud computing and other technologies combined to achieve the connectivity of various smart devices in the home, the devices on the cloud registration, through the mobile terminal to achieve remote control of a solution. Among them, speech recognition technology is particularly prominent, the combination of home and speech recognition technology, we can achieve the barrier-free communication between people and home to achieve "voice control" function, greatly improve the convenience of life, but also to meet the needs of consumers and enhance people's well-being. As a result, speech recognition technology has great prospects for development now and in the future.

2 Smart Home

2.1 Concept

Smart home is a product derived from information technology under the background of information age. It is mainly based on the use of Internet of things technology, daily residence as a platform, the use of generic cabling technology, network communication technology, security technology, automatic control technology and audio and video technology to effectively combine modern digital technology and household products, so that the home can maximize the development Play its various functions to provide people with a more comfortable, safe and convenient living environment.

2.2 Technical Features

The technical characteristics of smart home are as follows:

[1] Smart home mostly uses home gateway and system software to build smart home platform system. The core content of smart home LAN is the home gateway, which plays the role of conversion and information sharing with the internal communication protocol of the home. At the same time, it also plays an important role in data exchange with the external communication network, and also plays an important role in the control of smart home.

[2] Smart home has a unified platform. Smart home integrates all functions of smart home terminal and home intelligence through computer technology, network communication technology and generic cabling technology, so that all smart home can run on a unified platform. This not only realizes the data interaction within the smart home, but also can identify the network instructions to prevent illegal intrusion, becoming the "firewall" of the information family.

[3] Smart home mainly uses external expansion module to interconnect with other home appliances. Through wired or wireless way, the home gateway can intelligently control the home appliances and lights with the help of external expansion module.

[4] It has a complete embedded system. With the continuous development and progress of smart home, it has changed from the earliest single chip microcomputer to embedded system control, which is more complete and intelligent in control technology.

3 Application of Intelligent Voice Interaction Technology in Smart Home

3.1 Application

In recent years, with the rapid development of science and technology, artificial intelligence has gradually entered the public field of vision, and human-computer interaction has gradually become one of the mainstream life patterns in the new era. As we all know, smart home is a new trend derived from it, that is, on the basis of the use of Internet of things technology, the use of intelligent voice interaction technology, the effective integration of modern digital technology and household products, to maximize its function, in order to provide people with a more convenient, safe and efficient quality of life.

Xiaomi's current AI layout is perfect, including Xiaomi AI speaker, Xiaomi Xiaoai speaker mini, etc. Among them, the Xiaomi AI speaker is regular and is currently used by most families. Xiaoai audio Mini is suitable for moving everywhere, such as student dormitories, temporary offices and so on. In addition, there is a more portable Xiaomi Xiaoai Bluetooth speaker portable version, which can be taken out of the outdoor at will. It can be said that Xiaomi intelligent speaker covers most of the use scenarios.

Although the application of speech recognition technology in smart home can bring users higher experience and convenience, we take the intelligent voice interaction technology as the main line and find the following problems from smart home.

3.2 Problems

As we all know, Xiaomi is a company specializing in research and invention of intelligent hardware and electronic products, but also a mobile internet company specializing in the development of high-end smartphones, Internet television, but also committed to the development of smart home ecological chain construction of innovative technology. According to the choice of consumers and the sales of the enterprise can be learned that Xiaomi can be regarded as one of the leading brands of smart home in China. Among them, the company's artificial intelligence AI speakers are particularly popular and used. The speaker enables humans to interact with machines through intelligent voice interaction technology, i.e. the "you ask me to answer" feature. In the network state, we can directly ask them real-time weather, road conditions, music playback and other functions, to achieve a true sense of human-computer interaction.

But through the actual use of the public, we can see through the investigation, the speaker can not fully recognize people's speech commands. Combined with the actual situation and through the examples in life, everyone in the speech speed, tone, accent, etc. are different, and even people in different regions will have different dialects when expressing language, so we use the smart home must have a better understanding, and on this basis to analyze and identify it. In other words, in the current language environment, smart devices at home must be more "know you". The most important of these is the recognition of the user's pronunciation habits, such as speed and accent, and there is still a lot of room for improvement in recognition and accuracy. Thus, we discovered the DTW algorithm by reading books and so on.

4 DTW Algorithm

DTW (Dynamic Time Warping) is called the time dynamic regulation algorithm. It is understood that there are many similar or distance functions exist in the time series data, of which dynamic time regulation algorithm is the most significant one. All the phonetics contained in a pronunciation and the correct sequence of phonetic connections make up the correct pronunciation at once. The duration of each of these phonetics is related to the phonetics themselves and the condition of the speaker [2]. When the input voice signal is lengthened or shortened until it is the same length as the standard mode, the recognition rate can be increased and the problem of sending the same tone but the pronunciation time is different [3]. This process is called time regulation. However, by understanding it, we find that it solves the problem of template matching with different pronunciation lengths [4], but the recognition efficiency and accuracy are not high, so we propose an improvement based on the original intelligent speech interaction technology, that is, to improve the local path limit to improve the efficiency of the DTW algorithm.

5 Improvement of DTW Algorithm

In view of the problems existing in the DTW algorithm, some improvements are made to it, and when the DTW algorithm is run, the recognition speed will be affected if the two compared time series are longer and the repetition in operation is high. In response to the above problems, we have adopted the following solutions. Assuming that the sequence length of the two compared time series data is relatively similar and the length is specified in advance, we should first establish a length find table based on one of the time series length as the criteria, so as to save the lower limit of the search range, so in the course of each operation, we only need to find the lower limit of the limit range in the previously obtained lookup table, thus determining a coordinate range, and in this range, through the slope can calculate the upper limit of the limit range. According to the existing obstacles in the original algorithm, that is, every step, it is possible to calculate the limit range of coordinates corresponding to it, so it is extremely troublesome to carry out such operations frequently. Thus, this cumbersome step can be effectively avoided by following the above approach, as long as it is done once in a pre-established time series length lookup table. At the same time, the operation of checking the length of a time series to find a table in a computer requires only one instruction cycle, and the original repetitive cumbersome steps can be reduced to a one-time operation calculation to get the expected results. It can be seen that this improvement not only in theory, but also in practice to ensure that the algorithm can improve the efficiency of the program to a certain extent after the improvement. At the same time, we also think that we can remove the original DTW algorithm specified in the voice first strict alignment of this standard, in other words, any one pronunciation of the first frame can be any other pronunciation of the start frame of all frames can be any match. Correspondingly, the last frame can also match the last frame of any other pronunciation [5].

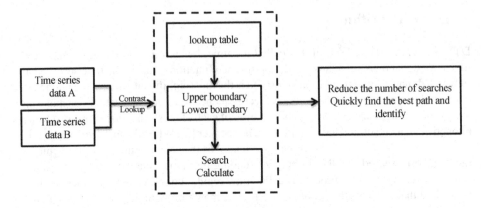

6 Improvement of Endpoint Detection Algorithm in DTW Algorithm

As we all know, the matching of speech recognition mainly uses two algorithms, DTW and HMM. However, through research and investigation, we found that because the DTW algorithm does not have an effective statistical method for training framework, it is not easy to use the low-level and top-level knowledge. In the speech recognition algorithm, it pales in comparison to the HMM algorithm in solving large vocabulary, continuous speech, and non-specific speech recognition problems. At the same time, this is related to the shortcomings of the speech recognition technology that we have discovered before, that is, the machine cannot recognize human language commands in smart furniture. Therefore, we have reason to believe that in order to solve this problem, we still have to change the DTW algorithm.

Through reading the literature, we found that the DTW algorithm still has some shortcomings, one of which is the sensitivity to the endpoint detection accuracy. In this regard, there are only two ways to solve this problem. One is to make changes from itself, such as reducing its sensitivity to endpoints by relaxing its front and rear endpoints; the other method is to use the outside of the DTW algorithm, as much as possible Accurately detect the endpoints of speech. In some literature, some authors have proposed methods to accurately detect endpoints through the study of short-time window functions and window lengths. When detecting the voice signal endpoints, it is usually judged by the method of multiplying the average amplitude value with the zero-crossing rate and the method of multiplying the average energy with it. If the length of the selected window is relatively small, then the precise position of the endpoint can be easily detected, but this will cause the algorithm to increase the amount of calculation and also reduce the recognition speed, and even mistake some noise for speech, leading to recognition error. On the contrary, if the selected window length is larger, the calculation speed and the efficiency of speech processing can be increased, noise can be skipped, and previous errors can be avoided, but this will reduce the detection accuracy of the endpoint. This problem is for the DTW algorithm. Very serious. Even so, the author of the literature gave a better solution strategy, which can not only improve the accuracy of the detection endpoint, but also avoid the problems caused by the window length being too long or too short, and achieved good results. The window length is variable. The voice strategy and algorithm are shown in the figure.

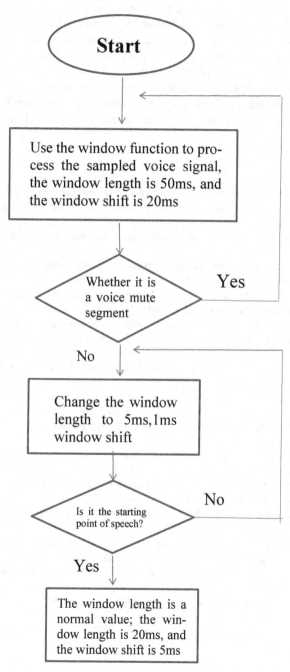

7 Conclusion

Based on the above research, we find the problem of intelligent voice interaction technology in the field of smart home, which leads to the improvement of DTW algorithm. In order to improve the machine's speech recognition technology and shorten the distance between human and intelligence, we start with improving the local path restriction and improving the efficiency of DTW algorithm, and find that this method is feasible, which can provide feasible suggestions for the subsequent improvement of smart home. I believe that in the future, intelligent voice human-computer interaction technology will be better and better, so that people have a more convenient and intelligent life.

References

1. Lin, Y.: Research on Dynamic Pricing of Internet of Things Platform – Taking Taxi Software Platform As An Example. Tianjin University, Tianjin (2015). https://doi.org/10.7666/d.y31 75477
2. Wenjie, W.: Application of speech recognition algorithm in vehicle robot. Digital User **25**(45), 70 (2019)
3. Tong, W.: Research and Implementation of Music Recognition and MIDI File Output Based on Android. University of Chinese Academy of Sciences (2013)
4. Qingdao Institute of Marine Technology, Tianjin University. Humming Retrieval Method Based on Deep Neural Network: Cn201811588112.8, 02 July 2020
5. Wenxuan, Z.: Design of smart home security system based on human-computer interaction. China New Technol. New Prod. **4**, 129–130 (2017). https://doi.org/10.3969/J.Issn.1673-9957. 2017.04.080
6. Bingbing, D., Jinshui, L.: On the development status and prospects of smart home. Smart City **5**(04), 21–22 (2019)
7. Tang, W.: Application of Intelligent Voice Technology Based on Cloud Service in Smart Home. Nanjing University of Posts and Telecommunications (2020)
8. Jing, Y.: Research And application of speech recognition technology in smart home. Satell. TV Broadband Multimedia **07**, 34–35 (2020)
9. Ying, C., Gongming, W., Lei, Y., Libing, X.: Analysis on application technology of speech recognition technology in smart home. Sci. Technol. Innov. **31**, 60–61 (2019)
10. Zhu, L., Zou, W.: Research on the construction of big data platform of tourist satisfaction based on Hadoop. Inf. Rec. Mater. **21**, 148–149 (2020)
11. Junzhi, W., Yan, W., Yi, S.: Intelligent home system based on voice interaction. J. Nanhua Univ. (Natl. Sci. Ed.) **34**(01), 60–67 (2020)
12. Shang, F., Dachen, S., Haixia, L.: An Improved algorithm for improving the efficiency of DTW. Comput. Eng. Des. **31**(15), 3518–3520 + 3525 (2010)
13. Su, H., Min, W., Bao, L.: An improved DTW speech recognition system. Western China Sci. Technol. **10**(01), 38–39 + 94 (2011)
14. Chun, W.: Research and implementation of speech recognition application system based on DTW. J. Jimei Univ. (Natl. Sci. Ed.) **02**, 104–108 (2002)
15. Changming, L., Feng, Y.: Research on improved DTW feature matching algorithm in speech recognition. J. North China Univ. (Natl. Sci. Ed.) **01**, 37–40 (2006)

Research on Risk Management of Digital Currency Based on Blockchain Technology in Mobile Commerce

Xinyu Li and Peiyan Zhou[✉]

School of Management, Jilin University, Changchun, China

Abstract. In the mobile era of blockchain 3.0, blockchain will no longer only exist in the virtual world, but will also exist in the actual environment of people's lives, and mobile commerce is the best aid to realize connection between virtual and reality. However, this kind of financial innovation also brings impact on financial security and challenges to the current financial regulatory system. As the underlying technology of digital currency, blockchain is essentially a decentralized database. Due to its special and ingenious design, blockchain has the characteristics of decentralization, immutability of information and anonymity. Therefore, digital currency based on blockchain has relatively high security, which can not only effectively reduce the high cost of issuing and circulating traditional banknotes, but also promote the transparency and convenience of transactions. At present, there are still some risks and challenges in the aspects of technology, law and financial system of digital currency, such as network security risk, lack of supporting laws and policies, impact on the current financial system, etc. This paper first briefly introduces the related concepts of blockchain and digital currency. Then it analyzes the advantages of blockchain-based digital currency and its application in the financial field. Next, it analyzes the risk characteristics of digital currency and points out the current major problems in supervision and gives corresponding risk management strategies with a view to providing help for the future sustainable development of blockchain technology and digital currency.

Keywords: Blockchain technology · Digital currency · Bitcoin · Risk management · Mobile security

1 Introduction

With the maturity of technology and concepts, the blockchain has entered the 3.0 mobile era. It is characterized by a programmable society, that is, the blockchain will no longer only exist in the virtual world, but will also exist in the actual environment where people live. Mobile commerce is the best aid to realize the connection between virtual and reality. Using the technical features and model concepts of the blockchain to construct the circulation system, payment system and credit system in the basic unit of e-commerce, greatly improve the user's service experience, while avoiding the risk of information leakage and simplifying the cumbersome process.

© Springer Nature Switzerland AG 2021
G. Salvendy and J. Wei (Eds.): HCII 2021, LNCS 12796, pp. 45–67, 2021.
https://doi.org/10.1007/978-3-030-77025-9_6

The origin of digital currency can be traced back to the late 1980s, when cryptography began to rise (Zhang et al. 2019). Therefore, many cryptography researchers began to construct a new kind of digital currency. This kind of early digital currency had an inevitable drawback: centralization (Zhang et al. 2019). However, digital currencies such as Bitcoin are not controlled by any central authority because of its characteristic of decentralization (Zhang et al. 2019). Accordingly, this kind of digital currency will not be attacked by single node, and the whole system is free from corruption. The obvious advantages of digital currency, such as fast payment speed and low (almost zero) cost, have greatly impacted traditional currencies (Huang 2019). However, external comments are divided into two kinds of opinion. Thus, in this paper, the background of the emergence of digital currency, the characteristics and possible risks are discussed based on the current financial innovation environment. The current situation and development trend of digital currency will be analyzed for the purpose of providing suggestions for the supervision of digital currency.

2 Research Method and Main Innovation

This paper mainly uses qualitative and contrastive analysis. This paper starts from the concept of blockchain technology and digital currency. Then characteristics and advantages of blockchain-based digital currency are discussed. After that, possible risks are analyzed combined with the application of blockchain. Then contrastive analysis is used for the purpose of analyzing current supervision situation of blockchain technology in financial field and finding out related problems in the supervision. At last, some regulatory recommendations for blockchain technology applied in the financial field are provided to give effective suggestions and countermeasures. The main innovation of this paper is to compare, summarize and classify the regulatory models of blockchain-based digital currency in different countries with the aim of finding out the common problems in the supervision of various countries and providing corresponding solutions.

3 Research Reviewed

From the present point of view, digital currency is still a new field. Researchers from domestic and foreign countries mainly discuss from the following aspects. Satoshi Nakamoto first proposed the concept of 'blockchain' in Bitcoin: A Peer-to-Peer Electronic Cash System published in 2008. This article provided a detailed introduction to the characteristics and functions of the blockchain technology. At the same time, a decentralized peer-to-peer direct transaction electronic cash system based on P2P network technology can be tried to establish. Furthermore, through the use of cryptography, time stamping and consensus mechanisms can be applied to ensure that the data can be traced and difficult to tamper with. The blockchain system of Bitcoin has been operating stably since it was launched in 2009. It can be said that this model design has been theoretically perfect. Shen Xin et al. (2016) and Shao et al. (2017) pointed out: Blockchain technology, as the underlying technical support of Bitcoin, can effectively solve the high cost and low efficiency caused by the distrust of multiple parties. Zhang (2016) stated that there would be legal risk, technical security risk and risk of anonymity because of the application of digital currency. Moreover, consumer right could be affected. Pu et al. (2017) comprehensively discussed the basic technology of blockchain and analyzed the platform architecture and characteristics of blockchain. In addition to the current most widely used financial field, it can also be used in logistics and transportation, medical health, and academic verification. Hui (2018) indicated that consumer right could be infringed because of the application of digital currency. He stated that consumer privacy problem also exists in blockchain financial sector, which will even aggravate the risk of consumer privacy infringement to some extent. Muharem (2019) claimed that Bitcoin is private currency and form competition relationship with government fiat currency, and thus has the nature of financial commodity. Zhang (2019) considered that there are anonymity risk, transaction risk and legal risk pertaining to blockchain-based digital currency. Faijan et al. (2019) considered that it is necessary to strengthen the regulatory system and coordinate international policy to deal with the risk. Loannis et al. (2019) considered that blockchain security technology system should be built to reduce risk. Besides, supervisory technology could be used to improve financial supervisory capabilities. Financial regulatory department should use financial technology to achieve the intelligentization of financial risk monitoring and improve the ability to predict financial risk. Ulrich (2019) discussed about the legal risk and risk of anonymity. He considered that anonymity risk may lead to financial fraud. Blockchain technology may be used as a method of illegal fund-raising and financial fraud, and digital currency has become the preferred currency dealing in illegal dark web. Belke and Beretta (2020) indicated that different from traditional banknotes, technical risk could be the major risk that may lead to the collapse of financial system in a short time. Furthermore, sandbox testing or other methods could be used to strictly verify the digital currency to be issued for the purpose of reducing risk.

4 Basic Conception of Blockchain and Digital Currency

4.1 Blockchain

In 2008, a mysterious man Satoshi Nakamoto released Bitcoin, bringing underlying technology-blockchain to the public view (Belke and Beretta 2020). Blockchain is a public form of bookkeeping that uses a digital ledger to allow individuals to share a record of transactions (Hui 2018). Blockchain is a type of incorruptible distributed ledger that allows information to be recorded and shared with a network of individuals (Hui 2018). In essence, blockchain is a public form of bookkeeping which makes use of internet technologies to instantly verify transactions that take place between individuals (Hui 2018). The public nature of blockchain means that every individual can view the transactions made by participants in that network. This means that participants can view the date, time, value of transactions, and the individuals involved, thereby creating a shared record or events (Ruan 2017). Figure 1 shows the extended characteristics of the block. The block is encrypted using a hash algorithm. Most people can participate together, making this mechanism a challenge to the exclusive centralized model of traditional exchanges (Satoshi Nakamoto 2018). Figure 2 shows the principle of blockchain mining. As shown in Fig. 2, the main steps are as follows: First, the "miners" collect unconfirmed transaction information from the entire network, incorporate it into a new block, and calculate a hash value based on the data of the previous block (Fu 2019). The hash value, which is a random number, is calculated by SHA256 algorithm to obtain a string of binary numbers with a length of 256, and then it is checked whether the string of numbers is lower than the target value (Fu 2019). If it does not meet the requirements, a large number of calculations must be performed to adjust the random number until the requirements are met (Fu 2019). In the end, this new block needs to be broadcast to the entire network and be verified (Fu 2019). If it passes, the new block will be created successfully, and it needs to be connected to the main blockchain and saved together (Fu 2019). The reward for successful creation of a new block is a certain amount of Bitcoin, which is initially 50 Bitcoins for each block and then halved every four years until all 21 million bitcoins are mined (Fu 2019).

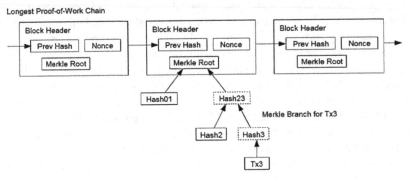

Fig. 1. The initial structure of blockchain (Source: Nakamoto 2018)

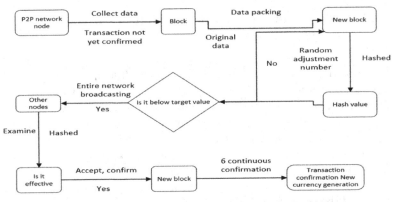

Fig. 2. The principle of Bitcoin mining (Source: Fu 2019)

4.2 Digital Currency

Digital currency is different from fiat currency. However, when digital currency is combined with real life in some kinds of situation, it begins to have value. Some of the most popular digital currencies include Dash, Bitcoin and Zcash. As of November 2018, there are 2486 cryptocurrencies listed in *Investing*, which did not include those that are issued but not listed or are not in circulation in the market (Liu 2017). Table 1 shows the comparison of paper money, electronic money and digital money.

Table 1. A comparison of paper money, electronic money and digital money (Source: Research Department of CICC)

Item	Paper money	Electronic money	Digital currency
Ownership	Ownership is the possession of paper money	Proof from the bank's book system	Ownership is the possession of the private key
Intermediary	P2P, no bank intermediary is required	Bank intermediary is needed for book keeping and settlement	P2P, no bank intermediary is required
Anonymity	Anonymous	Need to register personal real information in detail	Anonymous
Account approval	Do not need approval	Application and approval	Do not need approval
Payment review	Do not need to review	Review is required, certain payment requests will not be processed	Do not need to review
Track record	Hard to track	Traceable	Traceable
Circulation cost	High	Relatively high	Relatively low
Payment efficiency	Relatively low	Relatively high	The most efficient

Table 2 is the interception of the top 10 digital currencies in market capital as at September 2018. Based on the table, it is clearly to see that the top 10 digital currencies have all exceeded $1 billion in market capital. The capital exceeded 184.7 billion US dollars. The total market capital of Bitcoin, Ethereum and Ripple, which rank the top three in market capital, has an absolute scale advantage. As at September 2018, the total capital of these three digital currency markets is 157.1 billion U.S. dollars, accounting for 85% of the total capital of the top 10 digital currency markets.

Table 2. Statistical analysis of digital money in the top 10 market capitals (Unit: US Dollar) (Source: https://coinmarketcap.com/)

No	Name	Market cap	Price	Volume (24h)	Circulating supply	Change (24 h)
1	BTC	113,176,562,505	6545.96	4,261,484,372	17,289,537 BTC	1.73%
2	ETH	22,169,630,044	216.93	1,739,139,544	102,197,910 ETH	3.33%
3	XRP	21,824,399,278	0.547377	2,002,632,721	39,870,907,279 XRP	20.52%
4	BCH	7,759,561,894	446.74	342,709,562	17,369,313 BCH	2.21%
5	EOS	4,887,356,727	5.39	658,971,340	906,245,118 EOS	4.11%
6	XLM	4,778,587,411	0.254316	105,602,673	18,789,946,755 XLM	6.8%
7	LTC	3,362,630,173	57.52	303,232,230	58,461,227 LTC	4.01%
8	USDT	2,828,411,142	1.01	3,165,192,216	2,806,421,736 USDT	0.71%
9	ADA	2,094,379,662	0.08078	71,368,233	25,927,070,538 ADA	5.4%
10	XMR	1,904,161,481	115.83	28,975,025	16,438,821 XMR	1.99%

5   Advantages of Blockchain-Based Digital Currency

5.1   Low Costs and High Payment Efficiency

In the stage of issuance, digital currency does not need to pay the cost of issuing real money (Ulrich 2019). Its storage and circulation change from physical storage to cloud storage and from traditional logistics to digital transfer respectively (Ulrich 2019). In addition, there is no need to recycle, count and dispute, which greatly reduces storage and circulation costs, and improves the convenience of trading activities (Wu 2018). At the transaction stage, digital currency is recorded electronically in a single transaction book, without the need to establish and maintain a personal account, which is not limited by time and space and with the characteristics of decentralization (Zhang 2018). Furthermore, it does not require a third-party clearing institution, which reduces the process of real currency transaction and can realize the rapid transfer of domestic and foreign funds conveniently and at low cost (Zhang 2018).

5.2   High Security

Without traditional centralized institutions, digital currency transactions identify and record all transactions through the P2P network and the database composed of many nodes (Thorsten 2019). Each mode is independent and equal in status, and the information sent can spread to the whole network (Thorsten 2019). Even if a node fails, the whole network communication will not be paralyzed1 (Li 2019). The information is transmitted using a one-way encryption algorithm, which ensures that the results are verified for accuracy and therefore cannot be forged or tampered with by other nodes (Li 2019).

5.3   Distributed Ledger

The biggest innovation of digital currency is its distributed ledger model (Li 2020). Based on blockchain technology, each node distributed in the payment system replaces the traditional credit intermediary for bookkeeping (Jia 2018). Each node in the system has a copy of all information in the blockchain, including the data and time of transaction, so it is impossible to forge or double payment (Jia 2018).

5.4 Decentralization

Decentralization means that the system operates without the need for intermediaries or banks to process financial transactions and users can exchange Bitcoin peer-to-peer (Zheng 2019). However, each transaction needs to be confirmed by other users, and only after the transaction has been approved by the whole network and formed a new block, the transaction is considered successful (Kenji and Mitsuru 2019). As a result, it takes longer to confirm a deal. This is not only a weakness of Bitcoin itself, but also an insurmountable drawback of the P2P referendum form (Kenji and Mitsuru 2019).

6 Anonymity

Because Bitcoin accounts are a long string of random letters and numbers, and the account generates without real-name authentication, it is impossible to trace any personal information about a user through an account (Kianieff 2019). In addition, one user can have different accounts, and there is no correlation between multiple accounts (Zhang 2016). Therefore, although the number of Bitcoins in one account can be calculated, it is impossible to know the number of Bitcoins in all accounts of a user, which effectively guarantees the privacy of customers (Zhang 2016). However, the anonymity of Bitcoin also provides convenience for illegal transactions, such as money laundering and drug trafficking, and makes it more difficult to levy taxes (Ruan 2017).

6.1 Transaction Irreversibility

Traditional banking systems allow transactions to be revoked to address issues such as regret or error (Faijan et al. 2019). However, in Bitcoin's exchange system, each transaction is either successful or unsuccessful and cannot be revoked (Faijan et al. 2019). This is designed to prevent the payer from taking advantage of the cancellation to the detriment of the payee and to prevent the collection of additional personal information due to the need to re-establish trust at the time of refund (Faijan et al. 2019). Therefore, the irreversibility of the transaction may adverse to the acceptance of digital currency by the public (Faijan et al. 2019).

6.2 Promote the Development of Inclusive Finance

First, digital currency can carry out remote transactions without using financial intermediaries and connect with various advanced technologies such as the Internet and Internet of Things (Huang et al. 2020). With the continuous development of technology, it can significantly improve the coverage and convenience of financial services and help change the current situation of weak basic financial services (Ulrich 2019). Second, financial services based on digital currency have the characteristics of small amount, convenience, low transaction cost, and less infrastructure and human resources to be invested, so they have outstanding advantages in the field of convenient services (Zheng 2019). Finally, digital currency can also effectively solve the problems of information asymmetry and black-box trading in Internet finance, which can promote the development of Internet finance, simplify the data processing process, and enable individual to enjoy the benefits brought by financial development (Zheng 2019).

6.3 Build an Efficient and Sound Financial System

Although digital currency system has the characteristics of decentralization, but all of its trading information can keep forever based on the distributed ledger (Wu and Li 2018). Therefore, each transaction is traceable through the supervision of backstage supporter, thus providing continuous comprehensive data basis for monetary policy. Then it is benefit to analyze and precise measure money velocity, flow direction and monetary structure through big data analysis. Furthermore, financial risks can be evaluated effectively and credit policy can be timely adjusted and optimized to better support the development of economy and society (Wu and Li 2018). On the other hand, blockchain-based digital currency is immutable and unfalsifiable, so the transaction information of every participant is truthfully recorded (Wu and Li 2018). Overall, through the transparent and rigorous big data system of digital currency, regulators have sufficient information advantages to build a more efficient and robust financial system.

7 The Application of Blockchain in Financial Field

As of February 2018, there are a total of 1286 global blockchain projects (Wu 2018). It is clearly shown in Fig. 3 that China's blockchain projects only account for 4.65 of the total number of global blockchain projects ranking the third in the world, behind the United States and Britain. According to the *Blockchain White Book 2018*, the trend of blockchain removing from virtual to real is obvious.

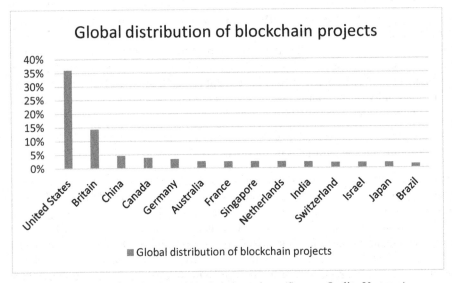

Fig. 3. Global distribution of blockchain projects (Source: Outlier Ventures)

It can be seen clearly in Fig. 4 that the application of blockchain projects in the financial field ranks first, and the Information and Communication field rank second, Underlying technology and infrastructure rank third, following with entertainment, energy and education industries.

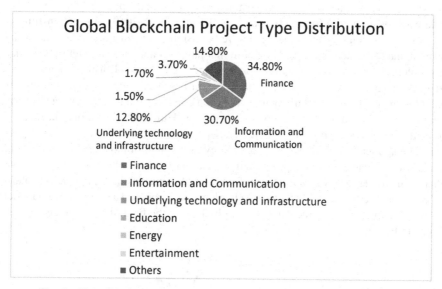

Fig. 4. Global blockchain project type distribution (Source: Outlier Ventures)

7.1 Application in Digital Currency

At present, digital currencies used in the field of Internet finance include Bitcoin, XRP, etc. (Jia 2018). With the development of blockchain technology, its role in the development of digital currency platforms has attracted the attention of institutions such as the Federal Reserve and the Bank of England (Jia 2018). The introduction of monetary policy system based on blockchain technology is useful to the macro-control of the financial market. For example, under the advice of the Bank of England, researchers from University College London proposed and developed a prototype legal digital currency system, namely the Central Banked Cryptocurrencies (Centrally Banked Cryptocurrencies)-RSCoin system in 2016 (Jia 2018). This digital currency is used to meet the needs of central banks. The emergence of this digital currency would allow blockchain technology to be endorsed by central banks in other countries. Since 2014, The people's Bank of China has set up research teams related to digital currency and blockchain technology. In the future, digital currency will also show good development prospects in China's financial field (Jia 2018).

7.2 Application in Payment and Settlement

Commercial bank act as payment intermediaries under the traditional payment and clearing mode. Payment and clearing in the financial field involves many institutions such as the central bank, the opening bank, etc. (Zhang and Xu 2018). Furthermore, overseas banks and corresponding banks are also cannot be ignored in the payment and settlement mode when dealing with foreign transactions (Loannis et al. 2019). As each institution has its own financial system, the agency relationship plays an important role in the payment and settlement system. The traditional payment and clearing method also has the problems of many nodes, complex process and high cost of clearing (Loannis et al. 2019). After the digital currency payment system based on blockchain technology is applied to the payment and settlement, people can conduct digital currency transactions without the need for third-party credit intermediaries (Hui 2018). Therefore, this kind of transaction system can improve the efficiency of cross-border and cross-regional payment. The application of blockchain technology in the field of payment and settlement can also make it easier to search payment information records, so the technology can also enhance the traceability of transaction information. Institutions including Deloitte have also conducted research on blockchain technology, and proposed a system design model and blockchain option contracts to try to apply them in the field of financial derivatives (shown in Fig. 5).

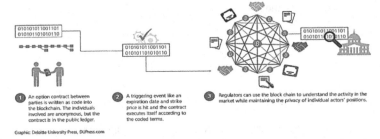

Fig. 5. Blockchain-based digital option contract model (Source: Deloitte 2016)

7.3 Application in the Field of Digital Direct Financing Platform

The establishment of digital securities system and equity-based digital crowd-funding platform is an important measure for the application of blockchain technology to digital direct financing platform. The establishment of securities system based on blockchain technology can reduce transaction costs, improve transaction speed and settlement speed (Huang et al. 2020). This technology can also guarantee the efficiency of investment divisions on the basis of avoiding the problem of information asymmetry. Digital direct financing platform can track the whole process of investment projects, which is convenient to let investors know the progress of projects in time (Huang et al. 2020).

7.4 Application in the Risk Management

The application of blockchain technology in risk management involves the following aspects, including the construction of digital credit investigation system, digital bill system and digital audit and internal control system (Huang 2019). Taking the digital credit information system of financial institutions as an example, the digital credit information system based on blockchain system has the advantages of high transparency and high efficiency (Huang 2019). Commercial banks can store customers' credit status through encryption (Li 2019). Customers of digital bill system can reduce the cost of system maintenance and system optimization while preventing the credit risk of enterprises (Li 2019).

8 Risks of Digital Currency

The use of digital currency can greatly reduce investment and simplify the payment and settlement process. However, issuing digital currency also faces certain risks.

8.1 Legal Risk

In the process of transformation to digital currency, the current legal framework is difficult to adapt to the management requirements of digital currency products and services because it is based on paper currency. Currently, from the legal perspective, there are no authoritative interpretations of the positioning, development and operating rules. Furthermore, there is also no legal regulation pertaining to intermediate service provider such as trading platform and intermediary institutions, etc. (Huang et al. 2020). Therefore, disputes of consumer rights and trade jurisdiction will not only harm the economic interests of the public, but also impact the traditional monetary system. At the same time, since the digital currency supervision system has not yet been established and there is no clear division of responsibilities, it is easy to create regulatory grey area, which allows criminals to take advantage of it (Ulrich 2019). On the other hand, different countries have different views on the legal status of digital currency, but digital currency is cross-border and cross regional circulation (Li 2019). Once there is a problem, it is difficult to have a unified regulatory measure to deal with. Furthermore, many criminals take advantage of the anonymity and decentralization of digital currency to engage in smuggling, drug trafficking, money laundering and other criminal activities, so the use of digital currency will bear certain legal risks (Li 2019). On the other hand, the consensus in any region of the world is that digital currency is a non-reality thing, applicable to the scope of legal management. However, no country or region has specific regulations regarding digital currency as a "medium of exchange" (Huang et al. 2020). If digital currency cannot be officially recognized as money by law, its illegal transactions will not be effectively monitored, which will affect the tax returns of digital currency merchants.

8.2 Speculative Risk

In 2017, the total market value of global digital currencies once exceeded US $600 billion, with an annual maximum increase of 3497.98% (Loannis et al. 2019). The types of digital currencies increased to 1334, showing a explosive growth in terms of both the total market value and the quantity (Loannis et al. 2019). In the case of bitcoin alone, growth in 2019 has reached more than 10 times (Loannis et al. 2019). While compared with the historical growth of bitcoin, this is negligible. The rise of digital currency has driven the whole grey industry chain. Financing through digital currency (ICO), establishing digital currency trading platform, private issuance of digital currency, etc. are all profiteering. Moreover, there are many irregular phenomena. Take bitcoin mining machine as an example, because mining machine manufacturers regularly limit the distribution of mining machines, there are many problems in the market. The premium between the mining machines in circulation on the market and those pre-sale on the official website is more than 100% at the peak (Thorsten 2019). Many speculators profited from the price difference. However, because the transfer of second-hand mining machinery is an agreement between individuals and there is no supervision, the price of mining machinery fluctuates greatly and thus lead to huge speculative risk.

8.3 Security Risk

All processes of digital currency are implemented via the Internet, so there is very high demand of computer and network technology. Regardless of the negligence or failure of algorithm design, system operation, equipment maintenance or external influences such as virus interference or hacker attacks, the digital currency system will be damaged, causing huge losses or even triggering systemic risks (Zhao et al. 2017). Therefore, when designing information system, the security of storage, transaction and circulation of digital currency must be solved first. Second, efficient processing is needed to deal with a large number of transactions. At present, the transaction frequency of blockchain is only close to 7 times per second, and there is still a certain gap in the frequency of hundreds of thousands of financial transactions per second (Wu and Li 2018). The *Jasper* project in Canada, which tested the issuance of digital currency, had problems in the second stage, such as slow transaction speed and system risks caused by newly added modules (Loannis et al. 2019). Table 3 displays some digital currency security events.

8.4 Anonymous Risk

The high level of anonymity and cross-border circulation of digital currency make it possible to completely avoid the banking system as long as there is the Internet (Kianieff 2019). Furthermore, cross-border transfer can be realized at low cost (Kianieff 2019). The real identities of both parties in the transaction are protected by cryptographic algorithms, which is convenient for criminals to transfer funds to conduct illegal activities (Hui 2018). Therefore, their true identities are difficult to trace, and it is difficult to effectively fight against crime without the cooperation of governments. Digital currency based on Internet technology is not subject to geographical restrictions due to the transnational

Table 3. Digital currency security events (Source: Zhang and Xu 2018)

Date	Event	Amount of loss (value at that time)
February 2014	850000 digital currency from the world's largest Bitcoin exchange operators 'Mt. Gox' were stolen and lead to bankrupcy	About US$350 million
March 2014	U.S. Digital Currency Exchange-'Poloniex' were stolen	Loss 12.3% of Bitcoin
January 2015	19000 Bitcoins were stolen from Bitstamp exchange	About US$5.4 million
June 2016	The largest crowd funding project in the blockchain industry *TheDAO* was attacked	About US$60 million
August 2016	About 120000 Bitcoins were stolen from the world famous Bitcoin trading platform *Bitfinex*	About US$65 million
March 2017	3831 Bitcoins were stolen from Bitcoin Exchange in South Korea	About 5.5 billion won
June 2017	A south Korean digital asset trading platform *Bithumb* was hacked.	Billions of won
December 2017	Mining Server *Nicehash* was attacked by hackers.	About US$ 63 million
January 2018	Japanese Bitcoin exchange *Coincheck* was attacked by hackers	About US$500 million
February 2018	Italian cryptocurrency exchange *BitGrail* suffers cyber attact	About US$170 million

characteristics of technology and device, making it difficult to accurately monitor the flow of funds. Using digital currency to arbitrage between different countries is also easy to evade sanctions, and thus increases the difficulty of supervision (Hui 2018). There are still a lot of blank in the content of regulatory level, which will inevitably lead to some criminals taking advantage of loopholes for personal gain (Fu 2019).

8.5 Transaction Risk

The transaction verification mechanism used by blockchain hides significant transaction risks, which can be used to carry out attacks such as double spend attack to complete transaction fraud (Zhang 2019). A "double spend attack" is the use of a single token in multiple transactions (Zhang 2019). It can be divided into two types according to the specific implement method, that are confirmation attack and tampering attack (Zhang 2019). The former is mainly through the use of transaction confirmation, payment confirmation and the time difference between the period and the current blockchain broadcast mechanism, relying on the sending of conflicting transaction information to implement fraudulent transactions (Wu 2018). The latter is to monitor the transaction information existing in the P2P network, tamper and forge the signature information and then broadcast to the network, so as to complete the double spend attack (Wu 2018).

8.6 Policy Risk

In the traditional paper money environment, once separated from the financial system, it is difficult to effectively monitor the operation of the base money, which affects the precision of setting monetary policy. After the introduction of digital currency, it will change the money supply and its structure, circulation speed, hierarchy and quantity, money multiplier, etc. (Zhao et al. 2017). On one hand, it can improve the accuracy of measurement and the intensity of monetary policy regulation. On the other hand, it will be a great challenge to the traditional monetary policy transmission mechanism and monetary policy tools, which still needs a lot of theoretical model construction and empirical research (Thorsten 2019).

8.7 Threaten Financial Stability

In theory, digital currencies could have an impact on the traditional monetary system, affecting not only the macro-control ability of the central bank, but also the revenue pf the government. Taking Bitcoin as an example, if digital currency becomes widely used, it will inevitably cause deflation because the total size of the money supply is constant and the speed of the money supply is decreasing (Meweters and Bruno 2016). The price of some digital currencies fluctuates sharply due to artificial speculation, which damages the confidence of holders and hinders their functions of circulation and payment. Therefore, supervision over artificial manipulation should be strengthened on the premise of not impeding the development and application of non-statutory digital currencies. Apart from a few countries, such as the United States and Germany, hold a positive attitude to non-statutory digital currency transaction, most countries are still cautious (Huang 2019).

8.8 Energy Risk

The cost of energy consumption is high. In the open network environment, multiple nodes can record new blocks, so it is necessary to solve the block conflict and data consistency problem. Therefore, it is significant to ensure that multiple nodes in the world participate in the bookkeeping simultaneously in order to maintain the security and reliability of Bitcoin blockchain data (Ruan 2017). However, the process of data sharing among multiple nodes is actually a high energy consumption process. At present, the calculation cost of the mining scheme provided by Bitcoin is so high, thus making it difficult to be widely used (Ruan 2017). Although the blockchain technology used in Bitcoin saves the cost of centralization, it also brings the cost of electricity consumption, which will also be a big obstacle to its adoption (Ruan 2017).

9 Current Supervision Situation of Digital Currency

Blockchain technology provides a safe and efficient method that can store any form of data on multiple platforms at the same time. Different industries and government departments have realized the development potential of this technology and started to use it in different fields. However, there are still differences in basic regulatory attitudes.

9.1 Rigid Supervision Model

Thailand regards all Bitcoin and other virtual currency transactions as illegal activities (Fu 2019). At present, due to the lack of applicable laws and relevant market control measures, Thai regulatory authorities regard Bitcoin-related activities as illegal, including the use and transaction of Bitcoin (Fu 2019). In June 2013, Bitcoin. Co. th, a Bitcoin startup in Thailand, suspended related transactions in order to adapt to the country's relevant policy orientation (Fu 2019). In March 2014, the central bank stated that Bitcoin was at risk but did not violate the law, and the company's Bitcoin business began to gradually resume (Fu 2019).

South Korea has gone from refusing to recognize Bitcoin's currency status to implementing blockchain innovation from top to bottom (Li 2020). At the end of 2015, Shinhan Bank participated in blockchain corporate financing (Li 2020). In February 2016, the central bank proposed in its report to encourage exploration and development of blockchain technology (Li 2020). In January 2018, KISA has started to build a blockchain ecosystem and plans to start pilot projects in core industries such as logistics and energy in April, and regard this technology as the fourth industry revolution (Li 2020). In March 2018, the "22018 TokenSky Blockchain Conference" was successfully held at the Hilton Hotel in Seoul, South Korea (Thorsten 2019). The South Korean government regards blockchain as the basic technology of the fourth industrial revolution, but there is currently no congressional legislation for digital currency supervision, only temporary regulations and administrative decrees designated by legal departments, financial commissions and other government departments (Faijan et al. 2019).

Russia's attitude has softened from a tough start, and starts to establish a legal framework (Huang et al. 2020). In 2014, the Russian Finance Ministry recommended banning the transaction of Bitcoin and cryptocurrency (Huang et al. 2020). In early 2016, the central bank considered the legalization and regulation of bitcoin exchanges (Li 2019). In January 2017, a roadmap for the development of "legalized' blockchain technology was submitted to the president (Li 2019). In order to promote the implementation of blockchain technology, Russian President Vladimir Putin, together with Ethereum founder Vitalik Buterin and blockchain experts from 15 countries, including the United States, India, Israel and Turkey, etc. discussed the future network protocol of blockchain and cryptocurrency (Li 2020). Russia is still in the exploratory period for blockchain (Li 2020). However, virtual currency transaction and possession will be legalized in Russia in the near future due to Putin's change of attitude towards blockchain technology and virtual currency (Li 2020).

Chinese government and enterprises have shown great interest and support the development of blockchain technology (Zhang 2019). The attitude towards digital currencies is restrained and rational since the core of Chinese economic development is stability (Zhang 2019). The central bank stated that Bitcoin does not have the attributes of indemnity and compulsion, so does not have the legal status of currency, and cannot be circulated as currency in the market (Li 2019). In November 2017, the State Council established the Financial Stability and Development Committee to strengthen the central bank's supervision and control of digital currency development (Li 2019).

9.2   Flexible Supervision Model

The European Commission is open to new technologies and actively promotes all parties to conduct research (Fu 2019). In April 2016, the European Digital Currency and Blockchain Technology Forum held an expo focusing on blockchain (Fu 2019). In addition, The European Commission has established an EU Blockchain Observatory and Forum (Fu 2019).

Germany was the first country to legalize Bitcoin (Wu 2018). In 2016, BaFin explored the potential applications of distributed ledger accounts, including their use in cross-border payments and the storage of data on transfers and transactions between banks (Wu 2018). Blockchain Bundesverband, a German blockchain lobbying advocacy organization stated that German government now wants to resolve regulatory issues as quickly as possible, and expects the benefits of blockchain to be realized in the German economy as much as possible (Wu 2018).

The United States classifies Bitcoin as a "commodity" and actively invests technology and finance to promote its research (Wu and Li 2018). In January 2015, the establishment of Bitcoin Exchange was approved, and the Bitcoin regulatory legislation was initially completed (Wu and Li 2018). In June 2015, BitLicense, the final version of the regulatory framework for digital currency companies, was released, and many regulatory institutions indicated their support for the development of blockchain technology (Li 2020). In June 2016, the Department of Homeland Security awarded subsidies to 6 companies devoting to government blockchain applications (Li 2020). At present, the United States has begun to be cautious and even resistance to digital currency exchanges (Li 2020). Although some exchanges have been licensed to trade, but the U.S. government has recently refused the registration of a number of digital currency companies (Li 2020).

In May 2016, Japan approved the digital currency regulation bill for the first time, and established the first blockchain industry organization, the Blockchain Cooperative Consortium (BCCC) (Fu 2019). In April 2017, it legalized the digital currency by revising the *Asset Settlement Act* (Fu 2019). Since then, Japan gradually becomes the country with the largest volume of digital currency transactions in the world, but the theft of Coincheck has aroused widespread concern about the security of exchanges by the government and the private sector (Fu 2019).

9.3 Regulatory Sandbox Model

The Monetary Authority of Singapore announced the establishment of the FinTech & Innovation Group (FTIG), which is mainly responsible for the supervision and development of new areas, managing risks, improving efficiency, and strengthening competitiveness (Faijan et al. 2019). At the same time, a "sandbox" test mechanism was proposed, which requires registration in the system for trial operation in advance (Faijan et al. 2019). Moreover, relevant companies can gain more freedom in innovation by pre-simulating operations to discover potential risks in time (Faijan et al. 2019). Singapore Prime Minister Lee Hsien Loong has publicly urged Singapore's financial sector to keep up with the development of blockchain technology, emphasizing supervision and encouraging innovation while maintaining industry trust and investor confidence (Kianieff 2019). Therefore, Singapore is far more open to regulatory policies for blockchain in financial sector than other Asian countries (Kianieff 2019).

10 Main Problems in the Supervision of Digital Currency

10.1 Lack of Key Legislation

From the aspect of the supervision of Internet finance in recent years, it is still unreliability. There is no relevant legislation or regulations for the supervision of the application of blockchain technology (Loannis et al. 2019). At present, there are legislative gaps in the issue of proof of rights in the blockchain and the legal attributes of smart contracts, subject of data rights and the restriction of their exercise, and information disclosure requirements for blockchain operating platforms (Loannis et al. 2019). Therefore, for disputes arising from the application of the blockchain, there are no specific laws and regulations for reference and protection (Ulrich 2019). If there is a loss of related interests, it may affect the enthusiasm of blockchain-related participants. The legislature temporarily maintains a relatively passive legislative attitude towards emerging things in the Internet field, which may be considering the protection and promotion of the market development of blockchain finance. However, it should still consider countermeasures for market regulation and dispute resolution. At present, there are still regulatory blind spots regarding whether there is any illegal use of blockchain operating platform in combating data and information transactions, anti-money laundering investigations, and terrorism fund flow reviews, or whether there are too low entry barriers and lax audits (Ulrich 2019).

10.2 Differences in the Regulation

Some countries currently advocate stricter regulatory measures for the digital currency market, but many countries are unwilling to impose strict restrictions on emerging markets at the risk of stifling innovative markets (Kenji and Mitsuru 2019). The regulation of cryptocurrency assets has raised issues relating to tax avoidance, money laundering, and financing of terrorism (Kenji and Mitsuru 2019). To a certain extent, cryptocurrency assets may have had an impact on the stability of financial markets. The United States is currently subject to a series of regulatory agencies that regulate financial products and transactions, which will not be conducive to the future environment for innovation (Loannis et al. 2019). Different countries hold different attitudes towards the blockchain. Actively explore the application of blockchain in different fields can promote economic development. At the same time, it can also identify potential risks as early as possible, and clarify specific supervision directions and objects of supervision. However, some countries will adopt relatively mandatory regulations in the initial stage which aims to minimize unknown risks, that is, taking full advantage of the blockchain within the scope of controllable risks. It is likely to affect the freedom of market development and the confidence of start-up entrepreneurs. Regarding rigid supervision and flexible supervision, one view is that while strengthening the supervision of individual financial institutions, the overall control of the market should always be paid attention to (Thorsten 2019). Another view is that market should be let free to adjust and minimize government intervention (Thorsten 2019). The strength of supervision will inhibit the development of innovation. The core is how to balance the degree of supervision and achieve the greatest regulatory benefits with the smallest regulatory cost.

10.3 The Protection of User Privacy Needs to Be Strengthened

Although the blockchain system has the advantages of transparency and inability to be tampered with, it is still subject to many challenges such as infrastructure, system design, operation management, privacy protection, and technology update. It needs to be considered in terms of technology and management as a whole. The immutable nature of blockchain technology makes transactions not regrettable, which means transactions cannot be cancelled or the account cannot be unfrozen. There will be conflicts between the centralized supervision method and the decentralized system. The current centralized monitoring model can monitor unidentified intrusions and verify the legality of transactions (Huang 2019). If illegal transactions are found, they can be interrupted in time, and unreviewed content will also be offline in time, except for the massive amount of data screening and manual individual identification (Huang 2019). However, if the system of the central organization is invaded by hackers, or a large-scale power accident occurs, which causes the system of the central organization to collapse, it is likely to lead to the leakage of user information and the loss of user property. Especially in the fields related to the privacy of users, such as insurance, medical care, etc. Although the relative security of data can be guaranteed in the decentralized system, it will also be shared in the entire system, and all users can browse other users' data.

10.4 Subsequent Disputes Involved in the Automatic Execution of Smart Contracts Need to Be Solved Urgently

The smart contract in the blockchain environment is to form an agreement with someone through the blockchain using cryptocurrency, and the agreement between the two parties does not need to be based on mutual trust (Fu 2019). When the preset conditions are triggered, the contract will be automatically executed according to the digital code converted from the agreed content (Fu 2019). Furthermore, the whole process cannot be interfered (Fu 2019). The completion of the contract will be recorded in the blockchain system according to the time stamp, and it cannot be tampered with or resumed

(Fu 2019). In the whole blockchain system, the transaction contents of both parties are also automatically identified by the system (Fu 2019). It does not need to rely on the existence of centralized servers, but runs through network nodes (Fu 2019). During the execution of the contract, the resources of both parties will be automatically obtained, and the system will be reasonably configured according to the agreed contents, and transmitted and run in the form of digital code (Fu 2019). The current smart contract cannot be effectively cancelled or abolished for the possible revocable contract or illegal contract (Zheng 2019). At present, there are no relevant provisions for the compensation mechanism of defective contract which has been automatically executed through the smart contract, and the technology at this stage cannot be completely separated from the participation of the court and the government (Zheng 2019). In addition, because the smart contract does not have a clear legal position, it is formally a contract established by changing the legal provisions into code entry (Zheng 2019). However, in essence, anonymity and encryption are basically unable to identify the contracting parties, and there is no relevant law or regulations to refer to (Zheng 2019). The technical principle of smart contracts can be seen in Fig. 6.

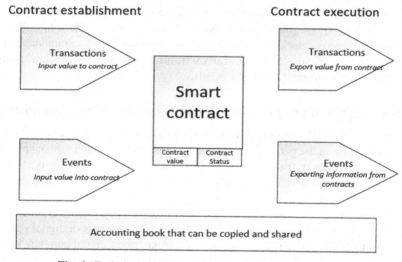

Fig. 6. Technical principle of smart contracts (Source: 36 Kr)

11 Regulatory Recommendations for Blockchain Technology in the Financial Field

11.1 Promote Relevant Regulatory Legislation of Blockchain Technology

Legislation should follow up with the development of technology in real time to avoid amplifying the adverse effects caused by the lag of legislation, so as to timely and effectively respond to market changes. First, for the enterprises involved in Internet finance, the threshold of qualification examination should be raised for the purpose of avoid the occurrence of market chaos. Second, strengthening the supervision of blockchain platform, and carrying out effective control through asset record mortgage or other forms. Third, urging and promoting the establishment of industry self-discipline and self-correction mechanism, and taking corresponding punishment measures for the behaviors that affect market fairness or damage the rights and interests of consumers. Fourth, complementing the new concept of blockchain technology to ensure that laws can be follow in the application process of blockchain technology in the financial field. On the other hand, it can also help the relevant departments to be more efficient in dealing with such disputes.

11.2 Establish Transboundary Joint Response Mechanism

The transboundary joint response mechanism should be established before the issuance of digital currency in order to deal with possible risks (Zhang and Xu 2018). Different from traditional financial risk events, digital currency based on information technology tend to show high concealments, high complexity, strong correlation, strong infectivity and other characteristics when risk events occur (Zhang and Xu 2018). Such risk characteristics put forward high requirements for emergency response and risk mitigation. Therefore, to deal with digital currency risk events, it is necessary to establish transboundary joint response mechanisms such as regulatory institutions, commercial banks and Internet enterprises, so as to provide early warning of potential risk problems, timely discover and deliver information of risk events.

11.3 Pay Attention to Legal Positioning and International Policy Coordination

At present, there are still a lot of problems to be solved in the legal and policy aspects of digital currency. From the perspective of legal arrangements and international policies, they are mainly shown in the following aspects. First, from the legal perspective, the conflict between the unique information technology nature of digital currencies based on different technology choices and the existing legal arrangements needs to be further clarified. At the same time, issues such as the identification of rights and responsibilities and the protection of consumers' rights and interests in the process of digital currency trading need to be further clarified to ensure the normal use of digital currency in trading activities. Second, from an international perspective, the attitudes and regulatory requirements of various countries in the world are very different at present. There is still not reach a consensus on digital currency among different countries. For example, China is actively seeking to issue digital currency first, but has strict restrictions on Bitcoin, ICO, etc., while Japan considers Bitcoin as a legal transaction currency. Changes in policy and regulatory requirements by any party in major countries or regions will have a significant impact on digital currencies. Therefore, there is still a lot of complex work to be done to coordinate digital currency as mature currency.

11.4 Use Regulatory Technology to Improve Financial Regulatory Capabilities

Traditional financial regulatory methods and tools have been unable to effectively regulate financial risks that generated by blockchain finance. Therefore, countries such as

Britain and the United States begin to use regulatory technology (RegTech) to improve the efficiency of regulation and reduce the cost of regulation (Zheng 2019). The practice of Britain and the United States can be used as a reference to introduce regulatory technology to strengthen effective supervision of blockchain finance (Zheng 2019). The specific regulatory framework should include the following aspects: First, digitalization of regulatory rules. Using big data and artificial intelligence technology to transform textual financial regulatory laws into digital regulatory rules through natural language processing (NLP) (Zheng 2019). On this basis, establish a complete digital regulatory rule base, combined with deep learning, algorithm and other technical means to detect own regulatory loopholes and improve the ability of financial supervision. Second, establish a regulatory application platform to effectively integrate the regulatory data of various departments and improve regulatory efficiency. Third, establish a comprehensive monitoring data acquisition system. Big data, cloud computing and artificial intelligence technologies are used to extract data and realize real-time update and interaction of financial regulatory data. Using cryptography and other data security technologies for data transmission to enhance the security and reliability of financial supervision data collection. Fourth, establish an intelligent financial risk judgement system. Financial regulatory authorities should make use of financial technology to realize the intelligentization of financial risk monitoring and improve the ability of financial risk prediction.

12   Conclusion

In this era when the real world is becoming more and more virtual and the virtual world is becoming more and more realistic, it is irrational to blindly suppress and pursue new things. Only to actively see the value of new things and alert to risks with right mindset, can promote the stability and harmonious development of the international financial system. Faced with the rapid changes in technology, opportunities should be seized to encourage enterprise innovation and fully release market vitality. At the same time, it is significant to avoid risks through reasonable management and control. Furthermore, test area can be used to provide feedback and continuously adjust the regulatory policy to better balance the long-term mechanism of supervision and the market. Through promoting and improving the regulatory legislation of blockchain technology, the barriers to entry of the blockchain industry are raised. Then potential risks and their characteristics are managed and controlled at different levels. At present, blockchain technology is still in the period of exploration. Governments and enterprises around the world are learning how to utilize blockchain technology. At this stage, the supervision efforts should be coordinated with actively explore the potential power of the new technology. At the same time, relevant policies and regulations should follow up and be adjust in real time, so that the blockchain technology can grow freely in a suitable legal framework, and take full advantage of its technological advantages while ensuring the stability of financial market.

Acknowledgments. The author would like to acknowledge and thank Prof. Zhou and all authors that provide useful thoughts and opinions for my final paper.

References

Belke, A., Beretta, E.: From cash to central bank digital currencies and cryptocurrencies: a balancing act between modernity and monetary stability. J. Econ. Stud. **47**(4), 911–938 (2020)

Faijan, A., Li, J.P., Shaik, S.A.: Potential of blockchain technology in digital currency: a review. In: 16th International Computer Conference on Wavelet Active Media Technology and Information Processing Wavelet Active Media Technology and Information Processing (ICCWAMTIP), pp. 85–91 (2019)

Fu, M.X.C.: The theory and practice of digital currency under blockchain-based on the case of Ripple. Ph.D. thesis, Shanghai Jiao Tong University, Shanghai (2019). Accessed 10 Jan 2021

Huang, G.H., Liu, D.W., Li, J.C.: Risk Identification and Supervision of Virtual Currency. Macroeconomy (2020). Accessed 10 Jan 2021

Huang, W.: The potential risks and model construction of blockchain technology applied to the derivatives market. Financ. Regul. Res. **2**, 97–109 (2019)

Hui, Z.B.: Research on the formation mechanism and risk supervision of digital encryption currency. Explor. Free Views **9** (2018)

Jia, M.M.: Bitcoin-based blockchain technology: opportunities and challenges in the financial sector. Financ. View **31**, 66–67 (2018)

Barrdear, J., Kumhof, M.: The macroeconomics of central bank issued digital currencies. Bank of England Staff Working Paper, vol. 605 (2016)

Kenji, S., Mitsuru, I.: How to make a digital currency on a blockchain stable. Future Gener. Comput. Syst. (2019). https://doi.org/10.1016/j.future.2019.05.019

Kianieff, M.: Blockchain technology and the law: Opportunities and Risks. Contemporary Commercial Law (2019)

Li, J.J.: Blockchain application risk and regulatory mechanism construction in the financial field. China Secur. J. (2020). 4th edn

Li, Y.: Research on the Legal Supervision of Digital Currency. Ph.D. thesis, Shandong Univeristy, Shandong (2019). Accessed 10 Jan 2021

Liu, W.: Digital currency issuance mechanism exploration and risk prevention based on international experience. Southwest Finance **51**(8), 51–58 (2017)

Loannis, L., Hacker, P., Eich, S., Dimitropoulos, G.: Regulating Blockchain: Techno-Social and Legal Challenges, 1st edn. Oxford University Press, Oxford (2019)

Mcweters, J., Bruno, G.: The future of financial infrastructure: an ambitious look of how blockchain can reshape finance. World Economic Forum (2016)

Ruan, X.D.: The development of digital currency and its risk prevention. New Economy Research, pp. 79–85 (2017)

Nakamoto, S.: Bitcoin: A Peer-to-Peer Electronic Cash System (2018). Accessed 10 Jan 2021

Thorsten, P.: International digital currencies and their impact on monetary policy: An exploration of implications and vulnerability. Hohenheim Discussion Papers in Business, Economics and Social Sciences (2019)

Ulrich, B.: Central bank digital currency: financial system implications and control. Int. J. Polit. Econ. **48**(4), 303–335 (2019)

Wu, H.: Regulatory research on the application of blockchain technology in the financial field, Ph.D. thesis, University of Chinese Academy of Social Sciences, Beijing (2018). Accessed 10 Jan 2021

Wu, T., Li, J.Q.: Research on the integration and development of blockchain and finance. Financ. Regul. Res. **12** (2018)

Zhang, B.: The application of blockchain technology in foreign countries and relevant recommendations. Financ. Technol. Time **5**, 35–38 (2016)

Zhang, S., Xu, X.: Research on risk management of digital currency based on blockchain. China Credit Card **12**, 45–48 (2018)

Zhang, X.H.: Research on legal risks and supervision paths caused by blockchain. Contemp. Econ. Manage. **11**, 79–83 (2018)

Zhang, Y.W.: Discussion on Digital Currency Risk Management Based on Blockchain. Modern Economic Information, 2rd edn (2019)

Zhao, Y., Zhang, X., Wei, B.Y.: Opportunities and challenges that blockchain technology brings to the financial market. China's prices, pp. 50–56 (2017)

Zheng, Q.F.: Blockchain technology, risk and regulation in financial markets. J. Qiqihar Univ. **44**(6), 44–48 (2019)

Developing a Mobile Learning Application for Preschooler

Yaw Hee Man, Su Mon Chit, and Abdul Samad Bin Shibghatullah[⊠]

UCSI University, Kuala Lumpur, Malaysia
abdulsamad@ucsiuniversity.edu.my

Abstract. Mobile learning is a trend method that people used to study online nowadays. There is a lot of different study methods in mobile learning. Although mobile learning has been widely used for primary school, secondary school or university and college but still yet to fully deploy in preschools age. Mobile learning can also be provided to preschoolers similar to university platforms, but for children or kids, game based mobile learning will be more suitable for them. This research will study the requirements of having a mobile learning application and to develop a mobile learning application for children age from 3 to 5 years old.

Keywords: Mobile learning · Preschools · Children · Kindergarten

1 Introduction

Mobile learning also known as M-learning is a mobility study method. M-learning is a new way to study and to access study material anytime and anywhere as long as learners are connected to the internet with a mobile device [1]. Mobile learning can be using handheld computers, or mobile phone which those are mobility and able to carry to anywhere. Mobile learning also includes the distribution and promotion of learning using mobile phones, and cell phones have gradually gained a role in secondary and higher education over the last five years [2]. Mobile learning is widely used in many areas such as teaching moral values [3], teaching financial literacy to children [4] as well as using mobile app as 3D augmented reality dictionary [5] for children. Mobile learning using portable computers is evidently relatively inexperienced in terms of both technology and pedagogy but is also evolving rapidly. Preschool is an early childhood programmed in which children combine learning with playing in a programmed run by professionally trained adults. Children are most often enrolled in childcare between the ages of three and five, while some classes can be attended by as little as two [6]. Nowadays, preschools are very common, and most parents send their children to preschool program before they enter primary school. This is to help their children to have a basic learning skill and adapt to the study environment easily. In this age of 20 century, Industrial 4.0 has been introduced and started being used in the whole wide world. Technology has a huge impact on children nowadays. Based on the results of media use and attitudes report 2019, it shows that YouTube has become the favorite platform for children who are between 5–15 [7]. This is exactly where they are during their preschool period. While they are using

© Springer Nature Switzerland AG 2021
G. Salvendy and J. Wei (Eds.): HCII 2021, LNCS 12796, pp. 68–84, 2021.
https://doi.org/10.1007/978-3-030-77025-9_7

technology to access YouTube, why not just access to the mobile learning application as well to continue their study at home. Mobile learning is known as M- learning. M-learning is an education that uses personal devices such as phones, laptops, or tablets. It can be very flexible and allow students to access the education material wherever and whenever they want to [8]. This M-learning application will provide children with a platform to study online without attending any physical class. With this application, children will no longer suffer the feeling of being apart with their beloved parents. The traditional way of children having preschool is their parents are required to send them to kindergarten which is expensive. Parents have to do many researches on which preschools are suitable to go and whether the location is suitable or not. For example, parents found the best preschool, but it is located very far. With this application developed, the best preschool can have this application to conduct their preschool and monitor the children via online. So that parents no need to worry about the location of the preschool. Author in [9] has mentioned the advantages for children having online learning such as the online learning system and the virtual education software could help the children to remember thing faster than usual and make them are more interested on study. This paper also mentioned that converting traditional teaching to online teaching for children is a good way to encourage them to proper use technology devices in this era of technology. Others than that, having online learning for children also could able to help them on balancing themselves between study and family interaction. According to the author in [10], by using mobile learning technology to the children will be much easier to capture their progress of learning outside the classroom through the features that provided in this technology such as audio recordings, videos, images or online notes. In this paper also mentioned that a huge different of future study environment will be adapting to all the new technologies and it could help children to learn how to practice their own social networking to the school environment. In this era of technology, many children start to use online learning tools such as game-based learning app or video learning app. M-learning should not only focus and develop for universities student since nowadays most of the children own a technology device. M-learning should consider developing for young children to prevent they overuse or misused the technology devices in an improper way. The aim of this project is to develop a prototype of M-learning that provide a platform for those children who are between 3 to 6 years old that have preschool so there is no need to attend physical class.

2 Literature Review

2.1 Mobile Learning

Mobile learning known as M-learning. It's basically E-learning but using mobile phone. Phone has been named as Mobile because its mobility. With M-learning, we can learn anywhere anytime just need a piece of hand phone would do [1]. This learning mode are growth rapidly especially in this covid-19 time. Every schools and universities have to close down due to the virus spreading and students has to attend E-learning. The Young generation has grown up on streaming platforms. Mobile learning is geared to the way millennials work and think. Yet there are so many benefits of M-learning that it will help all generations [1]. Mobile learning requires networking through wireless networks, mobile telecommunications networks or both for copying, uploading and/or online work, and links to institutional systems such as virtual learning environments (VLEs) and information systems management systems (VLEs) (MIS).

2.2 Word Puzzle

Based on the research found, word puzzle is a fantastic way to let your children learn and assisting their study in a surprising way. Word puzzle not only for children to have fun, it can help to occupy their time and train their brain to think and their memorizing skills. There are few advantages of having word puzzle for children when they were small. The first one, word puzzle helps to improve their understanding and spelling. Word puzzle usually come with pictures, so children would easy to understand the verb meaning by looking at the picture instead of some dictionary. Spelling improvement will be done by word puzzle as word puzzle required a certain knowledge of spelling the words. With word puzzle, children will clearly memorize and understand the word easily [11].

Secondly, word puzzle able to train child's work pace [11]. Although some simple word puzzle but different level has different difficulties of puzzle. With facing different difficulties of puzzle, the process time of children take to answer the question will be train. Slowly, children's work pace will get a better improvement and they are able to answer question quickly and correctly. With answering question correctly, they need a good self-esteem. Word puzzle would help to improve their self-esteem as well. Author in [12] has mentioned that, as a parent helping their child to solve some problem or help them to learn new thing would be able to increase their self-esteem. For example, parents could spend some time to play the word puzzle with their child. At the same time, praising or motivating given by parents are the key who brings up the children's self-esteem

2.3 Color Training

Color learning not only learning the name of the colour. Colour is very attractive and sensitive to our eye. What colour children like could affect their lifestyle and thinking even their learning skills. Learning colours are important as learning shapes. Based on [13], learning colours actually a cognitively complex task for very young children. Teaching them to identify different colours are helping them to identify the objects that appears to their environment. For example, children will learn how to request a Red Apple from their parents, or a Yellow Pikachu that they like. Children unable to identify more colours like adult do. But they will know what colour they like that which are more comfortable to them. By learning colours will help to increase their creativity. Learning colours are the basic for children, after learning how to identify colours, they can proceed to colouring. Colouring will have different learning outcomes and training for children.

2.4 Sound Training

In terms for children to learn and remember thing faster. Sound learning is the way to archive this. Memory functions in a very unique way. Memory first is store inside our brain by encoding the information. After encoding, then we will store it into our brain. When we want to remember it back, we will recall it. This is how memory works [14]. Learning things by seeing the objects and listening the sound, we will automatically store the sound with the object into our brain same as children. When we want to recall it back, the sound will recall automatically. So, this is the reason that sound learning could increase our memorizing skills and cause children to learn faster and remembering thing easier. Based on the research found that children have a sensitive ear sensing than adults [15]. Children will learn faster and easier than usual if the study material come with sound.

2.5 Game Based Training

Game based learning is a type of learning style which used game to learn it when children playing the game. Games have been used as a learning tools for centuries like chess game and so on [16]. The central principle behind game-based learning is to teach through repetition, loss, and achievement of goals. According to psychologist Judy Wills, "Students retain what they learn when the learning is associated with strong positive emotion." Children learn something when it is fun enough [17]. Based on the research found, there are quite a number of advantages of using Game based learning for children [18]. First of all, the main benefits of game-based learning are it could increase children memory capacity. Second was game-based learning could help to improve children's thinking and problem-solving skills. Most game required player to answer quickly or within a time given. So, children could practice their thinking speed and solving skills throughout the game. The last benefits which are quite helpful in developing children knowledge is help children to become computer fluency people. Due to this era is global with technologies, children will learn how to use technology one day. By letting them to play game will help them to understand how the technology works is.

2.6 No Scoring Games

There is one article that written by one of the reports from Tribune and he mentioned that every kid can win without scoring [19]. This is because kids will drop out when they think they need to win. They have such a feeling of pushy by looking at the final score. Without score, kids can have their fun during the game. With funs, children learn. By not having the score, young players should only concentrate on playing the game and understanding the rules; do not care about the results. This application was developed without any scoring system. This is because this application is focussed to let children learn and have fun during the game. To prevent children who can't answer well in this game and they feel depress, so scoring will be removed in this application. Matters in the progress not to the outcome.

3 Methodology

This research uses qualitative research method to gather requirements and prototype to develop the model. Qualitative research method is the research method which only collect non-numeric data and then analyze it [20]. What this prototype who done research from qualitative method is literature review. Literature review can be considered as qualitative research as because literature view able to show the interrelation and the concept of the topic. Basically, all the basic requirements and the benefits of some activities will be gathered and discussed. This is to have a clear direction while developing the prototype. For example, the benefits of not having scoring methods in these kinds of application, the benefits of providing game puzzle for children and son on. Others related application that on the market will be reviewed and gather their application details as well for the references of developing this prototype. By all the information gathered, we would know whether the prototype should include scoring system or not. After the application prototype has been developed, a more detailed qualitative methodology will be done to collect feedback from different people. This part of methodology aims for three different categories which age between 4–12, 13–40 and lastly 40 and above. Different age of people has different view and perspective for this application. Their feedbacks are really mattering to make this prototype to be perfect enough for children.

4   Result and Findings

Throughout the research by using the method that mentioned previously, we found that mobile learning is quite new for preschools. Most of the mobile learning for preschools are playing puzzle game, coloring game and so on. By having this data, we can do based on what we have in the market and what we do not have. At the meantime, mobile learning through game are more benefits from just mobile learning. This is because game is always fun compare to textbook learning or even E-learning which looking at an Electronic version of textbook. Learning while play game are more fun and more challenging for children. It's able to be triggered children learning skills and train their memory capacity.

After the research done, we found that there are pros and cons on having scoring system and not to have scoring system. With scoring system in the game of the children playing could help them to enter a competitive mood and challenge their processing skills and solving skills. Competitive game has competitors. But if children did not meet their own expectation or satisfaction, children might easy to get depress and lost confident from the game. This might affect their childhood learning mood. On the other hand, without scoring system of the game that children play will let children to be more relax compare to those which with scoring system. Without the score, its mean without competitors. Children can have fun and enjoy the game. When children have fun, they learn. This is to let children to be more focus on learning while playing but not playing with winning.

Moreover, game puzzle is very easy, but difficulties option has to be included to compatible with different children who have different level of knowledge. So, in our prototype, level of difficulties will be including as well. Since the application are design for children, the UI design of the prototype will keep it simple and colourful. Some cute cartoon background will be implied to the prototype to attract children's interest. This prototype will try to reduce as many buttons as possible. So, it's easier and user friendly to children who are less than 6 years old. Tidy and clean background and user interface is the requirement for this prototype. Following are the results of the questionnaire from all my respondents. Based on the Fig. 1, most of the participants have knowledge on what mobile learning is.

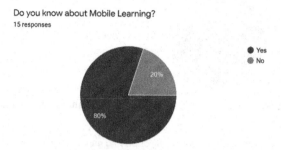

Do you know about Mobile Learning?
15 responses

● Yes
● No

20%

80%

Fig. 1. Knowledge on mobile learning

Based on Figs. 1, 2, 3, 4, 5, 6 and 7, respondents' comments and feedbacks has given a good direction on developing the prototype. By having all these feedback and agreement, a prototype application named FYP2 has been developed.

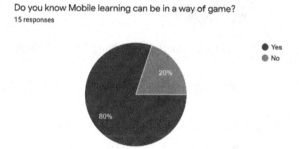

Do you know Mobile learning can be in a way of game?
15 responses

● Yes
● No

20%

80%

Fig. 2. Knowledge on game based mobile learning

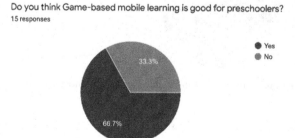

Do you think Game-based mobile learning is good for preschoolers?
15 responses

● Yes
● No

33.3%

66.7%

Fig. 3. Perception on game based mobile learning

Do you agree that mobile learning applications could help children to spend their time on a mobile devices in the right way?
15 responses

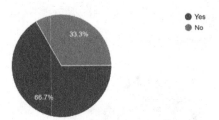

Fig. 4. Perception on game based mobile learning for children

Do you prefer preschoolers learn in a way of playing games or studying the textbook?
15 responses

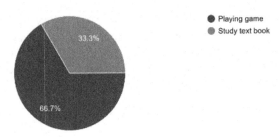

Fig. 5. Perception on game based learning for preschoolers

Do you agree that by having this mobile learning application, children will learn faster and effectively?
15 responses

Fig. 6. Perception on efficiency game based mobile learning

Figure 8 shows the first page when users enter to the application. This page is to introduce this application to the users and prompt user to confirm enter to this application. Header of this page will be welcoming users to this application. There's a button will prompt user to click on it as to continue to next page.

If there is a new application for children to play and have fun while learning, will you consider using it?

15 responses

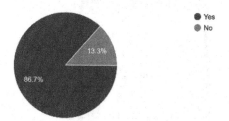

Fig. 7. Perception on usage of game based mobile learning

Fig. 8. Main Page of the application

Figure 9 show all the available activities in this application. Word puzzle 1 and word puzzle 2 are defined as level one and level two for this word puzzle game. Word puzzle 1 can be known as easy and puzzle 2 can be known as hard. The last section is colour training. This is to direct to the page of colour learning in this application.

Figures 10, 11, 12, 13 and 14 show all the 5 questions included in level one. All of these questions are focussing on the vowel letters in English which is A, E, I, O and U. Different questions comes with different picture that represent the question. User just have to type in the correct answer with big letters will pass the game.

Figures 15, 16, 17, 18 and 19 show all the 5 questions as well in level two. But the difficulties upgraded to 4 letters verb in this level. Starting from question 4 which is page 4, difficulties has been increased as two alphabets are missing and users need to answer the two letters correctly to pass the question.

From Fig. 20 we can see there is six boxes with six different colours. This page is to teach children by recognizing colour and how it pronounces. User can touch and click on any boxes with colours. System will automatically read out the colour accordingly to

Fig. 9. Menu

Fig. 10. Game Interface Page 1

the colour that users select. For example, user clicked on the red box. System will read out "RED" once user click it. System will read any colours that according to what user has selected.

Figure 21 shows the question 1, page 1 from puzzle level one. Once user click the blank answer box in the question, the keyboard will automatically be jumped out and prompt user to enter the correct answer. Next, users will use the on-screen keyboard to

Fig. 11. Game Interface Page 2

Fig. 12. Game Interface Page 3

key in the correct answer. After user key in the answer, user is required to click on the check answer button to check answer. System will check the answer whether it is match to the correct answer or not. If not match with the correct answer, toast box will show and users need to answer it again. User may seek help from their parents or friends. If the answer is correct, toast box with well-done will be shown. After the toast box appear,

Fig. 13. Game Interface Page 4

Fig. 14. Game Interface Page 5

the page will automatically jump to the next page and this function will loop until the end of the level and goes back to the menu page.

Evaluations are carried out on this prototype application that has been developed in order to test the system and ensure that it meets the objectives of the study and the requirements defined, as well as to identify any additional issues that must be addressed. The phase of evaluation consists of four step which is unit testing, integration testing,

Fig. 15. Game Interface Level 2 Page 1

Fig. 16. Game Interface Level 2 Page 2

system testing and user acceptance testing. The first three phase which is the unit testing, integration testing and system testing are going to test all the functional requirement whether it is meet or not. The last phase of testing, user acceptance testing is going to test all the non-functional requirement.

Target participants of this user acceptance testing phase is each group 10 person. Each group represent different group which is diploma, undergraduate and working

Fig. 17. Game Interface Level 2 Page 3

Fig. 18. Game Interface Level 2 Page 4

people. This is to collect a more generally feedback from different perspective. These 30 participants are required to install the APK file in their android phone and test out the application. Once they finish testing the application, a google form will require to fill in by them. This google form consist of 10 questions which ask for their opinion, comments and satisfaction for this prototype application.

Fig. 19. Game Interface Level 2 Page 5

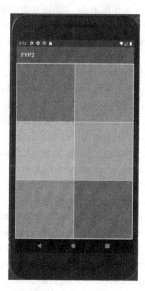

Fig. 20. Colour learning

From the survey, most of the respondent felt that the interface of this application should be improve to attract children's attraction. Next, most of the respondent suggest to increase the number of questions and shuffle the questions as well.

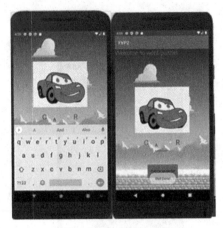

Fig. 21. Puzzle Level 1 Page 1

5　Conclusions and Recommendations

Most of the objectives has been successfully achieved. This prototype application able to solve the problem of children are boring while learning, children are able to have fun while during learning. Children no longer need to listen to teacher's boring lecture or reading other learning materials. The objectives of this application is let children to learn in a very fun environment. This objective has been successfully achieved by using game to attract children and let them have enough of fun during learning. This prototype application able to let children to have fun while learning new words. Necessary background study was done and analyzed in detail. Throughout all the research, I can define my own requirements for this prototype clearly. After all the data was gathered and analyzed, the prototype was designed based on all the data and requirement that gathered beforehand and according to the specifications as well. The evaluation of this prototype application also done by letting a number of participants to review the application. With my prototype application, children able to learn some new words starting from vowels. Children's able to play game as learning. This could help them to relax while studying. There is a very simple user interface which very easily understand by users. User are able to easily understand how to play the game by just looking at the interface itself. In this prototype, some java algorithm has been used to check answer of user enter it and some audio file has been imported into this application. Audio file is to let children learn how to read out the specific color. Though the study's objectives have been met and the prototype application has been successfully built and being evaluated, there will still bound to be some limitations to both the study itself and the prototype application developed. Nothing is perfect and this project are not excluded. Only practices make perfect, that's why this application prototype need to have evaluation to keep improving and make it better. First of all, due to time constraints, the long-term effect of using this application could not be studied. Next, the application is not fully complete as some of the planned-out feature may be excluded from the prototype application. The limitations that are known from the prototype applications are: User cannot enter lower case letter as the answer; User do not know their final score after they answer all the answer; The application interfaces are very poor and lack of attraction; The application lacks of questions; The program was evaluated on a small number of physical devices, meaning that its output on other devices could not be checked because the code could be processed differently by different devices, which could cause some application conflicts.

References

1. Priscila, What is Mobile Learning (m-learning)? Definition explained (2020). https://www.easy-lms.com/knowledge-center/lms-knowledge-center/mobile-learning/item10388. Accessed 15 Jan 2020
2. Traxler, J.: Defining, discussing, and evaluating mobile learning: the moving finger writes and having writ.... Int. Rev. Res. Open Distance Learn. **8**(2) (2007). https://doi.org/10.19173/irrodl.v8i2.346
3. Jian, N.L.M., Mon, C.S., Subaramaniam, K.: Adoption of mobile technology in teaching moral values to children: a study in Malaysia. In: 2020 IEEE 10th Symposium on Computer Applications & Industrial Electronics (ISCAIE) (2020). https://doi.org/10.1109/iscaie47305.2020.9108827
4. Hong, Y.S., Mon, C.S., Shibghatullah, A.S.: Impacting financial literacy for children using mobile application: a requirement analysis. Proc. Mech. Eng. Res. Day **2020**, 156–157 (2020)
5. Mon, C.S., Subaramaniam, K.: Understanding the requirement of a 3D aided augmented reality mobile app dictionary for children. Int. J. Technol. Enhanc. Learn. **12**(4), 447–457 (2020)
6. HealthofChildren, "Preschool," (2020). http://www.healthofchildren.com/P/Preschool.html. Accessed 15 Jan 2020
7. OfCom, "Children and parents: media use and attitudes report 2019" (2019). https://www.ofcom.org.uk/research-and-data/media-literacy-research/childrens/children-and-parents-media-use-and-attitudes-report-2019
8. Beal, V.: Mobile learning (M-learning) (2020). https://www.webopedia.com/definitions/mobile-learning-m-learning/
9. Galy, E., Downey, C., Johnson, J.: The effect of using e-learning tools in online and campus-based classrooms on student performance. J. Inf. Technol. Educ. **10**(1), 209–230 (2011). https://doi.org/10.28945/1503
10. Sharples, M., Milrad, M., Arnedillo-Sanchez, I., Vavoula, G.N.: Mobile learning: small devices, big issues. Technol. Learn. Princ. Prod. 233–249, January 2009. https://doi.org/10.1007/978-1-4020-9827-7
11. Olivier, K.: 9 Reasons Your Child Should Do Word Puzzles EVERY DAY (2017). https://www.worksheetcloud.com/blog/9-reasons-your-child-should-do-word-puzzles-every-day/. Accessed 15 Jan 2021
12. Raisingchildren, "About self-esteem: children 1-8 years" 2017. https://raisingchildren.net.au/toddlers/behaviour/understanding-behaviour/about-self-esteem. Accessed 15 Jan 2021
13. Katie, Why learning colors and shapes is so important for young children (2018). https://www.giftofcuriosity.com/why-learning-colors-and-shapes-is-so-important-for-young-children/. Accessed 15 Jan 2021
14. Pinola, M.: The Science of Memory: Top 10 Proven Techniques to Remember More and Learn Faster (2019). https://zapier.com/blog/better-memory/. Accessed 15 Jan 2021
15. PURO, "How children are more sensitive to noise" (2018). https://purosound.com/blogs/the-sound/how-children-are-more-sensitive-to-noise#:~:text=Children's ears are sensitive%2C with, more vulnerable to loud noise. Accessed 15 Jan 2021

16. Cahill, G.: "Why Game-Based Learning?" (2020). https://thelearningcounsel.com/article/why-game-based-learning. Accessed 15 Jan 2021
17. Tynker, "The Power of Play: How Kids Benefit from Game-Based Learning" (2020). https://www.tynker.com/blog/articles/ideas-and-tips/the-power-of-play-how-kids-benefit-from-game-based-learning/. Accessed 15 Jan 2021
18. TeachThought, "6 Basic Benefits Of Game-Based Learning" (2013). https://www.teachthought.com/technology/6-basic-benefits-of-game-based-learning/. Accessed 15 Jan 2021
19. Keilman, J.: With no score, every kid can win (2013). https://www.chicagotribune.com/news/ct-xpm-2013-06-26-ct-x-0626-keilman-column-20130626-story.html. Accessed 15 Jan 2021
20. Bhandari, P.: An introduction to qualitative research (2020). https://www.scribbr.com/methodology/qualitative-research/#:~:text=Qualitative research involves collecting and,generate new ideas for research. Accessed 15 Jan 2021

Transformation the Business of eCommerce Through Blockchain

Uttam Kumar Roy[1](✉) and Weining Tang[2](✉)

[1] E-Commerce Technology, Information Engineering Department,
Huzhou University, Huzhou, China
[2] Business Department, Huzhou University, Huzhou, China
twnly@zjhu.edu.cn

Abstract. Cryptocurrency, decentralization and distributed ledger made the Blockchain technology unique and robust. Bitcoin was the first blockchain-based cryptocurrency. Moreover, It became the synonym of digital/virtual currency and this technology opened a new era. It is not only the digital currency technology but also it offers many significant possibilities, which offer secure, fast, smooth and trust in today's eCommerce system. Many companies are implementing the technology and achieve the potential of security, speed and smooth transactions. Today's eCommerce highly depends on faster logistics, error-free transaction and protection of the user's data. Maintaining cybersecurity issues and giving the best user experience through UI is the first concern of today's eCommerce platform. Blockchain solves these problems by giving extra layers of personal data security and keeping the confidential bank data safe. Using the blockchain technology, singer, video content creator or any digital artist can get benefits. This paper includes a subjective review of Blockchain in E-commerce (physical and digital goods) and the possibilities, risks, future of this technology.

Keywords: eCommerce · Blockchain · Cryptocurrency · Business

1 Background

In 1834 Charles Babbage had designed a new analytical machine which can store, transfer, and adding numbers [1]. The machine did not come into reality at that time but generally considered the first computer because of program-controlled functionality. Charles Babbage considered the father of the computer. Moreover, in 1960 mainframe computer was introduced by IBM. Mainframe computer was a centralized system. It worked as a central data hub, responsible for data processing; more simply it could connect less powerful devices in the mainframe system to get powerful output.

Later on, the personal computer and the internet were introduced. In a traditional based internet system, a server store and process the data. Any computer/devices with an internet connection through the wired or wireless connection can connect to the web, and the web connection shows information from the relevant server [2, 3]. World Wide Web made it more convenient. With by unique domain system, anyone can see the

© Springer Nature Switzerland AG 2021
G. Salvendy and J. Wei (Eds.): HCII 2021, LNCS 12796, pp. 85–91, 2021.
https://doi.org/10.1007/978-3-030-77025-9_8

public information shared by the domain owner. The server runs through by individual or corporation, more like the server is also a centralized system.

Ecommerce website data is stored in a server where it has a central authority. Authorized admin can shut down the website, can make any changes anytime. Any irresponsible action of the admin can make the website data vulnerable. The website can be built using fake ownership and steal customers banking data and preferences. Simultaneously, many websites are getting hacked by hackers and lose valuable data, which raises customer security concerns. Hackers sell the database in the black market. The data can be used to harass an individual or can use for political purposes.

In 2001, Bram Cohen, an American computer programmer, introduced torrent file sharing, a new way to share files without servers. The files split into chunk. By using torrent supported software, anyone's local computer's hard disk work as a server [4].

The primary idea of the torrent was similar to the blockchain. However, there are some significant differences which make the blockchain so immutable, secure, anonymity. The torrent file-sharing does not depend on any particular server. Rather than it depends on the peer to peer network, in this technology, a file from the internet is downloaded and stored in the computer's local disk; then the computer works as a server. The more the downloads means the more seeders.

Nevertheless, the process used to share copyrighted items. As it has no centralized server system, the files cannot be deleted for any dispute. Moreover, it is not easy to find the location of the seeders.

In 2008 Satoshi Nakamoto introduced a new digital currency named bitcoin; [5] worked as a peer to peer electronic cash system. However, this technology was better than the torrent file-sharing; this coin's main objective is decentralized finance system and preventing double-spending. Hash and distributed ledger features made this bitcoin unique. Torrent file-sharing does not have distributed ledger features; any information can deliver through the torrent file-sharing. Torrent is like copying information; more downloads mean more copies, and more copies added more seeders. However, blockchain is to prevent copying information. The torrent file gets lost if there are no seeders of the file.

In blockchain technology, files do not get lost even it is a p2p network. This is why blockchain is powerful. This bitcoin made a significant change in the tech world and finance history. The popularity of this coin went higher, and no one could ever guess. The price of this one bitcoin rises from 1 dollar to 46000 dollars within nine years. It introduced the new technology Blockchain; a decentralized system. There are three types of blockchain such as public blockchains like Bitcoin and Ethereum; Private blockchains like Hyperledger and R3 Corda; Hybrid blockchains (a combination of public and private blockchain) like Dragonchain. The payment processing of this technology is faster, safer and hassle free than other payment gateway method.

This technology reduced the time and intermediary cost and increase trust in digital currency technology. It broke the boarder barrier for payment processing. There is no need to depend on any exchange agency, but money can be sent or exchange knowing the wallet number. At the same time, it hides users' identity; it is difficult to find out who is behind the account. As the cross-border can be done faster and safer, so it gets popularity very fast. Later on, blockchain-based cryptocurrency such as Ethereum become very famous and it introduces smart contracts. The technology added an extra security layer in eCommerce- not only in payment processing, but also in logistics.

This review paper aims to determine how much change the technology made in eCommerce and the popularity of blockchain-based eCommerce platform, finding out the challenges and guessing this technology's future.

2 Blockchain Technology in eCommerce

Finance is the main point of interest in eCommerce system. A smart eCommerce ecosystem entirely depends on Finance. Moreover, the development of eCommerce solely depends on faster transaction and trust. The error-free and hassle-free transaction makes the real deal.

Money makes the real value of the product. Selling creativity through the digital platform become one of the most significant business. Some years ago selling physical CD drive was a big business. However, as the internet has risen and music and artwork became digitalized, pirated things have also risen. The creator did not get enough value for their contribution because of piracy. Blockchain hashing opened a new door for the artist. The technology can enable the copyright effectively in creative work.

In a traditional website, the artist shares their art for selling. However, the problem is that 30–40% of commissioned need to transfer to the website holder; and an artist account can be removed, denied, and censored by the website's admin authority anytime.

If we consider the traditional video platform business system where creators post any videos And creators make money by monetizing their content. Some years ago, the system was not sophisticated. Anyone can upload videos on the video platform without the consent of the original creator. Now many video platform sites developed new AI to find duplicate, reuse and copyrighted content.

A blockchain-based video platform solves those complicated problems giving the real credit to the content creator.

The current traditional eCommerce's sellers are dependant on the payment gateway. These payment gateways give the exchange rate, and sellers or buyers have no choice to select different money exchanger. In the current eCommerce system, the payment gateway process the money when a customer buys a product. Moreover, the payment gateway contacts the relevant banking system to complete the transaction. The gateway usually charges 3–5% of the transaction. Some payment gateway charges more than 5% of every transaction. A customer also can give fake dispute, and the seller can lose the real money. If the transaction is a cross-border payment, it takes more than three days for some payment gateway.

Moreover, if this product is physical, the customer can show the shipment receipt as a proof of sending the goods to the customer. However, it gets complicated if the product is digital. Usually, service like Mastercard and Visa are faster, but the central authority can control the spending, restricting payment.

To process the transaction, payment gateway collects the customer's data, and they also contact the banking system with those data. In this data travel, there are risks to data stealing, hacking, losing customers money. A traditional based credit card such as Mastercard, Visa, is easy to fulfil the transaction in a minute. However, if the card data goes to the wrong hand, all money can be pulled out from the credit card. This is why customers do hesitate to buy from any eCommerce site; trust is a significant factor here. At the same time, the product can be lost; the website can be faked. So the eCommerce sector only depends on some big company; big companies can monopoly the system. It is hard to build trust for a new eCommerce site if they want to sell something cheaper.

Despite the facts, traditional based eCommerce sites are still very famous.

Here are the introduction of some Blockchain-Based business model which are making significant changes:

2.1 Libry

Libry is a marketplace for all kinds of digital contents; and their digital contents, including movies, games, books, pictures. Libry allows people to create a decentralized database. It is a protocol based system which allows to build apps and interact with digital content. Users can host their work on decentralized peer to peer network, it uses the protocol, and the creator can set the price or make it for free.

In the traditional video platform site; the creator can add their videos to a site such as youtube, Instagram, Facebook etc. Moreover, those sites are the central authority of those content; their business model is advertising-based. Moreover, videos can be demonetized anytime, or creator account can be shut down anytime by the admin. Nevertheless, a platform like libry has no central authority, no centralized servers; it works as a peer to peer system; so no one can prevent a transaction for videos. It means that users get full control of their contents [6].

2.2 Steem

Steemit is a site for the content creator to share their ideas, work. And registered users or creators can earn rewards by commenting or posting content, generating new coin steemit. It is powered by steem blockchain and steem cryptocurrencies. This website read and writes content to the Steem blockchain, making the content an immutable blockchain ledger. Users or content creators get steem digital tokens as a reward for their contribution. A registered user can earn steem digital token by posting, getting the upvotes from the platform's users, by voting, curating. Furthermore, users can also purchase steem tokens using bitcoin, ether or bitshares tokens.

Medium also serves with a similar concept. However, Medium has a central authority to show which content to share with their users; Medium's post goes through some curator. If the curator thinks that the post will value the users, they allow their platform to share that post.

However, in steemit, no one has this kind of control; users are the primary decision-maker.

This is the difference between a traditional based author community and blockchain-based steemit [7].

2.3 D Tube

A traditional-based video streaming site focuses on personal data collection and pressure of delivering the right ad to the right person. So a traditional based video streaming site solely depends on the advertising because that is their real business. Nevertheless, a decentralized tube or D tube is built on cryptography, transparency, open-source, and decentralized technologies to win user trust. It is an ad-free site tokenized business model; D tube does not collect user's data. It works as a reward system. Users or creators get the reward for their videos, rank their videos by upvoting.

D tube has no demonetization or account shutdown policy; once the user opens an account and upload the content, the contents cannot be deleted. There is no censorship in the content. Users earn coin by watching uploading sharing and commenting on the videos; censorship powers totally on users' hand [8].

2.4 Monetha

Monetha is a financial services company that increases confidence and probability of success in any financial interaction. By using blockchain technology, it is secure and private to control digital identity, by using their service, a person can own their personal without being dependant on service providers. The information is protected by cryptography technology. All the sensitive information encrypted, securely exchange data without intermediary and without worrying about data compromising. Their target is to improve the way people, business and government interact, open new opportunities without risking privacy and security. Users have the full right to the data and full control over it. No central authority can censor identity.

Monetha also works for eCommerce development; the product includes goods and services. Buyers can buy products like traditional eCommerce sites and using digital coins without worrying about hacking their data. And after getting the right product, buyers can go through the reputation system; the reputation system cannot be fabricated as like traditional eCommerce site. Sellers also can build a reputation in this system and can share their reputation with all other platforms. Monetha's trust and reputation system let the seller establish a trusted merchant. As it is decentralized and customers can only review after buying the real product; so there less worry about fraudulent and scam. Monetha payment gateway also helps to process the payment.

It works with the businesses of any size, and helps the business to start their blockchain journey; as it is a modular platform for blockchain development, it guarantees the secure and tampers proof exchange of public and sensitive information. It features-include comprehensive data management such as shared registry, digital identity, sensitive data, and digital ownership confirmation; rich reporting includes data analysis, data visualization, API access, and multiple data sources; their predictive analysis includes custom-tailored insights and behavioural segmentation, real-time fraudulent behaviour detection. The fundamental basis of trust in Monetha platform is Smart Contracts [9].

2.5 AORA

Aora is a blockchain-based buying platform for cross-border eCommerce and end to end crypto shopping. Users can buy products from online marketplaces in the USA and China using cryptocurrencies from anywhere in the world. Aora works as a third party to purchase goods on behalf of the user [10].

3 Challenges

There is no doubt that this decentralized technology is beneficial for the e-commerce platform. Simultaneously, it raises the issues of sharing inappropriate content to the people, as it is a decentralized system so that no one can control the content. However, maybe the Ethereum smart contracts may solve this problem.

In the payment system, it is difficult to find the transaction maker's identity; it also raises money laundering, illegal drug transporting, and human trafficking and opens door for illegal businesses.

Another challenge is the technology's availability; without a smartphone and internet connection, the system can break anytime.

Still, the blockchain-based digital coin considers as illegal in many countries. So the payment process in these countries are not possible legally.

The government can still stop all digital coin transactions; So the coin development only depends on the governments' interest.

4 Findings

Because of the features of Security, immutability, faster transaction, and encryption, stored data are hard to steal; no other technology can beat the blockchain technology yet.

There is a trust issue for a new eCommerce platform; there are many agencies who provide fake reviews and testimonials for a product; and at the same time the platform recommending products to the users by knowing their search history, cookies, and browsing product history. And traditional based eCommerce site owner have control to show the users some particular product if they want. They can also add fake reviews. In a blockchain-based e-commerce system users do not need to worry about privacy concern. Users can control the data they want to share, and at the same time users can find out the product recommendation based on their interest.

Blockchain system users cannot overwrite the reviews, and it is challenging to add fake reviews without buying the product because the system has inline some condition. In this way, it is easy to build trust.

There is no need any middleman for exchanging the payment. So the buyers or sellers do not need to worry to pay extra fees. Moreover, there is no way to cancel or shutdown the account. In the current system, the banking authority can freeze users' account in a minute but in the digital blockchain system is not possible; it all depends on the conditions or in the smart contracts. There is no worry about losing money. As it cuts down the extra intermediary cost, so the seller can give the product by discounted price, which is profitable for the buyer.

In a subscription-based system for the artist, the revenue model is not very transparent; still, it is on the system's hand. But in a decentralized system revenue is clear and transparent so that the artist will not get any revenue loss.

In the traditional market, still many products get lost in transportation; anyone can fabricate the product, and it is challenging to track. But in a blockchain based system, courier service provider can easily find out where the products were fabricated or lost or tampered.

5 Conclusion

eCommerce growing as the technology grows. It will change continuously based on the customers' interest. As it is still a new technology to the people; so the developers are continuously trying to adopt it with the system. Still, there are many gaps, such as bitcoin system mining machine's power consumption is high. The currency such as bitcoin price is still not stable, the price ups and downs so fast. Many blockchain based eCommerce site are still depend on the traditional based eCommerce site. Acceptance of blockchain based currency is the biggest factor. And blockchain based video platform are still not much popular as like traditional based video system. Still, many companies are testing the blockchain technology in eCommerce to improve logistics; QR based system also made a big change in this industry already. Hopefully, in the future integrating blockchain technology with AI will open some new doors in eCommerce also. It is still uncertain how this blockchain technology revolutionize international trade; where bitcoin has become a game changer already. As the SAAS (software as a service), XAAS (anything as a service), IAAS (identity as a service), BAAS (backup as a service) getting popularity day by day, and artists are joining subscription based model eCommerce website; if blockchain technology shows something promising, artist/creators will move as fast as possible in the blockchain based website; because of transparency, security and privacy.

References

1. Bromley, A.G.: Charles Babbage's analytical engine, 1838. In: Annals of the History of Computing, vol. 4, no. 3, pp. 196–217, July-Sept 1982. https://doi.org/10.1109/mahc.1982.10028
2. Levergood, T.M., et al.: Internet server access control and monitoring systems. U.S. Patent No. 5,708,780, 13 January 1998
3. Collins, W.H., Cubbage, A.D., Ahluwalia, I.S.: Internet server and method for providing access to internet e-mail and internet web pages. U.S. Patent No. 6,424,828, 23 July 2002
4. Choffnes, D.R., Bustamante, F.E.: Taming the torrent: a practical approach to reducing cross-ISP traffic in peer-to-peer systems. ACM SIGCOMM Comput. Commun. Rev. **38**(4), 363–374 (2008)
5. Nakamoto, S.: Bitcoin: A peer-to-peer electronic cash system. Manubot (2019)
6. Libry homepage. https://lbry.com/
7. Steemit homepage. https://steemit.com/
8. Dtube homepage. https://d.tube/
9. Monetha homepage. https://www.monetha.io/
10. Aora homepage. https://coin.aora.com/

Task Characteristics and Participants' Creative Performance in Crowdsourcing Contexts

Yuan Sun[1(✉)], Zhoujian Fan[1], and Anand Jeyaraj[2]

[1] School of Business Administration, Zhejiang Gongshang University, No. 18, Xuezheng Street, Hangzhou, Zhejiang, People's Republic of China
[2] Raj Soin College of Business, Wright State University, Dayton, OH 45435, USA

Abstract. Crowdsourcing refers to the use of public power to achieve the specific goals of companies, which is an important source for companies to achieve open innovation. With the rapid development of Internet technologies, companies and individuals increasingly participated in crowdsourcing activities, and the crowdsourcing community is becoming crowded. Numerous submissions by crowdsourcing participants increase the evaluation costs for companies and may be of variable quality. Therefore, improving participants' creative performance to ensure high-quality submissions has become a key issue for crowdsourcing service providers. In recent years, the application of digital technologies is remodeling the original crowdsourcing mode to optimize the user experience, reflected in the task design. Based on work design theory and self-determination theory, this paper offers a framework to explain how task characteristics affect participants' creative performance. Specifically, new technologies will strengthen participants' motivation through three task characteristics—i.e., autonomy, feedback, and diversity—which will subsequently improve participants' creative performance. We propose to conduct empirical research using a crowdsourcing platform to examine the research model. The findings of our research will be helpful for organizations to draw high quality submissions from crowdsourcing participants.

Keywords: Crowdsourcing · Task characteristics · Motivation · Creative performance · Digital technology

1 Introduction

Modern information technologies such as Web2.0 have fueled the growth of crowdsourcing platforms such as Innocentive and Mturk into various sectors. It is estimated that tens of millions of participants are active in the crowdsourcing market around the world and many participants earn income through their participation in crowdsourcing activities. For instance, 3% of the 200000 registered users of Hackone, a crowdsourcing platform, earn more than $100000 a year.

Over the past two years, a large number of participants have swarmed into the crowdsourcing communities. The user experience afforded by the crowdsourcing platforms is profoundly affecting participants' creativity levels, which is directly related to the quality of the submissions. It has been observed that low quality solutions have flooded the

© Springer Nature Switzerland AG 2021
G. Salvendy and J. Wei (Eds.): HCII 2021, LNCS 12796, pp. 92–99, 2021.
https://doi.org/10.1007/978-3-030-77025-9_9

crowdsourcing market (Acar 2019). In order to improve the overall creativity quality of participants, crowdsourcing platforms aim to ameliorate participants' experiences in crowdsourcing, especially related to system upgrades and process optimization. Since the core of crowdsourcing lies in task allocation and completion, crowdsourcing system design based on task optimization has become the key goal of platform service providers. For example, the Chinese crowdsourcing service provider ZhuBajie reduces the costs of task search by improving the graphical user interface of web pages while the design company Lkker optimizes the task process through embedded project management software. A number of successful experiences show that the new technology and business model optimize the original task characteristics, giving participants greater task autonomy, task feedback and task variety, which improved participants' creativite performance (Martinez 2015).

This study aims to explore how crowdsourcing task characteristics through technology empowerment affect the participants' creative performance. Participants' motivations are considered a key mediator in this process. According to the self-determination theory, participants have spontaneous motivations that are not driven by external forces (Wu and Gong 2020). When these motivations are satisfied or strengthened, they will demonstrate a higher level of creative performance.

2 Theoretical Background

2.1 Crowdsourcing and Creative Performance

Crowdsourcing is defined as outsourcing work to undefined groups through open competition rather than specifically designated employees (Boons et al. 2015). Early crowdsourcing usually employed telephone, email, and other forms to solicit opinions. However, Web 2.0 and related information technologies provide a significant opportunity for crowdsourcing in recent times, and the realization of open innovation through crowdsourcing has become an important opportunity for organizations (Chua et al. 2015).

The application of digital technologies to crowdsourcing presents key challenges to organizations. Unlike more centralized forms of open innovation, organizations do not identify or evaluate the individuals involved in advance. Rather, they assume that individuals with initiative and skills within the crowdsourcing population will choose to effectively solve the tasks themselves (Piller and Walcher 2006). However, not every optional member has the ability to solve problems (Afuah and Tucci 2012). As a result, digital open innovation activities usually generate a large number of ideas of variable quality, which implies variable creative performance. Crowdsourcing platforms require a significant amount of time for scheme filtering, which could lead to the selection of wrong ideas due to the limited attention and cognition of organization's management (Piezunka and Dahlander 2015). In order to avoid crowding and better practice open innovation, a deeper understanding of individuals and their contributions is needed (Bogers et al. 2016).

2.2 Work Design Theory

Different ways of work design have been proposed by management scholars based on a long tradition of research on physical activity of workers to work motivation in the 1970s.

Work design is a significant consideration for a range of individual, group, and organizational outcomes (Grant and Parker 2009). Crowdsourcing research covers a wide range of incentives and incentive programs that may motivate the creative potential of groups. These design attributes trigger the creative efforts of participants through virtual co-creation experiences and serve to attract them to crowdsourcing platforms in the future (Piller and Walcher 2006). Morgeson and Humphrey (2006) proposed characteristics related to three dimensions of work design. In crowdsourcing contexts, motivational task characteristics through incentives serve as the main mechanism to influence participants' motivation and creative performance. Further, since crowdsourcing tasks are largely knowledge-based, participants may be encouraged to fully demonstrate their ability and knowledge. These explain why organizations may attempt to solve their problems through crowdsourcing efforts. Task autonomy, task feedback, and task variety are the task characteristics most frequently considered to influence participants in crowdsourcing contexts.

2.3 Crowdsourcing Motivation

Self-determination theory is a method of human motivation and personality (Zhao and Zhu 2014). It uses traditional empirical methods and highlights the importance of internal resources of human evolution for personality development and behavior self-regulation (Ryan et al. 1997). It assumes that motivation is better regarded as a continuum, with intrinsic motivation at one end and extrinsic motivation at the other (Alam and Campbell 2017). There are various forms of motivation between the two ends, namely internalized extrinsic motivation. von Krogh et al. (2012) divided motivation into intrinsic motivation (idealism, altruism, kinship, interest), internalized extrinsic motivation (reputation, reciprocity, learning, self-use) and extrinsic motivation (occupation, reward). In the context of crowdsourcing, we divide motivation into intrinsic motivation, internalized motivation, and extrinsic motivation. Intrinsic motivation is to gain pleasure and sense of achievement by participating in crowdsourcing, internalized motivation is to learn knowledge and accumulate reputation by participating in crowdsourcing, and extrinsic motivation is to get reward by participating in crowdsourcing.

3 Research Model

Figure 1 shows the research model examined in this study, which proposes relationships between task characteristics and performance mediated by motivation.

3.1 Effects of Task Characteristics on Participant's Motivations

Autonomy. Task autonomy includes three aspects: the freedom of work arrangement, decision-making and working methods. Different from the traditional offline work, crowdsourcing participants have a higher degree of freedom, can choose or refuse to participate in a certain type of work, and flexible working hours (Zheng et al. 2011). As crowdsourcing service providers have launched multi-platform applications and synchronized workflow, participants can freely choose the work platforms. When participants realize that they can exercise self-control and the right of free choice, they will have

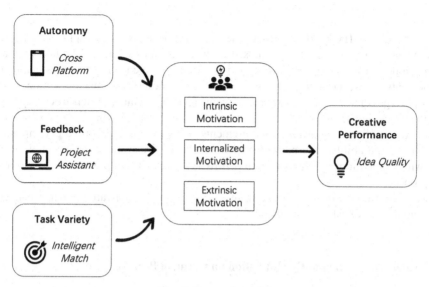

Fig. 1. Research model

greater motivation and ability, freely choose their own areas of expertise and innovative tasks, improve their sense of self achievement (intrinsic motivation) in the process of task participation, and fully learn the relevant knowledge in different fields to obtain better performance (internalized motivation), and invest time and energy to complete the task to get paid and gain professional reputation (extrinsic motivation). Therefore, we propose:

H1. Autonomy is positively associated with (a) intrinsic motivation, (b) internalized motivation and (c) extrinsic motivation.

Feedback. Feedback reflects the extent to which tasks provide direct and clear information about the effectiveness of task performance (Morgeson and Humphrey 2006). Tasks in crowdsourcing competitions may involve multiple proposal submissions, and feedback from the competition sponsors plays an important role in mobilizing the enthusiasm of participants (Martinez 2015). Crowdsourcing platforms have developed project assistants to achieve project docking between crowdsourcing participants and ensure immediate task feedback. Such task feedback can enhance participants' self-efficacy and self-presentation (intrinsic motivation), help participants evaluate and improve their plans and enhance their knowledge (internalized motivation), and enable participants put forward solutions more in line with the task expectation and win the competition (external motivation). Therefore, we propose:

H2. Feedback is positively associated with (a) intrinsic motivation, (b) internalized motivation and (c) extrinsic motivation.

Variety. Task variety refers to the extent to which a job requires employees to perform diverse tasks at work. It may be more interesting and competent to involve participants in different kinds of work (Morgeson and Humphrey 2006) so as to participate more actively in creative activities. In the crowdsourcing context, participants have a greater choice of tasks, and the number and type of tasks are higher compared to offline task platforms (Afuah and Tucci 2012). Through the optimization of platform graphical interface, participants can be more widely exposed to different kinds of tasks. The task recommendation systems based on big data and artificial intelligence technologies can help participants choose the appropriate tasks, increase task variety, and ensure accurate push. Multiple types of tasks can improve participants' crowdsourcing experience because participants can choose the task combination they are interested in (intrinsic motivation), put forward different knowledge requirements, which helps to improve participants' knowledge and ability (internalized motivation), and fully evaluate their own abilities and win competitions by choosing competitive tasks (extrinsic motivation). Therefore, we propose:

H3. Task variety is positively associated with (a) intrinsic motivation, (b) internalized motivation and (c) extrinsic motivation.

3.2 Effects of Participant's Motivation on Creative Performance

In crowdsourcing contexts, participants have a higher level of self-determination and the impacts of intrinsic motivation and internalized motivation will be further improved. Participants can choose different task combinations and work across different knowledge domains and improve their abilities. They can participate in a variety of interesting or challenging tasks to gain a sense of pleasure and achievement. Such positive feelings and abilities will enable participants to propose constructive solutions in crowdsourcing tasks, thus influencing creative performance. Extrinsic motivation emphasizes that participants get paid in the process of participation and improve their professional reputation (von Krogh et al. 2012). Participants will receive economic rewards should their solutions be of higher quality and selected by organizations. Participants with extrinsic motivation will actively participate in crowdsourcing tasks and strive to generate innovative ideas and enhance creative performance to earn material rewards. Prior research has demonstrated the positive impact of external motivation (Zou et al. 2020). Therefore, we propose:

H4. (a) intrinsic motivation, (b) internalized motivation and (c) extrinsic motivation is positively associated with creative performance.

4   Method

4.1   Platform

We chose the Chinese crowdsourcing design platform *Lkker*[1], which has nearly 50000 senior participants. Since its inception, the platform has served more than 8000 organizations. Different from other crowdsourcing platforms, *Lkker* uses independent project management authority to better connect the two sides of crowdsourcing platforms to promote high-quality submissions. *Lkker* actively engages in digital transformation: it

---

[1] Website: https://www.lkker.com.

actively develops and debugs mobile application software to realize seamless connection of crowdsourcing task management, improves communication efficiency in process management such that participants can receive timely performance feedback (Fig. 2), improves original web services, optimizes the operation interface, and uses artificial intelligence technology to achieve task distribution and evaluation.

Fig. 2. New version of *Lkker* integrates new technologies such as multi device synchronization, intelligent matching, and project management

4.2 Case Study

The purpose of this study is to explore the impact of task design characteristics of crowdsourcing platforms on participants' creative performance. We propose to conduct a pilot case study of participants on *Lkker*. We plan to conduct semi-structured telephone interviews with participants regarding task characteristics of the platform and how the application of new technologies can strengthen these characteristics. We will code and discuss the interview data to further clarify the relationships between task characteristics, motivation, and creative performance.

4.3 Empirical Research

Based on the case study findings, we propose to conduct a large-scale study using questionnaire surveys. This study draws on the measurement of variables in SSCI area I literature, which will be set up for the Chinese context using translation and back-translation methods. The questionnaire will be distributed to the participants of several typical tasks by organizations.

5   Conclusion and Future Research

Although crowdsourcing has become an important source of open innovation, the crowdsourcing community encounters solutions of variable quality, which can adversely affect the reputation of crowdsourcing service providers. Since crowdsourcing efforts rely on the release and completion of tasks, improving task experiences and creative performance of participants to promote high-quality submissions is a significant and urgent problem for crowdsourcing service providers. This paper puts forward a research model, selects typical Chinese crowdsourcing service providers, and strives to empirically examine the relationships between task characteristics, motivation, and creative performance to uncover usable knowledge for crowdsourcing providers.

Acknowledgements. This work was supported by Zhejiang Provincial Philosophy and Social Science Leading Talent Cultivation Project (21QNYC14ZD) and the Project of Key Research Institute of Humanities and Social Sciences at Universities-Modern Business Research Center of Zhejiang Gongshang University (2020SMYJ03ZC), Special Funds Project for Promoting the Level of Running Local Colleges and Universities in Zhejiang Province (Interdisciplinary Innovation Team Building of Internet and Management Change). This research is the achievement of New Key Specialized Think Tank of Zhejiang Province (Zheshang Research Institute).

References

Acar, O.A.: Motivations and solution appropriateness in crowdsourcing challenges for innovation. Res. Policy **48**(8), 13 (2019)

Afuah, A., Tucci, C.L.: Crowdsourcing as a solution to distant search. Acad. Manage. Rev. **37**(3), 355–375 (2012)

Alam, S.L., Campbell, J.: Temporal motivations of volunteers to participate in cultural crowdsourcing work. Inf. Syst. Res. **28**(4), 744–759 (2017)

Bogers, M., et al.: The open innovation research landscape: established perspectives and emerging themes across different levels of analysis. Ind. Innovation **24**, 1–33 (2016)

Boons, M., Stam, D., Barkema, H.G.: Feelings of pride and respect as drivers of ongoing member activity on crowdsourcing platforms. J. Manage. Res. **52**(6), 717–741 (2015)

Chua, R.Y.J., Roth, Y., Lemoine, J.F.: The impact of culture on creativity: how cultural tightness and cultural distance affect global innovation crowdsourcing work. Admin. Sci. Q. **60**(2), 189–227 (2015)

Grant, A.M., Parker, S.K.: Redesigning work design theories: the rise of relational and proactive perspectives. Acad. Manage. Ann. **3**, 317–375 (2009)

Martinez, M.G.: Solver engagement in knowledge sharing in crowdsourcing communities: exploring the link to creativity. Res. Policy **44**(8), 1419–1430 (2015)

Morgeson, F.P., Humphrey, S.E.: The work design questionnaire (WDQ): developing and validating a comprehensive measure for assessing work design and the nature of work. J. Appl. Psychol. **91**(6), 1321–1339 (2006)

Piezunka, H., Dahlander, L.: Distant search, narrow attention: how crowding alters organizations' filtering of suggestions in crowdsourcing. Acad. Manage. J. **58**(3), 856–880 (2015)

Piller, F., Walcher, D.: Toolkits for idea competitions: a novel method to integrate users in new product development. R&D Manage. **36**, 307–318 (2006)

von Krogh, G., Haefliger, S., Spaeth, S., Wallin, M.W.: Carrots and rainbows: motivation and social practice in open source software development. MIS Q. **36**(2), 649–676 (2012)

Wu, W., Gong, X.: Motivation and sustained participation in the online crowdsourcing community: the moderating role of community commitment. Internet Res. **31**, 287–314 (2020)

Zhao, Y.C., Zhu, Q.H.: Effects of extrinsic and intrinsic motivation on participation in crowdsourcing contest a perspective of self-determination theory. Online Inf. Rev. **38**(7), 896–917 (2014)

Zheng, H.C., Li, D.H., Hou, W.H.: Task design, motivation, and participation in crowdsourcing contests. Int. J. Electron. Commer. **15**(4), 57–88 (2011)

Zou, L.F., Wei, S.B., Ke, W.L., Wei, K.K.: Creativity of participants in crowdsourcing communities: the effects of promotion focus and extrinsic motivation. J. Database Manage. **31**(3), 40–66 (2020)

Design City Trip Management App in the Kuala Lumpur Context During Pandemic Covid-19: A Preliminary Research Case

Chee Ling Thong[1(✉)], Su Mon Chit[1], Lee Yen Chaw[2], and Chiw Yi Lee[3]

[1] Institute of Computer Science and Digital Innovation, UCSI University, Kuala Lumpur, Malaysia
{chloethong,chitsm}@ucsiuniversity.edu.my
[2] Faculty of Business and Management, UCSI University, Kuala Lumpur, Malaysia
chawly@ucsiuniversity.edu.my
[3] UCSI College, UCSI University, Kuala Lumpur, Malaysia
leecy@ucsicollege.edu.my

Abstract. During the Covid-19 pandemic, it is challenging for travel agency manager to manage multiple city trips simultaneously, at the same time practice standard operating procedure (SOP). There are numerous mobile applications used by travel agency to enhance customer service quality, however there is a lack of mobile application (app) for city tour management to assist manager in managing multiple trips and maintain SOP. The purpose of this study is to provide a mobile platform that enables managers to obtain real-time trip information of any registered car driver while monitoring car drivers and current trip status. The primary sources of data are based on earlier study to capture user requirements. It has also identified issues include poor communication and time coordination between the manager, driver and tour guide. Observation and document analysis are the secondary sources of data. By observing existing mobile applications including e-hailing and tourism apps, main features are identified, and extensional part are presented. Document analysis as research tool to understand Covid-19 SOP in Malaysia. The research findings help to conceptualize user requirements and user interfaces are designed. Device-based testing is adopted in a research case to validate the functional requirements of the app. The manager found the app is usable and capable to monitor multiple trips simultaneously by viewing real-time data to achieve zero-physical contact with the car driver. However, a permanent network connection is required to update data. For future work, app possesses offline and online capability features will be proposed to resolve the issue.

Keywords: Covid-19 · Pandemic · Travel agency · Mobile application · Tourism

1 Introduction

Tourism industry is one of the most affected industries globally during the Covid-19 pandemic. Many travel agencies are unable to continue or sustain their business during lockdown period in year 2020 due to pandemic. According to Papadopoulos and

G. Salvendy and J. Wei (Eds.): HCII 2021, LNCS 12796, pp. 100–112, 2021.
https://doi.org/10.1007/978-3-030-77025-9_10

friends [1], it is essential for Small and Medium Enterprise (SMEs) to have plans in place for securing business continuity particularly in using digital technologies (DT). There are two schools of thought to business continuity using DT. The first school of thought emphasizes that DT directly enables business process and services are up and running (continuity) and second school of thought having in place appropriate mechanisms through support system that ensure key business processes and staff interactions can be conducted digitally. Both school of thoughts aim in assisting SMEs stay connected and facilitate their working situation. However, the drawback of the schools is related to user and data privacy and it is beyond the discussion of this study. In this study, DT (or Information System, IS) is defined as a group of computer tools that are used to collect, process and store data. Organization uses and depends on IS to support their day-to-day operations, interact with people and manage their workforce. IS also provides a solid foundation to increase efficiency and productivity of an organization and ultimately it contributes to the success of an organization [2]. According to Ghita and friends [3], IS is one of the application types and it implies a mobile application which enables user reads remote data object such as passenger information system in a synchronous and asynchronous way from a local or central storage.

During the pandemic, healthcare researchers or scholars are able to contribute directly to fighting Covid-19 virus by introducing vaccines. Although IS researchers cannot solve pandemic problems directly, they are able to provide timely knowledge and insight that can contribute to global effort to flatten the curve of Covid-19 spread particularly in practicing physical distancing and contact tracing using mobile application. For example, a mobile application namely "MySejahtera" is developed and used in Malaysia to trace close contact of Covid-19 patients, by doing so it helps to block the virus chain. Mobile application for health consultation developed by a group of researchers in Indonesia [4] has made public easier to access to health care service without leaving their home. According to the world bank population 2018 [5], Indonesia being the fourth popular country in the world has confirmed Covid-19 cases (as of May2020) 0.007% of the total population [4]. The mobile application enables Indonesian to access health services in the form of online health consultation with doctors or specialist, purchase medicine and medical equipment without traveling to hospital.

Although there are numerous mobile apps for customer service enhancement, there is a lack of mobile tracking applications for manager in travel agency [6]. The study aims to design mobile Car application (app) for travel agency based on earlier study, at the same time it also validates the functional requirements. The mobile Car app is capable in tracking the multiple trips status and plan multiple trips simultaneously. In this study, a research case is used and travel agency who located in Kuala Lumpur (KL) is performing device-based testing to validate the requirements.

2 Literature Review

2.1 Pandemic and Tourism

The World Health Organization (WHO) has provided general advice for travelers since the outbreak of Covid-19 which includes personal and hand hygiene, respiratory etiquette, maintaining physical distance of at least one meter apart from others and use of a mask as appropriate. Sick travelers and persons at risk such as senior citizens and individuals with serious chronic diseases or underlying health conditions, should avoid international travelling to and from areas infected by covid-19 [7]. Likewise, Malaysians are required to comply with the health SOP provided by the Ministry of Health (MoH), such as social distancing, wearing face masks and practicing personal hygiene routines by using hand sanitizer during pandemic [8].

The tourism industry in Malaysia has been hit badly since the country declared Movement Control Order (MCO) nationwide on the 18th March, 2020. All activities that involving mass assembly such as religious, sports, social and cultural were mandated to cease operation temporarily. In addition, Malaysians have been barred from leaving the country whereas restrictions placed on the entry of all tourists and foreign visitors into Malaysia tourists have been imposed in order to curb the increase in covid-19 cases [9]. The situation was improved in June to September 2020 where Malaysians enjoyed much more relaxed conditions for about 3 months. Unfortunately, covid-19 cases surged in several districts within the region. Thus, On the 14th October, 2020, the Malaysian government announced that Selangor, Kuala Lumpur, and Putrajaya to be placed under the Conditional Movement Control Order (CMCO) to prevent the virus from spreading to other districts. This means movements across districts, would no longer be allowed [10]. To highlight the severity of local Covid-19 spread, districts in Malaysia are classified into four types of zones based on the number of cases reported in the area. For example, a district in Malaysia that reports above 40 local Covid-19 cases within the past 14 days will be declared as a red zone which means more stringent SOPs are required such as closure of schools and ban travelling across states or inter-district [11]. A district that reports between 21–40 Covid-19 cases is classified as orange zone whereas recorded covid-19 cases between 1 to 20 then the district is considered in yellow zone. Green zone is without any recorded Covid-19 case. Dr Noor Hisham, Director General of Health Malaysia has advised those living in either red or orange zone to stay at home, unless there is a need to go out and attend to urgent matters, then it is essential to comply with the SOP [12].

The tourism sector contributes greatly to the country's economy, recording an expenditure of RM92.6 billion in 2019, reported by the Tourism Satellite Account data from the Department of Statistics [13]. However, Uzaidi Udanis, the president of Malaysia Tourism Council revealed that tourism industry has experienced lost amounting around RM45bil in the first six months of 2020 due to the Covid-19 pandemic [14]. To revive the domestic tourism, Senior Minister of Defence, Ismail Sabri Yaakob announced recently of the "green travel bubble" initiative which has been effective on the 20th November, 2020. The news is well received by local tourism players as well as the general public. Under the travel bubble programme, people from green zones can travel to other zones that are marked green [15]. Green zone means zero Covid-19 cases reported in the past 14 days. The color zoning is applied to large districts in each state in the federal MOH's updates, although individual state health departments also publish Covid-19 statistics and color zones according to sub-district [16]. Datuk Seri Nancy Shukri, Minister of Tourism, Arts and Culture advised Malaysians to take this opportunity to travel responsibly and always adhere to the SOPs and the new norms while traveling [14].

To keep the economy moving and to invigorate the tourism sector, it requires all Malaysians to work together. As said by Dr Noor Hisham, Director General of Health Malaysia, "This is the only way to break the chain of Covid-19 infection in the community. Every one of us must work together and comply with the SOP. If there is no space for the virus to be transmitted, it will die on its own after two weeks" [13]. Hence, complying with SOP such as social distancing, wearing mask and personal hygiene is critical to stop the pandemic.

As of 10th January, 2021, only five districts in Peninsular Malaysia are classified as green zones following the recent increase in Covid-19 cases.

The five green zone districts are Jerantut and Lipis in Pahang, Langkawi (Kedah), Jeli (Kelantan) and Hulu Terengganu (Terengganu) [17]. The country has continuously recorded four digits Covid-19 cases reported each day for more than 30 days [18]. Malaysia reported a fresh record high number of confirmed Covid-19-infected individuals at 3,337 on the 14th January, 2021, which brought the country's cumulative figure of Covid-19 cases to 147,855 [19]. A total of 15 Covid-19-related deaths were reported on the same day, which brought the nation's cumulative number of Covid-19-related fatalities to 578 [Ibid].

Refer Table 1 for the number of covid-19 cases reported daily from 11th January 2021 to 15th January 2021 [20, 21].

Table 1. Covid-19 new cases daily for Kuala Lumpur, Malaysia [20, 21]

Date	Number of new cases
15/1/21	401
14/1/21	257
13/1/21	289
12/1/21	326
11/1/21	204

2.2 Mobile App to Complement/Enhance SOP

In this section, observation is made on existing mobile apps related to the research objective including tourisms app and e-hailing app. The common features of these apps are observed and extendable parts are analyzed. During pandemic, mobile applications such as MySejatera can be downloaded from GooglePlay, Appstore, Apps Gallery and Gamma. One of the functions in MySejahtera is MySejahtera Travel. It is a function built for Malaysian and Non-Malaysian travelers who are visiting or returning to Malaysia. This app is built based on new SOP of Malaysian Government developed during Covid-19 pandemic to control Covid-19 virus spread while opening Malaysian International borders to travelers [22]. The function ensures health declaration form is completed before arriving Malaysia, performing arrival check-in by scanning QR code, issuance of digital "Home Surveillance Order" (HSO) to user profile, perform daily self-assessment throughout 14-day quarantine period, reminder is given to user for lab test on the 13th day and visit district health department to end HSO and end 14-day quarantine completion period at district department [23] (Fig. 1).

Fig. 1. Check in.

Another tourism mobile app namely KLOOK is observed. KLOOK is a Hong-Kong-based in-destination services booking platform which provide customized features for different countries and destinations. Its features include e-ticket and discounts for popular location attractions with best price, multiple options for car rentals, train tickets and airport transfers, etc. During the pandemic, the travel industry in one the sectors which has severely impacted thus it needs swift respond to adapt to the new normal [24]. Hence, KLOOK has look into more domestic travel to cater the needs of traveler. KLOOK now offer more functions such as staycation packages to choose among 60 hotels in Hong Kong. Although KLOOK offers more features for local travelers, it has limited features to track the locations of traveler and contact tracing during this pandemic situation.

Grab is a Singaporean multinational ride-hailing company which initially offers transportation service but later expanded to more services such as food delivery and digital payments services via a mobile app. In conjunction with Covid-19 pandemic, Grab has introduced (GrabProect) which promote new safety features, updated safety policies and transport hygiene kits, to driver as well as passenger towards promoting the hygiene standards in the ride-hailing industry. The company now have more than two million driving partners, 68 million mobile app downloads and 3.5 million daily rides B [25]. Grab is just an e-hailing app which traveler can book a trip from one destination to another and it does not offer a plan for tourists to travel to a city. Like Grab, another e-hailing app proposed in Malaysia is Ezcab. Ezcab allows users to book a taxi to go from one destination to another. Ezcab has extended its service to delivery with maximum of 50kg from one place to another [26]. However, it does not offer a plan for tourists new to a city, and the user can only select a specific destination and a specific starting point. Table 2 presents the summary comparison among tourism and e-hailing apps.

Table 2. Comparison among tourism and e-hailing apps

Name	Type	Main features	Operational domains to extend
Grab	e-hailing app	Grab app assigns taxis and private hire cars to nearby commuters through a location-sharing system and a car to offer a ride to users. The company makes money by taking a cut of the booking fees. The App can be used for ride booking, food delivery and e-payment	Does not offer a plan for tourists new to a city, and the user can only select a specific destination and a specific starting point
EzCab	e-hailing app	Malaysia based e-hailing app which allows users to book to go from one destination to another. Ezcab has extended its service to delivery with maximum of 50kg from one place to another	Does not offer a plan for tourists new to a city, and the user can only select a specific destination and a specific starting point
MySejahtera	Tourism app	Users can perform health self-assessment on themselves and their families and can monitor their health progress throughout the COVID-19 outbreak. MySejahtera enables Ministry of Health (MOH) to monitor users' health condition and take immediate actions in providing the treatments required. MySejahtera Travel possess feature that enables tourist to declare their health condition	Does not offer features to plan for a trip or book facilities for tourists
KLOOK	Tourism app	In-destination services booking platform. Discounts and e-tickets for tourist destinations and places of interests near you. Multiple options for car rentals, train tickets and shared/private airport transfers	Not suitable to use during pandemic as no contact tracing or registration of travelers through App. No stringent hygienic measures

3   Methodology

In order to achieve research objectives in this study, methodology used are primary sources and secondary sources of data. Primary sources of data include requirement analysis based on the past study on mobile application for travel agency [6]. This instrument focuses on identifying travel agency manager expectations in managing multiple trips and can help to make the app more useful and user-friendly. Secondary sources of data include observation of two types of mobile applications: e-hailing mobile applications and tourism mobile applications. The common functions of these mobile applications are observed, and extendable parts are understood. Observation is also able to help researchers to identify functional requirements and graphical user interface design of mobile applications to be used by travel agency manager. Document analysis as part of secondary sources of data is reviewing documents which include SOPs for Covid-19 from WHO and KKM. Reviewing documents are able to help researchers to conceptualize the requirements of WHO and KKM as generic "rules and regulations" during Covid-19 pandemic. Consequently, an appropriate user interface of car mobile application is designed and it is developed using agile development method. User evaluation is conducted using device-based testing by a travel agency manager. One renown travel agency which is located in the capital city of Malaysia, Kuala Lumpur is selected as a research case. According to Papadopoulos and friends [1], a scenario (or research case) is used as an important tool for organization learning. Agile software development methodology which is the most common and appropriate methodology found in developing mobile application in this crisis. By adopting this practice, it incorporates the ability to change due to fast changes environment during pandemic and also feedback from users or manager are incorporated.

4   Results and Discussions

This section is divided into three subsections: 1) Design and Implementation of the proposed mobile car application which include user interface design and application logic; 2) Device-based testing results; and 3) Discussion.

4.1   Design and Implementation

The findings in earlier study show key features of mobile apps for travel agencies which possess trip scheduling feature and enables the manager to track location of the driver in real time based on pre-determined route. The background research and requirement analysis mentioned enable the researchers to gather requirements for the City Tour management application. Once user requirements and "rules and regulations" are identified, it helps to make the proposed mobile application more useful and user-friendly. The fundamental information is used by researchers to develop the mobile application with the functionalities and user interface design. Meanwhile, the system flow or business logic and architecture of the application are designed.

According to study conducted by Too et al. [6] in travel agency, issues identified between the manager, driver and tour guide are poor communication and coordination.

This is mainly due to lack of location-based information of the driver. The desirable features provided by the travel agency in earlier study are trip scheduling and location tracking for multiple destinations.

It is found that the regulations or SOP are updated daily by Ministry of Defence Malaysia during the period of Recovery Movement Control Order (RMCO) and Conditional Movement Control Order (CMCO) based on Covid-19 conditions according to the districts and color of zone area. It is also discovered that Malaysian Tourist Board encourages domestic tourism in order to boost the local economy.

4.2 User Interface Design

They are two key users of the mobile app: manager and driver. Figure 2 shows manager interaction with the system and Fig. 3 shows driver interaction with the system.

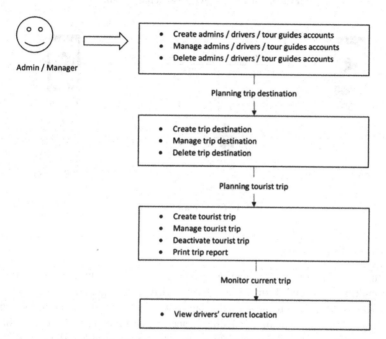

Fig. 2. Manager interaction with the system.

As to the basic features to be implemented, the application is based on client-server architecture which contains back-end server and database as well as front-end client. Server application is using Node.js together with MongoDB database. Client application is developed using Vue framework with Vuetify UI library. Client application can be deployed into three different platforms: Browser, Android and iOS mobile application. The overall architecture is presented in Fig. 4. In order to deploy to Android and iOS, Cordova is needed to run mobile Car web application which is similar to native application.

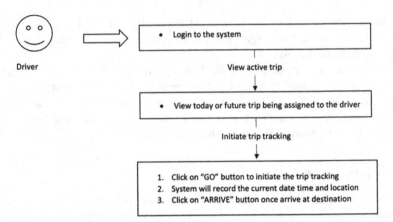

Fig. 3. Driver interaction with the system.

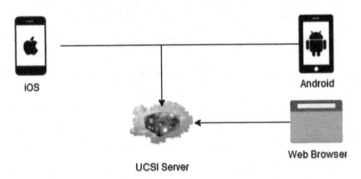

Fig. 4. System architecture

4.3 Business Logic Design

In this study, the mobile Car application allows admin staff (manager) to schedule and manage multiple trips and destinations, manage drivers and generate daily trip report. Figure 5 shows the main business logic. The sequence of the events is firstly manager needs to register or log in using the available account and then uses this car application to create accounts for driver and tour guide. To schedule and publish the trips schedule, manager need to enter information such as destination, picture of destination, date and time, driver and tour guide name and tourist name list. In normal or default mode, all trips are automatically activated. However, manager is able to de-activate the trip in the event that the trip has ended or cancelled. The app allows managers to publish a request consisting multiple trip plans and enable manager to manage trips by editing the trip information such as destination and view trip status including drivers' "start and end time" of the trip. Manager makes use of the app to read remote data in a synchronous way from central storage. Car drivers who are engaged in providing transportation service to travel agency are allowed to use app to activate the trip by clicking "GO" button when ready to go and system will record date, time and current location. When car driver arrives at destination by clicking "ARRIVE" button, date and time are recorded. These information of the trips are then reflected and shown in the app of the manager and manager are able track the trips of multiple destinations with different car drivers who are engaged in providing transportation services.

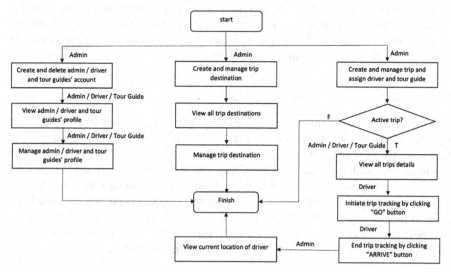

Fig. 5. Business logic design

4.4 Device-Based Testing Result

There are several testing environments for mobile application. According to Ghita Kouadri Mstefaori and Faisal Tariq [3], the construction of mobile application test environment involves high costs and complexity. Furthermore, setting up a mobile application test environment for multiple applications on each mobile platform for a range of devices is tedious, time-consuming and expensive. In this study, Android device is used in local test environment though this mobile application testing environment is less common and expensive. This environment is chosen and considered as the most appropriate during Covid-19 pandemic as it provides real insights into the functioning of the application. As recalled, there are SOP to be complied during pandemic, and it is discovered that performance of real mobile devices used in this study is better than other virtual option such as emulation-based testing, crowd-based testing or cloud-based testing. Android device is selected as the mobile platform for the device-based testing because it is less expensive compare to iOS devices. Three Android devices are purchased, and the test is performed under the actual conditions using mobile networks. One travel agency manager and driver have participated in this test during pandemic in November 2020. The scheduled multiple trips are UCSI University which located in Cheras to Kuala Lumpur International Airport (KLIA), Cheras to KL International Airport 2 (KLIA 2), KLIA to Cheras and KLIA 2 to Cheras. The trips are well-planned and able to be completed as scheduled. This is because traffic condition during CMCO in Malaysia is rather smooth and airport condition is less hectic due to country borders are opened to certain countries only. However, the respond time of driver application is rather slow. When "start" button is tapped in the driver application, it is insensitive due to network quality or coverage around airport in Sepang is unstable. This result in manager need to redo the entire scheduling process for one mistake made. Travel agency manager commented that it is better to allow to amend mistake made, else the resetting process is rather time-consuming. The limitation of device-based testing is it cannot cover all other mobile brands and operating systems (OS).

4.5 Discussions

The application is tested during the implementation phase. The main purpose of testing is to identify errors using the preliminary research case, so that researchers can improve the application and making it more reliable. For Android devices, it is important to run on various devices with different versions of OS. The application is first tested in devices with lower configurations and then high configurations including screen resolutions. The researchers have to ensure that the application is able to function adequately on different mobile phones. The test focuses on testing the business logic of the mobile Car application. The test is divided into three parts: code stability, functional test and cross-functional test. Table 3 shows the test cases of the application.

Table 3. Selected test cases of the application

Test mode	Case no	Input	Output
User login/register (Manager and driver)	1	Wrong password	Alert message is displayed
	2	Leave empty fields	Alert message is displayed
	3	Validation of user input	Not validated
Publish a request (Manager)	1	Date, time, name of driver and tour guide	Trip information is indicated
	2	View current location of driver	Successful
Accept the request (Driver)	1	Accept and view trip information	Successful
	2	Start and End trip	Successful
Modify status (Manager)	1	Cancel destination	Successful
	2	Edit trip	Successful

Synchronization is the main error occurs during testing phase which include sending and retrieving data from the database. The thread needs to perform time-consuming tasks with unstable network. This problem is in line with B. Koniig-Ries [27] that reliable operation of mobile applications during movement in space is a challenge for mobile app developer. When a mobile device switches from one radio cell (network) to another, loss or limitation of connectivity is not unusual and should be handled by the architecture of mobile application [28]. Architecture proposed by Ghita Kouadri Mostefaoui and Faisal Tariq [3] for mobile application is model-driven design process as it is an online-and offline capable mobile application architecture. It is able to solve the said problem. However, it needs evaluation of mobile app delivery in connection to market and for feature enhancement. Another proposed solution is asynchronous task need to be added so that it can resolve this problem in future work. Other enhanced functions such as format validation and remembering password need to be included in order to maintain reliability.

5   Conclusion

The mobile Car application has met the requirements set by the of travel agency which is able to manage multiple trips at different locations or destination by manager. At the same, this working application has considered all necessary functions to maintain SOP during Covid-19 pandemic. In future work, some features of the mobile Car application could potentially improve using machine learning technique such as detecting common problems face by manager in managing multiple trips and provide recommendations. One of the advantages of using machine learning algorithm is that as the amount of data increases, learning also increases. Consequently, accurate recommendations are provided by mobile Car application.

References

1. Papadopoulos, T., Baltas, K.N., Balta, M.E.: The use of digital technologies by small and medium enterprise during COVID-19: implications for theory and practice. Int. J. Inf. Manage. **55**, 102192 (2020)
2. Susanto, H., Leu, F.Y., Chen, C.K.: The Emerging Technology of Big Data: Its Impact as a Tool of ICT Development. CRC Press Taylor & Francis Group, Boca Raton (2019)
3. Mostefaoui, G. K., Tariq, F.: Mobile Apps Engineering: Design, Development, Security and Testing, pp. 36–39. CRC Press, Taylor and Francis Groups, Boca Raton (2019)
4. Setiawan, R., Zainul, K., Faruq, A., Qassandra, C.: Design mobile application for health consultation during pandemic Covid-19. Int. J. Adv. Trends Comput. Sci. Eng. **9**(4), 4241–4244 (2020)
5. World Bank, Population (2018). https://databank.org/data/download/POP.pdf. Accessed 20 Jan 2021
6. Too, W.G., Thong, C.L., Chit, S.M., Chaw, L.Y., Lee C.Y.: Features of mobile tracking apps: a review of literature and analysis of current apps compared against travel agency requirements. In: Salvendy, G., Wei, J. (eds.) Design, Operation and Evaluation of Mobile Communications. HCII 2020. Lecture Notes in Computer Science, vol. 12216, pp. 107–120. Springer, Cham. https://doi.org/10.1007/978-3-030-50350-5_10
7. World Health Organization (WHO). Public health considerations while resuming international travel. https://www.who.int/news-room/articles-detail/public-health-considerations-while-resuming-international-travel. Accessed 30 Dec 2020

8. Government extends conditional MCO until June 9. https://www.theedgemarkets.com/article/government-extends-conditional-mco-until-june-9. Accessed 1 Nov 2020
9. Malaysia announces movement control order after spike in Covid-19 cases. https://www.thestar.com.my/news/nation/2020/03/16/malaysia-announces-restricted-movement-measure-after-spike-in-covid-19-cases. Accessed 30 Oct 2020
10. CMCO in Selangor, KL and Putrajaya from 14–27 October. https://www.theedgemarkets.com/article/conditional-mco-be-implemented-selangor-kuala-lumpur-putrajaya-oct-14. Accessed 30 Dec 2020
11. Updated List of COVID Red Zones, EMCO Areas, And Places With Confirmed Cases In Malaysia. https://www.klook.com/en-MY/blog/covid-19-red-zones-malaysia/. Accessed 20 Dec 2020
12. True colours: If you live in a Covid-19 red or orange zone, stay home! https://www.nst.com.my/news/nation/2020/11/637820/true-colours-if-you-live-covid-19-red-or-orange-zone-stay-home. Accessed 2 Jan 2021
13. Travel bubble for safe domestic holidays. https://www.nst.com.my/news/nation/2020/11/645239/travel-bubble-safe-domestic-holidays. Accessed 2 Jan 2021
14. Tourism Ministry reveals recovery plans for pandemic-hit travel sector. https://www.thestar.com.my/lifestyle/travel/2020/11/23/tourism-ministry-reveals-recovery-plans-for-pandemic-hit-travel-sector. Accessed 27 Dec 2020
15. https://www.malaysiakini.com/news/551844. Accessed 29 Dec 2020
16. NSC Mulls Free Movement Between Green Districts, States For Tourism. https://codeblue.galencentre.org/2020/11/16/nsc-mulls-free-movement-between-green-districts-states-for-tourism/. Accessed 31 Dec 2020
17. Stay home, only 5 Covid-19 green zones left in the peninsula. https://www.freemalaysiatoday.com/category/nation/2021/01/10/stay-home-only-5-covid-19-green-zones-left-in-the-peninsula/. Accessed 15 Jan 2021
18. https://www.moh.gov.my/. Accessed 15 Jan 2021
19. Covid 19: Malaysia reports fresh record high of 3,337 new cases, 15 deaths. https://www.theedgemarkets.com/article/covid19-malaysia-reports-3337-new-cases-15-deaths. Accessed 15 Jan 2021
20. https://mysejahtera.malaysia.gov.my/. Accessed 16 Jan 2021
21. https://ukkdosm.github.io/covid-19. Accessed 16 Jan 2021
22. MySejahtera Travel (2020). https://mysejahtera.malaysia.gov.my/doc/MYSJ_Travel_Kit-EN.pdf. Accessed 16 Jan 2021
23. CodeBlue (2020). https://codeblue.galencentre.org/2020/06/10/nsc-sops-moot-mysejahtera-app-for-contact-tracing/. Accessed 16 Jan 2021
24. KLOOK (2020) (Simon Yuen). https://www.marketing-interactive.com/quick-responses-matter-how-klook-reshapes-tourism-in-the-future. Accessed 16 Jan 2021
25. Grab (2020). https://www.grab.com/sg/. Accessed 16 Jan 2021
26. EzCab (2020). https://ezcab.com.my/services/. Accessed 16 Jan 2021
27. Koniig-Ries: Challenges in mobile application development. IT-Inf. Technol. **51**(2), 69–71 (2009)
28. Pandya, R.: Mobile and personal communication systems and services. In: IEEE Series on Digital e Mobile Communication. Wiley, Hoboken (2004)

Towards Efficient Distance Studies: Online Course Management System (CMS)

S. M. Topazal, Kamal Ali Alezabi[⊠], and Chee Ling Thong

Institute of Computer Science and Digital Innovation, UCSI University, Cheras,
56000 Kuala Lumpur, Malaysia
kamal@ucsiuniversity.edu.my

Abstract. Information and communication technologies (ICT) have influenced almost every area of human activity and every part of their daily lives in today's world. It has also reduced physical and time limits and has easily described one attention and has a lot of developments in the teaching process. For instance, the Course Management System (CMS) is a structured system for handling the registration and enrollment of a new student as well as classes in the course. To prevent the risk of data loss and overcome the dilemma of current systems, this computerized system can store and back up all the data in the database. The paper aims to build a stable yet reliable framework for end-users. In addition, to address the issue in current systems, this paper outlines the evaluation and implementation of a CMS. This initiative would allow the university to expand its reach by reducing costs, minimizing operator errors, and saving time. The proposed Course Management Systems & administrator would, however, be able to manage the course, register new students, and reset the student password. Many advantages have been provided by the proposed system, including portability, remarkable flexibility, and so on. By using personal interview and online questionaries, the finding has shown CMS has become safe and it concludes that the general age is excellent and reduce time waste, degrade paper base work, and encourage to use online-based course registration and online learning platform and what functions and features the system could have.

Keywords: Course Management System (CMS) · Learning Management System (LMS) · Information and Communication Technology (ICT)

1 Introduction

In today's world, information and communication technologies (ICT) are available in the majority of fields where we have daily activities [7]. The generation of students born with digital technology brings with them a significantly different approach to learning. A CMS provides a broad scope to educational processes. It has reduced physical and time edges and it has easily described one attention and it has a lot of developments in the teaching process [2, 8]. The use of CMS is a relatively recent feature of university study or higher education and it becomes strongly integrated into course registration systems in many universities enter the world [10]. A typical CMS will offer namely user registration,

© Springer Nature Switzerland AG 2021
G. Salvendy and J. Wei (Eds.): HCII 2021, LNCS 12796, pp. 113–125, 2021.
https://doi.org/10.1007/978-3-030-77025-9_11

file exchange, student details, and chat rooms authentication, tests and surveys, wikis, creation of static web pages, chat rooms, and photo galleries. An advanced CMS can offer most of the components necessary for more commonly, distance learning, it can be used to help traditional classroom courses. Many drawbacks on CMS emphasized that this format was initially introduced as a far-reaching learning tool, but it has changed its function in the creation and serves as an assisting media medium in the classroom and teaching as well as a contact platform for teachers and students outside the classroom. Especially purpose for online course registration (course add and drop), a new student registration, and teaching and learning in future [2, 8].

Therefore, the acquisition object of the development of the CMS was doubtful, as the use of the program itself is for more physical learning than for long-distance education. Nevertheless, whatever role the CMS started playing, researchers also noted many advantages of implementing CMS [6, 10]. Meanwhile, CMS can provide a lecturer with a set of study tools, and a framework that accesses the relatively easy creation of subsequent teaching, course content, and includes students taking the courses [3, 9]. However, CMS is significant in growing teaching and learning experiences for common lessons, combined learning, and online courses. Especially, CMS plays a significant role in course management, communication between students and teachers, conducting teaching and learning tasks and it makes it possible for students in accessing lecturer notes. Moreover, CMS also aid to **facilitate academic staff in sharing students' works with their classmates, student assignment, and take back** to the response to them [2].

1.1 Problem Statement, Aim and Objective

The study identifies that while most technologically wealthy universities of the world are using CMS, the CMS as an addition to traditional means of instruction doesn't necessarily much improvement, implementation, and maintenance cost. The CMS like a whiteboard, WebCT, Moodle, and blackboard, etc. Initially, e-learning students have 60% faster-curved contrast to classroom counterparts. Consequently, all universities in the whole world should facilitate instructors, administration, and students with CMS. The study also displays that procedures and policy should be made and instructing should be offered for instructor's activities, registration process, and student's responsibilities. The interface is simple, easy to use and it does not have many buttons while it's access to the blackboard, all the courses are here. The course that needs to be accessed is selected (clicked) to perform a function with a notification [2]. The key problem is the ability to learn between students, but lecturers teach them identical content in one classroom [2, 9]. Students are assessed and entered fairly, while students should not have the same abilities to grab learning skills. Lecturers evaluate their students by using some questions but most of the time the question out of the context and students are not able to see all courses, which are offered in a semester as well the subsequent semester. The CMS does not estimate the tuition fees for any particular subject. Moreover, students also feel confused about their subject tuition fees [5]. The basic aim for developing the prototype named "Course Management System" is to make the whole process of Course registration, course adds and drop, new student registration, and e-learning platform atomized in university and providing a new and easy to use system for all users. Therefore, online resources and materials are the key resources for academic staff, presentations, teaching materials, syllabus, files, exams, and everything. The CMS aims to achieve the following objectives: To shorten the time and effort of preparing the course list and student identity and to fully automate the course list and registration number creation process. The general object research aims to improve an adaptive e-learning program to allow students to solve problems and answer questions based on their skill or speed. In addition, the students can be enrolled in their subject freely by staying anywhere and the admin creates a new student registering. To minimize using paper and environmental pollution. The admin can create sessions, courses, and the department. The students will be able to enroll his/her course and edit their profile as well as change password. The admin can create session/s, course, semester, and the department. The admin also can view student's login activities.

2 Literature Review

The CMS program integrates several web tools, Learning Management System (LMS) or Virtual Learning. In tradition, the course registration process is offered by most of the universities, where an employee is provided by pen and paper-based [14]. Now automated online course registration process to save the cost and upgrade the student services, and an atomized registration system [9]. Moreover, the communication between the Personal Digital Assistants (PDA's) and the server is the easiest because of the wireless technology involved with them but sometimes the PDA-based system increases the student's additional cost and it never provides any real-time feedback from the student [1]. The CMS allows the admin to add new student and their course enrollment. Afterward, is logged into the system, the admin can add, edit, delete, and display all details about the students [9]. The student can be able to register their selected course with a unique pin code that will be provided by the admin. When a student successfully enrolled their courses then, the student will be able to view their enrolled course name, session, department, semester, and the enrollment creation date as well as, print their course details [1]. The CMS can be providing a lecturer with a set of study tools, and a framework which accesses the relatively easy creation of subsequent teaching, course content, and includes students taking the courses [9, 13]. The system architecture is focused on functions that are very stable and scalable.

We have studied some of the existing CMS systems such as Brickfield Asia College (BAC) and International Islamic University Malaysia (IIUM) Course Management Systems. Those systems have some imperfection in terms of system functionality such as lacking live chat and security. In our proposed system, student enrolls her/his course must use a unique pin code that will only be available from admin. In this way, the student course registration process is going to be secure from a third-party. Moreover, as illustrated in Fig. 1, the proposed system employs the live chat function while the student will be performed chatting with the admin if they face any troubles during their course registration. The student can communicate in two ways, WhatsApp and Messenger which allow the student to register from anywhere and anytime.

Besides, the overall architecture of the proposed system is examined along with the implementation behind the functions and features. The use case descriptions are used to illustrate the actions of the user and it has also an activity diagram that represents the

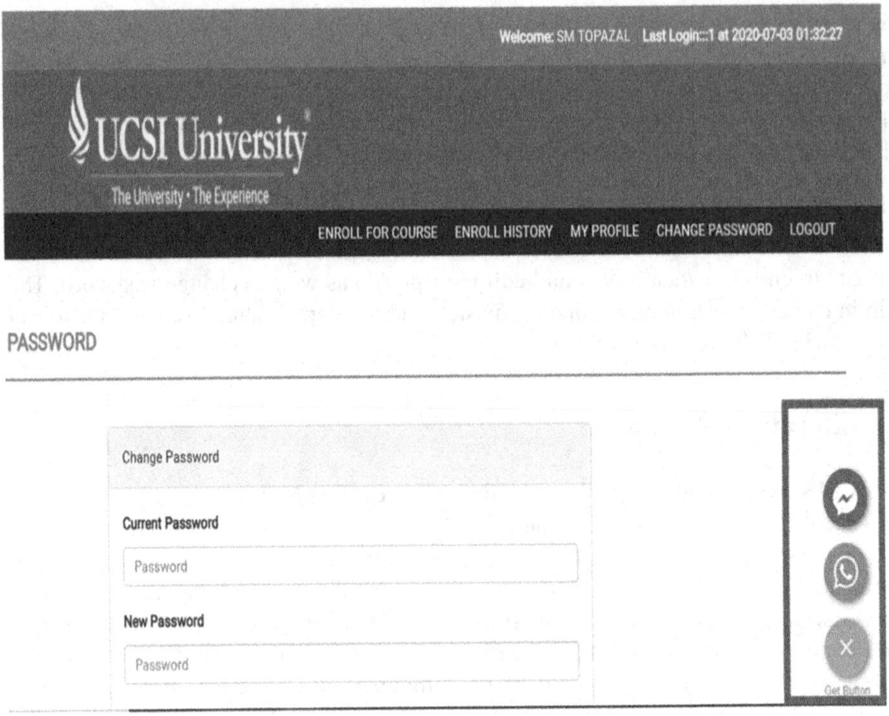

Fig. 1. The live chat feature in the proposed system

interactive dimensions of this structure and illustrates the flow from one activity to the others. The class diagram is a stable diagram type that illustrates the structural design by displaying the relationship between classes (class, attribute, operation).

Use case diagrams are usually used to illustrate the activities (use cases) that can be performed by the users of the system. Figure 2 represents the use case diagram for the Course Management System which will have two actors namely the student and the admin who can perform a variety of actions. Firstly, the student has needed to log in to the system before access. If the student will be felt any hesitate during the system accessing time, they should be performed by live chat with the admin. Students can access in manage course registration and change login password. Finally, the student must perform to log out from the system when they want to leave. Once the student logs out from the system then it must be recorded by the database that the admin able to see their log history. The admin has also needed to authenticate the system before entering. The admin enables to use and access all the functionalities such as add, update, and delete the session, semester, department, and course, manage student registration, view enrollment history, view student logs history, manage course registration, and change student password as well as log out option. Below Fig. 3 displays the class diagram with several attributes that can use by admin and student. The login has the structure of the database table in which login is connected to the admin and student. The student has to connect with the admin and message (live chat). But most of the relationship with

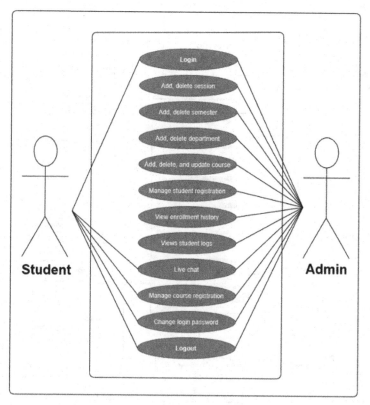

Fig. 2. Use case diagram

the admin. Likewise, the admin has a direct relationship with the department, student registration, course enrolment, course add-delete, and session, and so on that, all are displayed in Fig. 3.

3 Research Methodology

In this study, the research methodology used to achieve research objectives is survey. A "survey" can in the form of a short paper-and-pencil feedback form or a personal interview [11]. Data were collected via an online questionnaire and interview. They were 125 respondents participated in the survey. The survey has been performed on social media exclusively likewise Twitter, Instagram, Facebook, and Course Network (CN). The purpose of the survey is to enable the researcher to gather requirements from the users and at the same time understand the current problems faced by the users. There are 12 questions in the online questionnaire, and it is divided into 4 sections. The four sections are: section A is "Demographic Section", section B is "users' ability", section C is user's prior experience and section D is open-ended questions.

The survey method is applying for data collection. This method provides quantitative data that needs to fulfill the research objectives. The research study is one of the

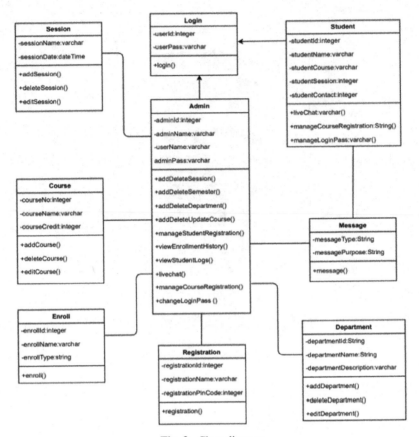

Fig. 3. Class diagram

most significant facets of measurement of social science. Conducting a survey has many advantages over performing physical interviews, where the effort and the time is efficiently reduced [4]. The area is calculated with the following formula (1) which is a Sample Size Calculator [12]. The total number of respondents in the group is university students. Using the formula (1), a population size of 125, a confidence level of 95%, and a margin of error of 1.96% yielded a sample size of 120 people [12].

$$\frac{\frac{z^2 \times p(1-p)}{e^2}}{1 + (\frac{z^2 \times p(1-p)}{e^2 N})} \tag{1}$$

Where N is the population size − 125, z is confidence level − 95, e is error − 1.96, p is sample size − 120.

After the sample size for the survey was calculated above, the survey questionnaires were mass distributed. Given the current situation of the global pandemic virus in the whole world as well as Malaysia, both surveys and interviews were asked through Google Form.

4   Results and Discussion

Following the creation of the designs, the coding phase begins, which includes implementing all the modules that are designed. Besides, the overall architecture of the system is examined along with the implementation of the functions and features. The data are collected, and the responses are provided with pie charts once respondents answer the survey. The collected data then provides a summary of the answers. A summary of responses is then generated from the collected data.

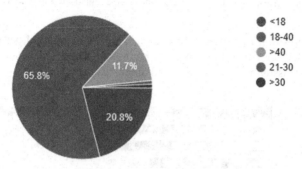

Fig. 4. Respondents' age range.

The Fig. 4 shows the respondent's age range from below 18, 18 to 40, and over forty years old. According to the diagram the majority 65.8% of respondents' age range between 18 to 40 years. While over 40 years old respondents are 11.7% the lowest.

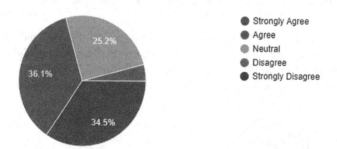

Fig. 5. CMS is helping to respondents learning experience.

Figure 5 presents the highest number of the participants 36.1% agreed with the CMS is helpful for their learning experience, but the corresponding proportion of 34.5% strongly agreed, 25.2% are neutral with them. However, approximately 4.2% of the respondents disagreed that CMS ever and never help them with their learning experience.

Figure 6 displays the maximum number of the participants 23.3% used daily (once or more per day), and few times in a week, opposite to did not use around 3.3%. The proportion of 20.8% used a few times in a month. Moreover, the corresponding to use once a week and a few times in a semester of 15% and 14.2% of the respondents,

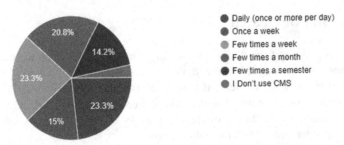

Fig. 6. Respondents to do use online course registration in (CMS)

respectively. Below Fig. 7 provides information about the majority of participants were 75.8% downloaded Docs, files, links. While the minimum number of 0.8% of respondents used to submit an assignment, do a quiz, and did not use anything.

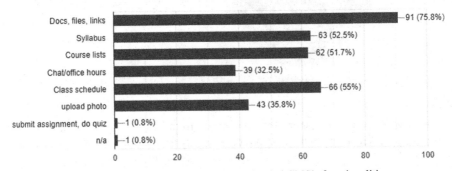

Fig. 7. Respondents have used or downloaded CMS's functionalities.

In other words, the corresponding proportion of 52.5% and 51.7% are used/downloaded syllabus and course list, respectively. The second highest 55% of the trend of respondents used class schedules, opposite to 32.5% chat/office hours. The proportion of 35.8% of the participants used to change their profile photos.

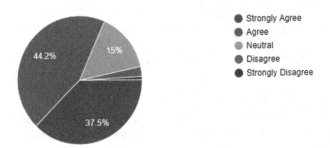

Fig. 8. Respondents are encouraged to implement the CMS in all institutions.

The above Fig. 8 illustrates the largest number of the participants 44.2% agreed with the implementation of the CMS in all educational institutions, opposite to 0.8% of respondents are strongly disagreed. On the other hand, the proportion of 37.5% strongly agreed, and 15% are neutral of the participants, while the respondents of 2.5% disagreed to implement this system. Overall, the questionnaire has shown a positive response from the respondents regarding the system. According to the survey, CMS has become safe, and it concludes that the general age is excellent and reduce time waste, degrade paper base work, and encourage to use online-based course registration and online learning platform and what functions and features the system could have.

4.1 Implementation

The web system is mainly developed using several types of platforms. The hosting server of the system is www.000webhost.com server supporting the MYSQL platform which is where the system database was developed using Structured Query Language (SQL) as a developing language and Personal Home Page (PHP) as a medium to maintain the connection between the system and the database in the server. The architectural Fig. 9 or layout framework depicts a structure and a database, and the software components needed for the development of a computer-based system. A system access device such as a laptop or a tablet, a smartphone is required for the user, and all the information of data is stored in the database. The UI design was one of the most significant tasks in this system. The user interface design aims to make it easier to use by the users (admin and student). The interface was created for both users (admin and student).

Fig. 9. The CMS's graphical user interface.

Above Fig. 9 illustrates the information about the Admin Main or Home page. After the successful login, the Admin shows various features in the menu bar, where the performance separately with the Session, Semester, Faculty, Course, Registration, manage students, enroll history, student logs, and logout. It ensures that the Admin will be able to use every displayed function. After the implementation, the researchers invited 125 respondents to perform evaluation on user satisfaction. The users are university students from 4 universities in Malaysia: UCSI University, City University, Limkokwing University, International Islamic University of Malaysia as well as Mahsa University. The evaluation of the system is performed to fulfil the user requirements gathered earlier. There were 4 questions asked in the evaluation and the results are presented in Table 1.

Table 1. User experience of evaluation

No	Question	User satisfactory				
		1	2	3	4	5
1	The CMS is user-friendly?	5	5	20	65	30
2	The CMS allows users to enroll in the course and enroll in student registration?	–	5	20	65	35
3	The CMS works efficiently, and time reduces?	–	–	10	35	80
4	The CMS functions sufficiently?	–	5	25	70	25

Table 1 gives the information about the outcome of the user satisfactory level of the course management system. The questionnaire on user acceptance is a Likert scale form. Fifteen participants were chosen from the questionnaire surveys participants to test the CMS System and then complete the user acceptance evaluation questionnaire.

The responses of the first question are shown in Fig. 10 below, it is about the user experience and user interface design. Approximately one-half percent of users agreed that the architectural design of the system is user-friendly. About one-fourth percent of testers strongly agreed that the system architecture design is easy to use and user-friendly and 16% of the users stayed neutral. However, four percent of users are expressed disagree and strongly disagreed.

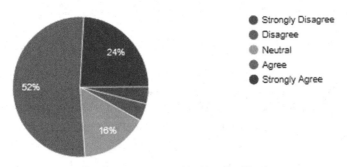

Fig. 10. User evaluation question No. 1

Question number 2 asked about the function of the system whether it helps the user to do course enroll and new student registration easier or not. Figure 11 shows that closely over one half of them is agreed to allow users to do course enrollment and new student registration easily. Exactly 28% of the users strongly agreed that the system makes it easy for users to course enrollment and student registration. On the other hand, four percent of them disagreed and 16% of the users remains constant.

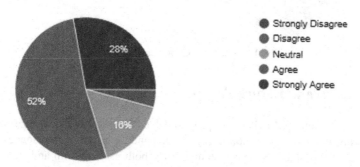

Fig. 11. User evaluation question No. 2

Question 3 asked about the efficiency of CMS and the reduction of time. Figure 12 shows that approximately two-thirds percent of the users agreed strongly that the system is efficient, and time is reduced. Below one-third percent of testers are agreed on the usefulness of the system and eight percent of users stayed neutral.

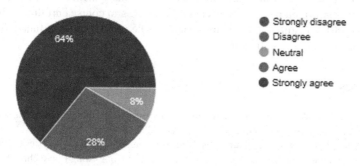

Fig. 12. User evaluation question No. 3

Finally, as illustrated in Fig. 13, exactly 56% of the testers agreed that the system's role is satisfactory. Approximately 4% of the users' disagreed and around 20% of the users are neutral and strongly agreed that the CMS is satisfactory for them. In general, every user is satisfied with the CMS and believes that the CMS meet their requirements.

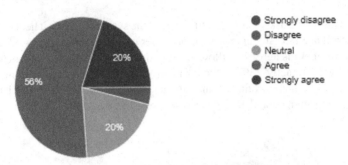

Fig. 13. User evaluation question No. 4

5 Conclusion and Future Works

In this paper, an efficient CMS has been proposed that can secure and recognize both users (student) who able to do online course registration and the admin who manages courses and registering new students. The system ensures both users (admin and student) will have only one way to be able to enter the system as long as the users (admin and student) are log in to the system. However, it does not matter how many times the student wants to add the course. In the other words, the system also allows the admin to fully maintain this system, where the admin can manage the course and a new student registration such as add course, session, and semester. The system has been developed according to the scope of the paper. Moreover, the developers also want to improve some of the key features of the current system. In the below the developers listed out their wishes for some of the future improvement: Auto-notification sends from the system to users (Admin and student). The confirmation e-mail sends after the successful course enrollment. Improve or add some of the features in the admin panel. Make online payment function for the student panel as well as admit card.

References

1. Andresen, M.A.: Asynchronous discussion forums: success factors, outcomes, assessments, and limitations. J. Educ. Technol. Soc. **12**(1), 249–257 (2009)
2. Chiu, S.K.: Perceptions of and attitudes towards a course management system at the Hong Kong Polytechnic University. Doctoral dissertation, The Hong Kong Polytechnic University (2019)
3. Chua, C.: Information Communication Technology. 149–168 (2019).
4. Daniel, E.: The usefulness of qualitative and quantitative approaches and methods in research-ing problem-solving ability in science education curriculum. J. Educ. Pract. **7**, 91–100 (2016)
5. Ekwonwune, E.N.: Design, and Implementation of an Online Course Management System. J. Softw. Eng. Appl. **12**, 21–33 (2019)
6. Goh, C.F.: Why do university teachers use e-learning systems? Int. Rev. Res. Open Distrib. Learn **21**, 136–155 (2020)
7. Issue, S.: Intelligent e-restaurant system with Wi-Fi, vol. 4, no. march, pp. 192–200 (2015)
8. Maher, D.: The use of course management systems in pre-service teacher education, pp. 196–213 (2019)

9. Reid, L.: Learning management systems: the game changer for traditional teaching and learning at adult and higher education institutions. Glob. J. Hum. Soc. Sci. G Linguist. Educ. **19**(6), 1–14 (2019)
10. Saputra, Y.: A study on course management system implementation in Indonesian higher education institutions (2018)
11. Base, K.: What is the research methods knowledge base ? Using the KB in a course about the author (2002)
12. Survey Monkey: Sample Size Calculator (2018). https://www.surveymonkey.com/mp/sample-size-calculator
13. Chua, C.C.: Information communication technology, pp. 149–168 (2019)
14. Palvia, S.P.A.: Online education: worldwide status, challenges, trends, and implications, pp. 233–241 (2018)

A Review on the Research of Producer Services Supply Chain in China

Siqi Yin[✉], Caihong Liu, Yi Xie, and Yu Shui

School of Business, Jiaxing University, Jiaxing 314001, China

Abstract. With the development of modern manufacturing industry, the division of production is more and more detailed, and the importance of producer services is more and more prominent. In order to clarify the development status and trend of China's producer service supply chain, based on the development status and problems of China's producer service supply chain, this paper analyzes the influencing factors of the collaboration of the production + service mixed supply chain from the connotation and characteristics of producer service supply chain. At the same time, the author thinks that the producer service supply chain of China is still in the development status quo, and the producer service industry of China's manufacturing industry is still in the situation of fighting alone. How to develop and strengthen the producer service supply chain of China's manufacturing industries.

Keywords: Productive services · Supply chain · Manufacturing

1 Introduction

China's the Eleventh Five-Year Plan emphasizes that we should vigorously develop the producer oriented service industry, refine and deepen the professional division of labor, reduce social transaction costs, and improve the efficiency of resource allocation, so as to realize the transformation of economic growth mainly driven by industry to driven by i-industry coordination [1]. The right choice to optimize China's industrial structure is to learn from the experience of developed countries, take the development of service outsourcing as a breakthrough, focus on the development of modern producer services, stimulate the linkage effect between producer services and manufacturing, promote the formation of effective industrial agglomeration of producer services, and promote the upgrading of local enterprises' industrial chain [2]. China's economic activities are changing from manufacturing industry as the center to service industry as the center, and the relationship between manufacturing industry and producer services is increasingly close [3]. There are two characteristics of manufacturing servitization: one is input servitization, that is, service elements play an increasingly important role in the total input of manufacturing; the other is output servitization, that is, service products play an increasingly important role in the total output of manufacturing. Producer services can improve the production efficiency of other elements of enterprises, so as to reduce the input of resource consuming elements or replace the input of resource consuming elements [4]. As a result, the healthy development of the manufacturing industry is

© Springer Nature Switzerland AG 2021
G. Salvendy and J. Wei (Eds.): HCII 2021, LNCS 12796, pp. 126–137, 2021.
https://doi.org/10.1007/978-3-030-77025-9_12

inseparable from the strong support of the producer service industry. At the same time, the trend of the service-Oriented industrialization of the manufacturing industry has gradually become clear.

At present, the development of producer services in China is relatively backward, and the lack of interaction mechanism between producer services and manufacturing industry, especially in the distribution network, logistics, financing and other aspects, has seriously affected the improvement of the competitiveness of manufacturing industry [5]. The research on producer service supply chain is still at the stage of concept definition and arrangement, and the research on the organic integration of manufacturing supply chain and service supply chain is relatively lacking, especially the quantitative research and empirical research [6]. For manufacturing enterprises, through the support of supply chain, reduce operating costs, through effective cooperation between enterprises to improve efficiency and flexibility become the key [7]. With the development of modern information technology, it is inevitable to improve the productive service level of manufacturing enterprises and cultivate a large number of professional producer service providers [8].

In view of the core status of producer services in manufacturing industry and the fact that producer services in China are relatively backward, it is very urgent to carry out relevant research. With the transformation of enterprises to service-Oriented manufacturing, the traditional manufacturing supply chain is gradually transformed into a hybrid supply chain with both manufacturing and service functions. In order to find out the current research situation and problems in China, this paper reviews the related research.

2 Definition of Connotation of Manufacturing Supply Chain

2.1 Definition of Producer Services Supply Chain for Manufacturing

In 1988, vandermenwe and Rada pioneered the concept of "Servitization of Manufacturing". The servitization of manufacturing is defined as the transformation of traditional manufacturing enterprises from simply providing tangible goods or goods and additional services to providing "goods service package" with customers as the center [9]. According to white (1999), servitization of manufacturing is a process of dynamic change, in which the role of manufacturer changes from goods provider to service provider [10]. Szalavetz (2003) thinks that servitization of manufacturing has two meanings: first, the efficiency of internal services is increasingly important to the competitiveness of manufacturing enterprises. Competitiveness comes not only from the efficiency of traditional manufacturing activities, but also from the effective organization and provision of internal services, and its importance and complexity are gradually increasing; second, the complexity and importance of external services related to goods to customers Increasing [11]. At the same time, China's academia has also given a lot of attention to the servitization of manufacturing. For example, Lei Lin and Guisheng Wu think that servitization of manufacturing is that manufacturing enterprises further strengthen and enhance the original service support activities in order to obtain competitive advantage. This kind of service enhancement is mainly manifested in two aspects: basic enhancement and promotion enhancement [12]. According to the content of services provided by enterprises, Jingmei Ma believes that servitization of manufacturing includes general value-Added services based on products and professional services separated from products [13]. Jiguo Liu and others believe that servitization of manufacturing refers to manufacturing enterprises' aim to obtain competitive advantage and change the value chain from manufacturing centered to service centered [14]. Dapeng Zhou believes that servitization of manufacturing is an economic trend of increasing proportion of input and output of service elements remanufacturing [15].

A classic definition of supply chain in academic circles is proposed by Professor Xiaoliang Li: "around the core enterprise, through the control of logistics, information flow and capital flow, from the purchase of raw materials to the production of intermediate products and final products, and finally by the sales network to deliver products to consumers, it is a whole chain composed of suppliers, manufacturers, distributors, retailers and final users Body function network chain structure". Here, the supply chain is oriented to manufacturing enterprises, around the logistics, its management purpose is to reduce costs and improve efficiency [16].

To sum up, its definition should be: in the process of transformation from product supply chain to product service supply chain, the role of supply chain itself will change, from only providing products to providing products and additional services, and then to providing the integration scheme of products and services. Therefore, the supply chain has also changed from a single product supply chain or services supply chain to a product service supply chain integrating products and services [17]. That is, the mode of integrated management of information, service process, service capability, service performance and service funds from the initial service provider to the final customer, which is dominated by productive services and formed for the generation and delivery of services.

2.2 Characteristics of Producer Services Supply Chain for Manufacturing Industry

The transmission and collection of services of each node depend on the flow and sharing of information. The flow in the whole supply chain is not physical products, but services. Of course, some services still depend on the physical flow of products, such as logistics services. But our research focuses on the flow of services. Service industry is an indispensable part of a country's development. The rapid development and prosperity of modern service industry has become an important symbol of a country's and regional economic modernization [18]. Manufacturing enterprises will produce different types of producer services around all aspects of product production. Manufacturing enterprises will produce different types of production service demand around all aspects of product production. Producer services supply chain is a complex system, but the reality exists in our economic society. Because service is intangible and difficult to measure, customers often participate in the process of service delivery. Service providers and customers have to communicate face to face. Therefore, the structure of the service supply chain is much simpler than that of the product supply chain. Compared with the operation mode of the product supply chain, there is only one service supply chain, that is, completely pulling and market reacting, which is determined by the non storability of the service and the diversity of the service demand. The manufacturing oriented producer service supply chain is a combination of the two. The span of supply chain nodes is different, so it has complexity.

It is also dynamic. The supply chain is composed of members with different executive functions. Its operation process involves logistics, information flow, capital flow and so on. It is closely related to the external environment and constantly interacts with the external environment [19].

Due to the needs of enterprise strategy and adapting to the change of market demand, node enterprises and service providers need to be updated dynamically. With more and more participants in the supply chain and wider geographical scope, supply chain management gradually changes from closed, static and linear structure to open, dynamic and network structure [20], This makes the manufacturing oriented producer service supply chain dynamic.

At the same time, it also has the characteristics of user oriented. User demand pull is the driving source of information flow, products and services, capital flow operation in the supply chain, is an essential part. Driven by customer demand, through the establishment of strategic partnership between enterprises in the supply chain, we can comprehensively improve the satisfaction of cooperation among enterprises, so as to achieve the goal of improving the satisfaction of end users [21].

Crossover is also an important feature. There are more cooperative enterprises in each node, the supply chain structure grows [22], and many supply chains intersect, which increases the difficulty of supply chain management and coordination.

3   The Influencing Factors of Supply Chain Coordination Between Manufacturing Industries and Producer Services in China

After the "integration of industrialization and informatization", China has puted forward the "integration of two industries" of advanced manufacturing industry and modern service industry for the first time. Recently, the national development and Reform Commission and other 15 departments jointly issued the "Implementation Opinions on Promoting the Deep Integration Development of Advanced Manufacturing Industry and Modern Service Industry", which provides direction in cultivating new formats and new modes of integration development and exploring new paths of integration development in key industries and key fields [23]. With the further development of producer service industry, producer service supply chain has been gradually formed. As one of the core work of establishing producer service supply chain, supplier selection has become an important part of its development and stability. The research of supply chain management has always been a research hotspot of scholars at home and abroad. However, the definition and understanding of supply chain management pay more attention to the transformation process of physical products in manufacturing industry, while the research of service supply chain management involving service transformation process is relatively less [24]. At present, the research of supply chain management has gradually started from product supply chain to service supply chain. According to the development status of producer services, this paper discusses how to evaluate and improve the performance of producer services from the perspective of supply chain management [25].

To build a modern economic system, we must develop the economy with high quality. The focus of economic development lies in the real economy, and the key and difficult point of developing the real economy lies in the manufacturing industry. "Proposal of the CPC Central Committee on Formulating the Fourteenth Five-Year Plan for National Economic and Social Development and the Long-Range Goals for the year 2035" proposes to promote the deep integration of modern service industry with advanced manufacturing industry and modern agriculture, and accelerate the digitization of service industry. With a new round of development of information industry and the transformation of global manufacturing industry from single production to "production + service", it is an inevitable choice to promote the high-Quality development of manufacturing industry to promote the symbiosis and coordinated development of manufacturing industry and service industry [26].

In the field of China's manufacturing industry, multinational companies occupy the high end of the industrial value chain by virtue of the comparative advantage of producer services, and earn high profits. However, the development of producer services in China is relatively backward, and there is no interactive mechanism between producer services and manufacturing industry, especially in the distribution network, logistics, The development of logistics finance can promote the interaction and cooperation between third-Party logistics enterprises, financial institutions and small and medium-Sized enterprises in the supply chain, so as to promote the interactive development of producer services and manufacturing industry in China, and realize the "seamless link" between them [27]. Supply chain enterprises, which constitute the whole social system, play a more important role in collaborative management. First of all, supply chain enterprises need to solve the basic and development problems of the supply chain through the overall management and control of the whole supply chain, and play a general role. Secondly, the supply chain enterprises need to analyze and coordinate the problems in each link of the supply chain, and constantly investigate the rationality of the business process, so as to achieve the effect of collaborative management. Finally, supply chain enterprises need to manage the implementation process of each link of the supply chain in order to improve the supply chain foundation. Through the collaborative management of the above three aspects, the whole supply chain can run more efficiently. A good information tracking and quick response mechanism is established in the supply chain system to alleviate the difficulty of production schedule control caused by the characteristics of collaborative production and outsourcing in the supply chain [28].

The coordination problem of Service-Oriented Manufacturing Hybrid Supply Chain (SMHSC) composed of vendors, Service providers and integrators and dominated by manufacturers. Product demand is affected by service effort level of service providers and market random factors. By using the Stackelberg game model, it is proved that the simple revenue sharing contract cannot coordinate the service-Oriented manufacturing mixed supply chain, but the service effort cost sharing model designed on this basis can coordinate. The results show that the effective parameters of revenue sharing and cost sharing must satisfy two linear relationships and a certain value range in the coordination of hybrid supply chain. Under such conditions, all participants of the hybrid supply chain can obtain excess profits and maintain the healthy operation of the supply chain [29]. In our daily life, it is not difficult to find such a situation, a company's products after research and development, production, after listing has no expected sales; its main products in the sales of one or two years later, the market began to decline. An enterprise's products have been sought after by many similar products as soon as they are listed on the market. Since an enterprise's products are listed on the market, it has never been a day of easy life. For two years, it has been on the verge of collapse [24].

Some people think that this is the current situation of fierce competition in the Chinese market. Therefore, many enterprises believe that the current market is becoming more and more difficult, and the opportunities are less and less. The upgrading of industrial structure is the focus of Jiangsu's economic development. The upgrading of manufacturing structure is inseparable from the support of producer services. The core of foreign trade supply chain management is to obtain competitive advantage in the form of an overall industrial chain. Supply chain management is the process of interaction between producer services and manufacturing industry. The industrial chain that gathers logistics, technology and information interacts with manufacturing industry under the coordination of foreign trade enterprises, and allocates resources reasonably with specialized division of labor, Knowledge and technology diffusion is the driving force for manufacturing industry to improve its technological capability and transformation and upgrading [30].

With the rapid development of producer services, collaborative management of service supply chain has attracted more and more attention. Under this background, this paper analyzes the characteristics of producer services supply chain, and uses the traditional supply chain model for reference, analyzes the basic model of collaborative management of producer services supply chain and the relationship between its components [31]. The key is to understand and control the market. This paper analyzes the composition and characteristics of the service supply network of manufacturing enterprises, and analyzes the ternary relationship and its changes under the producer service supply network, so as to clarify the new requirements of manufacturing enterprises for suppliers under the producer service supply network. Then, based on the classification dimension of Kraljic matrix, the classification system of producer services for manufacturing enterprises oriented to service strategy is established, and the Kraljic matrix classification method based on DEA linear programming is introduced, The producer services of service-Oriented manufacturing enterprises are divided into four types: Strategic producer services, bottleneck producer services, leverage producer services and non critical producer services. Through questionnaire survey, eight commonly used producer services are located in each type of service [32].

Enterprises must have market awareness in order to better integrate into the market. The goal of an enterprise can only be achieved through the market. Due to the fluctuation of the market, the competitiveness of enterprises has been transformed into the competition between supply chains. In the modern market economy environment, all the will and behavior of enterprises must meet the needs of the market, take users as the core, better meet the needs, better integrate into the supply chain of producer services, meet the needs and improve competitiveness. The key to China's transformation from a big manufacturing country to a powerful manufacturing country is continuous innovation to integrate the production chain and service supply chain. In the era of change is the only constant, innovation is the normal operation of enterprises, in order to better integrate the supply chain and producer services supply chain, in an invincible position in the competition [33].

4 Analysis on the Application of Producer Services Supply Chain in China

In 1999, Edward G. Anderson and Douglas J. Morrice began to apply the theory of supply chain to the field of service [34]. Service supply chain has gradually developed into a new research direction in the field of supply chain. In order to meet the needs of globalization, many Chinese enterprises have focused on the global layout of supply chain. The trend of supply chain globalization is more and more obvious, and it is becoming the key content of a new round of national competitiveness [35]. Under the penetration and integration of information technology, China's producer service supply chain is accelerating its development and extension. In practice, some industry supply chains show agile response speed, efficient collaboration ability, accurate matching efficiency and powerful service functions, which help enterprises enter a new space of cost reduction and efficiency increase [36]. At present, the competition in the field of manufacturing industry has focused on the front-End R&D and back-End marketing and other service links. The extended development of service supply chain makes the proportion of professional services in modern service industry, such as logistics and marketing, technology R&D, human resource development, software and information services, financial services, accounting and auditing lawyers, higher and higher [37]. The service mode is diversified [38]. For example, Xumei Zhang and others conducted a pricing equilibrium analysis in view of the situation that mobile phone manufacturers and telecom operators jointly launched "product + service" contract mobile phones, considering network externality, service level, mobile phone price adjustment ratio of telecom operators and other factors [36]. Shenzhen Langhua enterprises carry out the "supply chain + business" cross domain service, relying on the operation mode of five platforms such as circulation business integration, private financial holding, cross-Border e-commerce, intelligent logistics and foreign trade comprehensive service, give full play to the enterprise resource integration and cross industry coordination ability, and provide service for customer enterprises in one or more businesses such as industry, finance, Internet, logistics and foreign trade For the third party supply chain solution system services. Due to the diversity of service types, the types of service providers are also relatively diverse. Different types of service providers provide differentiated services at different stages. Some service providers need to integrate services and products into product service systems and provide them to customers, while others can directly face customers [39]. They are mainly concentrated in developed areas. The distribution pattern of location agglomeration of producer services shows that producer services are closely related to the level of urbanization. The agglomeration effect of producer service industry is more obvious than that of manufacturing industry, which is mainly concentrated in a few big cities or metropolitan areas [40]. Because the agglomeration trend of production services is determined by the natural needs of human contact and information uncertainty, legal, advertising and accounting services are more concentrated in the central business district of metropolis. Therefore, the more developed countries and regions have formed a set of development models and promotion methods suitable for the region through years of manufacturing service practice. In contrast, the less developed regions have a slower development of producer service supply chain.

In recent years, many high-Tech parks and logistics parks have been set up in various provinces and cities of China, and the construction of CBD has been strengthened one after another, all of which are aimed at forming industrial cluster effect. But throughout the country, producer service clusters are mostly based on low cost, and their innovation ability and ability to participate in international competition are not strong. In addition, in the construction of various parks, the concept of regional cooperation is lacking, and the phenomenon of low-Level repeated construction is very common [41].

Although the Chinese government, industry associations and scholars have made some achievements in the research and implementation of producer services, it is still in its infancy, mainly focusing on tracking and learning foreign models, and has not yet put forward a systematic theoretical framework with Chinese characteristics System and implementation methods, the leading advantages of regional industrial cluster model in promoting industrial development have not been fully reflected, most of the clusters are large but not strong, and the effect is not obvious [42]. On the whole, China's supply chain is still in its infancy. Affected by the backward management concept, imperfect credit mechanism, lack of industry standards, serious institutional constraints and policy barriers, and insufficient basic support, there are still many problems in process optimization, business collaboration, technology promotion, risk prevention and green development, which need to be solved [37].

The Yangtze River Delta has become the largest base for China to undertake the transfer of global manufacturing industry. The development of headquarters economy based producer services in Shanghai can provide good support for the development of manufacturing industry in Shanghai and its Yangtze River Delta [43]. Service supply chain has become an important way to transform economic growth and improve the competitiveness of service industry. So it is a new way to optimize the structure of service industry to transform the traditional service industry structure through service-Oriented supply chain. Service supply chain management is committed to reduce costs and improve efficiency. Service oriented enterprises guide the supply chain management mode, which creates a good opportunity to improve the overall competitiveness of the service industry. Service supply chain management can not only reduce the actual cost of providing services, remove the obstacles affecting the provision of high-Quality services, but also effectively improve the satisfaction of enterprise customers and general consumers [44]. Producer service supply chain can summarize the mode of Shaangu, that is, through service integrators, all kinds of suppliers can be provided It integrates with end customers, and provides a comprehensive service system based on capability management, demand management, supplier relationship management, customer relationship management, service delivery management, and capital and financing management [45]. In the producer service industry cluster base, through the establishment of long-Term cooperative relationship between service enterprises, strengthen forward or backward network economic ties and cultivate common service enterprise culture, improve the degree of interdependence of service enterprises in the cluster base, so as to increase mutual trust, reduce the uncertainty from outside the cluster base and reduce transaction costs [46]. For service providers, since they become part of the product service system from the production stage, it is beneficial for different types of service providers to serve customers in the subsequent stages, which not only promotes the development of producer services, but also provides a way to realize the value-Added of product follow-Up services and forms a long-Term profit value-Added point [47]. On the other hand, with more and more producer service enterprises gathering, the service products that can be provided are continuously enriched, the industrial chain is continuously extended, and the correlation between industries is continuously improved, which can optimize resource allocation, reduce service costs, and increase the social welfare level of service enterprises and service employees [39]. The adoption of supply chain management mode can really enable enterprises to win the market with the lowest cost, the fastest speed and the best quality, and what benefits is not an enterprise, but an enterprise group [1]. Therefore, in the operation process of service supply chain, service providers pay more attention to creating value with customers and stakeholders, rather than realizing value through one-Way product transfer like the original industrial supply chain. Therefore, in the service supply chain, any upstream enterprise should regard customers as a key link in the value network. Not an isolated entity. That is to say, the customer is regarded as a kind of resource of enterprise value realization, rather than the service object of enterprise value realization. In the model of service supply chain, demand is the main line instead of product [48]. In this situation, the effective strategic interaction between supply and demand becomes a kind of dynamic ability that must be possessed to obtain sustainable competitive advantage. This ability enables enterprises to increase their knowledge of customer status and preferences.

Servitization of manufacturing is the inevitable result of the development of productive forces. The penetration of manufacturing into service is the only way for manufacturing enterprises. The most important service object is enterprises, and service should go to enterprises [49]. Producer service supply chain is a complex system, but the reality exists in our economic society, service is intangible and difficult to measure, customers often participate in the process of service delivery, service suppliers and customers have to communicate face to face, so the structure of service supply chain is much simpler than that of product supply chain [50]. Therefore, it is necessary and inevitable to promote the development and improvement of producer service supply chain.

5 Conclusion

Compared with the traditional supply chain, the service flow and logistics of producer service supply chain coexist at the same time. The service flow is heterogeneous, dynamic and uncertain, which is difficult to describe and evaluate quantitatively [51]. China's economically developed regions, such as the eastern region, should give full play to the role of the market and promote the integrated development of manufacturing and producer services, so as to drive the industrial transformation in the western region [52]. Most of the research focuses on the traditional product manufacturing industry. On the definition and understanding of supply chain management, more attention is paid to the production and transformation process of physical products in the manufacturing industry, while the research on service supply chain management involving service transformation and delivery process is relatively less [53]. Chinese manufacturing enterprises should constantly make the supply chain mode and service mode innovated. The establishment of manufacturing supply chain based on collaborative services such as enterprise procurement, logistics and service is the inevitable way to improve the operation efficiency and management level of manufacturing supply chain and enhance the competitiveness of enterprises.

Acknowledgments. This research was supported by the SRT project of Jiaxing University in China (Grant No. CD8517203088).

References

1. Wang, Z.X.: The strategic choice of developing producer services. International Trade Forum **4**, 1–7 (2006). (in Chinese)
2. Liu, Z.B.: Developing modern producer service and adjusting and optimizing structure of manufacturing. J. Nanjing Univ. (Philos. Humanities Soc. Sci.) **5**, 36–44 (2006). (in Chinese)
3. Lu, Z., Liu, Y., Wang, Q.: Strategy selection of China's producer services industries development-based on the view of industrial interaction. China Ind. Economy **8**, 5–12 (2006). (in Chinese)
4. Zhang, H.P.: The development of producer services and industrial integration. Discussion Modern Econ. **05**, 77–80 (2008). (in Chinese)
5. Jiang, Q.E., Liu, J.F.: Analysis of logistics finance in improving interactive development between productive service industry and manufacturing industry. COMMERCIAL Res. **03**, 174–177 (2010). (in Chinese)
6. Zhang, J.J., Zhao, Q.L., Xing, D.N.: Research on product service supply chain: from product dominant logic to service dominant logic. China Bus. Market **33**(02), 93–100 (2019). (in Chinese)
7. Cao, Y.P.: An analysis of the effective ways to optimize the supply chain of manufacturing enterprises. Modern Bus. Trade Ind. **24**, 27–28 (2010). (in Chinese)
8. Chen, S.Z.: The strategic choice of developing producer services in China. Econ. Rev. **02**, 62–65 (2010). (in Chinese)
9. Vandermerwe, S., Rada, J.: Servitization of business: adding value by adding services. Eur. Manag. J. **6**(4), 314–324 (1988)
10. White, A., Stoughton, M., Feng, L.: Servicizing: the quiet transition to extended producer responsibility. Technical Report, Tellus Institute, Boston, MA (1999)
11. Szalavetz, A.: Tertiarization of Manufacturing Industry in the new Economy: Experiences in Hungarian companies. Hungarian Academy of Sciences Working Papers, vol. 134 (2003)
12. Lin, L., Wu, G.S.: Service-based product differentiation: one mechanism of service-enhancement. Res. Quant. Econ. Technol. Econ. **8**, 137–147 (2005). (in Chinese)
13. Ma, J.M.: Research on Upgrading Mechanism and Economic Effect of Chinese Outsourcing Enterprises. Beijing; China Social Sciences Press (2018). (in Chinese)
14. Liu, J.G.: Servitization and related categories: a comparison based on literature review. J. Hubei Univ. Econ. **7**(4), 69–73 (2006). (in Chinese)
15. Zhou, D.P.: Research on Manufacturing Servitization–Cause, Mechanism and Effect. Shanghai: Shanghai Academy of Social Sciences (2010). (in Chinese)
16. Hu, Q.Y., Hu, D.J.: Modern supply chains: definition and configuration. Supply Chain Manag. **1**(1), 35–45 (2020). (in Chinese)

17. He, Z., Chen, J.H., Yao, S.J.: Game analysis about incentive of information sharing in product servitization supply chain. China Mech. Eng. **3**, 346–351 (2014). (in Chinese)
18. Zhu, Y.F., Meng, Z.Q.: Analysis on the characteristics of service supply chain and countermeasures to improve its competitiveness. Northern Econ. **10**, 20–21 (2008). (in Chinese)
19. Zhang, W.S.: Adaptive supply chain characteristics and complexity analysis. China's Collective Econ. **10**, 66–67 (2015). (in Chinese)
20. Wang, J.Y.: Modern supply chain: evolution characteristics and development strategy. MacroEconomic Res. **07**, 97–106 (2019). (in Chinese)
21. Ma, X.A., Feng, Y., Tian, P.: Supply chain customer requirement deployment. Ind. Eng. Manag. **04**, 11–15 (2002). (in Chinese)
22. Zhao, Q.Q.: Analysis on the risks and countermeasures of supply chain management in manufacturing enterprises. Logist. Purchasing China **20**, 77–78 (2020). (in Chinese)
23. Yan, Y., Han, Q.: "Two Industry Integration" of Manufacturing Industry and Service Industry Helps High Quality Development. People's Daily - People's Daily Overseas Edition, 20 November 2019. (in Chinese)
24. Zhang, N.: Construction and analysis of supply chain management model of producer services. China Market **45**, 56–57 (2012). (in Chinese)
25. Yang, J.Y., Wen, C.: Supply chain collaborative planning based on hybrid method. Comput. Eng. Sci. **34**(4), 180–185 (2012). (in Chinese)
26. Supply Chain Collaborative Management under E-commerce (2018). https://www.xzbu.com/3/view-14871004.html. (in Chinese)
27. Jiang, Q.E., Liu, J.F.: Analysis of logistics finance in improving interactive development between productive service industry and manufacturing industry. COMMERCIAL Res. **000**(003), 174–177 (2010). (in Chinese)
28. Yan, Y., Han, Q.: The integration of manufacturing industry and service industry helps high quality development. People's Net - People's Daily Overseas Edition, 20 November 2019. (in Chinese)
29. Zuo, F.J., Zhang, Z.F., Fan, B.B.: Research on coordination of service-oriented manufacturing hybrid supply chain. Modern Manuf. Eng. **01**, 43–50 (2019). (in Chinese)
30. Xu, C.Y., Liu, X.L.: Research on the relationship between foreign trade supply chain management and producer services. Modern Econ. Inf. **000**(012), 167–168 (2018). (in Chinese)
31. Wu, D., Lu, Y.X.: Analysis of supply chain mode of producer services based on collaboration. Inf. Weekly **20**, 0345–0345 (2018). (in Chinese)
32. Liu, F.: Research on Producer Service Supplier Management of Manufacturing Enterprises Oriented to Service Strategy. Xi'an University of Technology, Xi'an (2014). (in Chinese)
33. Liu, J.: Research on Supply Chain logistics Management System Based on Collaborative Service. Chengdu, University of Electronic Science and Technology (2010). (in Chinese)
34. Anderson, E.G., Morrice, D.J., Lundeen, G.: Stochastic optimal control for staffing and backlog policies in a two-stage customized service supply chain. Prod. Oper. Manag. **15**(2), 262–278 (2006)
35. Liu, Z.Z.: Current situation and problems of China's supply chain development. MacroEconomic Manag. **05**, 63–70 (2019). (in Chinese)
36. Yuan, H.: Research on the relationship between service supply chain and service outsourcing. Econ. Res. Guide **04**, 14–15 (2008). (in Chinese)
37. Zhu, Y.F.: Research on Construction and Competitiveness Evaluation of Service-Oriented Supply Chain. Zhejiang University of Technology, Zhejiang (2008). (in Chinese)
38. Zhang, X.M., Guo, J.R., Zhang, L.L.: Research on the connotation and operation mode of modern manufacturing service. Res. Sci. Technol. Manag. **29**(9), 227–229 (2009). (in Chinese)

39. Dan, B., Luo, X., Liu, M.L.: Product service supply chain model based on manufacturing and service process integration. J. Chongqing Univ. (Soc. Sci. Edn.) **22**(1), 99–106 (2016). (in Chinese)

40. Li, J.F., Bi, D.D.: Review of foreign research on producer services. Foreign Econ. Manag. **26**(11), 16–19 (2004). (in Chinese)

41. Dan, B., Jia, L.H.: Development experience of foreign producer services and its enlightenment to China. Prod. Res. **16**, 87–88 (2008). (in Chinese)

42. Li, H., Gu, X.J., Qi, G.N.: Development mode of modern manufacturing service industry and china's development strategy. China Mech. Eng. **23**(7), 798–809 (2012). (in Chinese)

43. Gao, Y.S.: Research on the Development Mode of Shanghai Producer Services Cluster. Beijing, University of Foreign Economic Relations and Trade Press (2009). (in Chinese)

44. Jin, L.Y.: Service supply chain management, customer satisfaction and enterprise performance. China Manag. Sci. **14**(2), 100–106 (2006). (in Chinese)

45. Song, H., Yu, K.K.: Structural innovation mode of service supply chain–a case study. Bus. Econ. Manag. **7**, 3–10 (2008). (in Chinese)

46. Wang, Z.F.: Research on Service Supply Chain Cooperation and Benefit Distribution. Chongqing University (2011). (in Chinese)

47. Ma, S.H.: On the influence of core enterprises on the formation of supply chain strategic partnership. Ind. Eng. Manag. **5**(1), 24–27 (2000). (in Chinese)

48. Wang, J.Q.: Research on Service Supply Chain Model Construction and Service Process Composition. Beijing Jiaotong University, Beijing (2008). (in Chinese)

49. Qi, G.N.: Four pressures give birth to manufacturing services. Informatization of China's Manuf. Ind. Appl. Edn. **1**, 14–15 (2009). (in Chinese)

50. Song, D.X., Weilai, H., Yang, X.: Management mode of producer service supply chain based on service outsourcing. Ind. Eng. **12**(2), 37–41 (2009). (in Chinese)

51. Lin, W.J., Jiang, Z.B., Li, N.: Service-oriented manufacturing hybrid supply chain. In: The Fifth National Conference on Complex Networks, Qingdao, Shandong, pp. 10–15 (2009). (in Chinese)

52. Fan, Z.M.: Promoting the integration of advanced manufacturing industry and modern service industry. Environ. Econ. z1, 16–19 (2020). (in Chinese)

53. Wang, K.Z., Jiang, Z.B., Lin, W.J., Xie, W.M.: Study on the hybrid supply chain management of service-oriented manufacturing. Soft Sci. **27**(05), 93–100 (2013). (in Chinese)

An Evaluation on Entity Extraction and Semantic Similarity Metrics to Facilitate Medical Text Analysis Based on WordNet

Qinwei Zhang and Runtong Zhang[✉]

Beijing Jiaotong University, Beijing 100044, China
{19120627,rtzhang}@bjtu.edu.cn

Abstract. This paper aims to evaluate the previous entity extraction methods and semantic similarity metrics in order to improve the entity extraction and semantic analysis process for narrative text in electronic medical records. With the dataset collected from Medical Information Mart for Intensive Care III (MIMIC-III), our results showed that WordNet-based lemmatization and Part of Speech tagging have more of a significant influence in medical text analysis. For the sematic similarity metrics, the experimental results show that the measure proposed by Lin, which is based on IC, has the highest correlation coefficient with the artificial dataset of $r = 0.727$. The metric combining Resnik and Tversky's measures, which is based on features as well as IC, also has relatively stable performance, which indicates that IC and feature are the factors should be particularly considered for the future research.

Keywords: Electronic medical records · Entity extraction · Medical text · Semantic similarity · WordNet

1 Introduction

The rapid development of hospital information systems has made it popular for the application of Electronic Medical Records (EMRs) to store and manage medical information [1]. In fact, not limited to the storage of patient-centered records, the widely used EMRs have become a useful resource for data analysis and decision-making in healthcare field. For example, they could help predict the risk, identify early signs of cancer, as well as assist medical staff in decision making with text mining [2, 3]. At present, leveraging Natural Language Processing (NLP) and machine learning techniques to analyze English EMRs has greatly reduced the workload in medical research.

In the era of digitalization, information retrieval (IR), which retrieves and sorts documents from large collections according to users' search queries, has been widely applied in the biomedical field such as building patient queue using EMRs [4]. For EMRs, each medical entity contains not only word information but also rich character information; therefore, effective combination of words and characters could be very important for medical entity extraction [5]. Statistics indicate that about 80% of the textual information

© Springer Nature Switzerland AG 2021
G. Salvendy and J. Wei (Eds.): HCII 2021, LNCS 12796, pp. 138–151, 2021.
https://doi.org/10.1007/978-3-030-77025-9_13

in English EMRs has not been effectively utilized due to narrative texts [6]. Moreover, professional medical terminologies in the medical records make the analysis of EMR text information even more challenging. Systematized Nomenclature of Medicine - Clinical Terms (SNOMED CT) [7] provides a unified data model for structured EMR and it is also recognized as the multilingual terminology standard internationally. Researchers have now compiled the Medical Text Extraction, Reasoning and Mapping System for EMR data through text encoding and mapping [8], but in order to better match with SNOMED CT terms, it is limited to medical terminologies therefore other important terms might be excluded.

Most of the entity extraction and similarity methods are proposed based on Word-Net, which is an electronic lexical database; in WordNet, words are divided into five categories: noun, verb, adjective, adverbs and function words; among them, nouns are stored according to the subject hierarchy; verbs are stored according to implicit relationship; adjectives and adverbs are stored according to multidimensional hyperspace [9]. For entity extraction, NLP such as tokenization or Part-Of-Speech (POS) tagging, has been developed to process clinical or biomedical documents [4]. To enhance the accuracy of disease inference, Guo et al. [10] proposed the term frequency-inverse document frequency (TF-IDF) model for the representation of the relationship between symptoms and diseases. In the extraction process, the functional words are likely to be stored in the database as a part of the syntactic components of the language [11]. For entity extraction, synonym recognition based on WordNet is also required to facilitate semantic analysis in the text. At present, apart from the similarity calculation methods based on path distance, Information Content (IC) and feature, there are also hybrid measures combining multiple factors mention above. For the most classical distance-based measures, which are Wu and Palmer [12] and Leacock and Chodorow [13] measures, they effectively utilize the hierarchical structure of WordNet, but the accuracy could be limited since the path value is a discrete value. The IC-based methods, such as the most representative ones by Resnik [14] and by Lin [15], have a stable performance; but it's solely based on the concept itself without considering its depth in the taxonomy. The attribute-based method, such as the metrics proposed by Tversky [16] and improved by Pirró [17], usually focus on the common features of the word pairs. There are also improved hybrid methods [18–20] which combining two or more factors, for example, the one which considers both Resnik's IC-based method and Tversky's feature-based method. The vocabulary in English EMRs covers a large number of written nouns, verbs and adjectives; moreover, the text is usually longer which requires shortening the calculation time and more stable and accurate calculation in synonym recognition. Thus, we carry out an evaluation for the several existing methods which could provide some directions for the future research on semantic similarity calculation for medical texts.

Therefore, this study aims to compare the existing entity extraction methods and semantic similarity calculation measures to facilitate medical text analysis. Based on WordNet [9], this study explores the effectiveness of different entity extraction methods and semantic similarity measures to improve the accuracy and stability of semantic research. The structure of this paper is organized as follows: The methods for the evaluation process of entity extraction and the similarity measures are elaborated in Sect. 2; the results of the experiments are described in Sect. 3. The main findings, related works and the limitations in the study are discussed in Sect. 4, and we conclude our work in Sect. 5.

2   Methods

2.1   Dataset

The dataset used in this study is from (Medical Information Mart for Intensive Care III) MIMIC-III [21] database of PhysioNet [22], and includes 100 detailed records of 52 patients from year 2001 to 2012. The content of the dataset includes patient information, allergies, chief complaint, history of present illness, past medical history, family history, social history, physical exam, pertinent results, discharge records, etc. The research is aimed to conduct the semantic similarity analysis of the entities extracted from the narrative text of the EMRs. Figure 1 shows the text and the entities needing to be identified and extracted, such as medication conditions, treatment methods, etc.

History of Present Illness	
The original	Ms. [**Known lastname 31**] is a 62 y.o. woman with primary progressive MS [**Name13 (STitle) 32**] in [**2143**] with spasticity s/p intrathecal baclofen pump placment in '[**64**]. s/p tracheostomy in '[**65**] [**1-8**] to chronic respiratory weakness. recurrent UTIs. aspiration PNAs. who presents after being found to be febrile and unresponsive at her nursing home. According to notes from [**Hospital6 33**]. the pt was found at her nursing home yesterday ([**3-26**]) AM. shaking her head repeatedly. subsequently becoming obtunded (presumed seizure). She was taken by EMS to [**Hospital1 34**] ED. . In the ED at [**Name (NI) 34**]. pts vitals were: Tm 103.6. HR 110-150s RR 12-18 SaO2 98-99%NRB. Soon after. pt supposedly seized in the ED. was given Ativan. Ambu'd and subsequently placed on SIMV ventilation. Pt was empirically started on Vancomycin. Levoquin. Ceftriaxone. Bactrim and Acyclovir. On exam. it was noted that the skin overlying the baclofen pump (RUQ) appeared inflamed. Labs were notable for a WBC of 25 with 68%polys and a bandemia of 20%. U/A with 50-100 WBC. +leukocyte esterase. +nitrite. LP was performed and CSF analysis showed 7.250 WBCs with 92% polys. glucose 10. TP 1440. and gm stain with many polys.
Entities extracted	62 y.o. woman, primary progressive MS, spasticity s/p intrathecal baclofen pump placement, obtunded, Tm 103.6, HR 110-150s, RR 12-18, SaO2 98-99%NRB Ativan, SIMV ventilation, Vancomycin, Levoquin, Ceftriaxone, Bactrim, Acyclovir, inflamed WBC of 25, 68%polys, bandemia of 20%, LP, CSF analysis, 7.250 WBCs, 92% polys. glucose 10. TP 1440, gm, many polys.

Fig. 1. Sample of entity extraction of EMR

To evaluate the efficiency of the WordNet-based measures for semantic similarity calculation, this study used the Natural Language Toolkit (NLTK) [23] and WordNet which is an English Lexical Database and built in NLTK. Moreover, the entity extraction part and semantic similarity metric part are processed on Jupyter Notebook and PyCharm respectively. The EMR text files are sorted according to the content, and divided into five tables (Admission, Patients, Case History, Physical Exam, and Discharge Records). The attributes of each table are shown in Fig. 2. The data are converted to csv files and imported to the database as an experimental dataset.

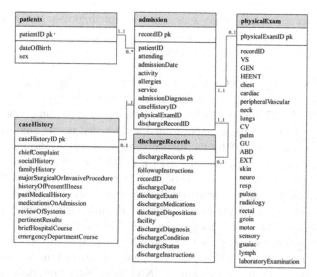

Fig. 2. Entity relationship diagram of the dataset

2.2 Medical Entity Extraction

Before applying the semantic similarity metrics for analysis, there are entities needing to be extracted. Medical entity extraction is a process to extract the entities in the EMR text by using NLP methods and obtaining terms such as disease characteristics, medication conditions, treatment methods, etc. For this part, data cleaning, punctuation removing, and other processes are applied before comparison. Next, stemming and WordNet-based lemmatization are applied for History of Present Illness and then, TF-IDF and WordNet-based PoS-tagging are tested for entity identification, as is shown in Fig. 3.

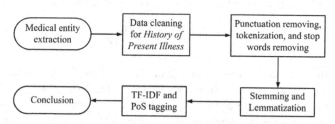

Fig. 3. Flow Chart of Medical Entity Extraction

First, an entity extraction study of structured text is conducted. Take the History of Present Illness from Table Case History in the dataset as an example. Data cleaning, punctuation removing, tokenization, and stop words removing are applied.

Second, both rule-based Stemming and dictionary-based (WordNet-based) Lemmatization are applied with the goal to transform a variant of a word and other derivative-related forms to its common base form. Stemming usually refers to a rough process that cuts off the end of a word and usually involves deleting the derived affix. Lemmatizing is based on WordNet and usually refers to the use of morphological analysis of vocabulary to find its original form, and is usually designed to remove only the end of the transformation and return the basic or lexicographic form of the word, which is also called lemma.

Third, medical entity extraction is performed. Due to the large amount of data, only the first 20 rows are presented. The methods are TF-IDF and PoS-tagging. In general, the weight of TF-IDF [24] consists of two parts: the first part calculates the normalized word frequency (Term Frequency, abbreviated as TF), that is, the number of times a word appears in a file divided by the total number of words in the file. The second part is the Inverse Document Frequency (IDF), which is calculated as the number of documents considered divided by the number of documents in which a particular word appears. PoS-tagging method is based on WordNet and can mark the PoS of a word, and the result of the tag is in a binary array format. Required labels will be picked from the binary array and stored in a binary sequence. When using PoS-tagging to extract the corresponding type of words, first we apply NLTK [25] to extract all the nouns in the text of the 10 samples as well as their types, and then extract the disease symptoms or medical treatment phrases in the form of "NNP, NN", which refers to "Proper noun (singular) + Noun (singular)". With the extracted terms such as time, disease level, or treating methods, text analysis will put them into a process to compare the characteristics of each record.

2.3   Evaluation for Semantic Similarity Estimation

The semantic similarity metrics evaluated are Resnik Similarity, Lin Similarity, Wu and Palmer Similarity and the hybrid Res-Tvr Similarity. The IC-based Resnik metric denotes how similar two word senses are, based on the IC of the Least Common Subsumer (most specific ancestor node) [14, 23]. The other IC-based metric, Lin Similarity [15, 23] returns a score of similarity based on the IC of the Least Common Subsumer and that of the two input Synsets and the relationship is given by the Eq. (1).

$$\text{sim}(c_1, c_2) = 2 \times \frac{\text{IC}(lcs)}{\text{IC}(s_1) + \text{IC}(s_2)} \tag{1}$$

Wu & Palmer Similarity is based on the depth of the two senses in the taxonomy and that of their Least Common Subsumer [12, 23]. The hybrid Res-Tvr Similarity integrates IC and attribute feature [14, 16]. The IC in the calculation of the total number of hyponyms also reflects the depth of the concept in the taxonomy: the greater the depth, the further away from the root node, the more specific the concept expressed, and the larger the IC value. It does not compare the two concepts horizontally, that is, by considering the shortest path, as Eq. (2) indicates.

$$\text{sim}_{res-tvr}(c_1, c_2) = (\alpha + \beta + \gamma) \times \text{IC}(msca(c_1, c_2)) - \beta \times \text{IC}(c_1) - \gamma \times \text{IC}(c_2) \tag{2}$$

Where $msca$ is the most specific common abstraction; α, β, γ are the different parameters in each category.

Another experiment is conducted to evaluate the effectiveness of each semantic similarity metrics. Here the artificial dataset collected by Pakhomov et al. [27], which consists of a list of term pairs that have been evaluated by various healthcare professionals to determine the degree of semantic similarity, is applied. The collected data is the average rating of semantic similarity between the pair of terms measured as the position of the finger touch on a bar displayed on a computer screen (VAS scale 0–1600: 0 - least similar, 1600 - most similar).

The correlation coefficient is applied to evaluate the correlation between the results of the metrics and the artificial dataset. Here the measures will be tested with the Pearson correlation coefficient [28] which reflects the degree of linear correlation between the two datasets. The correlation coefficient of the sample is indicated by r whose value is between -1 and $+1$, as Eq. (3) indicates:

$$r = \frac{\sum_{i=1}^{n} (X_i - \overline{X})(Y_i - \overline{Y})}{\sqrt{\sum_{i=1}^{n} (X_i - \overline{X})^2} \sqrt{\sum_{i=1}^{n} (Y_i - \overline{Y})^2}} \tag{3}$$

Where n is the sample size, X_i, Y_i and $\overline{X}$, $\overline{Y}$ are the observed values and means of the two variables respectively. The larger the absolute value, the stronger the correlation between the variables.

3   Results

Experiment results are obtained from the MIMIC-III dataset mentioned in the last section by calling the functions from WordNet and NLTK. For the semantic similarity section, the calculated and the artificial similarities of the tested term-pairs are evaluated by their Pearson correlation coefficients.

The results of Stemming and Lemmatizing are shown in Table 1 with the first column showing the original text and the second column showing the cleaned text. As for entity extraction, part of the TF-IDF output in the sparse matrix format is as shown in Table 2. The value of 0 in the matrix stands for the terms that do not appear in the document respectively or which have an IDF equal to 0, that is, the terms appear in all the documents. Finally, the results of extracting the disease symptoms or medical treatment phrases in the form of "NNP, NN" with PoS-tagging are in Table 3.

For the evaluation of semantic similarity measures, here we test the 4 metrics below, which are the methods proposed by Resnik, Lin, Wu and Palmer and the hybrid one. Table 4 lists the similarity value calculated by each measure as well as the artificial dataset. The Pearson correlation coefficient values for each measure are listed in Table 5 and Fig. 4 displays the scatter diagrams of the results for each methods. The measure proposed by Lin has the highest Pearson correlation value with the artificial dataset of 0.727, which is greater than the IC-based methods by Resnik (0.722), the feature-based hybrid method (0.726) and the distance-based method by Wu and Palmer (0.712).

Table 1. Properties results of data cleaning with stemming and lemmatizing.

EMR No	Body_Text	Body_Text_Clean	Stemmed (Rule-based)	Lemmatized (WordNet-based)
1	54 year old female with recent diagnosis of ulcerative colitis on 6-mercaptopurine. prednisone 40–60 mg daily. who presents with a new onset of he…	[54, year, old, female, recent, diagnosis, ulcerative, colitis, 6mercaptopurine, prednisone, 4060, mg, daily, presents, new, onset, headache, neck…	[54, year, old, femal, recent, diagnosi, ulcer, coliti, 6mercaptopurin, prednison, 4060, mg, daili, present, new, onset, headach, neck, stiff, pat…	[54, year, old, female, recent, diagnosis, ulcerative, colitis, 6mercaptopurine, prednisone, 4060, mg, daily, present, new, onset, headache, neck,…
2	61F w/ sign PMH for UC s/p colectomy. Stage II breast cancer presented on day 13 of second cycle of chemotherapy with fever to 100.6 at home w/ se.	[61f, w, sign, pmh, uc, sp, colectomy, stage, ii, breast, cancer, presented, day, 13, second, cycle, chemotherapy, fever, 1006, home, w, severe, r…	[61f, w, sign, pmh, uc, sp, colectomi, stage, ii, breast, cancer, present, day, 13, second, cycl, chemotherapi, fever, 1006, home, w, sever, rigor…	[61f, w, sign, pmh, uc, sp, colectomy, stage, ii, breast, cancer, presented, day, 13, second, cycle, chemotherapy, fever, 1006, home, w, severe, r.
3	Ms. [**Known lastname 31**] is a 62 y.o. woman with primary progressive MS [**Name13 (STitle) 32**] in [**2143**] with spasticity s/p intrathecal…	[ms, known, lastname, 31, 62, yo, woman, primary, progressive, ms, name13, stitle, 32, 2143, spasticity, sp, intrathecal, baclofen, pump, placment…	[ms, known, lastnam, 31, 62, yo, woman, primari, progress, ms, name13, stitl, 32, 2143, spastic, sp, intrathec, baclofen, pump, placment, 64, sp,…	[m, known, lastname, 31, 62, yo, woman, primary, progressive, m, name13, stitle, 32, 2143, spasticity, sp, intrathecal, baclofen, pump, placment,…
4	Pt was in USOH. awaiting R THR. collapsed while celebrating a funeral mass. was down for 1 min prior to EMS arrival. found to be pulseless. atrial…	[pt, usoh, awaiting, r, thr, collapsed, celebrating, funeral, mass, 1, min, prior, ems, arrival, found, pulseless, atrial, activity, noted, stips,…	[pt, usoh, await, r, thr, collaps, celebr, funer, mass, 1, min, prior, em, arriv, found, pulseless, atrial, activ, note, stip, occasion, wide, qr,…	[pt, usoh, awaiting, r, thr, collapsed, celebrating, funeral, mass, 1, min, prior, em, arrival, found, pulseless, atrial, activity, noted, stips,…

(continued)

Table 1. (*continued*)

EMR No	Body_Text	Body_Text_Clean	Stemmed (Rule-based)	Lemmatized (WordNet-based)
5	This 51 year-old female was admitted to an outside hospital with chest pain and ruled in for myocardial infarction. She was transferred here for…	[51, yearold, female, admitted, outside, hospital, chest, pain, ruled, myocardial, infarction, transferred, cardiac, catheterization]	[51, yearold, femal, admit, outsid, hospit, chest, pain, rule, myocardi, infarct, transfer, cardiac, catheter]	[51, yearold, female, admitted, outside, hospital, chest, pain, ruled, myocardial, infarction, transferred, cardiac, catheterization]

Table 2. Part of TF-IDF results of the sample.

EMR No	...	Resp	Respir	Respiratori	Respond	Respons	Result
1	...	0.000000	0.000000	0.000000	0.066577	0.000000	0.000000
2	...	0.000000	0.000000	0.045682	0.000000	0.000000	0.000000
3	...	0.000000	0.000000	0.000000	0.000000	0.000000	0.000000
4	...	0.000000	0.000000	0.000000	0.000000	0.000000	0.000000
5	...	0.000000	0.000000	0.000000	0.000000	0.000000	0.000000
6	...	0.000000	0.000000	0.000000	0.000000	0.000000	0.000000
7	...	0.094191	0.000000	0.000000	0.000000	0.000000	0.000000
8	...	0.000000	0.000000	0.000000	0.000000	0.000000	0.000000
9	...	0.000000	0.000000	0.000000	0.000000	0.000000	0.000000
10	...	0.000000	0.000000	0.000000	0.000000	0.000000	0.000000
11	...	0.000000	0.000000	0.000000	0.000000	0.000000	0.000000
12	...	0.000000	0.08805	0.000000	0.000000	0.000000	0.000000
13	...	0.000000	0.000000	0.075011	0.000000	0.000000	0.000000
14	...	0.000000	0.000000	0.041684	0.000000	0.000000	0.062012
15	...	0.000000	0.000000	0.000000	0.000000	0.000000	0.000000
16	...	0.000000	0.000000	0.000000	0.000000	0.000000	0.000000
17	...	0.000000	0.000000	0.000000	0.000000	0.000000	0.000000
18	...	0.000000	0.000000	0.097740	0.000000	0.000000	0.000000
19	...	0.000000	0.000000	0.000000	0.000000	0.000000	0.000000
20	...	0.000000	0.000000	0.051426	0.000000	0.076504	0.000000

Table 3. Specific terms extracted from the sample by applying WordNet-based PoS-tagging.

EMR No	The terms
1	['UC treatment']
2	['II breast', 'PMN count', 'CVL placement']
3	['SIMV ventilation', 'CSF analysis', 'Micro lab', 'CSF sample', 'B strep', 'SC line', 'MCA infarct']
4	['O2 saturation', 'Chest tube', 'White count', 'ABG later', 'EKG change', 'ST segment', 'MI protocol', 'Heart rate', 'Lasix today', 'White count', 'Postoperative day', 'Blood pressure', 'White count', 'Urine output', 'White count', 'ID perspective', 'Postoperative day', 'Postoperative day', 'Postoperative day', 'Postoperative day']
5	['Parkinson disease', '[**Last']
6	['Prednisone taper', 'Sputum sample', 'Chest x-ray', 'CT angiogram']
7	['M w/', 'ETOH abuse', 'IV valium', 'Banana bag', 'CIWA monitoring']
8	['EtOH abuse', 'UGI bleed', 'EtOH withdrawal', 'EtOH intox', 'RLL opacitiy']
9	['Per review', 'IV lasix']
10	['C2 fracture', 'L breast']

Table 4. Comparison between the Different Measures.

c_1–c_2	Pakhomov	Resnik	Lin	Res-Tvr	Wup
uremia – aspirin	256	0.596	0.043	2.376	0.200
erythema – tremor	316	0.596	0.047	3.543	0.174
chills – snoring	322.5	0.802	0.066	4.228	0.286
seizures - insulin	332.75	0.596	0.050	4.351	0.235
overeating - seizures	396.5	2.036	0.169	5.599	0.400
uremia - pyorrhea	551	9.489	0.656	10.747	0.900
hypothyroidism - infertility	598	6.016	0.466	8.742	0.750
photopsia - headache	632	5.081	0.509	10.601	0.556
sleeplessness - agitation	882.5	5.577	0.489	9.737	0.750
catatonia - lethargy	890	4.235	0.334	7.181	0.625
pallor - iron	901.75	0.596	0.050	4.243	0.250
thirsty - hunger	935.75	2.298	0.189	5.767	0.375
avitaminosis - starvation	984.75	6.016	0.470	8.856	0.545

(continued)

Table 4. (*continued*)

c_1–c_2	Pakhomov	Resnik	Lin	Res-Tvr	Wup
brochitis - pneumonia	1019.75	9.403	0.683	11.319	0.917
hunger - starvation	1134.5	11.208	0.945	14.937	0.941
candidiasis - mycosis	1151.25	13.367	0.985	15.476	0.941
starvation - anorexia	1176.75	6.016	0.446	8.198	0.667
brucellosis - zoonosis	1195.75	7.787	0.583	10.089	0.800
dizziness - vertigo	1287	13.367	1.000	15.668	1

Table 5. Pearson Correlation Coefficients.

Method	Pearson correlation ($r =$)
Resnik	0.722
Lin	0.727
Res-Tvr	0.726
Wu and Palmer	0.712

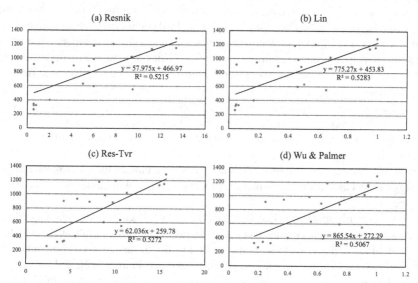

Fig. 4. Scatter diagrams of the results. Vertical axis represents the similarity value of artificial dataset while horizontal axis represents the corresponding metrics

4 Discussions

As it can be observed in Table 1, Lemmatizing results are much clearer than that of Stemming. The WordNet based Lemmatizing can retrieve the synonym of the object word. For example, the suffix letters of the word "severe" is mechanically deleted and is extracted as "sever", while Lemmatizing can recognize "severe" correctly. For the output of TF-IDF in Table 2, for example, for the 18th medical record (0.097740), the 13th (0.075011), the 20th (0.051426), the TF-IDF value of the word "respiratory", as shown in Table 2, is higher than the rest of the sample, hence the corresponding patients of these samples are presumably to have respiratory diseases. Similarly, PoS-tagging can extract text entities in the medical record with other forms. According to the structuring analysis of the medical record text, the same method can be applied to extract terms such as "(WBC (indicator)} {25 (numerical)}", "{primary (degree)} {progressive MS (measure)}", {heavily (status)} {calcified (symptom)} {left main (part)}. Therefore, it can be concluded that the TF-IDF method is mainly used for keyword extraction in texts and the amount of computation is larger, while for the entity extraction of EMR text, it is more practical to use PoS-tagging. For the experiment of the proposed similarity metric, it is found that the IC-based measure has higher accuracy and more stable correlation.

In the field of NLP, text extraction research on English EMRs covers tokenization, named entity recognition, semantic analysis, disambiguation, etc. Regarding entity extraction, Tang et al. [29] designed a TLink extraction module that includes multiple modes. The main research directions found in the study is that time expression extraction needs to identify and standardize the text strings which represent time and duration, which could be identified with tagging. Lester et al. [30] conducted a retrospective observational study using TF-IDF and structural topic model (STM) to categorize the online reviews from Yelp in order to examine the characteristics of patient experience in community pharmacies through pattern exploration techniques of the unstructured free-text data. The results revealed 9 topics that influenced patient experiences at community pharmacies including waiting time, service attitude, and physical store characteristics. Guo et al. [10] presented the term TF-IDF model for the representation of the relationship between symptoms and diseases to enhance the accuracy of disease inference, and the results illustrate that the model with TF-IDF representation performs better than the one with only Word2Vec symptom. Moreover, other methods such as tokenization or PoS-tagging, has also been developed for processing clinical documents or biomedical literature [4].

For the semantic analysis of EMR, at present, the WordNet-based semantic similarity measures are mainly based on distance, IC or features, and there are also hybrid metrics which combines multiple factors among them. For the distance-based approaches, the most classical ones are the metrics proposed by Wu and Palmer [12], and by Leacock and Chodorow [13], which effectively utilize the hierarchical structure of WordNet; however, their accuracy is limited for the path length is a discrete value. The three new improved models proposed by Ashaee et al. [31] work by giving weights to WordNet hierarchical edge, which eliminate the previous problem but meanwhile, ignores other paths and the number of hyponyms as well as the other factors that affect the similarities. The IC-based methods are mainly developed from Resnik measure [14], which is based on the common IC of the two concepts, but it only calculates the IC of their least common subsume. Later, Zhou et al. [18] improved the IC-based measure proposed by Sanchez by introducing the relative depth, which solved the problem of IC of the two concepts with the same hypernym and different hyponyms structures and numbers being equal, but its parameters need to be determined through experimental debugging under actual conditions. The feature-based method is determined by calculating the number of common features that the two concepts share, such as Tversky model [16]. The larger the number is, the greater the semantic similarity will be. Based on the three categories above, there are also hybrid methods. Li, et al. [19] proposed that the metrics could combine information sources nonlinearly, including structural semantic information and IC, and the experiment suggests better results than the general measures; but it also has disadvantage that the parameters require to be settled each time in different scenarios. Therefore, here we evaluate those metrics to find out the factors should be particular considered when processing medical text.

However, there are still limitations in this paper. First, more comprehensive comparison considering the shortest path, common IC, respective attribute features and the depth in the taxonomy could be realized, which might have a more targeted result for EMR texts. Second, research on the entity extraction in English medical record text such as PoS-tagging can also be used for EMRs in Chinese; especially the existing Jieba tokenization tool makes it more efficient. But since the WordNet database is only for English and French vocabulary, the research in this paper has great limitations for Chinese EMRs in both entity extraction and semantic similarity calculation. Therefore, future research can focus on the vocabulary classification tree in Chinese to extract entities and calculate semantic similarity in Chinese.

5 Conclusions

This paper evaluates the current entity extraction methods in analyzing EMR text based on the MIMIC-III database. For NLP of medical texts, the results indicated that lemmatization has a more significant influence than stemming with lexical normalization; moreover, it is found that PoS-tagging is more practical with the structured entity extraction. Then, for the sematic similarity metrics, the results show that the measure proposed by Lin, which is based on IC, has the highest correlation coefficient with the artificial dataset. The metric combining Resnik and Tversky's measures, which is based on features as well as IC, also has relatively stable performance. Improved similarity metrics could focus on IC and feature factors, moreover, reducing the complexity of tuning and traversing of the multi-way tree should also be considered.

Acknowledgments. The authors would like to thank those who had done previous studies in the field of entity extraction and semantic analysis. This work was inspired in part by their contributions. The authors would also like to thank Doctor Donghua Chen for whose instructions for this research are highly appreciated.

References

1. Sun, W., Cai, Z., Li, Y., Liu, F., Fang, S., Wang, G.: Data processing and text mining technologies on electronic medical records: a review. J. Healthcare Eng. **5**, 1–9 (2018)
2. Hirst, C., Hill, J., Khosla, S., et al.: The application of natural language processing (NLP) technology to enrich electronic medical records (EMRs) for outcomes research in oncology. Value Health **17**(03), A6 (2014)
3. Segura-Bedmar, I., Colón-Ruiz, C., Tejedor-Alonso, M.Á., Moro-Moro, M.: Predicting of anaphylaxis in big data EMR by exploring machine learning approaches. J. Biomed. Inf. **87**, 50–59 (2018)
4. Wang, Y., Wu, S., Li, D., Mehrabi, S., Liu, H.: A part-of-speech term weighting scheme for biomedical information retrieval. J. Biomed. Inf. **63**, 379–389 (2016)
5. Gao, Y., Wang, Y., Wang, P., Gu, L.: Medical named entity extraction from chinese resident admit notes using character and word attention-enhanced neural network. Int. J. Environ. Res. Public Health **17**(5), 1–17 (2020)
6. Linguamatics: The World'S Leading NLP Text Mining Platform for Health Sciences. https://www.linguamatics.com/healthcare. Accessed 19 May 2020
7. IHTSDO, SNOMED CT Starter Guide. https://www.snomed.org. Accessed 12 Sep 2020
8. Zhou, L., Plasek, J.M., Mahoney, L.M., et al.: Using medical text extraction, reasoning and mapping system (MTERMS) to process medication information in outpatient clinical notes. In: 2011 AMIA Annual Symposium Proceedings, Minnesota, USA, pp. 1639–1648 (2011)
9. Fellbaum, C.: WordNet: An Electronic Lexical Database, 1st edn. MIT Press, Cambridge (1998)
10. Guo, D., Duan, G., Yu, Y., Li, Y., Wu, F., Li, M.: A disease inference method based on symptom extraction and bidirectional long short-term memory networks. Methods **173**, 75–82 (2020)
11. Miller, G., Charles, W.: Contextual correlates of semantic similarity. Lang. Cogn. Process. **6**(01), 1–28 (2007)
12. Wu, Z. and Palmer, M.: Verbs semantics and lexical selection. In: Proceedings of the 32nd Annual Meeting on Association for Computational Linguistics, Kyoto, Japan, pp. 133–138 (1994)
13. Leacock, C., Miller, G., Chodorow, M.: Using corpus statistics and WordNet relations for sense identification. Comput. Linguist. **24**(01), 147–165 (1998)
14. Resnik, P.: Using information content to evaluate semantic similarity in a taxonomy. In: International Joint Conference on Artificial Intelligence, Montreal, Quebec, Canada (1995)
15. Lin, D.: An information-theoretic definition of similarity. In: Proceedings of the Fifteenth International Conference on Machine Learning (ICML), Madison, Wisconsin, USA, pp. 296–304 (1998)
16. Tversky, A.: Features of similarity. Psychol. Rev. **84**(02), 327–352 (1977)
17. Pirró, G.: A semantic similarity metric combining features and intrinsic information content. Data Knowl. Eng. **68**(11), 1289–1308 (2009)
18. Zhou, Z., Wang, Y., Gu, J.: A new model of information content for semantic similarity in WordNet. In: International Conference on Future Generation Communication and Networking Symposia, IEEE Computer Society, Hainan, China, pp. 85–89 (2009)
19. Li, Y., Bandar, Z.A., McLean, D.: An approach for measuring semantic similarity between words using multiple information sources. IEEE Trans. Knowl. Data Eng. **15**(04), 871–882 (2003)
20. Dong, C., Yan, J., Fang, L., Shi, B.: Measure semantic distance in WordNet based on directed graph search. In: International Conference on E-Learning, E-Business, Enterprise Information Systems, and E-Government, Las Vegas, Nevada, USA, pp. 57–60 (2009).

21. Johnson, AEW., Pollard, TJ., Shen, L., et al.: MIMIC-III, a freely accessible critical care database. Scientific Data **3**, 1–9 (2016)
22. Goldberger, A.L., Amaral, L.A., Glass, L., et al.: Physiobank, physiotoolkit, and physionet components of a new research resource for complex physiologic signals. Circulation **101**(23), 215-e220 (2000)
23. WordNet Interface. https://www.nltk.org/howto/wordnet.html. Accessed 10 Dec 2020
24. Erra, U., Senatore, S., Minnella, F., Caggianese, G.: Approximate TF–IDF based on topic extraction from massive message stream using the GPU. Inf. Sci. **292**, 143–161 (2015)
25. Jha, N. K.: An approach towards text to emoticon conversion and vice-versa using NLTK and WordNet. In: 2nd International Conference on Data Science and Business Analytics (ICDSBA), ChangSha, Hunan, China, pp. 161–166 (2018)
26. Ingvaldsen, J., Veres, C.: Using the WordNet ontology for interpreting medical records. In: CAiSE'04 Workshops in connection with the 16th Conference on Advanced Information Systems Engineering, Knowledge and Model Driven Information Systems Engineering for Networked Organizations, Proceedings, Riga, Latvia, vol. 3, pp. 355–358 (2014)
27. McInnes, B.T., Pedersen, T., Pakhomov, S.V.: UMN medical residents similarity/relatedenss set (UMNSRS-Similarity and UMNSRS-Relatedenss): semantic similarity and relatedness between clinical terms: an experimental study. In: AMIA Annual Symposium proceedings, Washington, DC, USA, pp. 572–6 (2010)
28. Mari, D.D., Kotz, S., Drouet, D.: Correlation and Dependence: An Introspection, 1st edn. Imperial College Press, London (2001)
29. Tang, B., Wu, Y., Jiang, M., et al.: A hybrid system for temporal information extraction from clinical text. J. Am. Med. Inf. Assoc. **20**(05), 828–835 (2013)
30. Lester, C.A., Wang, M., Vydiswaran, V.G.V.: Describing the patient experience from Yelp reviews of community pharmacies. J. Am. Pharmacists Assoc. **59**(3), 349–355 (2019)
31. Ahsaee, M.G., Naghibzadeh, M., Naieni, S.E.Y.: Weighted semantic similarity assessment using WordNet. In: International Conference on Computer and Information Science (ICCIS), Chongqing, China, pp. 66–71 (2012)

Investigating Issues Related to VAT Collection and Management in Chinese Mobile Commerce

Peiyan Zhou[✉] and Xiaochun Lin

Jilin University, Jilin, People's Republic of China

Abstract. The virtual nature of the transaction object, the borderless scope of the transaction and the asymmetry of the transaction information under the mobile commerce transaction model have certain impact on the original VAT collection and administration system in China. By comparing the VAT systems of the OECD, the EU and other countries, and taking into account the actual economic development of China, this paper explores the problems of VAT collection and administration in China. The issue of VAT collection efficiency in China is explored in terms of clarifying the determination criteria, building a new collection model, taking advantage of big data and improving tax compliance.

Keywords: Electronic business · Electronic · Mobile and ubiquitous commerce

1 Introduction

With the development of the digital economy and modern communication technology, mobile commerce has been favored by many Chinese companies as a new business model and this mode of transaction is gradually penetrating into people's lives. Personal consumption has become more convenient and the tax revenue generated by individual consumers has increased. The emergence of the platform economy has also disrupted the traditional way of doing business and transaction patterns of brick-and-mortar enterprises, further expanding the scope of transactions and further enhancing the convenience and mobility of business operations. The resulting domestic and cross-border transactions in China have generated a huge source of tax, creating new VAT tax collection challenges for the government.

In recent years, mobile commerce has become an increasingly important part of China's economic development, with a variety of transaction models generating huge economic flows. The boom in online trading platforms has contributed to the future development of mobile commerce. However, due to the virtual nature of online transactions, the borderless scope of transactions and the information asymmetry between the two parties, there are a series of problems in the taxation and administration of VAT on mobile commerce transactions in China and internationally. The rapid development of mobile commerce and the immaturity of the relevant tax regulations have exacerbated the severity of the problems, such as the lack of clear criteria for determining the taxable entity, the lack of definition of the tax location and tax jurisdiction, the vague criteria

G. Salvendy and J. Wei (Eds.): HCII 2021, LNCS 12796, pp. 152–166, 2021.
https://doi.org/10.1007/978-3-030-77025-9_14

for determining the nature of the business, the significant information asymmetry and the imperfection of the overall VAT collection and administration system, which have made the government face great challenges in VAT tax collection and administration. Based on the possibility of future development of mobile commerce and the importance of tax collection and administration to the country's development, it is of great significance to understand accurately the legal policies related to mobile commerce, clarify the VAT collection and administration aspects of mobile commerce, and improve the tax registration and inspection system for China's tax security.

2 Current Situation of VAT Collection and Administration Development of Mobile Commerce in China

2.1 Definition and Current Situation of Mobile Commerce

Mobile commerce is a kind of economic transaction activity based on wireless communication, in which the supply and demand sides of the transaction are not completely fixed, including tangible and intangible product transactions. In a broad sense, all e-commerce transactions conducted with mobile devices can be called mobile commerce, and the development of the digital economy has extended the scope of mobile commerce. It shifts the old fixed-location model of transaction processes confined to traditional network connections to a mobile interconnection model with frequent movement of financial information across regions. The digital economy is defined as a series of economic activities in which the use of digitised knowledge and information is a key factor of production, modern information networks are an important carrier, and the effective use of information and communication technologies is an important driving force for efficiency improvement and economic structure optimization in the G20 Digital Economy Development and Cooperation Initiative. The digital economy uses the network as a carrier, big data as a basic element, and uses the characteristics of high digitization and informatization to promote enterprise development. In 2019 China's digital economy has reached 35.8 trillion yuan, accounting for 36.2% of GDP, and the total scale and growth rate of China's digital economy is among the world's top. At present, Chinese scholars' research on mobile commerce mainly focuses on "mobile" and "commerce", which not only breaks through the traditional industrial economy of offline transactions in the form of fixed locations, but also adds "mobile" to e-commerce. With the economic trading platform as an intermediary, mobile consumers can directly use their terminal devices to conduct consumption activities at any time and place, breaking through the traditional restrictions of fixed sales locations; further breaking down the boundaries of digital goods and services, enterprises through the platform for mixed sales of goods and services; through the third-party financial institutions to pay for goods, reducing the traditional trading model of wholesalers and other links to join. At the same time, digital enterprises have changed the old mode of fixed registration place, through the network for registration, the use of network domain name changes and the construction of virtual website and other forms, resulting in the enterprise registration place and service provision place is not the same.

The development of mobile commerce has now gone through three generations. With the development of network communication technology, mobile commerce has greatly changed people's lifestyle in terms of shopping and trading with its convenience and efficiency, forming a huge tax source. However, the region-free and borderless nature of mobile commerce transactions and the digitisation of transaction objects have further amplified the tax loopholes built on the traditional VAT collection model and challenged the traditional VAT system and collection mechanism in each country. The digitalisation of the subject matter of user transactions has also become increasingly evident, breaking down the physical and spatial barriers of the traditional transaction model; the complexity of the transaction chain makes it easy for the collection authorities to determine the scope and attribution of taxation based on the "destination principle" or the "place of consumption principle". In this regard, the characteristics of mobile commerce, such as the multiplicity of participants, the hidden nature of trade information and the digital nature of products, do not create new taxation problems, but rather highlight the existing problems under the influence of the environment.

2.2 Policies on VAT Collection and Administration in China

For physical enterprises, offline physical transactions can avoid the difficulties of collection and administration caused by the unclear subject matter of the transaction and the ambiguity of where the transaction takes place, while the registration system for major physical enterprises also reduces the cost of tax collection and administration. China's current taxation system has introduced detailed and clear regulations on the collection and administration of traditional VAT but does not provide for VAT-related issues in mobile commerce.

As far as the scope of taxation is concerned, the Provisional Regulations of the People's Republic of China on VAT stipulate that units and individuals who sell goods or processing, repair and fitting services, sell services, intangible assets, real estate and import goods in the People's Republic of China are VAT payers and shall pay VAT. Mobile commerce transactions include transactions of tangible products and intangible products. Transactions of tangible products have clear transaction targets and can be managed with reference to the existing VAT collection and management policy, while intangible sales transactions mainly in the digital industry spawned by the digital economy are faced with the problem of ambiguous transaction targets. The digital economy relies on intangible assets, and part of China's tax policy on intangible assets can define the VAT collection and administration issues in the course of digital economy transactions, but the definition of digital goods and services is not yet available.

As far as the place of taxation is concerned, the Provisional Regulations of the People's Republic of China on VAT provide for the following points. Firstly, if the seller of the transaction is a fixed business, it shall file a tax return with the competent tax authority where its establishment is located; if the head office and branch offices are not located in the same county (city), they shall pay tax separately to the competent tax authority where their respective establishments are located. Secondly, if the seller of the transaction is a fixed business operator selling goods or providing taxable services in a foreign county (city), it should file a tax return to the tax authority in charge of the place where the establishment is located after obtaining a tax administration certificate for the outbound business activities; if no tax return is filed, it should file a tax return to the tax authority in charge of the place where the sale or the service takes place; thirdly, if the seller is not a fixed business operator, it should file a tax return to the place where the sale or the service takes place. At present, for the sale of tangible products under the mobile commerce model, the purchaser needs to obtain the goods by post or pick-up, so the "mobile" nature of the transaction under this form of transaction is mainly reflected in the sales side. For intangible sales, China has not yet regulated the tax declaration of the possible virtual transaction locations, which has led some enterprises to avoid tax through virtual sites and platform transactions on the internet, resulting in a loss of tax sources.

2.3 Current Status of VAT Research on Mobile Commerce

At present, the issue of VAT collection and administration under the mobile commerce transaction model has not been widely discussed, but there are more studies on the collection and administration issues under the digital economy, e-commerce and other related economic forms. Li (2017) proposes the challenges faced by the VAT system under the digital economy in the light of the EU tax reform experience; Zhou and Li (2018) propose the new requirements for the development of the collection and administration methods under the platform economy. Dale (2018) proposes that the latest EU tax reform is conducive to ensuring the implementation of VAT collection principles. Chen et al. (2019) conduct a study and comparative analysis of the VAT system involving relevant transactions in China, taking into account the characteristics of cross-border digital transactions, and improve the cross-border VAT system by clarifying the nature of the transaction, the criteria of the taxing place and "reverse taxation"; Zhang (2020) proposes that from the perspective of the EU VAT reform, the VAT system can be improved in the In the context of digital economy, VAT tax compliance can be enhanced in several aspects, such as system, cost and information platform construction. While maintaining the characteristics of online transactions, mobile commerce adds the feature of "mobile", which further blurs the location and nature of transactions, and requires further exploration of VAT collection and management in this mode.

2.4 VAT Collection and Control Issues for Mobile Commerce

The development of mobile commerce has expanded the means of transaction, and through online trading platforms, transactions can flow across regions without the need for intermediate transit links or customs borders. The complexity of transactions makes it more difficult to collect data. Virtual platforms and third-party trading platforms obscure tax information and make it difficult to obtain the complete chain of business transactions, and the direct interface between platforms and tax collection agencies may lead to "adverse selection". The development of digitalisation of the subject matter of transactions has blurred the definition of digital services and digital goods. The mismatch between the development of the tax system and the pace of development of mobile commerce, as well as the differentiation and specialisation of policies, has led some companies to avoid tax by choosing to shift their place of incorporation. The difference between "taxation at the place of consumption" and "taxation at the place of production" is even more pronounced in the process of mobile commerce transactions, with double taxation and double non-taxation restricting the normal operation of the tax system. In addition to the problem of double taxation, the reasonable allocation of tax revenue in the process of cross-regional transactions is also a bottleneck in the orderly development of VAT collection and administration in mobile commerce in China.

3 International Practice in the Collection and Administration of VAT on Mobile Commerce

As a result of the rapid development of mobile commerce and the integration of the global digital economy, cross-border transactions have become increasingly active and new transaction models have become new engines of economic development. The development of mobile commerce on an international scale has led to the need for tax regulators to regulate the digital transactions generated therein on a universal and equitable basis. However, the traditional VAT collection model is difficult to adapt to current transactions of complex goods and services, and the development of cross-border mobile commerce transactions poses a huge challenge to VAT collection in various countries. At present, China has not introduced VAT provisions for mobile commerce transactions, and no international proposals have been made to address the issue. The relevant provisions are still unclear. Issues such as the location of transactions, digital trading platforms and digital products and services in mobile commerce transactions have been explored in a number of studies. Internationally, the OECD, the EU and other countries have proposed corresponding policies for digital transaction services, including the worldwide BEPS action plan, the introduction of a digital services tax and changes to the scope of cross-border VAT transactions, all of which have provided references to the development of mobile commerce tax collection and administration.

3.1 OECD Tax Policies

The development of the digital economy and mobile commerce has had a huge impact on the widespread collection of both direct and indirect taxes internationally. In addition to the challenge of effective tax collection and administration, there is also an urgent need to resolve the issue of how to reasonably allocate tax on transactions. In view of the increasing popularity of cross-border digital trade, the OECD, as an advocate of global tax reform, has issued plans and reports with an overarching effect, which should be used as a basis for adjusting specific measures in each country.

The OECD's first action plan on Base Erosion and Profit Shifting, "Address the tax challenges of the digital economy", points out that the digital economy itself does not show specific BEPS issues, but only the impact of its many features on BEPS. 2018 OECD "Interim Report" points out that the digital economy Three main factors affect the value creation process, namely cross jurisdictional scale without mass, heavy reliance on intangible assets, and the principle of the importance of data and user participation. In 2019, the OECD has proposed in a "public consultation paper" a response to the challenges of the digital economy, namely user engagement, marketing intangible assets and economic salience.

In recent years, the OECD has issued a number of documents on the administration of VAT in international trade, including adherence to the principles of cross-border trade neutrality in VAT and the principle of place of consumption tax jurisdiction to determine the administration of cross-border goods and services. 2019 saw the OECD report "The Role of Digital Platforms in the Collection of VAT/GST on Online Sales", which included the following issues in the context of digital transaction models Platforms fulfil tax obligations to tax collection authorities instead of the parties to the transaction; enhance cross-border tax information sharing and cooperation between tax collection authorities and trading platforms, etc.

3.2 EU Tax Policy

The European Commission has introduced a number of reforms to VAT collection in response to the fact that cross-regional trade and personal consumption in mobile commerce has increased the cost of VAT collection on an international scale. Weaken the barriers to cross-regional and cross-border VAT collection by establishing a range of VAT collection systems. Improving the feasibility of tax collection through an integrated collection process and the effectiveness of VAT tax collection through enhanced cooperation. Although the EU VAT reform focuses on cross-border business, its operational mechanism involves the intermediary role of the trading platform and the asymmetry of transaction information and other tax collection difficulties that may be encountered in mobile commerce transactions.

In 2019, EU Council Directive 2019/1995 introduced a "one-stop" taxation system. This system applies to both sales between EU countries and transactions between non-EU countries. Under this system, the transaction process is split into two stages, with the digital platform acting as a transit medium for the declaration and payment of VAT. In addition, the e-tax platform allows for a one-off declaration without the need for multiple registrations, and non-EU member states can choose to register for tax and make VAT payments between any EU member states where their transactions take place; EU member states must register for tax at the place of registration. At the same time, counterparty tax credits can also be collected through the platform. This system is complemented by the introduction of a special scheme for small businesses, a law on online transactions and administrative cooperation to facilitate a more rapid development of the system.

The VAT "reverse taxation" mechanism. In order to combat irregularities in digital transactions, the EU has proposed the adoption of a "reverse taxation" system in member states, whereby the seller's tax liability is replaced by the buyer's tax declaration at the seller's tax authority. This approach would reduce tax evasion and avoidance by taking advantage of VAT benefits. However, due to the flexibility of individual consumers and the changeable nature of their transactions, it is less efficient for them to take the initiative to register with the tax authorities, and the cost of collection and administration is generally too high for the tax authorities.

The EU's "one-stop" tax collection system and "reverse taxation" mechanism are part of the improved VAT registration system for digital products, which to a certain extent improves VAT collection and administration information and reduces collection costs; the new tax administration system also allows for close involvement of various authorities in VAT administration and improves collection and administration efficiency.

3.3 Other Countries

In the face of the rapid development of the digital economy, in addition to major organizations such as the OECD and the EU, which are promoting policies on VAT collection and administration, other countries internationally are also making adjustments to their own systems. In the case of digital transactions in mobile commerce, countries such as the UK, France and Australia have taken measures to assist tax collection by expanding platform-assisted services.

Some countries, such as the UK, France and Italy, have proposed that VAT on digital goods and services be collected and paid by trading platforms on their behalf, in order to improve the efficiency of VAT collection and administration and reduce government supervision costs. Australia requires the payment of Goods and Services Tax (GST) for the sale of goods or provision of services within the country, or the import of goods or services, which is similar in nature to China's VAT. The Australian government has also established data sharing and information exchange registers with some digital platform companies to improve tax compliance of digital trading platforms. In response to the facilitation of the flow of low-value goods across borders, New Zealand has changed its previous policy of exempting low-value imported goods from VAT and introduced VAT on digital products and cross-border transactions, while suppliers with annual sales of more than NZ$60,000 are required to file tax returns. The New Zealand GST Act also sets out in detail the criteria for determining consumer status for e-commerce services and specifies the basis for the levy.

The Korean government has implemented an e-tax policy, established an information sharing platform and has largely made invoices paperless by 2017. In addition, the Korean government requires e-commerce businesses to pay an additional 10% VAT in addition to the basic tax. Singapore has also specified that from 2020 onwards, GST will need to be levied on offshore service providers for inbound purchases of offshore digital services; it also specifies a minimum standard amount for taxation of digital services.

In the current environment, major international organizations and countries are adjusting their existing tax systems based on the principles of tax neutrality, tax completeness and tax convenience. The EU's "one-stop" taxation system and reverse taxation measures are conducive to clarifying the effective tax information of both parties to a transaction under mobile commerce and alleviating the tax injustice under the subject matter of digital transactions. Tax completeness means ensuring complete tax collection and avoiding tax evasion by enterprises using the existing tax system; tax convenience means reducing the complicated registration procedures in the tax collection process and simplifying the VAT taxation mechanism. In response to these two principles, digital trading platforms, as intermediaries in the process of mobile commerce transactions, not only establish a mechanism for information sharing between enterprises and tax collection and administration authorities, but also facilitate the regulation of tax information disclosure at source. However, the improvement of the international tax system under mobile commerce and the digital economy still faces problems such as high operating costs and low tax compliance by individual consumers, and further improvements are still needed internationally in terms of simplifying tax collection and administration procedures, promoting digital tax development and strengthening administrative cooperation.

4 Challenges to VAT Collection and Administration in Mobile Commerce

In recent years, under the influence of the digital economy, China's mobile commerce transaction model has developed rapidly, and domestic consumption and cross-border transactions have formed a certain scale, which has already made a certain impact in the international arena. However, the current development of China's digital economy and mobile commerce is not matched by the efficiency of VAT collection and administration, and there are a series of challenges.

4.1 The Criteria for Determining the Subject and Object of Taxation Need to be Improved

Therefore, it is necessary to improve the combination of online and offline supervision mode and make the monitoring of internet tax sources a key breakthrough point, focusing on monitoring the taxable subject of mobile sales. Under the mobile commerce transaction mode, more and more transactions are completed through the online digital space, so there may be problems in both the taxation subject and the taxation object. In terms of the tax subject, in order to protect the privacy and security of both parties to the transaction, some important information has to be encrypted during the transaction, which raises questions about the authenticity of the real transaction and the electronic transaction documents of the mobile commerce transaction. At present, a large number of small-scale enterprises and individual trading entities conduct transactions through the mobile commerce model. Due to the lack of timely follow-up by the tax administration, phenomena such as setting up virtual websites, not registering on the platform and multiple dependencies are frequent, which increase the difficulty of VAT tax administration and identification. With regard to taxable objects, as a large number of intangible products are traded digitally under the mobile commerce transaction model, distinguishing digital services from digital goods has become a primary issue to improve the efficiency of VAT collection and administration, for which China has not yet provided a clear definition. With regard to the main characteristics of digital products, the taxable object of digitalisation can be divided into various categories according to whether it can be stored or not, and whether it can be transferred twice, etc. Therefore, the taxation criteria for the subject of the transaction need to be further improved.

4.2 Difficulty in Determining the Place of Taxation and the Scope of Tax Territorial Jurisdiction

The place of registration of a taxable enterprise and the place where taxable acts are performed are relatively independent concepts in China. The place of registration of an enterprise is the registered address of the business license of the enterprise, which generally refers to the location of the main office of the company; however, the current VAT regulations in China have not yet provided a clear definition of the place where commodity transactions and services are performed. According to the Provisional Regulations on Value Added Tax (VAT), the VAT administration in China determines the place of taxation according to criteria such as the place of establishment or residence and the place where the taxable act takes place. As it is more difficult for economic actors at both ends of the transaction chain to transact directly across regions under the real economy model, the place of tax collection and administration is based on the location of the establishment or the place where the taxable act takes place. With the development of the digital economy, under the mobile commerce model, both parties to a transaction are more likely to transact through platforms built on the internet and no longer through offline physical transactions. While tangible product transactions are subject to changes in location on the sales side, intangible product transactions are subject to changes in location on both the sales side and the transaction side, making the taxation and administration of intangible product sales more complex. The mismatch between the traditional place of taxation and the place where the economic benefits are generated has prompted some enterprises to choose to change the nature of their business and shift their place of incorporation to a low-tax country to avoid paying taxes, resulting in tax losses in the place where the business takes place and highlighting the contradictions in tax collection and administration.

At present, a large number of transactions in China adopt the tax location standard of paying taxes at the location of the registered office. The main features of the mobile commerce transaction model make the traditional taxation standard no longer applicable, and transactions through the network platform have to a certain extent weakened the necessity of the permanent establishment, and both sides of the transaction conduct transactions by building a platform, using the modification of the server site to change the location of the actual transaction occurring under the general platform monitoring, weakening the digitalization of goods and services also exacerbates this weakening effect. The characteristics of the mobile commerce model make the Territoriality Principle clearly flawed, as there is no Permanent Establishment in the traditional sense of a platform-mediated transaction, making it difficult to determine the true location where the goods or services are transacted.

4.3 Unclear Criteria for Determining the Nature of Business for VAT Administration

There are two main issues regarding the business nature of the subject of taxation: the determination of the homogeneity of transactions between mobile commerce transactions and physical transactions; and the determination of the differences in transactions of digital goods and services under the mobile commerce model.

The rapid development of Internet technology and the emergence of various special forms of platform transactions have made it difficult for tax policies to follow up in a timely manner. For example, the sale of electronic journals is not subject to the same level of taxation as the sale of paper journals, which, driven by profit and the digital age, can have a sales diversion and profit-seeking effect that can greatly limit the development of the book industry. However, it is also important to consider whether the additional services that exist when the new digital industry is essentially the same as the traditional industry will make a difference in facilitating the economic benefits.

Under the mobile commerce transaction model, there are not yet clear criteria for whether the subject of a digital transaction is classified as a digital service or a digital good, which provides a way for companies to avoid tax. For example, if digital music is purchased through a trading platform, from the perspective of digital goods, the consumer is provided with a reusable and storable commodity, and the tax collection authority should levy VAT at the same rate as the purchase of goods; from the perspective of digital services, the consumer is provided with digital music in the form of additional services, including high sound quality and priority experience, and in this respect is provided with a service. Due to the lack of relevant tax policies, companies are somewhat selective in the case of digital transactions through platforms, and the criteria for determining digital products and services need to be further improved.

4.4 Difficulty in Obtaining Information for VAT Administration and Significant Information Asymmetry

Under the mobile commerce model, there are more diverse transaction modes, more complex transaction chain links and more complicated transaction networks. The single transaction model from producer to intermediary to consumer, which existed in the past in the real economy model, has been gradually replaced by multiple transaction parties and agents, mainly including sales through one or more intermediaries, direct sales to consumers through an agent platform, or a crossover between the two. The diversification and flexibility of transaction forms have made tax collection and management information on online and platform transactions more concealed and difficult to capture, making it difficult for tax authorities to accurately grasp information on tax sources, and the information asymmetry between tax collectors and taxpayers has become more pronounced. In addition, tax authorities are also subject to information cost dilemmas in the process of VAT collection. The authenticity of the identity of transaction subjects and the virtual nature of the location where transactions take place and other new features under the mobile commerce transaction model make it more difficult to effectively supervise VAT. The large amount of information asymmetry also leads to the risk of adverse selection and exacerbates the difficulty of collection.

4.5 The VAT Tax Collection and Administration System is not yet Perfect

China's VAT tax collection and administration system for mobile commerce is not yet perfect and has not yet developed tax services to match it. For example, under China's traditional VAT collection and administration model, the tax collection agency collects VAT from legal entities such as enterprises and does not collect VAT from individual consumers. However, with the development of mobile commerce transaction models and more convenient personal consumption, the share of such consumers has grown rapidly and tax leakage has intensified. The new transaction model also poses a challenge to the traditional VAT collection period, as online transactions through platforms create a time lag in the temporary storage of payments for goods, a situation that tends to lead to inconsistencies in the timing of revenue recognition for businesses, thus making tax collection and administration more difficult.

In summary, the main reasons for the VAT taxation and administration problems of mobile commerce in China are that the rapid development of mobile commerce is not well matched with the taxation and administration system; and the scope of the traditional

VAT definition needs to be adjusted. Firstly, China's taxation system is lagging behind in terms of the complexity of the mobile commerce transaction chain, the identification of tax subjects for cross-regional transactions and the determination of the nature of taxable objects; secondly, with the accelerated development of the digitization of the economy and the convenience of the internet, the economic flows arising from direct personal consumption are accelerated and VAT collection and administration lacks attention to the field of personal consumption; thirdly, the regulatory system is not yet perfect and mobile commerce transaction models, where virtual servers and proxy transactions are commonplace, have created serious information asymmetry problems and challenged the collection efficiency of tax collection authorities.

5 Measures to Improve the Effectiveness of VAT Collection and Administration Under the Mobile Commerce Model

5.1 Clarifying the Basic Determination Criteria for VAT Levy

With the development of mobile commerce and the digital economy, the VAT subject matter, subject matter of transaction, place of taxation and nature of services in intangible product transactions need to be followed up in a timely manner to match the current popular trend of digital products and services.

Adding the definition of VAT payer, the Provisional Regulations of the People's Republic of China on VAT stipulate that "units and individuals who sell goods or processing, repair and fitting services, sell services, intangible assets, real estate and import goods within the territory of the People's Republic of China are VAT payers and shall pay VAT in accordance with these Regulations". With the development of mobile commerce, there is a need for detailed regulations on VATable acts of taxpayers, including digital goods and digital services; and for cross-border platform transactions, there is also a need to adjust China's tax policy to align with international standards.

The place and time of taxation for digital goods and services should be adjusted according to the nature of the taxable entity. For cross-border platform consumption within China, the tax sharing rules can be improved by adopting the tax sharing between the place of consumption and the place of production; for cross-border mobile commerce transactions in China, the principle of the place of consumption should continue to be effectively promoted, and the provisions of the principle of the place of consumption for digital goods and services should be further clarified to avoid distorting the consumption choice in order to safeguard one's tax rights and interests. Due to the virtual and cross-regional nature of mobile commerce, the determination of the tax location needs to rely more on the development of big data, advance consideration of possible situations such as setting up virtual servers and frequent domain name changes, and to strengthen the cooperative management of cross-regional and international network issues within China in response to this issue.

5.2 Exploring New Standards for VAT Collection and Administration and Building a New Model of Tax Collection and Administration

China has now taken measures to innovate a new model of tax collection and administration by using commissioned agents and establishing a tax credit evaluation system, combining online collection with offline collection. However, online collection is mainly based on the recording of transaction information, and the main tax collection still needs to be carried out offline by tax collection authorities. As a result, the current collection system still fails to meet the economic development in the mobile commerce model.

The VAT taxation model is shared between the place of production and the place of consumption. At the level of the tax collection and administration model, the traditional VAT definition can be adjusted in response to the current characteristics of China's economic development by adopting a shared VAT taxation model between the place of production and the place of consumption and improving the cross-regional tax sharing rules. The tax subject of the same transaction will be changed from a single producer to a joint consumer and producer. Under the traditional transaction model, merchants in the place of consumption purchase goods from enterprises in the place of production and then sell them to individual consumers in the place of consumption, and the double consumption chain results in both the place of production and the place of consumption of goods being taxed at the same time; under the mobile commerce transaction model, the transaction chain no longer requires intermediaries or manufacturers in the place of consumption to make secondary sales, and individual consumers can directly purchase goods in the place of production through the platform, directly affecting the VAT collection in the place of consumption. The adoption of the shared taxation model between the place of production and the place of consumption can, on the one hand, clarify the issue of where the VAT tax belongs under mobile commerce transactions and, on the other hand, promote the balance of tax revenue between the two places.

Third party collection model. The traditional producer's periodic tax return can be extended to a third party such as a platform party to pay tax on behalf of the producer under the development of mobile commerce transactions. The prevalence of digital products and services makes the traditional measurement of physical transaction targets no longer fully applicable, and the transaction information held by the trading platform as a medium of exchange is more accurate. With the development of big data, real-time information statistics and tax payments are also possible.

5.3 Enhancing Data Sharing with the Help of Big Data and Blockchain Technology

Individual consumers are the bulk of consumption in the digital economy and it is a future trend for third-party platforms to collect this tax on their behalf. With the development of big data and the obvious role of individual consumption in driving China's economic growth, it has become both possible and necessary for tax collection authorities to accurately collect VAT from individual consumers. The development of big data and blockchain technology, with its features of traceability, traceability and non-tamperability of transactions, can ensure the accuracy of transaction data and provide guidelines for the improvement of the VAT collection and administration system. Tax collection and administration authorities can monitor tax-related acts of mobile commerce, broaden the scope of information search, break down information barriers and complete cross-regional tax collection and administration.

In cross-border mobile commerce transactions, the platform side can grasp more comprehensive information on the transaction chain, and Chinese tax collection authorities can directly interface with the platform to realize simultaneous real-time updates of platform transaction information and the tax collection system, thus fully grasping the behavior of transaction subjects and increasing tax transparency. The development of big data and blockchain technology is therefore a prerequisite for the implementation of this policy.

5.4 Combining Satellite Navigation Systems to Identify the Location of the Transaction

The networked and virtualized location of transactions has led to a significant divergence between where goods are produced and where they are consumed. Whereas the location of the sales side of tangible products can change in real time without the restrictions of the transaction, the sale of intangible products faces difficulties in determining the location of both the sales side and the consumer side. Suppliers and consumers can complete transactions quickly through the trading platform, regardless of the location of the transaction. How to accurately determine the location of each transaction and clarify the tax jurisdiction is one of the key elements in coordinating VAT collection and management. Positioning systems such as the BeiDou Satellite Navigation System (BDS) have navigation and positioning and data communication functions. The future development trend of mobile commerce can be combined with satellite positioning systems to authorize platforms to determine the actual location of each stage of a transaction and accurately capture the location of the supplier's revenue under the networked nature of the transaction through methods such as precise single-point positioning. Digital goods and services can be combined with consumer habits through a location-based system, taking into account information such as where the mobile network is used and the location of the payment address, to clarify where goods and services are supplied, where goods transactions and services take place, and where supply-side revenue is generated; ethical issues such as user privacy and security in the transaction chain also need to be considered.

5.5 Improving Tax Collection and Administration Contracts for Mobile Commerce to Enhance Tax Compliance of Tax Payers

Effective fulfillment of tax contracts under the mobile commerce transaction model is a prerequisite for smooth tax collection and administration by tax authorities. Based on the current development trend of mobile commerce in China, it should be promoted from several aspects, including tax information management, comprehensive coverage of tax links, and limiting the interest relationship between trading platforms and enterprises. Firstly, tax collection and administration authorities should connect with major trading platforms, establish a transaction information transmission network, and adjust the current form of tax collection and administration of periodical declarations to introduce a form of timely declarations and real-time registration. Secondly, the tax collection authorities should carry out comprehensive supervision of the transaction chain, including the inclusion of individual consumers in the scope of tax supervision to achieve reverse supervision. A database of consumer information should be gradually established to dovetail with the tax collection and management platform, so as to fully realize the tax collection and management authorities' comprehensive control of the information. Thirdly, improve the regulation of trading platforms, limit the transfer of interests between trading platforms and enterprises, realize the authenticity and traceability of transaction information, and give full play to the role of third-party platforms. Use the law to stipulate their obligation to pay on behalf of others and gradually strengthen the taxation department's co-ordinated management of VAT collection.

6 Conclusion

Against the backdrop of the rapid development of the digital economy and mobile commerce, the large number of tax sources generated by individual consumers through platform transactions has a significant impact on different regions within China as well as on the countries where cross-border transactions take place. In the face of the digital impact, most countries around the world have adjusted their previous VAT regimes to accommodate the development of the modern economy. For the adjustment or otherwise of China's VAT system, after taking into account the OECD, EU and other countries' reform measures, it is also necessary to adapt to the current development of China. This paper provides some thoughts and suggestions on how to promote the reform of China's VAT tax system, including clarifying the scope of digital goods and services, improving tax compliance of taxpayers and ensuring tax neutrality and effectiveness in the collection and administration process, starting from the mismatch between the policies and models in China's current VAT collection and administration process and the development of modern economy. Only if everything from the VAT policy system to the collection and administration measures are adapted to China's development model can we better promote the development of China's tax governance and safeguard the country's tax rights and interests.

References

Zhang, Y., Zong, R.: International comparison and reference of tax collection and management of cross-border direct e-commerce (in Chinese). Int. Taxation China **11**, 75–79 (2020). https://doi.org/10.19376/j.cnki.cn10-1142/f.2020.11.013

Chen, L., Wang, T., Luo, Z.: International experience reference of VAT on cross-border digital transactions (in Chinese). Int. Taxation China **02**, 31–35 (2019). https://doi.org/10.19376/j.cnki.cn10-1142/f.2019.02.006

Zhou, K., Li, X.: Innovation of tax governance system in the platform economy (in Chinese). Taxation Res. **12**, 73–77 (2018). https://doi.org/10.19376/j.cnki.cn11-1011/f.2018.12.013

OECD: Statement by the OECD/G20 Inclusive Framework on BEPS on the Two-Pillar Approach to Address the Tax Challenges Arising from the Digitalisation of the Economy, January 2020. OECD/G20 Inclusive Framework on BEPS, OECD, Paris (2020). www.oecd.org/tax/beps/statement-by-the-oecd-g20-inclusive-framework-on-beps-january-2020.pdf

UNCTAD: Digital Economy Report 2019. https://unctad.org/webflyer/digital-economy-report-2019#tab-2

Wang, Y.: An analytical framework of the impacts of a digital economy on tax institution and tax division——also on the core proposition of tax reform (in Chinese). Taxation Res. **11**, 67–75 (2020). https://doi.org/10.19376/j.cnki.cn11-1011/f.2020.11.011

Wang, W., Zhu, C.: Meeting the challenges of the digital economy: from a VAT on production to a tax on consumption and production (in Chinese). Taxation Res. **12**, 61–67 (2020). https://doi.org/10.19376/j.cnki.cn11-1011/f.2020.12.009

Competitive Intelligence in Technological Innovation: An Exploratory Study

Peng Zhou[✉]

Jiaxing University, Jiaxing, Zhejiang, China

Abstract. [Purpose/Significance] This paper makes an exploratory study on the competitive intelligence activities in technological innovation, trying to find out the use mode, function and influencing factors of competitive intelligence in technological innovation. [Method/Process] Through literature review, eight research questions are drawn out, and the corresponding interview outline and questionnaire are designed. Field interview and questionnaire survey are carried out on 43 high-tech enterprises in Jiaxing City of China, and descriptive statistical analysis is carried out on the returned questionnaires. [Result/Conclusion] (1) The most frequently used intelligence in technological innovation is direct competitor intelligence, followed by indirect competitor intelligence, and finally potential competitor intelligence. (2) There is no total difference in the use of competitive intelligence between incremental innovation and fundamental innovation, but there are structural differences. (3) The most frequently used competitive intelligence is in the commercialization stage, followed by the creative stage, and finally the development stage. (4) The main way for enterprises to collect competitive intelligence is through direct way, less through indirect way. (5) In technological innovation, enterprises are more concerned about the current state of competitors than the future state (6). The support of competitive intelligence for technological innovation ideas is mainly reflected in effectiveness, followed by feasibility, and finally novelty. (7) The role of competitive intelligence in technological innovation is mainly in improving products, followed by improving the marketing. (8) The main factors affecting competitive intelligence activities in technological innovation are individual factors, followed by organizational factors.

Keywords: Technological innovation · Competitive intelligence · Competitor · Information

1 Introduction

Technological innovation is essentially a kind of speculative activity, and its failure rate is quite high. Most technological innovation activities end in failure. The reason is that technological innovation faces great uncertainty, such as technological uncertainty, market uncertainty, policy uncertainty and resource uncertainty. Therefore, how to reduce the uncertainty in technological innovation has become a problem that enterprises must consider and deal with. With the continuous practice of enterprises and the continuous exploration of academic circles, it is gradually realized that intelligence can reduce the

© Springer Nature Switzerland AG 2021
G. Salvendy and J. Wei (Eds.): HCII 2021, LNCS 12796, pp. 167–181, 2021.
https://doi.org/10.1007/978-3-030-77025-9_15

uncertainty in technological innovation. Intelligence activity is the basis and premise of technological innovation. From a certain point of view, technological innovation is an information processing process.

Many achievements have been made in the research on the relationship between intelligence and technological innovation, such as the status and role of intelligence in technological innovation, the acquisition, diffusion and use mechanism of intelligence in technological innovation. These studies have undoubtedly greatly deepened people's understanding of this phenomenon, but there is a big limitation in the existing research, that is, there is no separate research on different types of intelligence. Although there are different terms in the research, such as strategic intelligence, competitive intelligence, technical intelligence and market intelligence, there are often overlapping, inclusion and mixing in the use of these terms. The difference of language understanding also leads to the confusion of variable measurement scheme. Therefore, how to further analyze their relationship with technological innovation and reveal their special mechanism in technological innovation on the basis of clearly defining each intelligence type is a problem that must be solved in deepening the research in this field.

Taking competitive intelligence as the research object and 43 high-tech enterprises in Jiaxing as samples, this paper analyzes the use, function and influencing factors of competitive intelligence in technological innovation by using exploratory research method, trying to provide some research ideas and inspiration for the academic circles, and also provide comparative research results for the follow-up research of other types of intelligence.

2   Literature Review

Competitive intelligence can be divided into broad sense and narrow sense. The broad sense of competitive intelligence refers to the research on competitive environment, competitors and competitive strategies, while the narrow sense of competitive intelligence refers to the research on competitors. Because the broad sense of competitive intelligence also includes market intelligence and technical intelligence, in order to distinguish, the competitive intelligence studied in this paper refers to the narrow sense of competitive intelligence, which is a kind of intelligence activities juxtaposed with market intelligence and technical intelligence.

Research on competitors is one of the driving factors of technological innovation, and bringing competitors research into the technological innovation process will improve the success rate of technological innovation [1–3]. Some empirical studies have proved that there is a positive correlation between competitive intelligence and technological innovation performance [4–6], and some empirical studies have shown that competitive intelligence is related to a higher level of new product quality [7–10].

Competitors are divided into direct competitors, indirect competitors and potential competitors [11, 12]. Direct competitors refer to the enterprises that have the same customer group and provide the same products; indirect competitors refer to the enterprises that have the same customer group and provide different but similar products; potential competitors refer to the enterprises that have the same customer group but adopt new products to meet the needs of customers, and potential competitors are subversive to the enterprises. Some studies found that compared with the analysis of direct competitors and indirect competitors, the identification and analysis of potential competitors is conducive to enterprises to adopt more open technological innovation activities [13–15].

Although competitive intelligence may be involved in all stages of technological innovation, some studies point out that the use of competitive intelligence is different in different stages of technological innovation. Hart and Baker [16] found that competitive intelligence is mainly used in the "development" stage, while Zahay et al. [17] found that competitive intelligence is used more in the "fuzzy front end" and "test, acceptance and release preparation" stages.

The dimensions of technological innovation conception evaluation include novelty, effectiveness and feasibility [18]. Novelty refers to the degree of difference between technological innovation conception and existing products, effectiveness refers to the ability of technological innovation conception to solve customer needs, and feasibility refers to the difficulty of transforming technological innovation conception into a real product. Some studies have preliminarily proved that there are differences in novelty, effectiveness and feasibility of technological innovation ideas obtained from the analysis of different types of competitors [19–21].

It is generally believed that the content of competitor analysis includes four aspects: competitors' future goals, self assumption, current strategy and resources and capabilities. Future goals and self assumption are the driving factors of competitors' future activities, current strategy is the ongoing activities of competitors, and resources and capabilities are what competitors can do. Compared with the current strategy and the analysis of resources and capabilities, the analysis of competitors' future goals and self assumptions in technological innovation is more important [1].

The shortcomings of the existing researches are: (1) most of the researches focus on the relationship between general intelligence and technological innovation, and competitive intelligence is usually regarded as a subset of intelligence, so there are few researches on the relationship between competitive intelligence and technological innovation; (2) competitive intelligence has not been subdivided into direct competitor intelligence, indirect competitor intelligence and potential competitor intelligence (3) the use of competitive intelligence in incremental innovation has not been compared with that in fundamental innovation; (4) although the use of competitive intelligence in technological innovation has been investigated by stages, the object of case study is relatively single, some of which are enterprises in the same industry; (5) the access and content preference of competitive intelligence in technological innovation have not been clarified; (6) the specific role of competitive intelligence in technological innovation has not been investigated in depth; (7) the influencing factors of competitive intelligence in technological innovation have not been paid attention to.

3 Research Design

3.1 Research Questions

According to the results of literature review, eight problems need to be further explored are put forward.

- Question1: to what extent different types of competitive intelligence are used in technological innovation?
- Question2: to what extent different types of competitive intelligence are used in incremental and fundamental innovation?
- Question3: is there any difference in the use of competitive intelligence in the three stages of technological innovation?
- Question4: what are the ways to obtain competitive intelligence in technological innovation?
- Question5: what are the competitors' preferences for the content of analysis (future goals, self assumptions, current strategies, resources and capabilities) in technological innovation?
- Question6: do technological innovation ideas based on different types of competitive intelligence have different characteristics?
- Question7: what are the specific functions of competitive intelligence in technological innovation?
- Question8: what factors affect the competitive intelligence activities in technological innovation?

3.2 Method

High tech enterprises are the main force of technological innovation. The intensity of technological innovation activities of these enterprises is relatively large, and the corresponding competitive intelligence activities are relatively sufficient. Therefore, it is more conducive to realize the intention of this study to select high-tech enterprises as the research object. The author visited six high-tech industrial parks in Jiaxing, including Jiaxing Science and Innovation Center, Jiaxing Intelligent Industrial Innovation Park, Xiuzhou Photovoltaic Town, Jiaxing Photovoltaic High-tech Industrial Park, China Electronic Technology (Jiaxing) Intelligent Industrial Park, and European and American Biotechnology Industrial Park. During the visit, firstly, through a brief exchange with enterprises, we screened out the enterprises suitable for participating in the survey, mainly excluding enterprises with weak innovation activities, enterprises in monopoly industries. Secondly, we consulted enterprises' intention to participate in the survey. Finally, we successfully visited 43 enterprises. The specific situation of sample enterprises and Respondents is shown in Table 1.

Table 1. Sample characteristics

Industry	Respondents
Software (20%)	General manager, deputy general manager and general manager assistant (36.7%)
New energy and new materials (16.7%)	R&D Manager, R&D Engineer (23.3%)
Electronics (13.3%)	Sales Manager, sales supervisor (16.6%)
Internet (13.3%) machinery (10%)	Technical manager, technical director (10%) It manager (6%)
Biology and medicine (10%)	Else (7.4%)
Else (16.7%)	

The survey is divided into two parts: the first part is the interview part, which is mainly to understand the general situation of enterprise technological innovation and discuss the terms related to technological innovation and competitive intelligence with the interviewees; the second part is the questionnaire part, which allows the interviewees to fill in the questionnaire on the spot. The questionnaire consists of 56 questions. The first four questions are used to collect the information of enterprises and respondents, and the remaining 52 questions are designed around research questions. The items in the scale all use the Likert seven point scale, and the numbers "1" to "7" indicate seven degrees from "very disagree (or very inconsistent)" to "very agree (or very consistent)".

The design and distribution of the questionnaire are based on Tencent questionnaire platform, and the respondents are required to fill in the electronic questionnaire. After the survey, the data were exported from Tencent questionnaire platform. The main way of data analysis is comparison, and the average value of each variable is used to represent its concentration degree, which is displayed by column chart or bar chart.

4 Data Analysis and Results

The research results correspond to the research questions, including the following eight aspects:

1. The use of different types of competitive intelligence in technological innovation

In technological innovation, there are obvious differences in the use of direct competitor intelligence, indirect competitor intelligence and potential competitor intelligence. From large to small, they are direct competitor intelligence (5.57), indirect competitor intelligence (4.13) and potential competitor intelligence (3.56), as shown in Fig. 1. Direct and indirect competitors are more likely to attract attention, while potential competitors are relatively easy to ignore. In the interview, individual enterprises indicated that they had not consciously thought about potential competitors, some enterprises reflected that they did not have effective means to identify potential competitors, and some enterprises thought that the analysis of potential competitors had little significance for technological innovation.

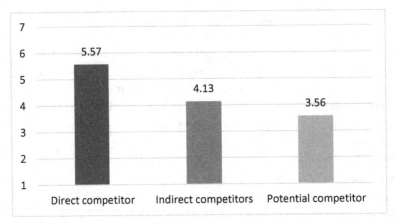

Fig. 1. The use of competitive intelligence in technological innovation

2. The use of competitive intelligence in incremental innovation and fundamental innovation

The degree of competitive intelligence use in incremental innovation and fundamental innovation is 4.44 and 4.39 respectively, and the difference is small, as shown in Fig. 2. This shows that the use of competitive intelligence has nothing to do with the change degree of technological innovation.

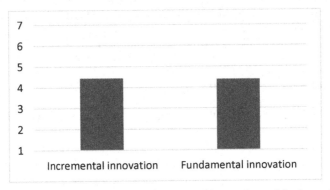

Fig. 2. The use of competitive intelligence in incremental innovation and fundamental innovation

Furthermore, in the two types of technological innovation, the distribution of the use degree of the three kinds of competitive intelligence is consistent, from large to small, they are direct competitor intelligence, indirect competitor intelligence and potential competitor intelligence, as shown in Fig. 3. In terms of the use of direct and indirect competitor intelligence, incremental innovation is greater than fundamental innovation; in terms of the use of potential competitors' intelligence, fundamental innovation is greater than incremental innovation. Fundamental innovation pays more attention to potential competitors, which is consistent with the research results of Murray et al. [13] and Guimaraes and Paranjape [14].

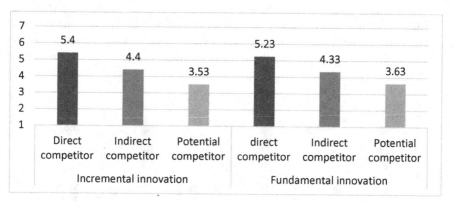

Fig. 3. The use of competitive intelligence in different types of technological innovation

Therefore, although there is no difference in the use of competitive intelligence between incremental innovation and fundamental innovation, the structure of the three kinds of competitive intelligence is not consistent in the two types of innovation.

3. The use of competitive intelligence in different stages of technological innovation

According to the degree of competitive intelligence use, the three stages of techno-logical innovation are: commercialization stage (4.88), creativity stage (4.59) and devel-opment stage (4.42), as shown in Fig. 4. This is inconsistent with the research results of Zahay et al. [17] and Hart and Baker [16]. These two studies show that competi-tive intelligence is used in the creative stage and development stage (including testing, acceptance), while competitive intelligence is not involved in the commercialization stage. The possible reason is that the sample enterprises of these two studies belong to a single industry, while the sample enterprises of this study come from multiple industries.

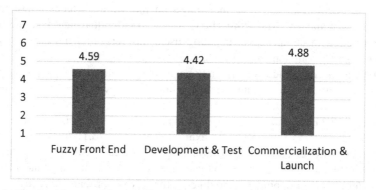

Fig. 4. The use of competitive intelligence in the three stages of technological innovation

In the three stages, the distribution of the three kinds of competitive intelligence use degree is consistent, and the order from large to small is direct competitor intelligence, indirect competitor intelligence and potential competitor intelligence, as shown in Fig. 5. From the dynamic point of view, the use of direct competitor intelligence shows an increasing trend; the change pattern of indirect competitor intelligence and potential competitor intelligence is as follows: the value of development stage is the smallest, the value of creative stage is larger, and the value of commercialization stage is the largest.

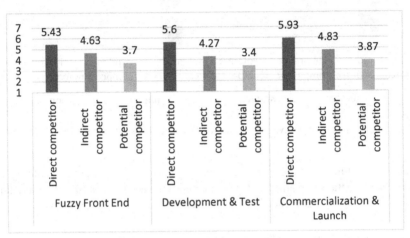

Fig. 5. The use of different types of competitive intelligence in different stages of technological innovation

4. Access to competitive intelligence in technological innovation

The questionnaire provides five options about the ways to obtain information in technological innovation: ①public information: including newspapers, journals, patents, standards, product manuals, company annual reports, government and industry association publications; ②Internet: including websites, social media, search engines and web crawlers; ③exhibition activities: including academic seminars, technology appraisal meetings and commodity expo ④third party: refers to individuals and institutions that have contacted with competitors, including users, lawyers, brokers, certified public accountants, stock commentators, banks, advertising companies, distributors, suppliers, industry authorities, industry associations, media, consumer organizations, quality inspection departments, storage and transportation departments, etc.; and ⑤consulting company or investigation company.

In technological innovation, the ways to obtain competitive intelligence are listed as public information (5.5), Internet (5.33), exhibition activities (5.1), third party (3.7) and consulting company (2.8) according to the amount of choices. As shown in Fig. 6, the use of the former three is much greater than that of the latter two, indicating that enterprises mainly prefer to collect opponent's intelligence directly rather than indirectly.

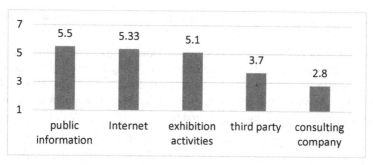

Fig. 6. Ways to obtain competitive intelligence in technological innovation

5. Content preference of competitive intelligence in technological innovation

In the process of technological innovation, the order of enterprises' attention to content of competitor analysis from large to small is resources and capability (5.3), current strategy (5.2), future goal (4.83) and self hypothesis (4.23), as shown in Fig. 7. The first two elements represent the current state of the enterprise, and the second two elements mainly represent the future state of the enterprise. Therefore, it can be considered that the enterprise pays more attention to the current state of its competitors than the future state. The score of self hypothesis is the lowest among the four factors (4.23), and the gap between self hypothesis and the other three factors is large, which indicates that enterprises are least concerned about competitors' opinions and judgments about themselves or the industry. This result is different from common sense. It is generally believed that technological innovation is future oriented and may pay more attention to the future state of competitors. In the interview, some enterprises pointed out that although the future goals and self assumptions of competitors are important, they are difficult to find and clarify, so they can only focus on the current strategies, resources and capabilities that are relatively easy to obtain, which may represent the common difficulties of some enterprises.

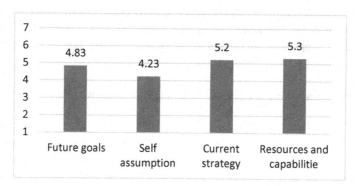

Fig. 7. Content preference of competitive intelligence in technological innovation

6. Characteristics of technological innovation conception of competitive intelligence

The characteristics of technological innovation ideas supported by competitive intelligence are ranked from large to small as effectiveness (4.66), feasibility (4.5) and novelty (4.45), as shown in Fig. 8. That is to say, the most prominent feature of technological innovation ideas brought by competitive intelligence is that they can meet customer needs, followed by easy implementation, and finally novelty.

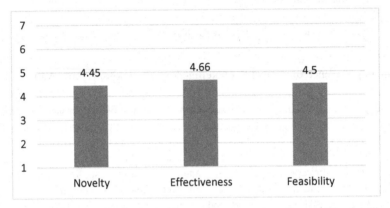

Fig. 8. Characteristics of technological innovation conception of competitive intelligence

Furthermore, in terms of the novelty, effectiveness and feasibility of technological innovation ideas, the three kinds of competitive intelligence have the same performance pattern, ranking from large to small according to the score: direct competitor intelligence, indirect competitor intelligence and potential competitor intelligence, as shown in Fig. 9. In every feature of technological innovation conception, the intelligence of direct competitors is superior to that of indirect competitors, and that of indirect competitors is superior to that of potential competitors.

According to the maximum and minimum values of the three kinds of competitive intelligence, the direct competitor intelligence most supports effectiveness (5.7) and least supports novelty (5.13); the indirect competitor intelligence most supports effectiveness (4.67) and least supports feasibility (4.4); while the potential competitor intelligence most supports novelty (3.66) and least supports feasibility (3.5).

7. The role of competitive intelligence in technological innovation

The role of competitive intelligence in technological innovation is pluralistic, and there are differences in degree, as shown in Fig. 10. The first is to reduce the risk of technological innovation (5.63). Competitive intelligence can reduce the uncertainty and thus reduce the risk, which has been verified, which is consistent with the mainstream view of the academic community. In the second, third and fifth place are improving product quality (5.56), increasing product differentiation (5.5) and shortening product development cycle (5.3), which are mainly related to the characteristics of new products.

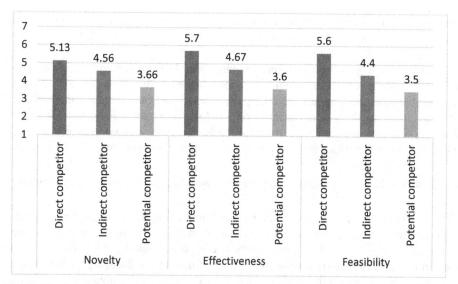

Fig. 9. Characteristics of technological innovation conception of different types of competitive intelligence

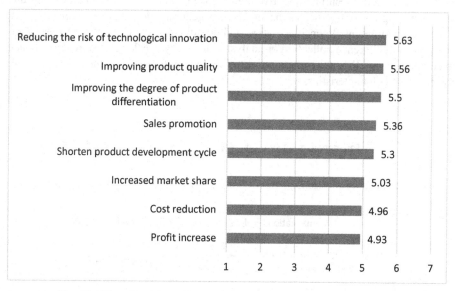

Fig. 10. The role of competitive intelligence in technological innovation

Among the remaining four, sales promotion (5.36) is in the fourth place, while increasing market share (5.03), reducing costs (4.96) and increasing profits (4.93) are at the end. These four functions are mainly related to the market. Why is the score of sales promotion higher than that of the other three? Some enterprises explain this way: after analysing the competitors, they adopt the way of price reduction to compete, so the sales increase, but the profit may not increase or even decrease. There are similar explanations for market share and cost. To sum up, the role of competitive intelligence is mainly to improve products, and then the market.

In this part, an open question is set to inquire about the role of enterprises in competitive intelligence other than questionnaire options. In the answers, "less detours", "faster" and "higher efficiency" appear more frequently, which indicates that an important role of competitive intelligence is benchmarking and surpassing, that is, to learn from the practices of excellent competitors to improve and perfect their own systems or strategies. This kind of benchmarking and surpassing can be applied to both products and markets.

8. Factors influencing competitive intelligence activities in technological innovation

The influencing factors of competitive intelligence activities in technological innovation are also diverse, and there are differences in degree, as shown in Fig. 11. Top management support (6.13) and the quality of competitive intelligence personnel (5.9) rank in the top two and are significantly ahead of the other influencing factors. These two factors mainly reflect the micro human will and ability. Informatization level (5.06), corporate culture (4.6) and organizational structure (4.53) are in the third, fifth and sixth place respectively. These three factors mainly reflect the characteristics of the organization. The competitor's anti competitive intelligence (4.7) is in the fourth place, and the score is not high, which indicates that enterprises generally do not pay enough attention to anti competitive intelligence activities, and do not cause enough trouble to the other enterprise's intelligence collection or analysis. Generally speaking, the greatest impact on competitive intelligence is the micro level of people, followed by the macro level of organizational characteristics.

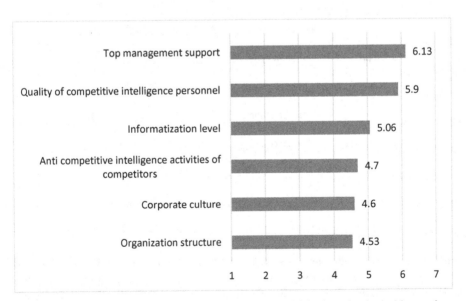

Fig. 11. Influencing factors of competitive intelligence activities in technological innovation

This part also sets up an open question to ask the influencing factors of competitive intelligence beyond the questionnaire options. Among the answers, "the nature of the industry", "the stage of enterprise development" and "the difficulty of intelligence collection" appear more frequently. In particular, "industry nature" is mentioned most frequently, which indicates that industry nature may affect the degree and mode of competitive intelligence development to a considerable extent. In other words, the influencing factors not only exist in the individual and enterprise level, but also exist in the industry level.

5   Conclusion and Future Research

Through the questionnaire survey and interview of 43 high-tech enterprises in Jiaxing City, this paper explores the competitive intelligence in technological innovation, which are mostly not involved in the current academic circles or involved but not deeply analyzed. The specific conclusions include the following aspects:

1. On the whole, the direct competitor intelligence is the most used in technological innovation, followed by the indirect competitor intelligence, and finally the potential competitor intelligence.
2. On the whole, there is almost no difference in the use of competitive intelligence between incremental innovation and fundamental innovation, but there are differences in the structure of the three kinds of competitive intelligence in the two types of innovation, that is, direct competitor intelligence and indirect competitor intelligence are used more in incremental innovation, while potential competitor intelligence is paid more attention in fundamental innovation.
3. In terms of different stages, enterprises use competitive intelligence most in the commercialization stage, then in the creative stage, and finally in the development stage. The distribution of the use degree of the three kinds of competitive intelligence in the three stages is consistent, from large to small are direct competitive intelligence, indirect competitor intelligence and potential competitor intelligence. From the dynamic point of view, the intelligence of direct competitors is increasing, while the intelligence of indirect competitors and potential competitors are basically in the shape of "U".
4. In technological innovation, enterprises mainly collect competitive intelligence through direct means (open information, Internet and exhibition activities), and seldom through indirect means such as third parties or consulting companies.
5. From the analysis content of competitive intelligence, in technological innovation, enterprises are more concerned about the current state of competitors (current strategy, resources and capabilities) than the future state (future goals, self assumptions).
6. The support of competitive intelligence for technological innovation ideas is mainly manifested in effectiveness, followed by feasibility, and finally novelty. The three kinds of competitive intelligence support each characteristic of technological innovation conception in the same distribution pattern, from large to small are direct competitive intelligence, indirect competitive intelligence and potential competitive

intelligence. As far as every kind of competitive intelligence is concerned, the intelligence of direct competitors most supports effectiveness and least supports novelty; the intelligence of indirect competitors most supports effectiveness and least supports feasibility; the intelligence of potential competitors most supports novelty and least supports feasibility.

7. The role of competitive intelligence in technological innovation is mainly in improving products, followed by improving the market.

8. Competitive intelligence activities in technological innovation are mainly affected by individual level factors, followed by organizational level factors, and there are also industrial level factors.

The main contributions of this paper are as follows: first, the competitive intelligence is separated from other types of intelligence, and the relationship between competitive intelligence and technological innovation is specially studied; second, the competitive intelligence is further divided into direct competitor intelligence, indirect competitor intelligence and potential competitor intelligence, and their use in technological innovation is investigated respectively. Because this paper is aimed at exploratory research, it has the inherent limitations of exploratory research, that is, the sample size is small, the conclusion can only be preliminary, and further empirical test is needed. In the future, the problems worthy of further study at least include: Are industry type, enterprise scale and product life cycle related to the use of competitive intelligence in technological innovation? Do three types of competitive intelligence have interactive effects on technological innovation performance? In technological innovation, are the concerns about competitors' future goals, self assumptions, current strategies, resources and capabilities related to technological innovation performance? Besides novelty, effectiveness and feasibility, what are the characteristics of technological innovation ideas supported by competitive intelligence? Are there still differences among the three kinds of competitive intelligence in these characteristics? Why does competitive intelligence improve products more than markets in technological innovation? In technological innovation, why do individual factors have stronger influence on competitive intelligence than organizational factors? These questions need to be answered by further descriptive or explanatory studies. In addition, we also need to study the market intelligence and technical intelligence in technological innovation, and compare the results of this study, so as to reveal the significance of different types of intelligence for technological innovation and the differences in the way of use.

References

1. Akroush, M.N.: An empirical model of new product development process: phases, antecedents and consequences. Int. J. Bus. Innov. Res. **6**(1), 47–75 (2012)
2. Liu, G., Ko, W.W.J., Ngugi, I., Takeda, S.: Proactive entrepreneurial behaviour, market orientation, and innovation outcomes: a study of small- and medium-sized manufacturing firms in the UK. Eur. J. Mark. **51**(11/12), 1980–2001 (2017)
3. de Waal, G.A., Knott, P.: Patterns and drivers of NPD tool adoption in small high-technology firms. IEEE Trans. Eng. Manag.nt **63**(4), 350–361 (2016)

4. Calantone, R.J., Schmidt, J.B., Song, X.M.: Controllable factors of new product success: a cross-national comparison. Mark. Sci. **15**(4), 341–358 (1996)
5. Bajaj, D.: Exploring market and competitive intelligence research as a source for enhancing innovation capacity. Coll. Q. **18**(3), 5 (2015)
6. Allameh, S.M., Naeini, S.G., Ansari, A., Kianpour, K., Nazari, Z.: Study the effect of competitive intelligence components on creating innovation. Int. J. Manag. Acad. **2**(1), 27–35 (2014)
7. Calantone, R.: An integrative model of the new product development process. J. Prod. Innov. Manag. **5**(3), 201–215 (1988)
8. Cooper, R.: Identifying industrial new product success: project NewProd. Ind. Mark. Manag. **8**(2), 124–135 (1979)
9. Cooper, R.G., Kleinschmidt, E.: New products, what separates winners from losers. J. Prod. Innov. Manag. **4**, 169–184 (1987)
10. Michael Song, X., Parry, M.E.: The R&D-marketing interface in Japanese high-technology firms. J. Prod. Innov. Manag. **9**(2), 91–112 (1992)
11. Tribby, M.E.: Competitive Analysis: The Direct and Indirect. John Wiley & Sons, New Jersey (2013)
12. Markkanen, S.: Competitor analysis for Feelback Ltd-A base for strategic decision making. Kuopio, Savonia University of Applied Sciences (2012)
13. Guimaraes, T., Paranjape, K.: Competition intensity as moderator for NPD success. Int. J. Innov. Sci. **11**(4), 618–647 (2019)
14. Murray, R., Millson, I., Wilemon, D.: The impact of changing markets and competition on the NPD speed/market success relationship. Int. J. Innov. Manag. **14**(5), 841–870 (2010)
15. Tadd, W., MingJer, C.: Indirect competition: Strategic considerations. Soc. Sci. Electron. Publishing **27**(34), 2774–2779 (2008)
16. Hart, S.J., Baker, M.J.: The multiple convergent processing model of new product development. Int. Mark. Rev. **11**(1), 77–92 (1994)
17. Zahay, D., Griffin, A., Fredericks, E.: Information use in new product development: An initial exploratory empirical investigation in the chemical industry. J. Prod. Innov. Manag. **28**(4), 485–502 (2011)
18. Franke, N.E., von Hipple, E., Schreier, M.: Finding commercially attractive user innovations: a test of lead user theory. J. Prod. Innov. Manag. **23**(4), 301–315 (2006)
19. Nemutanzhela, P., Iyamu, T.: The impact of competitive intelligence on products and services innovation in organizations. Int. J. Adv. Comput. Sci. Appl. **2**(11), 38–44 (2011)
20. Gawer, A., Cusumano, M.A.: Industry platforms and ecosystem innovation. J. Prod. Innov. Manag. **31**(3), 417–433 (2014)
21. Boniface, O.: Using customer-product competitor analysis as drivers for a business' reconfiguration and market repositioning. J. Contemporary Manag. **14**(1), 385–415 (2017)

User Experience, Acceptance
and Impact of Mobile Communications

Accessibility Challenges of Video Conferencing Technology

Nicole Anderson[✉]

School of Computing, Weber State University Ogden, Ogden, UT, US
nanderson1@weber.edu

Abstract. This paper discusses some of the accessibility challenges posed by current video conferencing technology with a specific focus on the Deaf community. There is a long way to go in making this technology fully accessible and inclusive for those with accessibility needs. The current state of the art is examined and areas of possible technological improvement discussed. Also discussed is the need to integrate into the technology cognitive aspects that force a correct and inclusive mental model by those participants without accessibility needs that are sometimes oblivious to or don't know how to overcome their own challenges participating in a diverse group using this software. While we realize the needs and methods of participation by different communities will not be exactly the same, we hope to push development in a direction that is more inclusive and more equitable. We consider how these ideas apply to the educational community and beyond.

Keywords: HCI · Accessibility · Mental models

1 Introduction

Video Conferencing Technology, such as Zoom, has made remote meeting attendance much more accessible for many users. Joining meetings from any location with a reasonable internet connection is now feasible and can be done with a few button clicks. Sharing materials is easy, and recording meetings for attendees or those unable to attend can be accomplished with minimal effort.

In some ways this technology has made meetings more accessible for those with specific accessibility challenges as well, but in other ways it makes them less inclusive for this population. We are going to zoom-in on a few groups of people with accessibility challenges in this paper, examine how well Zoom Video Conferencing meets the needs of these populations, and consider how the technology might be improved to create a more positive experience for these groups and for all participants.

2 Experiences with Video Conferencing Technology

2.1 One-on-One Meetings

Let's first consider the current experiences of users of video conferencing technology. In much of this paper, we will focus on Zoom as it is the most popular technology for

© Springer Nature Switzerland AG 2021
G. Salvendy and J. Wei (Eds.): HCII 2021, LNCS 12796, pp. 185–194, 2021.
https://doi.org/10.1007/978-3-030-77025-9_16

remote meetings, and also most frequently identified as the most accessible of the major players in this realm.

Our primary accessibility focus will be on the population of Deaf and hard-of-hearing individuals, although we will touch on other accessibility needs as well. It is easy to understand some of the challenges the Deaf individuals may face in using Zoom. American Sign Language, or ASL, is frequently used for face-to-face communication with this population. ASL is a gesture based, three-dimensional language. When forced onto a screen, it is still possible for individuals to communicate using ASL. However, it is more challenging to interpret the signs and it can be more taxing to do so than when face-to-face. Some Deaf individuals are able to read lips. At the time of this writing, we are in the thick of COVID-19, and many people are wearing masks in the workplace and at school, making lip reading an impossibility. Regardless, only a portion of the Deaf and hard-of-hearing population communicate this way. Deaf individuals are often highly skilled at adapting to new challenges and new situations. After all, they have been frequently required to do so. Let's consider the other side of the coin.

Imagine, if you are a hearing person, communicating with a Deaf individual on Zoom. It is likely that even if the conversation is intended for just the two of you, there will be a third person present: an interpreter. With any conversation, there is a different dynamic when a third person is listening in. In this case, the dynamic of the conversation changes even more dramatically. When speaking to an individual one-on-one, you focus not only on what that individual is saying, but their facial expressions and body language. With an interpreter in the picture, literally, the interpreter often become the visual focus of both of the individuals in the conversation. For the Deaf individual, they must focus on the interpreter as they are the only person speaking their language. For the hearing individual (or at least for the author), by default we focus on the person speaking aloud. The software draws attention to the interpreter. Losing all of this context, no hints from the speaker's body language, no changes in tone, etc., can pose a challenge for the hearing individual in correctly interpreting the words presented as fully. This could be referred to as a mental screen.

2.2 The Mental Screen and Display Biases

The idea of the mental screen was introduced by Shlomo Benartzi, a behavioral economist, in his book The Smarter Screen: Surprising Ways to Influence and Improve Online Behavior [1]. The idea of a mental screen is that our minds focus on what or whoever commands our attention. On our physical screen, the Zoom software only reinforces this mental screen we already struggle to overcome.

This is also related to Benartzi's idea of display biases. In Zoom, depending on our settings, the person speaking aloud is brought into a large box at the forefront, or alternately their smaller box is highlighted in gallery mode. In the case of video conferences, we have been trained to look at the biggest box in the center, or in the case where we have a row of potential speakers, the one highlighted at any given moment. Our already existing display bias is reinforced by the software. As UX designers, we know how powerful the choice of location in which we put an element on the screen matters.

The point we are making here is that when using Zoom for a one-on-one meetings, we already have identified an enormous amount of challenges for both the Deaf and hearing individuals in the conversation. Large group meetings pose even more challenges.

2.3   Large Group Meetings

Next let's consider a larger meeting situation. One thing that all individuals may notice when they use video conferencing technology is that some of the human aspects of meetings feel different. There is not the time sitting around the table prior to everyone arriving where small talk is made. There are less "how are you's" and we often learn less personal information about others we regularly attend meetings with when the focus tends to more stay on the meeting topics at hand. In addition, just like in one-on-one meetings, it is more difficult to see and interpret the body language of others attending. Additional effort must be made to notice who is waiting to speak, and to pick up on cues as to when it is a good time to add one's own two cents to a discussion without interrupting or beginning to speak at the same time as others. These human aspects can be magnified for individuals with disabilities.

Again, considering a different angle, individuals without specific accessibility needs may not find themselves skilled at forming the correct mental model when interacting with Deaf individuals using video conferencing technology. For example, by default in Zoom, the individual speaking out loud is pinned as the primary largest picture to appear on screen. We reiterate that you can instead choose gallery mode if you wish to see many individuals presented in the same sized boxes on your screen. But when speaking with a Deaf individual, the interpreter is identified by the technology as the speaker, and the Deaf individual may *not even be shown on the screen*. This is actually more likely to happen to Deaf individuals than for other, as Deaf individual's often use their interpreter in both directions, to interpret the words of others and to interpret their words into spoken language. That is, of course, not always the case, as many Deaf individuals do speak aloud. However, for an individual that always signs, they may chose to mute themselves to avoid making noise that the other attendees would hear by muting their microphone. When they do this for the entire meetings, they are likely to be given a lower priority screen position if they are on the screen at all. Again, the mental screen is an issue. Another challenge that may exist is related to the five senses theory. We'll explore that next.

2.4   The Five Senses Theory

Jinsop Lee, an industry designer, introduces the five senses theory [2]. He describes how good design uses as many senses as possible, so that we aren't leaving out someone because they lack one sense. When we interact with someone with an accessibility challenge on Zoom, we often limit a second sense when one is missing. For example, for a Deaf individual, they aren't using their sense of hearing. But when we take the camera focus off of them, we limit the visual sense for both the instructor and the student since typically the best eye contact and observations are made when the speakers are highlighted. Our goal should be instead to enhance the senses and capabilities of our users, rather than limit them. In order to facilitate this, let's move on to a discussion of some known best practices for utilizing existing video conferencing technology.

3   Best Practices Using Existing Technologies

One of the first strategies we would like to discuss to make meetings more accessible is enabling participation for all. For individuals with hearing impairments, knowing when to participate in a meeting may be more difficult. We suggest setting some ground rules for participation in online meetings. Users often jump in verbally when they want to share. Consider requiring everyone to digitally raise their hand, as is enabled in Zoom, before speaking. Even better, use a tool such as the Trace Online Hand Raising Utility (https://tohru.raisingthefloor.org) to allowed those wishing to speak to be queued in the order of requests.

Alternately, consider using the waterfall method for participation. This technique involves the instructor asking a question, giving time to all participants to come up with an answer and type their response into the chat, and then asking them to hit enter at the same time. Then answers can be reviewed and equal participation opportunity is ensured.

Another technique involves slowing down the meeting. Try to pace the meeting appropriately, allowing individuals the time they need to take advantage of any assistive devices or allowing time for interpretation. In a similar vein, making sure participants are speaking one at a time rather than interrupting each other can also be helpful. In addition, taking notes or minutes and sharing those with all meeting participants upon conclusion of the meeting can provide the opportunity for all participants to catch up on any information they may have missed. To take this one step further, record the meeting and providing both the electronic version as well as a transcript of the meeting to participants upon its conclusion. If time permits, review the transcript for accuracy and to make sure all speakers were identified properly in case follow-up questions are later required.

During the meeting it is important to be cognizant of the types of specific needs and challenges of your participants. When considering individuals with visual impairments, we started by looking at Zoom's documentation to see if these needs were addressed. It was indicated that "Zoom ensures that its products are operable and perceivable for users with visual impairments." Of course, supplemental tools such as screen reads which read text aloud are available [3]. However, meeting participants may speak at the same time others when participating in the chat. For a Blind participant, listening to both simultaneously is not reasonable. Content shared via screen sharing would prove challenging for this population. In addition, the authors have noticed that many visually impaired individuals appear to use sound more deeply that sighted individuals. Some of the clues generally available in face-to-face interactions, such as where a person is sitting, and whether an individual that typically sits at a particular location has joined the meetings (typically audible with sliding chairs and books hitting the table) are not available in online remote video conferencing.

Of course, there are so many different types of disabilities or needs that users may have. Physical impairments may restrict typing in chat or participating on a whiteboard.

Limited technological resources may prove a challenge for some. Let's examine some general accessibility practices that may assist a variety of users.

We have noticed that universities are one group introducing their own best practices for accessibility using Zoom. Let's take a look at a couple of examples. San Francisco State University recently published an Article titled "Best practices for accessibility and user experience when using Zoom for meetings and classes." [4] Here are their suggestions for the instructor with respect to ensuring that their meeting or class is accessible for all participants.

1. Enable the Closed Captions feature on your account for any meetings or classes that will require closed captions.
2. Send out the Zoom Keyboard Shortcuts ahead of time.
3. Describe visual content that is displayed will help anyone with a vision or cognitive disability, as well as someone that may have needed to call in due to a local internet outage.
4. Provide instructions on how participants can ask questions.
5. Send any resource links you post in Chat via email as well.
6. Confirm the best polling technology in advance.
7. Describe what you are annotating if using the Whiteboard feature.

Let's look at another example. One the most comprehensive lists we found was from Yale University [5]:

1. Enable the Closed Caption Feature
2. "Spotlight"ASL Interpreters
3. Manually Create Breakout Rooms When Using Interpreters
4. Slow Down your Pace
5. Enable "Always Show Meeting Controls"
6. Enable the "Mute Participants Upon Entry" Feature
7. Communicate Keyboard Shortcuts
8. "Remember to describe images and other visual content that's displayed
9. Provide instructions on how participants can ask questions
10. Send any resource links you post in Chat via email as well
11. Limit use of the Zoom polling feature
12. Describe what you are annotation gif using the Whiteboard feature
13. Record Your Zoom Session

We could certainly compare with additional universities' best practice lists and we encourage you to do so. Instead, we will jump into some of our take-aways from the various suggestions. There are a few common threads, such as enabling closed captioning and communicating shortcuts. But we also observe that these lists are inconsistent. We note that it is a big undertaking for the instructor or presenter to understand and remember all of the things they should do to ensure their meeting is accessible. We also noticed that not all institutions provided these guidelines, include our home institution.

Following these guidelines may allow all users to participate in meetings and courses to a certain degree, especially as observers, but it certainly is still challenging for those with accessibility needs to participate to the same degree as the other users. We commend universities on making effort in the right direction, but we don't believe the approaches we just examined will be enough to overcome the mental screen of the other participants. For example, let's consider a situation of an individual with a speech disability asking a question via chat. Sure, this feature will enable them to ask their question. But it won't put the spotlight on them as the person asking the question to the same degree that it would someone that asked the question aloud. In a large online classroom, the faculty may not know the names of all students so they may not be able to have a mental picture of who is asking the question even if students have their cameras on. We would like to see growth where meeting accessibility needs is a two way street. Students with accessibility needs can participate as actively as others, and faculty can have a similar mental model regarding their engagement in the course.

Since, for the most part, universities are all using the same technology, best practices don't seem like they should be institution specific. We would like to see a standardized best practices list and we would like to see these features made easier to use and made standard practice for individuals' delivering meetings.

Again, we note that at the time of writing, while COVID-19 is present, the need for the use of Zoom-like technology is amplified, as less in-person communication is generally desired. Thus, some of the challenges of utilizing these technologies are doubly amplified. Some have noted an increase in digital accessibility awareness due to COVID-19. In fact, a recent survey by Deque Systems indicated that the majority of senior-level, U.S.-based accessibility practitioners across many industries reported an increased awareness of the impact of accessibility on digital channels at a time when there was also a huge (83%) increase in the importance of digital channels within their organizations [6]. We hope that due to this, we will see improvement in best practice guidelines, as well as the development of additional technologies to aid in achieving accessibility goals.

4   Upcoming Technologies

Next, let's take a look at some currently available and upcoming technologies designed to make meetings and courses more accessible. There are add-on tools that can be used in conjunction with Zoom. For example, there is a product called Otter Voice Meeting Notes [7] that provides live transcription during a meeting. Viewing closed captioning would assist some individuals in understanding what was being said, but not in being active participants. The first road block to using this technology, especially for a student, would be the price.

Another add-on tool for Zoom [8] allows helpful keyboard shortcuts for controlling meeting alerts, for opening add on dialogs, and for focusing in and out of the remote controlled screen. While this seems helpful, we again would like to see the burden of equal participation shifted away from the user when possible.

A new piece of remote course delivery software coming on to the horizon is called Class for Zoom. In a later section we discuss accessibility in education, but we believe that some of the strategies used in this technology could be helpful in education as well as professional settings. Teach for Zoom [9] intends to allow a space where "Teachers don't get lost in the grid view and have a dedicated Podium space. TA's and presenters can be moved to the from of the class." The authors think this technology, specifically presenting two individuals side-by-side at the "front" of the remote classroom could be helpful in highlighting side-by-side the person signing and the translator.

In the sample meeting shown on the next page from the Class Technologies website, imagine the teacher or meeting chair in the left column and the translator and person signing in the positions on the top right. This side-by-side visual could help everyone in both noticing when someone is signing, being able to read their expressions, and still allow the translation and important of the translator come trough in the communication. This particular tool also support hand raising where individuals are queued in the order they have raised their hands. We may suggest modeling this in a different way for a traditional meeting, but the idea still holds. We should take turns while speaking, and want to allow individuals with or without accessibility needs equal spots in the speaking queue (Fig. 1).

Fig. 1. These is a sample meeting from the Class for Zoom website.

Another tool provided by this software is participation tracking. The description on this feature reads that "All participants can be listed in order of their class participation time (amount of time the student talks in class)". This could be a useful tool for all meeting to ensure that all individuals, including those with accessibility needs are given the opportunity to participate.

Regardless of whether this particular software is adopted, we believe that software that enables a user interface where the participants can be actively highlighted is one crucial step in the right direction. We hope to see additional technologies integrate these concepts as well.

5 Accessibility in Education

Course accessibility and inclusivity can be aided by having the savvy to configure some of our existing technologies to operate with these goals in mind. New technologies can also be developed to support these needs. To produce the best solutions, we should move the process of thinking about how to support our students with accessibility needs to a time frame long before a course begins. Since the types of needs are diverse, this is a big ask but also a big opportunity. The opportunity may be even greater in online coursework where the use of communication tools is already baked into the design of the course.

We already know equity and equality are not the same thing when it come to students with accessibility needs, or in general for that matter. But even when we utilize current modifications available to students, there is room to grow in producing equity in HCI and more broadly CS education. Since the types of needs are diverse, this is a big ask but it is also a big opportunity.

While there is inadequate representation of gender and race in CS (which includes or at least overlaps with HCI), students with disabilities make up a fair share of our students [10]. We, however, tend to not produce a curriculum that is equitable and inclusive for them.

These students are often directed to an office of disability or accessibility services and accommodations to be granted are reported back to instructors, typically after a course has begun. Some accommodations are small, such as extended time on exams, and an instructor can easily provide them. But we would like to be bold enough to suggest that the accommodations often being provided are not equitable. We believe we as a community with significant technical skills should work toward providing more equitable, more inclusive tools to support many types of accessibility challenges. The outcomes as well as the process should meet the needs of all of our students. This includes making sure one of our core pieces of course delivery software, our video conferencing software, adequately supports these students.

The authors' personal experiences specific to meeting with a Deaf student via video conferencing technology during office house included challenges in making sure all communication used the correct tone, adjusting our mental models to reflect that we were communicating with the student rather than the interpreter when using available tools, and working to make sure the student felt included and supported in the course, not just that course content was technically accessible to them. We owe all students not just content delivery, but engagement and connection.

After this experience, we believe course accessibility and inclusivity can be aided by having the savvy to configure some of our existing technologies to operate with these goals in mind. To produce the best solutions, we need to make sure we are designing and using the best tools to support the needs of all students. Improving video conferencing technology stands out as one of the biggest opportunities to support our goals. Let's next consider some new potential development areas that could assist in moving in the right direction.

6   Areas for New Development for Education and Beyond

With gesture recognition technology growing [11, 12] we hope to see new developments in this area. Considering our Deaf meeting participants, if interpretation could be performed accurately by gesture recognition software, this could reduce the need to have an interpreter available and could also help other users focus on the speaker using sign language rather than the interpreter. Historically, this has been attempted but never fully achieved or never utilizing methods that can easily serve as an add-on to our current video conferencing technology [13, 14].

Natural language processing has also improved significantly in recent years. This allows for automatic transcription of meetings. We would suggest the creation of a tool that generates a live sign language video as others are speaking. Even better, as augmented and virtual reality are growing in capability, we envision this happening in a three-dimensional environment to make this type of communication less taxing.

As designers, let's put people front and center in our designs, both literally and figuratively. We need to find a way to make sure software users, including users of video conferencing technology, see the individuals they are communicating with. This means centering them in our UI designs. This means assisting in enabling a mental model that doesn't cause a mental screen. These are challenging tasks. We ask this community to help address this need.

7   Advocacy Needed

Potentially more difficult than the technological challenges we need to overcome is the simple prioritization of accessibility in both education and corporate models. Resources must be allocated to meet these needs. Effort must be made by users and developers. Funds must be set aside to purchase appropriate assistive software and hardware as well as to perform research and development of these technology.

The reality is, we all need accommodations. They may be permanent, such as in the case of many physical disabilities, but they may also be temporary such as in the case of an illness or accident. When we put measures in place to accommodate people and allow wider participation, we all benefit. Let's advocate for universal design in our remote meeting software, and in software in general.

8   Conclusion

Current video conferencing technology, like Zoom, has a long way to go to support all users, particularly those with accessibility needs. The needs and shortcomings are particularly visible within educational environments. In this paper, we have introduced a few methods to best utilize current technologies, and we hope we have also inspired the development of new technologies and instilled the goal of keeping accessibility in one's mind eye both when creating new technology and when interacting with a broad population which includes those with accessibility needs using these technologies.

References

1. Benartzi, S.: Saving for tomorrow. In: 2011 TED Conference. https://www.ted.com/talks/shl omo_benartzi_saving_for_tomorrow_tomorrow
2. Lee, J.: Designing for all 5 senses. In: 2013 TED Conference. https://www.ted.com/talks/jin sop_lee_design_for_all_5_senses?language=en
3. American Foundation for the Blind. "Screen readers." https://www.afb.org/blindness-and-low-vision/using-technology/assistive-technology-products/screen-readers. Accessed 12 Feb 2021
4. SFSU Best practices for accessibility and user experience when using Zoom for meetings and classes. https://athelp.sfsu.edu/hc/en-us/articles/360045071674-Best-practices-for-accessibi lity-and-user-experience-when-using-Zoom-for-meetings-and-classes
5. Yale: Usability & Web Accessibility. https://usability.yale.edu/web-accessibility/articles/zoom. Accessed 12 Feb 2021
6. Deque Systems, How is COVID-19 Impacting Digital Accessibility. https://www.deque.com/covid-19-digital-accessibility-report/. Accessed 12 Feb 2021
7. Otter AI Home Page. https://otter.ai. Accessed 12 Feb 2021
8. NVDA. https://addons.nvda-project.org/addons/zoomEnhancements.en.html. Accessed 12 Feb 2021
9. Class for Zoom Homepage. www.class.com. Accessed 12 Feb 2021
10. Rivers, E.: Women, minorities, and persons with disabilities in science and engineering. National Science Foundation (2017)
11. Zhang, X.-H., et al.: Improvement of dynamic hand gesture recognition based on HMM algorithm. In: 2016 International Conference on Information System and Artificial Intelligence (ISAI). IEEE (2016)
12. Willems, D., et al.: Iconic and multi-stroke gesture recognition. Pattern Recogn. **42**(12), 3303–3312 (2009)
13. Li, Y.: Hand gesture recognition using Kinect. In: 2012 IEEE International Conference on Computer Science and Automation Engineering. IEEE (2012)
14. Liang, R.-H., Ming, O.: A real-time continuous gesture recognition system for sign language. In: Proceedings third IEEE International Conference on Automatic Face and Gesture Recognition. IEEE (1998)

Technology Craving and Withdrawal: Exploring Compulsive Mobile App Use

Jeffrey A. Clements[✉]

Weber State University, Ogden, UT 84201, USA
jeffclements@weber.edu

Abstract. To date, very little research has looked at the cravings and withdrawal individuals may experience for certain mobile apps. Research has demonstrated that some individuals may be classified as addicted to various mobile apps. Current research has difficulty explaining why some individuals have difficulty controlling their addictive behaviors while others do not (Abrams 2000), primarily because they have not taken technology craving into account. Accounting for technology craving in models of technology use is important as craving has the potential to drive addictive behaviors. This study explores the roles of technology craving and technology withdrawal in compulsive mobile app use.

Keywords: Compulsive · Craving · Withdrawal

1 Introduction

1.1 Compulsive Mobile App Use

The World Health Organization (1989) defines addiction as the use of something for relief, comfort, or stimulation, and which often continues, in part, due to cravings when it is absent. It has also been defined as compulsive use that is not necessary, accompanied by some impairment of health or social functioning (Institute of Medicine (U.S.). Committee to Identify Strategies to Raise the Profile of Substance Abuse and Alcoholism Research 1997). A behavioral addiction involves engaging in a specific behavior for relief, comfort, or stimulation, and which results in discomfort or unease of some type when discontinued (Porter and Kakabadse 2006).

The most comprehensive definition of technology addiction within MIS research is defined as "a psychological state of maladaptive dependency on the use of a technology to such a degree that the following typical behavioral addiction symptoms arise: (1) salience—the technology dominates a user's thoughts and behaviors; (2) withdrawal—negative emotions arise if a person cannot use the technology; (3) conflict—the use of the technology conflicts with other tasks, which impairs normal functioning; (4) relapse and reinstatement—a user is unable to voluntarily reduce the use of the technology; (5) tolerance—a person has to use the technology to a greater extent to produce thrill; and

© Springer Nature Switzerland AG 2021
G. Salvendy and J. Wei (Eds.): HCII 2021, LNCS 12796, pp. 195–206, 2021.
https://doi.org/10.1007/978-3-030-77025-9_17

(6) mood modification—using the technology offers thrill and relief, and results in mood changes" (Turel et al. 2011).

While the discussion of technology addiction is not new, very little research on compulsive technology use has been done. Research from 1985 on the behavioral addiction of playing electronic games warned that this phenomenon appears to be an "instance of new technology producing an activity that has the necessary features to give it potential for excess, and catching society unawares before it can anticipate the dangers and instigate the sorts of controls that have grown up around more traditional pursuits, such as drinking alcohol or gambling" (Orford 2005). More recent research along this stream has looked at how personality relates to the negative effects of employee technology addiction on a continuum ranging from problematic use to pathological use (Buckner et al. 2012). Buckner et al.'s work (2012) demonstrated that in general the five factor model could predict some aspects of problematic use, but in general could not predict pathological use. Similar work viewing addiction on a continuum has also studied the addiction phenomenon ranging from pathological computing addictions to non-pathological high engagement computing activities (Charlton and Danforth 2010).

Though research related to compulsive technology use exists, there has been a consistent lack of clear terminology in research looking at behavioral addictions to some form of technology (Clements and Boyle 2018). Compulsive technology use has been studied as information addiction (Pratt and Palloff 1999), mobile email addiction (Turel and Serenko 2010), problematic internet use (Davis et al. 2002), computer addiction (Charlton and Danforth 2010), and internet addiction (Yellowlees and Marks 2007). Yellowlees and Marks (2007) found those with impulse control and addictive disorders are especially at risk for using the Internet in problematic ways.

The theory of flow perspective (Csikszentmihalyi 1998) states that IT facilitates a mind state in which people are so intensely involved in an activity, that nothing else seems to matter. In this state the experience itself is so enjoyable that individuals will do it even at great cost, for the sheer sake of doing it (Csikszentmihalyi 1998). The concept of flow is a demonstration of the kind of focused attention and stimulation connected to behavioral addiction (Porter and Kakabadse 2006).

Research has shown that addictive behaviors often occur alongside other addictions. Alcoholics are often heavy smokers, and smokers tend to drink more coffee; heroin users frequently use various other drugs plus alcohol (Peele 1989). This has also been shown to be the case with workaholism and technophilia (technology addiction) in that the behavior of the workaholic serves to trigger technophiliac behaviors (Porter and Kakabadse 2006). There is a compounding effect in that the strength of one addiction serves to strengthen the other. This highlights why certain technology platforms can be so addictive. If a single IT platform—such as a smartphone—can facilitate and enable multiple addictions (e.g., Facebook addiction, email addiction, Angry Birds addiction), then that particular IT platform will compel high levels of use from the technophiliac.

Compulsive technology use is defined herein as spontaneous interaction with technology that is unintentional, uncontrollable, effortless, and efficient (Clements and Boyle 2018).

1.2   Technology Craving

Compulsive technology use has only recently begun to be identified by MIS researchers. Most related research has examined similar phenomena such as problematic internet use, internet addiction, and obsessive-compulsive use. Compulsive technology use represents a stage of system use which is driven by something other than behavioral intent. Compulsive technology use encompasses a stage of use which has moved beyond the initial acceptance of a technology and moved beyond the intentional decision to continue using a technology (i.e., continuance). It is a type of technology use which has extended beyond goal orientation and intentionality (Clements and Bush 2011).

Craving refers to the episodic stimuli of spontaneous and intrusive thoughts about wanting or needing a desired object. Research has demonstrated that cravings can drive behavior non-rationally (Saladin et al. 2006). Individuals can experience cravings for a variety of things. To date, very little research has looked at the cravings individuals may experience for certain technologies. Current research has difficulty explaining why some individuals have difficulty controlling their addictive behaviors while others do not (Abrams 2000), primarily because they have not taken technology craving into account. Accounting for technology craving in models of technology use is important as craving has the potential to explain addictive behaviors (Abrams 2000; García-Rodríguez et al. 2011).

Craving has been defined as a subjective experience within one's awareness that reflects retrieval from the memory systems of a strong learned desire to satisfy an actual or perceived need (Kozlowski and Wilkinson 1987). Craving is generally viewed as an intense desire or urge to obtain an appetitive target (Kavanagh et al. 2009). When a person experiences a craving episode, spontaneous and intrusive thoughts about wanting or needing a desired object are triggered by processes outside of the individual's awareness. These intrusive thoughts are associated with a sense of anticipation for pleasure, stimulus or relief (Kavanagh et al., 2009). Research on craving has examined the role craving plays in mediating addictive behaviors (Abrams 2000). This research highlighted that correctly conceptualizing craving would be useful in understanding why some individuals—under certain circumstances—have difficulty controlling their addictive behaviors, while others do not.

It is important to discuss the distinction between types of cravings. Following the distinction proposed by Ferguson and Shiffman (2009), there are two forms of cravings—background cravings, and episodic cravings. Background craving refers to the relatively steady experience of craving over the course of hours, days, or weeks. In a technology context, a Twitter user, after a period of time of not checking their tweets, will experience a background craving for information until he/she finally checks-in. In contrast, episodic craving refers to periods of time defined by intense cravings—involving spikes and surges. These intense episodes are triggered by stimuli associated with the behavior. In the context of a mobile app, the example of the Twitter user's phone repeatedly vibrating to indicate incoming tweets can serve to produce episodic craving.

1.3 Technology Withdrawal

Withdrawal is the combination of physical and mental effects that a person experiences after they stop using something they have a compulsion for or an addiction for. Generally, this has been studied along with drugs and alcohol. However, a person may experience withdrawal from technology. Withdrawal from technology refers to the negative emotions arise that if a person cannot use a particular technology (Turel et al. 2011).

The foundation of much of this type of research comes from the work on problematic internet gaming (Kaptsis et al. 2016) This phenomenon is characterized by aversive or unpleasant physical or psychological states that happen when a person stops gaming. This is consistent with the typical definition of withdrawal in dependence syndromes in that cessation produces mounting tension until the behavior can be completed again. This process is thought to be behavioral and chemical as compulsive behaviors can trigger dopamine release. In turn dopamine exposure changes other brain areas, such as the amygdala which can boost negative emotions, such as fear, anxiety and stress when the compulsive behavior ends, leaving addicts seeking the behavior again simply to escape the pain of withdrawal (Zastrow 2017).

In general, technology withdrawal refers the negative emotions a person experiences when they are faced with the absence of their technology object of desire. When a person can't access his or her favorite app or they have run out of virtual coins or they have lost their phone etc., unease, discomfort, stress, and malaise can ensue. In essence, the same types of physical symptoms found in those experiencing mild chemical withdrawal can be found in the personal experiencing technology withdrawal.

2 Hypothesis Development

2.1 What Drives Compulsive Use - Craving

Craving has the potential to drive addictive and compulsive behaviors (Abrams 2000; García-Rodríguez et al. 2011). Cues associated with previous behaviors can result in episodic craving (Ferguson and Shiffman 2009). Most classic behavioral theories point to the importance of an external stimulus to initiate action. Hull's Stimulus Response Theory (1943) and other theories of classical conditioning suggest that all behaviors must first be primed or cued before the behavior can be engaged. Technology can provide the necessary external priming stimuli in the form of embedded lights, vibrations, alarms. These triggers serve to provide behavioral stimuli. These technology features serve as external behavioral initiation mechanisms, or triggers which set behaviors into motion (Simon 1947).

These technology-enabled triggers can present themselves in a number of forms. Take for example today's smart phone device. Consider the variety of indicator lights of varying colors, and flashes of varying intensity. Consider the innumerable combination of vibration sequences, visual alerts, symbols, or messages. Consider the variety of audible sounds, beeps, tones and rings. All serve the purpose of signaling to their human operator, "Hey…I have something for you… Look at me… Listen to me… Pick me up… Interact with me." This has important implications for the design of a technology as technology-enabled triggers can be purposefully incorporated into a system to act as mechanisms of behavioral initiation. This point is reflected in recent calls for information systems research that is design science oriented (Hevner et al. 2004). Once the behavior is primed and initiated there are psychological processes which provide guidance and persistence for the action in the form of craving.

More recent research building on incentive conditioning suggests that when behavioral triggers are associated with a rewarded response, the value associated with the reward becomes ingrained and conditioned into the triggers themselves. (Neal et al. 2006) Thus as the behavior is subsequently performed the triggers themselves begin to carry value enough to motivate action in the form of craving (Kavanagh et al. 2009). The behavior is driven because the past reward conditioning has established the necessary cognitive context-response associations, and the context becomes embedded with the motivational force for responding (Wood et al. 2002).

An information system or technology can serve as the context for individuals to perform a variety of behaviors. Research on smartphone use shows that automatic checking behaviors emerge and are reinforced by the quickly accessible informational rewards provided by the smartphone (Oulasvirta et al. 2012). If an information system or technology can provide sufficient technology-enabled triggers then people interacting with those systems or technologies will have increased technology cravings. In turn our increased cravings will drive future behavior.

H1: Mobile App Craving will be positively associated with compulsive mobile app use.

2.2 What Drives Compulsive Use – Withdrawal

Research has shown that withdrawal is associated with a variety of negative states such as depressed mood, elevated anxiety, inability to experience pleasure, and disturbed sleep (Heilig et al. 2010). While not identifying the phenomenon as withdrawal, researchers found that excessive smart phone users had poor subjective well- being and disturbed sleep (Li et al. 2015).

Similar research has found excessive social media use to be linked with depression and anxiety (Primack et al. 2017). Again, while not explicitly calling out the withdrawal symptoms, it is clear researchers are seeing withdrawal in people who are compulsively using mobile applications. Without intervention, withdrawal states lead to future repeated compulsive behaviors. This means that those experiencing high levels of withdrawal will also see future compulsory behaviors increase. Formally stated:

H2: Withdrawal will be positively associated with compulsive mobile app use.

3 Research Methodology

3.1 Research Design

For several reasons, this study uses survey research design. First, a survey design provides a way to tap into the perceptual variables of interest. These perceptual constructs are thereby quantified so that comparisons can be made and inferences can be drawn about the relationships between the variables in the population. Previous research on psychological constructs such as technology habit have used survey items to assess behaviors that are not easily observable.

Second, a survey design provides the advantage of identifying attributes of a large population from a subset of individuals (Fowler 2002). The main purpose of a survey is to generalize from a sample to a population so that inferences can be made about some behavior (Babbie 1990); in this case compulsive technology use. Therefore, this study will be able to sample a subset of the population to learn more about what drives compulsive technology use in the greater population.

As compulsive technology use is a behavior that individuals perform in a variety of settings with their personal technology devices, a controlled experiment could prove unwieldy in accurately capturing the phenomenon. Therefore, it would be difficult to make inferences about the population based on an experiment which does not accurately reflect the phenomenon of compulsive technology use.

Third, a survey design allows for standardized measurement that is consistent across all respondents to ensure that comparable information is obtained. Meaningful statistics are desired to examine the extent to which variability in the drivers of compulsive technology use account for variability in compulsive technology use. Without such standardized measurement, meaningful statistics cannot be produced (Fowler 2002), and any relatedness present between the variables of interest in a given individual would not be comparable to those of another individual.

Table 1. Technology craving items

Craving – an intense desire or urge to obtain an appetitive target (mobile app)	
Measure	Source
I often spontaneously think about this app	Newly developed
I sometimes feel an urge to use this app	
I find myself thinking about this app	
I have experienced feelings of craving associated with my use of the app	

New measures were developed and used to measure technology craving. A total of four items were developed for the survey instrument. Items were scored using a 7-point Likert type scale ranging from strongly agree (1) to strongly disagree (7).

New measures were developed and used to measure technology withdrawal. A total of four items were developed for the survey instrument. Items were scored using a 7-point Likert type scale ranging from strongly agree (1) to strongly disagree (7).

Previously validated scales (Clements and Boyle 2018) to measure compulsive technology use were used in this study. Items were scored using a 7-point Likert type scale ranging from strongly agree (1) to strongly disagree (7).

Table 2. Technology withdrawal items

Withdrawal – negative emotions associated with the lack of access to technology (mobile app)	
Measure	Source
I would feel annoyed if my access to this application was blocked	Newly developed
I would feel distressed if I was not able to access this application for an extended period of time	
I would feel I was missing out if I was not able to access this application for an extended period of time	
The thought of never being able to access this application would cause me anxiety	

Table 3. Compulsive technology use items

Compulsive technology use- spontaneous interaction with technology (mobile app) that is unintentional, uncontrollable, effortless, and efficient	
Measure	Source
I Choose this app without even being aware of making the choice	Clements and Boyle (2018)
I unconsciously start using this app	
Using this app is something I do without even being aware of it	
I find myself checking in with this app without explicitly planning to do so	
I often feel compelled to use this app	
I often feel I spontaneously use this app	
I feel I must use this app	

3.2 Hypothesis Testing

Data collection was via a web-based survey. Student participants from a United States based university were invited through email to take part in the study. In total 443 student (response rate = 0.71) completed the survey including 195 males and 248 females.

A partial least squares – structural equation modeling (PLS – SEM) approach was utilized to test the measurement and structural model. The primary objective in using this approach is maximizing the total explained variance in the dependent variables while evaluating the data quality as determined by the measurement model characteristics.

Before testing the structural model, I assessed the construct dimensionality of the measures and the factorial validity of the latent constructs. This was done in two phases. The first phase consisted of a principle components analysis (PCA) using SPSS to rigorously analyze construct dimensionality as it cannot be measured directly with PLS but is assumed to be there a priori (Gefen 2003; Gerbing and Anderson 1998). The second phase consisted of using Smart PLS to assess two elements of factorial validity—convergent validity and discriminant validity—as suggested by authors (Gefen and Straub 2005). These two elements are critical components of construct validity (Straub et al. 2004).

Next, I tested the measurement model with PLS to assess factorial validity by conducting a confirmatory factory analysis in which the pattern of loadings of the measurement items on the latent constructs were specified in the model. Results of the CFA showed that all measurement items loaded with significant t-values on the latent constructs as an indication of convergent validity (Gefen and Straub 2005). To assess the discriminant validity of the measurement model I examined the correlations of the latent variable scores with the measurement items. This showed that all items loaded highly on their specified factor and not highly on other factors.

Table 4. Cross-loadings

Cross-loadings	Compulsive	Craving	Withdrawal
CU2	0.868	0.434	0.372
CU3	0.887	0.467	0.361
CU4	0.879	0.481	0.384
CU5	0.876	0.542	0.390
CU6	0.780	0.443	0.360
CU7	0.775	0.542	0.493
Crave1	0.488	0.894	0.541
Crave2	0.552	0.889	0.560
Crave3	0.516	0.926	0.521
Crave4	0.516	0.873	0.527
Withdraw2	0.331	0.465	0.850
Withdraw3	0.474	0.590	0.931
Withdraw4	0.444	0.550	0.914

To further assess discriminant validity, I conducted an average variance extracted (AVE) analysis. This test determines discriminant validity by examining whether the square root of the AVE for each latent construct is larger than any correlation among any pair of latent constructs (Fornell and Larcker 1981). Results indicated that the AVEs were well above the .50 threshold and that the square roots of the AVEs were consistently larger than any other correlation Results of this type provide further evidence of discriminant validity (Chin 1998).

After concluding the measurement model was sound, I next assessed the structural model in SmartPLS (Ringle et al. 2005). The first step in assessing the structural model is done by calculating the R2 values of the endogenous latent variables, and then examining path scores to determine the strength of the relationship.

Table 5. Construct reliability/validity

Construct	Cronbach's alpha	rho_A	Composite reliability	Average variance (AVE)
Compulsive	0.920	0.923	0.938	0.715
Craving	0.918	0.919	0.942	0.802
Withdrawal	0.882	0.909	0.926	0.808

Compulsive technology use had an R^2 value of 0.36. Next, I examined all the individual path coefficients of the structural model. These values can be interpreted as standardized beta coefficients of OLS regressions. The path from craving to compulsive use had a score of 0.46. The path from withdrawal to compulsive use had a score of 0.19.

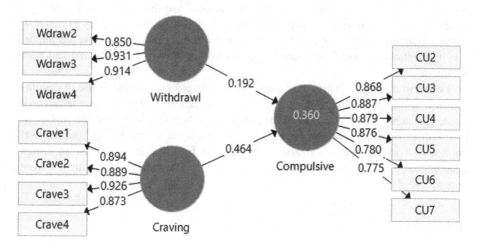

4 Discussion

4.1 Implications and Directions for Future Research

Hypothesis 1 stated that mobile app craving would be positively associated compulsive mobile app use. Results from the model testing are in support of this. Individuals experiencing increased cravings seem to be more compulsively using their mobile app of choice.

Hypothesis 2 stated that mobile app withdrawal would be positively associated with compulsive mobile app use. Though the results from the model testing are indeed in support of the hypothesis, the effect was rather small. Whether this was an artifact from the survey instrument or whether individuals under report, it is hard to say. However, people that experience withdrawal type episodes are indeed experiencing higher levels of compulsive mobile app use.

Understanding the phenomenon of compulsive technology use has several theoretical implications. From a research standpoint, this fills a gap in the call for research with a design science orientation (Hevner et al. 2004) as elements of technology design can drive behaviors. Understanding the technology features which enable high levels of compelling interaction will allow for the study of and design of high use voluntary type technologies. Current IS usage models and theories have had difficulty explaining technology use in this voluntary use paradigm. This study reflects "an important assumption that seems to be missing in the IS literature on continuing IT use, namely, that IT itself may be one of the most important triggers of automatic IT use behaviors" (de Guinea and Markus 2009).

Another contribution stems from the further development of the concept of compulsive technology use as a new IS dependent variable. There has been a growing interest in IS research to understand an individual's continued use well after initial adoption (Clements 2015). Paired with this is the notion that much technology use occurs outside of an organization's mandate to use a particular technology. A large portion of post-adoption technology use can be classified as personal use that is voluntary in nature. Research has yet to fully address how individuals engage with technology in this new context. Furthermore, accounting for craving and withdrawal in this context has important implications as behavior is driven be means that are very non-rational and very automatic.

Future work should continue to study how craving affects individuals use of systems and how it might negatively affect positive work-related behaviors. Another area of future research in in the area of withdrawal. This study barely scratched the surface of how withdrawal can drive usage behavior. Future studies of how technology withdrawal impacts individuals and organizations might prove fruitful. Future studies on design features that might enable this phenomenon and how this might be eliminated from systems are also warranted.

References

Abrams, D.B.: Transdisciplinary concepts and measures of craving: commentary and future directions. Addiction **95**, S237-246 (2000)

Babbie, E.R.: Survey Research Methods. Wadsworth Publishing Company, Belmont (1990)

Buckner, V.J.E., Castille, C.M., Sheets, T.L.: The Five Factor Model of personality and employees' excessive use of technology. Comput. Hum. Behav. **28**, 1947–1953 (2012)

Charlton, J.P., Danforth, I.D.W.: Validating the distinction between computer addiction and engagement: Online game playing and personality. Behav. Inf. Technol. **29**, 601–613 (2010)

Chin, W.W: The partial least squares approach for structural equation modeling (1998)

Clements, J.A.: Beyond habit: the role of sunk costs on developing automatic is use behaviors. J. South. Assoc. Inf. Syst. **3**(1), 17–37 (2015)

Clements, J.A., Boyle, R.J.: Compulsive technology use: compulsive use of mobile applications. Comput. Hum. Behav. **87**, 34–48 (2018)

Clements, J.A., Bush, A.A.: Habitual is use and continuance. In: Southern Association for Information Systems Proceedings, p. 16 (2011)

Csikszentmihalyi, M.: The flow experience and its significance for human psychology (1998)

Davis, R.A., Flett, G.L., Besser, A.: Validation of a new scale for measuring problematic internet use: implications for pre-employment screening. Cyberpsychol. Behav. **5**, 331–345 (2002)

De Guinea, A.O., Markus, M.L.: Why break the habit of a lifetime? Rethinking the roles of intention, habit, and emotion in continuing information technology use. MIS Q. 433–444 (2009)

Ferguson, S.G.: Shiffman, S: The relevance and treatment of cue-induced cravings in tobacco dependence. J. Subst. Abuse Treat. **36**(3), 235–243 (2009)

Fowler, F.J: Survey Research Methods. Sage, Thousand Oaks (2002)

Fornell, C., Larcker, D.F.: Evaluating structural equation models with unobservable variables and measurement error. J. Market. Res. **18**, 39–50 (1981)

García-Rodríguez, O., Ferrer-García, M., Pericot-Valverde, I., Gutiérrez-Maldonado, J., Secades-Villa, R., Carballo, J.L.: Identifying specific cues and contexts related to 125 smoking craving for the development of effective virtual environments. Cyberpsychol. Behav. Soc. Netw. **14**, 91–97 (2011)

Gefen, D.: Assessing unidimensionality through LISREL: An explanation and an example. Commun. Assoc. Inf. Syst. **12**, 2 (2003)

Gefen, D., Straub, D.: A practical guide to factorial validity using PLS-graph: tutorial and annotated example. Commun. Assoc. Inf. Syst. **16**, 109 (2005)

Gerbing, D.W., Anderson, J.C.: An updated paradigm for scale development incorporating unidimensionality and its assessment. J. Market. Res. **25**, 186–192 (1998)

Heilig, M., Egli, M., Crabbe, J.C., Becker, H.C.: Acute withdrawal, protracted abstinence and negative affect in alcoholism: are they linked? Addict. Biol. **15**, 169–184 (2010)

Hevner, A.R., March, S.T., Park, J., Ram, S.: Design science in information systems research. MIS Q. **28**, 75–105 (2004)

Hull, C.L: Principles of Behavior: An Introduction to Behavior Theory. Appleton-Century, New York (1943)

Institute of Medicine (U.S.). Committee to identify strategies to raise the profile of substance abuse and alcoholism research: dispelling the myths about addiction: strategies to increase understanding and strengthen research. National Academy Press, Washington, D.C. (1997)

Li, J., Lepp, A., Barkley, J.: Locus of control and cell phone use: Implications for sleep quality, academic performance, and subjective well-being. Comput. Hum. Behav. **15**, 450–457 (2015)

Kaptsis, D., King, D.L., Delfabbro, P.H.: Gradisar, M: Withdrawal symptoms in internet gaming disorder: A systematic review. Clin. Psychol. Rev. **43**, 58–66 (2016)

Kavanagh, D.J., May, J., Andrade, J.: Tests of the elaborated intrusion theory of craving and desire: features of alcohol craving during treatment for an alcohol disorder. Br. J. Clin. Psychol. **48**, 241–254 (2009)

Kozlowski, L., Wilkinson, A.: Use and Misuse of the Concept of Craving by Alcohol, Tobacco, and Drug Researchers. Br. J. Addict. **82**, 31–36 (1987)

Li, J., Lepp, A., Barkley, J.E.: Locus of control and cell phone use: Implications for sleep quality, academic performance, and subjective well-being. Comput. Hum. Behav. **52**, 450–457 (2015)

Neal, D.T., Wood, W., Quinn, J.M.: Habits—a repeat performance. Curr. Direct. Psychol. Sci. **15**, 198–202 (2006)

Orford, J.: Problem Gambling and Other Behavioural Addictions. Academic University Press, Cambridge (2005)

Oulasvirta, A., Rattenbury, T., Ma, L., Raita, E.: Habits make smartphone use more pervasive. Pers. Ubiquit. Comput. **16**, 105–114 (2012). https://doi.org/10.1007/s00779-011-0412-2

Porter, G. and N. K. KakabadseL HRM perspectives on addiction to technology and work. Journal of Management Development 25, 535–560 (2006).

Pratt, K., Palloff, R.M.: Building Learning Communities in Cyberspace: Effective Strategies for the Online Classroom. Wiley, Hoboken (1999)

Primack, B.A., et al.: Use of multiple social media platforms and symptoms of depression and anxiety: a nationally-representative study among US young adults. Comput. Hum. Behav. **69**, 1–9 (2017)

Ringle, C.M., Wende, S., Will, A.: SmartPLS–Version 2.0. Universitat Hamburg, Hamburg (2005)

Simon, H.A.: Administrative Behavior: A Study of Decision-Making Processes in Administrative Organization. Macmillan, New York (1947)

Saladin, M.E., Brady, K.T., Graap, K., Rothbaum, B.O.: A preliminary report on the use of virtual reality technology to elicit craving and cue reactivity in cocaine dependent individuals. Addict. Behav. **31**, 1881–1894 (2006)

Straub, D., Boudreau, M.-C., Gefen, D.: Validation guidelines for IS positivist research. Commun. Assoc. Inf. Syst. **13**, 380–427 (2004)

Turel, O., Serenko, A.: Is mobile email addiction overlooked? Commun. ACM **53**, 41–43 (2010)

Turel, O., Serenko, A., Giles, P.: Integrating technology addiction and use: an empirical investigation of online auction users. Mis Q. **35**, 1043–1061 (2011)

Wood, W., Quinn, J.M., Kashy, D.A.: Habits in everyday life: thought, emotion, and action. J. Pers. Soc. Psychol. **83**, 1281–1297 (2002)

Yellowlees, P.M., Marks, S.: Problematic internet use or internet addiction? Comput. Hum. Behav. **23**, 1447–1453 (2007)

Zastrow, M.: News feature: is video game addiction really an addiction? Proc. Nat. Acad. Sci. **114**(17), 4268–4272 (2017)

The Use of mPOS in Mexico

Sunday Adewale Olaleye[1] and Manuela Gutiérrez-Leefmans[2(✉)]

[1] Oulu Business School, University of Oulu, 90570 Oulu, Finland
[2] Universidad de las Américas Puebla, 72810 Cholula, Mexico
maria.gutierrez@udlap.mx

Abstract. Economies around the world are migrating to either "cashless" or "less cash" models. Latin America is no exception. Mexico, with its considerable population and large economy, including many small and medium enterprises, already offers a variety of mPOS brands. Despite this, most literature on cashless societies has focused on developed countries and other innovative emerging nations such as Nigeria, leaving the Latin American region out of its scope. This paper presents a model of mPOS use in Mexico based on a survey of graduate and undergraduate students. Using structural equation modelling (SEM) variables such as lifestyle, ease of use and carbon footprint produced interesting results. The study finds that users' lifestyle is the highest predictor of mPOS in Mexico. Also, carbon footprint predicts mPOS use while the user's perception of ease of use did not predict the mPOS use. The study also concludes that mPOS in Mexico will promote a green environment and make Mexican society healthy. Managerial wise, this study suggests that the mPOS service providers in Mexico should pay closer attention to mPOS users' lifestyle. Besides, mPOS service providers should consider the carbon footprint and lifestyle when addressing their product to a specific customer segment.

Keywords: mPOS · Lifestyle · Ease of use · Carbon footprint · Emerging economy · Cashless

1 Introduction

As economies migrate to cashless technologies, mobile point of sale technology (mPOS) has attracted the researcher's attention. This development is valid for a variety of developed countries and some emerging ones. However, that is not Mexico's case, a country with a vast population and many small and medium enterprises, where mPOS technology has been around for about ten years. Although cash is still in use, the country's insecurity and more recently, the pandemic may be encouraging users to use cashless technologies.

Worldwide consumers are using cards for payments more frequently and even for small transactions [1]; a behavior which is driven, in part, by more people holding cards (in emerging market economies (EMEs) and greater availability of point-of-sale (PoS) terminals. Traditional POS terminals used to be fixed and installed on counters. However, according to [1], lower-cost smartphone or tablet-based POS terminals have emerged,

© Springer Nature Switzerland AG 2021
G. Salvendy and J. Wei (Eds.): HCII 2021, LNCS 12796, pp. 207–218, 2021.
https://doi.org/10.1007/978-3-030-77025-9_18

encouraging even smaller businesses to invest in them. In addition to the economic incentive behind cashless technologies a growing concern for our environment may also be contributing to their adoption.

A mobile Point of Sale (mPOS) is an electronic device, which uses an internet connection and a credit/debit card to process payments for goods and services through a mobile phone. It is therefore a simple and inexpensive way for small businesses to process payments. For users, this technology requires them to carry less cash. Although there is considerable research on new payment systems, we see more news articles than scientific studies on mPOS. This is particularly true for the Latin American context, where the literature is scant.

In Mexico, we constantly see mPOS companies advertised to small and medium enterprises (SMEs). Micro, small, and medium enterprises represent 99.8% of total business units in the country [2]. It is therefore crucial for such businesses to have access to cheaper payment methods (the cost of an mPOS terminal varies between $299 and $3,999 Mexican pesos with commission starting at 3%) with quick processing times (cash available within three days) without having to go through a bank. Some mPOS terminals also allow the business owner to defer payments, which represents an advantage for the customer but a higher cost for the business.

There are currently 10.8 million mPOS users in Mexico and this number is expected to grow to 19.6 million by 2024 [3]. Although this may seem like a small number compared to the country's population, it will represent a penetration rate of 14.6%. If we compare this to the mPOS transaction value globally, according to the same source, China is in first place (with the highest penetration) and Mexico is in 13th place.

Researchers have been concerned with the study of new technologies to replace cash. [1] analyzed payment methods from cash and standard cards, contactless cards, RFID stickers and mobile payments (NFC and remote). This study found that the most popular electronic payment method in history was contactless cards (used in offline mode and without printing paper slips). This method is even faster than cash. However, [4] find that few societies are close to a "cashless" or even "less cash," model. In fact, there has been a resurgence in the use of cash that appears to be driven by store-of-value motives rather than by payment needs. While there may still be an interest in cash, the current pandemic has brought about concerns with hygiene, reinforcing the usefulness of cashless methods. Cashless technologies also offer a partial solution to Mexico's crime problem and its concern with safety. Not carrying cash can be an attractive option for citizens.

Understanding of the factors that affect the use of this technology among Mexican consumers is essential. Our research question is: *What is the impact of ease of use, carbon footprint and lifestyle on mPOS use in the context of a developing economy such as Mexico?* We constructed a survey with 249 responses and used structural equation modelling (SEM) to confirm that risk is the highest predictor of mPOS awareness in Mexico. This paper begins by presenting a review of the literature on the topic, focusing on the variables of ease of use, carbon footprint and lifestyle. In the methodology section, we present the sample, questionnaire development, measurement model and assessment. The final part of the paper presents the results along with a discussion section that considers practical and policy implications.

2 Reviewed Literature and Hypotheses Formulation

Some research streams have used well-known theories to explain the adoption and use of mPOS technology, such as UTAUT, TAM or TPB. This paper presents a model of mPOS use in Mexico using ease of use, carbon footprint reduction, and compatibility with lifestyle. Hence, the three variables proposed were used to hypothesize on mPOS technology due to their relevance in the mobile context.

2.1 Lifestyle

An important stream of literature on lifestyle and technology, has looked at the effectiveness of novel ICTs, such as Internet and mobile applications to improve lifestyle and is therefore found commonly in medical journals [5, 6]. That is, it has focused on the effect of the technology on a healthy lifestyle. Other literature streams have focused on studying the role of technology on digital lifestyles in an educational context. Such is the work of [7], who study the 'digital lifestyle' afforded by technologies and how this impact on students' values and attitudes, their level of digital literacy, and approach to their studies. They find that the 'digital lifestyle' did not always create a balanced way of life. This is because connectedness to information, abilities to engage in the uses of technologies in multiple contexts and while completing other tasks, as well as student's expectations of speed and reliability impacted at times on their personal, social, and emotional lives. Therefore, technology appears to be affecting the personal lifestyle.

A third stream of literature is the one that looks at the effect of lifestyle in the adoption of a technology. For example, studies that find that lifestyle patterns have a significant impact on mobile banking applications users [8]. Other recent studies have highlighted the age and generational difference between users as factors that determine technology adoption [9]. Student populations are usually young and have slightly different lifestyles to older ones, however a mix of students that includes graduate ones can provide a wider view where lifestyles may vary. However, not only students but most humans globally engage in mobile activities either for personal or work matters. Hence, lifestyle is an important variable to hypothesize on mPOS technology due its relevance in the mobile context and we therefore define it as:

H1: Personal lifestyle has a positive impact on the use of mPOS.

2.2 Reduction of Carbon Footprint

The carbon footprint left by the production of good and the delivery of services is a growing global concern, and the use of mobile technologies is no exception. Energy consumption and carbon emissions may concern mobile users. Considering the increase in the number of mobile phones in use in the world today, the carbon footprint of such technology becomes an important concern. In 2020, there are 14.2 billion devices in use and by 2023 that number is expected to grow to 16.8 billion [3].

Annual per capita carbon emission targets have been established in the global and production of carbon emissions is projected to decline between 2010 and 2030 in all G20 economies except China, India, Indonesia, the Russian Federation, Saudi Arabia, and

Turkey [10]. Mexico performs under the current policies and NDC scenarios, however, it was responsible for 1.5% of global greenhouse gas GHG emissions in 2017 [11].

Researchers have shown that ICT adoption can in fact contribute to a reduction in energy consumption and CO_2 impact [12]. Recent data indicate that there is more potential for carbon emissions reduction in other sectors, which could deliver carbon savings five times larger than the total emissions from the entire ICT sector in 2020 [13].

There is a considerable amount of research on "green IT" [14–17], that is, on the effects of technology on carbon emissions and studies on IT policies and their impacts on IT production and use [18]. The impact of individual attitudes on the adoption of carbon-reducing technologies has been studied before [10] and although there is a body of IS research, which looks at this, [19] finds that more empirical research on the factors influencing adoption of green technologies is needed. The current pandemic showing the effects of carbon footprint on our ecosystem and health may impact the use of technology. The study of user knowledge and care about carbon footprint is therefore useful and can be stated as:

H2: Perceived knowledge of a reduced carbon footprint has a positive impact on the use of mPOS.

2.3 Ease of Use

Ease of use is "the degree to which a person believes that using a particular system will be free of effort" [20]. Ease of use is a variable that has been traditionally studied following the UTAUT model. An example of this is the work of [21], who finds that ease of use significantly impacted on users' trust in mobile social software for recreational purposes and its eventual use. TAM was used by [22] to show that ease of use significantly impacts the adoption of mobile technology and should therefore be studied with caution.

Perceived ease of use and attitude were found to be jointly responsible in determining the subscribers' intention to use of 3G mobile service [23]. Other research on convenience has found it tends to be the most affecting perceptions of consumers on usefulness and ease of use [24] in a mobile commerce context. Perceived ease of use also affects customer satisfaction [25], and one can, therefore suggest it will affect the use of technology. This is important information for software developers to pay more attention to mPOS' ease of use function.

Different results are presented by [26], who find that we found that ease of use was less significant in understanding repurchase intention to use mobile technologies. Our study focuses on the user's use of the technology when presented with it as a form of payment, it is then interesting to find out if users consider ease of use an important factor when using mPOS. Hence, the last hypothesis formulation is as follows:

H3: Ease of use has a positive impact on the use of mPOS.

3   Methodology for the Study

This study adopts quantitative methodology [27] to generate knowledge and create understanding about mPOS and how it affects the Mexican society. It helps to learn about student population and to examine questions about the tertiary students as the sample population. Earlier study has used tertiary students to identify the online shopping behaviour [28].

The data analysis was done using the SmartPLS (v. 3.3.3) statistics software. Descriptive statistics were used to illustrate the basic features of the data, and inferential statistics were used to probe the assessed questions, proposed model, and formulated hypotheses were tested with SmartPLS bootstrapping with 5000 subsamples and two-tailed with a significance level of (0.05).

3.1 Questionnaire Design

The questionnaire was designed and administered in Spanish (the official language in the country), but later translated the gathered data into English Language through a native speaker with proficiency of both Spanish and English language. Also, the questionnaire was managed through Qualtrics online survey platform. 5-point Likert scale characterize the questions with minimum of disagree (1) and maximum of strongly agree (5) and established on the earlier studies. The study adapts and reuses the lifestyle variable with modification from [29]. Likewise, the variable of Carbon footprint from [12, 19, 30]; and ease of use from [31]; and mPOS use from [32].

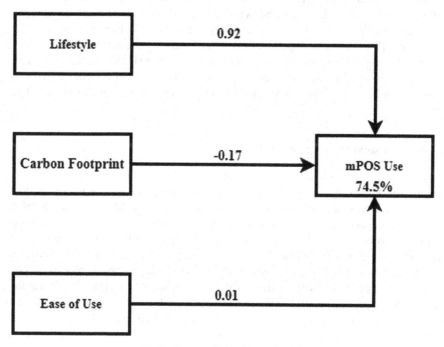

Fig. 1. Proposed mPOS use model.

3.2 Sampling for the Study

The study is based on a survey of undergraduate and graduate students. The survey was directed to students from the Universidad de las Américas, Puebla (UDLAP), one of the country's best private universities in Mexico. The university has a student population of 10,000. Therefore, the study has a 320-person sample size, with an 85% confidence level, and a 4% margin of error. Out of the 320-questionnaire administered, only 249 were relevant after the data cleaning process. The study used SPSS v. 26 for descriptive analysis and the results show that the age group that are younger than 21 accounts for 1 (0.4%), age bracket 21–25 years old accounts for 234 (94%) while age group 26 and above accounts for 14 (5.6%). The participants age bracket 21–25 dominate the survey. Regarding technology proficiency, 9 participants fall to the category of a beginner (3.6%), 122 participants are technology proficient at intermediate level (49%), 113 are advanced users (45.4%) and only 5 participants are technology proficient at expert level (2%). Majority of the participants are intermediate technology users (details in Table 2).

4 Results

mPOS is inevitable for a country like Mexico with population of 127.6 million. mPOS disruptions is advancing to replace the traditional point of sale and it is extremely useful to prevent long queue in the stores and its portability and cost effectiveness are of importance to the retailing stores. The interoperability of mPOS with other systems is another strength of mPOS. A recent paper confirmed the interest of the corner store owners in using mPOS adaptation that they called Point of Sale Tablet (POST) in Baltimore City, Maryland. The study utilised descriptive statistics and carried out a variance structural equation modelling [33]. This study reports the results under measurement and structural model.

4.1 mPOS Use Measurement Model

The use of partial least square structural equation modelling (PLS-SEM) is progressing with SmartPLS data analysis software because of its simplicity and user-friendly interface [16, 34]. This study considered the data quality based on different metrics before embarking on structural equation modelling and take a cue from the study of [35]. The results of measurement model shows that the composite reliability of the three variables conform to the established thresholds of 0.7 and average variance extracted also conform to the thresholds of 0.5. The study tests the internal consistency and establishes the convergent validity of the variables utilized. The factors loading were above 0.5. Regarding the effect size of the variables, compatibility with lifestyle had the highest effect size of 0.975, followed by reduction of the carbon footprint with 0.102 while the ease of use had no effect size. As related in the existing literature, compatibility with lifestyle had large effects while carbon footprint had small effect size on mPOS use [36]. Table 1 and 3 gives full account of the quality criteria of this study.

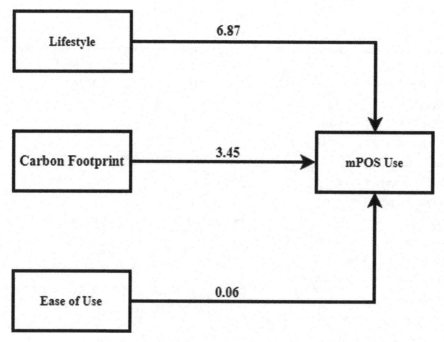

Fig. 2. mPOS use model.

4.2 MPOS Use Structural Model

This study used three independent variables (compatibility with lifestyle, reduction of carbon footprint and ease of use) to predicts mPOS use with three hypotheses (H1–H3). That is, mPOS use (H1) in Mexico is compatible with user's lifestyle ($\beta = 0.92$, T = 6.87, P = 0.001). Also, the mPOS use in Mexico reduces the carbon footprint and promote green environment ($\beta = -0.17$, T = 3.45, P = 0.001) and perceived ease of use of mPOS device increases its use in Mexico ($\beta = 0.01$, T = 0.06, P = 0.954). The ease-of-use p-value is greater than 0.05 and the hypothesis was rejected. On the other hand, compatibility for the lifestyle is the highest predictor of mPOS use. The hypotheses formulated for compatibility for lifestyle and reduction of carbon footprint was accepted (Figs. 1, 2 and Table 4). The model of mPOS use explained 74.5% of the variance.

Table 1. Measurement threshold for mPOS use model.

Variables and items	Factor loading	$f2$	Composite reliability	Average variance extracted
Lifestyle		0.975	0.893	0.736
Lifestyle 1	0.873			
Lifestyle 3	0.861			
Lifestyle 4	0.841			
Carbon footprint		0.102	0.960	0.923
Carbon footprint 1	0.939			
Carbon footprint 3	0.981			
Ease of use		0.000	0.920	0.793
Ease of use 2	0.808			
Ease of use 3	0.934			
Ease of use 4	0.924			
mPOS use		–	0.964	0.931
mPOS use 1	0.965			
mPOS use 2	0.964			

Note: The authors removed the variables that had low threshold (<0.5).

Table 2. mPOS use demographic values.

Demographic	Indicator	Frequency	Percent
Age	Younger than 21	1	0.4
	21–25 years old	234	94
	26 and above	14	5.6
Technology proficiency	Beginner	9	3.6
	Intermediate	122	49
	Advanced	113	45.4
	Expert	5	2

Table 3. mPOS use discriminant validity values.

	Carbon footprint	Ease of use	Lifestyle	mPOS
Carbon footprint	0.960			
Ease of use	0.499	0.890		
Lifestyle	0.424	0.842	0.858	
mPOS	0.220	0.694	0.851	0.965

Table 4. Tested hypotheses

	Original sample	Standard deviation	T statistics	P values	Hypotheses validation
Lifestyle -> mPOS use	0.917	0.133	6.873	0.001	Accepted
Carbon footprint -> mPOS use	−0.174	0.050	3.450	0.001	Accepted
Ease of use -> mPOS use	0.009	0.155	0.057	0.954	Rejected

5 mPOS Results Discussion

Small businesses and individuals are moving towards alternative payment system in Mexico due to the pricey fees charged by the existing banks and due to the bank's excessively complicated administrative procedure. Despite the benefits of alternative payment system, there is still a gap in mPOS adoption, use and continuous use in Mexico. For instance, a study [37] proposed a mPOS fourteen (14) years ago with added value of construction and maintenance cost reduction. After fourteen (14) years some countries are still in between acceptance and resistance of the alternative payment solution. This study employed descriptive, measurement and structural statistics to explain the phenomenon of mPOS and to answer the research questions. The study intends to know why compatibility with lifestyle, reduction of carbon footprint and ease of use are the determinants of mPOS use in Mexico. Earlier research defined compatibility as "perceived cognitive distance between an innovation and precursor methods for accomplishing tasks" [38]. Inferring from the earlier definition, this study define compatibility with lifestyle as a behaviour of mPOS users based on their preference. This study found the compatibility with lifestyle as the highest predictor of mPOS use and this result align with the recent study of [39]. The corresponding study found that customer lifestyle compatibility influences intention to use the food delivery apps. The higher the perception of compatibility with lifestyle, the higher the mPOS use. The effect of carbon footprint is a global phenomenon [40]. Another study found that exposure to information supporting the conspiracy theories reduces participants of the study intentions to reduce their carbon footprint. Reduction of carbon footprint predicts the mPOS use which indicates that the higher the perception of carbon footprint reduction, the higher the mPOS use. Contrary to other results, ease of use is not significant in this study. This result aligns with the study of [31]. This result shows that understanding how to use the mPOS is not yet clear for the Mexican. The study also concludes that mPOS in Mexico will promote a green environment and make Mexican society healthy. Theoretically, this study integrates user's habits and green driver to showcase mPOS use model. First, this study shows the direct relationship of compatibility with lifestyle and reduction of carbon footprint as drivers of mPOS use. This result shows path to cashless and green economy in Mexico.

5.1 mPOS Use Managerial Discussion

Managerial wise, this study suggests that the mPOS service providers in Mexico should pay closer attention to mPOS users' lifestyle. Besides, mPOS service providers should consider the carbon footprint and lifestyle when addressing their product to a specific customer segment.

5.2 mPOS Use Limitations and Future Discussion

This study was only limited to the University students and a single country but since mPOS disruption is a global phenomenon, the future researcher should test the model of this study in other countries. The researcher should add some psychology variables such as anxiety, mood, and satisfaction to add the perspective of emotional attachment to mPOS.

References

1. Polasik, M., Górka, J., Wilczewski, G., Kunkowski, J., Przenajkowska, K., Tetkowska, N.: Time efficiency of point-of-sale payment methods: empirical results for cash, cards and mobile payments. In: Cordeiro, J., Maciaszek, L.A., Filipe, J. (eds.) ICEIS 2012. LNBIP, vol. 141, pp. 306–320. Springer, Heidelberg (2013). https://doi.org/10.1007/978-3-642-40654-6_19
2. INEGI. Estadísticas a propósito del día de las Micros, Pequeñas y Medianas Empresas Comunicado de Prensa, 25 June 2020. https://www.inegi.org.mx/contenidos/saladeprensa/aproposito/2020/MYPIMES20.pdf
3. Statista. Forecast number of mobile devices worldwide from 2019 to 2023 (2020). (in billions). https://www.statista.com/statistics/245501/multiple-mobile-device-ownership-worldwide/
4. Bech, M.L., Faruqui, U., Ougaard, F., Picillo, C.: Payments are a-changin' but cash still rules. BIS Quart. Rev. (2018)
5. Afshin, A., et al.: Information technology and lifestyle: a systematic evaluation of internet and mobile interventions for improving diet, physical activity, obesity, tobacco, and alcohol use. J. Am. Heart Assoc. 5(9), (2016)
6. Wang, J., Cai, C., Padhye, N., Orlander, P., Zare, M.: A behavioral lifestyle intervention enhanced with multiple-behavior self-monitoring using mobile and connected tools for underserved individuals with type 2 diabetes and comorbid overweight or obesity: pilot comparative effectiveness trial. JMIR mHealth uHealth 6(4), (2018)
7. McMahon, M., Pospisil, R.: Laptops for a digital lifestyle: The role of ubiquitous mobile technology in supporting the needs of millennial students. In: Educause Australasia (2005)
8. Al-Dmour, R., Dawood, E.A.H., Al-Dmour, H., Masa'deh, R.E.: The effect of customer lifestyle patterns on the use of mobile banking applications in Jordan. Int. J. Electron. Market. Retail. 11(3), 239–258 (2020)
9. Yu, C.S.: Using e-lifestyle to analyze mobile banking adopters and non-adopters. J. Global Inf. Technol. Manage. 18(3), 188–213 (2015)
10. Lin, S.M.: Reducing students' carbon footprints using personal carbon footprint management system based on environmental behavioural theory and persuasive technology. Environ. Educ. Res. 22(5), 658–682 (2016)
11. UN Environmental Programme. Emissions Gap Report 2019 (2019). https://www.unenvironment.org/resources/emissions-gap-report-2019

12. Gelenbe, E., Caseau, Y.: The impact of information technology on energy consumption and carbon emissions. Ubiquity **2015**, 1–15 (2015)
13. The Climate Group. McKinsey Company, SMART 2020: Enabling the low carbon economy in the information age (2020). https://www.theclimategroup.org/sites/default/files/archive/files/Smart2020Report.pdf
14. Murugesan, S.: Harnessing green IT: principles and practices‖. IT Prof. **10**(1), 24–33 (2008)
15. Fuchs, C.: The implications of new information and communication technologies for sustainability. Environ. Dev. Sustain. (10)3, 291–309 (2008)
16. Cohen, M.C., Lobel, R., Perakis, G.: The impact of demand uncertainty on consumer subsidies for green technology adoption. Manage. Sci. **62**(5), 1235–1258 (2016)
17. Du, K., Li, J.: Towards a green world: how do green technology innovations affect total-factor carbon productivity. Energy Policy **2019**(131), 240–250 (2019)
18. Kraemer, K.L., Dedrick, J., Melville, N.P., Zhu, K. (eds.) Global e-Commerce: Impacts of National Environment and Policy. Cambridge University Press, New York (2006)
19. Dedrick, J.L.: Green IS: concepts and issues for information systems research. CAIS **27**(1), 11 (2010)
20. Davis, F.D.: Perceived usefulness, perceived ease of use, and user acceptance of information technology. Manage. Inf. Sci. Quart. **13**(3), 319–340 (1989)
21. Chinomona, R.: The influence of perceived ease of use and perceived usefulness on trust and intention to use mobile social software. Afr. J. Phys. Health Educ. Recreat. Dance **19**(2), 258–273 (2013)
22. Kaasinen, E.: User acceptance of mobile services: value, ease of use, trust and ease of adoption (2005)
23. Suki, N.M., Suki, N.M.: Exploring the relationship between perceived usefulness, perceived ease of use, perceived enjoyment, attitude and subscribers' intention towards using 3G mobile services. J. Inf. Technol. Manage. **22**(1), 1–7 (2011)
24. Bendary, N., Al-Sahouly, I.: Exploring the extension of unified theory of acceptance and use of technology, UTAUT2, factors effect on perceived usefulness and ease of use on mobile commerce in Egypt. J. Bus. Retail Manage. Res. **12**(2) (2018)
25. Ohk, K., Park, S.B., Hong, J.W.: The influence of perceived usefulness, perceived ease of use, interactivity, and ease of navigation on satisfaction in mobile application. Adv. Sci. Technol. Lett. **84**(2015), 88–92 (2015)
26. Amoroso, D.L., Lim, R.A.: Exploring the personal innovativeness construct: the roles of ease of use, satisfaction and attitudes. Asia Pac. J. Inf. Syst. **25**(4), 662–685 (2015)
27. Prihatiningtias, Y.W., Wardhani, M.R.: Understanding the effect of sustained use of cloud-based point of sales on SMEs performance during covid-19 pandemic. Indonesian Account. Rev. **11**(1) (2021)
28. Ofori, D., Appiah-Nimo, C.: Determinants of online shopping among tertiary students in Ghana: an extended technology acceptance model. Cogent Bus. Manage. **6**(1), 1644715 (2019)
29. Kim, K., Kim, G.M., Kil, E.S.: Measuring the compatibility factors in mobile entertainment service adoption. J. Comput. Inf. Syst. **50**(1), 141–148 (2009)
30. Brown, J.R., Guiffrida, A.L.: Carbon emissions comparison of last mile delivery versus customer pickup. Int. J. Logist. Res. Appl. **17**(6), 503–521 (2014)
31. Shaw, N.: The mediating influence of trust in the adoption of the mobile wallet. J. Retail. Cons. Serv. **21**(4), 449–459 (2014)
32. Kim, C., Tao, W., Shin, N., Kim, K.S.: An empirical study of customers' perceptions of security and trust in e-payment systems. Electron. Commer. Res. Appl. **9**(1), 84–95 (2010)
33. Olaleye, S.A., Salo, J., Sanusi, I.T., Okunoye, A.O.: Retailing mobile app usefulness: Customer perception of performance, trust and tension free. Int. J. E-Serv. Mob. Appl. (IJESMA) **10**(4), 1–17 (2018)

34. Olaleye, S.A., Sanusi, I.T., Mark, F.S., Salo, J.: Customers' loyalty to tablet commerce in Nigeria. Afr. J. Sci. Technol. Innov. Dev. **12**(2), 217–229 (2020)
35. Hair, Jr., J.F., Hult, G.T.M., Ringle, C., Sarstedt, M.: A Primer on Partial Least Squares Structural Equation Modeling (PLS-SEM). Sage Publications (2016)
36. Carson, C.: The effective use of effect size indices in institutional research. In: Proceedings of the 2004 American Society for Engineering Education Annual Conference & Exposition, pp. 41–48 (2012)
37. Kwon, O., Shin, H.C.: Mobile point-of-sales system. Convergence Secur. J. **7**(3), 87–93 (2007)
38. Karahanna, E., Agarwal, R., Angst, C.M.: Reconceptualizing compatibility beliefs in technology acceptance research. MIS Quart. 781–804 (2006)
39. Belanche, D., Flavián, M., Pérez-Rueda, A.: Mobile apps use and wom in the food delivery sector: The role of planned behavior, perceived security and customer lifestyle compatibility. Sustainability **12**(10), 4275 (2020)
40. Olaleye, S.A., Sanusi, I.T.: The need for green companies in Nigeria: a study of electronic invoicing. Afr. J. Inf. Syst. **11**(1), 1 (2019)

Augmented Reality-Based Dance Training System: A Study of Its Acceptance

Javid Iqbal[1]([✉]) and Manjit Singh Sidhu[2]

[1] Institute of Computer Science and Digital Innovation (ICSDI), UCSI University, Kuala Lumpur, Malaysia
`javid@ucsiuniversity.edu.my`
[2] Department of Informatics, College of Computing and Informatics (CCI), Universiti Tenaga Nasional (UNITEN), Kajang, Malaysia

Abstract. Blending the user environment with digital information in a real-world scenario is characterizes as Augmented Reality (AR). In the field of learning and training, there are many state-of-art learning theories that focus on behaviorism, cognitivism and constructivism domains. Therefore, we aim to develop an AR based Dance Training System (ARDTS) for teaching psychomotor skills (voluntary dance movements) based on the category of constructivism learning theory. The dance training systems based on AR fall under the category of cognitivism learning theory, where the learner is provided with the feedback for a subsequent training session based upon the output of the previous session (history of performance). On the other hand, the proposed ARDTS is developed based upon the information flow model of constructivism learning theory where the feedback is based upon learner's actions, self-learning and overall competence making it distinctive in comparison to the existing systems. ARDTS is investigated and validated for user acceptance based upon the Technology Acceptance Model (TAM). This multiplayer fun-filled dance training system with interactive feedback and guidance mechanism is the ultimate outcome that eventually is evaluated and validated for user acceptance.

Keywords: Augmented Reality · Dance training · Kinect

1 Introduction and Motivation

AR is a computer vision (CV) discipline which is characterized as blending the user environment with digital information in a real-world scenario. On the other hand, Virtual Reality (VR) offers a complete digitally built virtual world, AR uses the actual world and overlaps supporting novel knowledge on top of that [1]. AR is employed as a complement to a standard curriculum, where graphics, text, audio, and video are superimposed into the real-time environment of the student. AR focuses on making human life easier by integrating virtual information not only to the present environment but also to any indirect view of the real-time scenario [2]. This research focused primarily on solving long-term learning retention and poor learning efficiency to master a dance skill through

© Springer Nature Switzerland AG 2021
G. Salvendy and J. Wei (Eds.): HCII 2021, LNCS 12796, pp. 219–228, 2021.
https://doi.org/10.1007/978-3-030-77025-9_19

AR technology based on constructivism learning theory and TAM. Self-learning and long-term learning retention have seldom been focused in AR based education till date for excelling in any art forms there is an intrigue necessity for the evolution of self-learning-based AR training systems. Moreover, the contribution of virtual reality and AR towards making human lives easier and comfortable still needs major research attention by the experts and research developers [3]. The need for self-learning AR based dance education serves as the main motivation of this research.

Therefore, this research focuses on providing a novel interactive NUI with visual cues and pose matching mechanism, so that it can provide long-term retention, for the dance trainee. Dance is a creative art, can be learned efficiently through engagement, motivation and peer-based competitive interfaces. The existing dance training system comparatively lacks this core essential feature for increased learning efficiency [4]. Therefore, the major motivation for this research is also increasing the overall learning efficiency by mastering the dance skills in comparison to the state-of-art techniques/systems.

2 Statement of the Problem

The existing training systems lacks behind major aspects of self-learning, poor efficiency and increase learning time has eventually motivated for the proposed research [5]. This research is aimed to address and fill all the above-mentioned research gaps through distinct and interactive AR based dance training system.

The research questions are to be answered and addressed through the research objectives and a novel interactive self-learning AR based dance training system is designed, developed, implemented and validated in this research. The performance metrics for comparative analysis are learning efficiency and learning time of the system in comparison with the state-of-art techniques/systems. The knowledge about the user's acceptance and perspective is aimed to be the ultimate outcome based on quantitative analysis and investigation of the influential factors.

The key research questions include improvisations of the existing AR based dance training mechanism followed by increasing the learning efficiency and influential factors for acceptance of novel ARDTS system. The corresponding research objectives deal with developing dynamic pose matching mechanism based on skeletal mapping for multiple users which is further validated using TAM. The research is aimed to achieve the outcome of novel interactive feedback mechanism comprising of visual cues and matching percentage for multi-user thereby leading to long-term learning retention NUI, increased learning efficiency and insights into user acceptance.

3 Design of the Study

An empirical research approach was designed and implemented in order to achieve the research objectives and meet the research goal. The research approach used is quantitative method and comparative analysis which helps to address the in-depth problems, research questions and the objectives. The quantitative method in this research will extract its data from the questionnaires distributed to the users. The participants were carefully selected and a pilot study was conducted in order to hone and enhance the robustness of the questionnaire and to achieve a higher degree of accuracy. The quantitative information is the data gathered from the TAM questionnaire as described in [6]. These questionnaires were designed according to the principle concepts underlying the current research and the literature.

The comparative analysis adopted in this research will help to compare the findings of previous researchers and hence can benchmark those findings to provide new findings and outcome. The empirical research design employed in the current research has been depicted in Fig. 1. The research design is a framework of approaches and methods to efficiently handle the research problem and to attain the objective of the study. Figure 2 depicts the flowchart for research design.

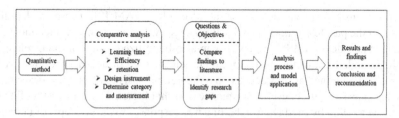

Fig. 1. Empirical research approach

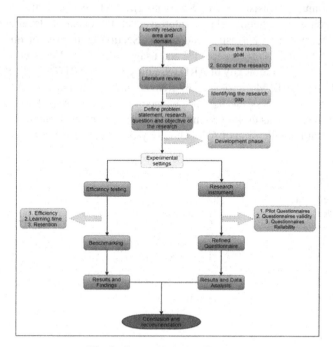

Fig. 2. Research design flowchart

4 Sampling Process and Techniques

Non-probability convenience sampling technique was employed throughout this current research. Convenience sampling is a non-probability sampling technique where subjects are selected by their convenient accessibility and proximity to the research domain [7] Preliminary analysis suggests that this approach has satisfied the criteria for the target population. The sample unit for this research is new dance learners from dance schools and university.

5 The Instrument Designs

The research instrument employed for the research is TAM [8]. These models have evolved over the past few years to provide the user's level of acceptance for technological applications and devices [9]. The TAMs can also be utilized as a tool to correlate and relate the intended use of the users with their actual usage of devices. In other words, they can also be defined as approaches on a theoretical basis to derive and describe the factors that cause and affect user's acceptance of technologies. The TAM was delineated during the year 1989 by Fred Davis labelling it as responses to the concepts of Perceived Usefulness (PU) and Perceived Ease of Use (PEOU) and their relativeness to the overall attitude towards using a system by the potential user.

The questionnaire consists of two Sections. The first Section is the demographic information such as age, gender, dance interest level, the expertise level and the percentage of dance learning curiosity. The second Section comprises of questions that deal directly with the ARDTS acceptance and usage, which are Perceived Ease of use, Perceived Usefulness, Complexity of ARDTS, Enjoyment of ARDTS, Self-efficacy, and Intention to Use. The TAM consists of 37 items which come under 6 TAM factors as depicted in Fig. 3, to assess the user acceptance of proposed ARDTS [6]. There are many research instruments employed in the literature for physical training or gamification consoles. But for validation of AR technology-based dance learning systems, it was

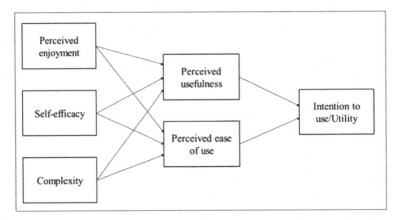

Fig. 3. TAM with external variables

found that TAM serves to be the best fit as it provides the knowledge on the willingness of users towards utilization and acceptance of the system [10].

6 Design of ARDTS

The design and implementation of ARDTS, which demonstrates the appropriate way of performing advanced moves with real-time feedback is depicted in Fig. 4.

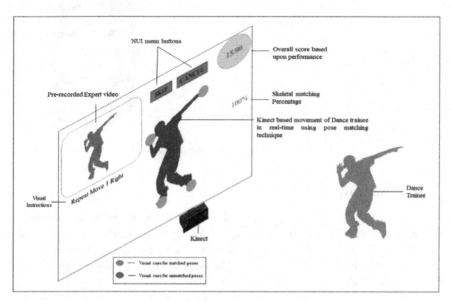

Fig. 4. ARDTS system model

The proposed Pose matching mechanism include the submodules of defining the joints of interest, the moving joints, body size factor, pose limit and matched pose for the scoring performance by the trainee are implemented and evaluated using the ARDTS.

The ARDTS system is designed and developed in a way which will provide ease of use to the new learner. In order to get rid of unwanted cables, wires, and mouse clicks, as in the existing systems, but functionality ARDTS supports Natural User Interface (NUI). NUI is a user interface for HCI, that the user operates through intuitive action of natural gestures. A click in ARDTS system is to touch the required button in NUI for 3 s to perform its operation. In order to make the menu buttons easily selectable, all the buttons are placed to the right-hand side of the user since the majority of the population are right-handed. Left-hand users are excluded from this chapter as depicted in Fig. 5.

Fig. 5. User interface of the proposed ARDTS

6.1 Single User Layout

As depicted in Fig. 6, the left top side of the screen is for the professional dancer's video and below the video, a subtitle textual cue, will queue which is used to display the next step to be performed through the session. The scoreboard is placed on the top right corner to motivate the dance learner. The skeletal matching percentage is placed at the right side of the dance learner. When the dance learner is performing his dance learning session, the screen has two 3D buttons on the top of the screen in order to select the option of skip/cancel. The following circumstances can serve the purpose of these options:

Skip: If the dance learner is not familiar with the dance move even after repeated training, he/she can skip the current move by clicking on the skip button, so that the video jumps to the next move.

Cancel: Can be opted at any point of time if the dance learner wants to change the dance style and dance level. The dance learning session can also be stopped through the selection of this button.

6.2 Multi User Mode Layout

After selecting the multi-dancer mode, the learner screen splits into two equals halves with two different matching percentage and scoreboard in order to calculate individual performance as shown in Fig. 7. The dominant dancer will be the dancer 1 since he takes the right side of the screen and he/she has access to the cancel and skip buttons. The dominant dancer is assumed to be on the right (although the order of appearance

Fig. 6. Single user screen of ARDTS

Fig. 7. Multi-user mode of ARDTS

determines the dominance). The left side is the Dancer 2 who will cooperatively be calibrated for the dance steps performed according to the expert of pre-recorded video. This option essentially serves to provide competition among peers and for constructive learning.

7 Statistical Analysis Method

The measuring instrument (questionnaires) used in this research is based upon TAM, in order to assess the overall acceptability of ARDTS. The questionnaire that was used as the research instrument comprises of 37 items which come under 6 factors primarily used to assess the newly developed ARDTS. The responses were scored on a 7-point Likert scale (strongly disagree to strongly agree). Individually the subjects were required to conduct a training session with the Kinect device. The researchers keenly monitored the session to track and recognise any problems that the participants experienced during preparation. Through the NUI and interactive audio input, the subjects were asked to choose from the level of competency and type of dance style. The time period for each of the session-performing subjects was dependent on the chosen dance style and level of competence. The initial design of the ARDTS was set up at M.G.R. University, Chennai.

8 Results

The ARDTS was tested for acceptability and usability among 86 subjects with the aid of TAM. This model was constructed based upon 37 items categorized according to 6 factors. The graphical representation in Fig. 8 depicts the standard deviation and mean for the categorized 6 factors. The research instrument was tested among the subjects, wherein the responses were recorded on a 7-point scale ranging from "strongly disagree to strongly agree". The statistical mean for each of the six TAM factors ranged from 4.14 (related to complexity of ARDTS) to 5.94 (enjoyment of ARDTS) respectively [5]. Through these statistical mean values, it can be notably concluded that the subjects have indicated stronger acceptance towards the usage of ARDTS. Moreover, the minimum value of mean score which is 4.14 falls in the category above "Neutral" along a 7-point scale and on the other hand, the maximum value (5.94) equates to "Agree" in a 7-point scale.

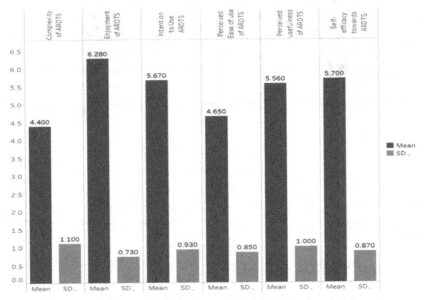

Fig. 8. The Mean and Standard deviation of ARDTS based upon six factors on TAM

The performance analysis for the comparison of proposed pose matching technique with the existing algorithms, in terms of frame level accuracy of matched poses has been tabulated in Table 1. Additionally, the proposed algorithm has lesser learning time in comparison to the existing techniques for mastering a particular dance style, as shown in Fig. 9.

Table 1. Performance analysis of the proposed system

Method	Accuracy	Learning time in secs
ARDTS skeletal mapping Mechanism (Proposed algorithm)	93.50%	120
Continuous Human Action Recognition (CHAR) [11]	92%	280
Pose Kinetic Energy [12]	91.90%	440
Actionlet [13]	74.70%	600
Sparse Coding [14]	65.30%	760

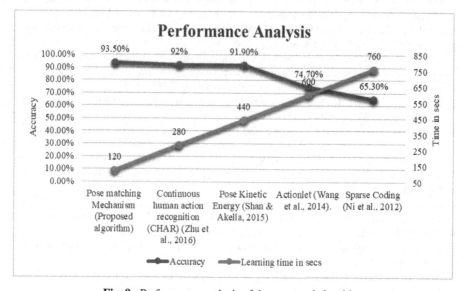

Fig. 9. Performance analysis of the proposed algorithm

9   Conclusion

The user acceptance rate of the proposed system is higher, clearly indicating likeliness of dance enthusiasts on contrary to other learning methods such as traditional training and video tutorials. The visual cues and interactive feedback for mastering a particular dance style as part of AR-based dance education in the constructivism learning theory have been demonstrated in this research. With the advancement of AR technology and the essence of skilful training, education mainly depends upon the training tools and learning environment in addition to the type of learning theory employed. The future of AR in the field of education and training has been envisioned to solve many existing technical challenges, but more importantly, it should also focus on creating a world-wide interest and impact for AR based training thereby leading towards a revolutionary impact on the overall e-learning education platform.

References

1. Milgram, P., Takemura, H., Utsumi, A., Kishino, F.: Augmented reality: a class of displays on the reality-virtuality continuum. Telemanipulator Telepresence Technol. **2351**, 282–292 (1994). https://doi.org/10.1117/12.197321
2. Azuma, R.T.: Predictive Tracking for Augmented Reality. February, 262 (1995). http://www.cs.unc.edu/techreports/95-007.pdf
3. Amin, D., Govilkar, S.: Comparative study of augmented reality SDK's. Int. J. Comput. Sci. Appl. **5**(1), 11–26 (2015). https://doi.org/10.5121/ijcsa.2015.5102
4. Fonseca, M.J., James, S., Collomosse, J.: Skeletons from sketches of dancing poses. In: Proceedings of IEEE Symposium on Visual Languages and Human-Centric Computing, VL/HCC, pp. 247–248 (2012). https://doi.org/10.1109/VLHCC.2012.6344537
5. Iqbal, J., Sidhu, M.S., Bin, M., Ariff, M.: AR oriented pose matching mechanism from motion capture data. Int. J. Eng. Technol. **7**, 294–298 (2018)
6. Iqbal, J., Sidhu, M.S.: A taxonomic overview and pilot study for evaluation of augmented reality based posture matching technique using technology acceptance model. Procedia Comput. Sci. **163**, 345–351 (2019). https://doi.org/10.1016/j.procs.2019.12.117
7. Sekaran, U., Bougie, R.: Research Methods for Business: a Skill-Building Approach. John Wiley & Sons Ltd., 7th edn. (2002)
8. Davis, F.D.: Perceived usefulness, perceived ease of use, and user acceptance of information technology. MIS Q. **13**(3), 319–340 (1989). http://www.jstor.org/stable/249008
9. Shore, L., Power, V., de Eyto, A., O'Sullivan, L.: Technology acceptance and user-centred design of assistive exoskeletons for older adults: a commentary. MDPI, Robot. **7**(1), 3 (2018). https://doi.org/10.3390/robotics7010003
10. Legris, P., Ingham, J., Collerette, P.: Why do people use information technology? A critical review of the technology acceptance model. Inf. Manage. Elsevier **40**, 191–204 (2003)
11. Zhu, G., Zhang, L., Shen, P., Song, J.: An online continuous human action recognition algorithm based on the kinect sensor. Sensors (Switzerland), **16**(2) (2016). https://doi.org/10.3390/s16020161
12. Shan, J., Akella, S.: 3D human action segmentation and recognition using pose kinetic energy. In: Proceedings of IEEE Workshop on Advanced Robotics and its Social Impacts, ARSO, pp. 69–75, January 2015. https://doi.org/10.1109/ARSO.2014.7020983
13. Wang, J., Liu, Z., Wu, Y., Yuan, J.: Learning actionlet ensemble for 3D human. IEEE Trans. Pattern Anal. Mach. Intell. **36**(5), 914–927 (2014). https://doi.org/10.1007/978-3-319-04561-0
14. Ni, B., Moulin, P., Yan, S.: Order-preserving sparse coding for sequence classification. In: Fitzgibbon, A., Lazebnik, S., Perona, P., Sato, Y., Schmid, C. (eds.) ECCV 2012. LNCS, vol. 7573, pp. 173–187. Springer, Heidelberg (2012). https://doi.org/10.1007/978-3-642-33709-3_13

Stakeholder Perceptions in the Context of Community Risk Reduction (CRR): Self-reported Hazards as Two-Way Communication Between First Responders and the Communities They Serve

Katelynn A. Kapalo[1](✉), Kevin P. Pfeil[1], Joseph A. Bonnell[2], and Joseph J. LaViola Jr.[1]

[1] University of Central Florida Orlando, Orlando, FL, USA
kate.kapalo@knights.ucf.edu
[2] Phoenix Fire Department, Phoenix, AZ, USA

Abstract. Due to rapid advances in technology, particularly location-based services, there has been an increase in the availability of self-reporting hazard tools and mobile applications. However, many challenges remain in understanding stakeholders' perceptions of community risk reduction (CRR) information systems and the impact these self-reports have on emergency response. This paper addresses the gap in the existing literature by combining theories and data from multiple disciplines. Existing research has traditionally focused on Wildland-Urban Interface (WUI), citizen science for Geographic Information Systems (GIS), and participatory mapping. Still, the extant literature does not comprehensively evaluate community stakeholders' perceptions and engagement in emergency preparedness efforts, particularly for applications intending to engage both civilians and first responders. More importantly, there is little existing research to better understand the relationships that exist between the first responders, technology, and residents they serve in their first-due areas. Consequently, this paper aims to provide an overview on how to best support multiple stakeholders and to foster more constructive communication between first responders and the communities they serve through technology mediated self-reporting tools.

Keywords: Community risk reduction · Emergency communications · User experience · Emergency response · Community engagement

1 Introduction

Due to recent advances in technology, people are connected now more than ever to their emergency services. The popularity of mobile applications has made community risk reduction (CRR) efforts further reaching. Recent developments in the area of mobile applications empower civilians to aid before emergency responders arrive on scene by

© Springer Nature Switzerland AG 2021
G. Salvendy and J. Wei (Eds.): HCII 2021, LNCS 12796, pp. 229–242, 2021.
https://doi.org/10.1007/978-3-030-77025-9_20

encouraging those certified in rendering cardiopulmonary resuscitation (CPR) to intervene [1, 2]. Additionally, some mobile applications create the opportunity for individuals to self-report medical data, similar to a digital medical alert bracelet, in case of emergencies. Seminal work in this area has summarized the impact of mobile applications in emergency response more broadly [3]. While the extant literature demonstrates the utility of applications for specific purposes, such as CPR interventions, most of this research takes the form of market research in industry, rather than a formal academic evaluation or approach. The goal of this paper is to outline some of the more important sociotechnical dimensions that can be conceptualized as an integrated framework for understanding how to support mobile and technology-mediated two-way communication between first responders and the community they serve.

2 Related Work

Trends in fire data indicate that the majority of fire-related deaths of both civilians and firefighters occur at the scene of residential structure fires [4]. As a result, there is a movement to increase the amount of data made available to first responders [5]. This additional information is not only to augment their understanding of residential structures in their first-due areas, but also as a way to engage citizens in hazard mitigation efforts. However, this movement is relatively understudied and presents new opportunities and challenges for all stakeholders involved in the collection, management, retrieval, storage, and security of this residential data.

To situate this paper in the extant literature, we will explore the existing models for CRR efforts. In particular, we examine how the Wildland-Urban Interface (WUI) community has successfully engaged citizens in risk reduction efforts to save lives and property. This paper will demonstrate the importance of understanding citizens and business owners' perceptions of the fire service. Specifically, we will examine the impact of the availability of residential structure data on first responders. One of the implications of these trends is that citizens may be reluctant to provide information if they do understand how and when it will be utilized. We also explore the impact of several sociotechnical dimensions (e.g., privacy, transparency, trust) on citizen engagement in CRR efforts.

It is important to operationalize the constructs and dimensions identified in this work. Although there is some debate depending upon the disciplinary lens through which these dimensions are evaluated, we leverage the existing definitions to further define this work. In this paper, community is defined as

2.1 Community Involvement: Current Domains and Directions

Citizen participation in risk-reduction activities has traditionally been shaped in two major ways. First and foremost, in terms of disaster and crisis response, citizens have been involved in the process to create more resilient communities through a focus on preparedness efforts [6]. We elaborate on this concept in further detail below. We begin with a broad discussion of public participation and then we move to other domains of public interest that have successfully implemented community involvement.

Emergency Preparedness. Across the literature, emergency preparedness is a common theme in the context of community participation in risk reduction efforts. For example, a large study in Atlanta focused on identifying and prioritizing fire inspections to reduce the risk of fire loss [7]. This approach leveraged machine learning techniques to better support fire agencies in identifying buildings at risk, consequently improving preparedness and mitigation efforts.

Home Visits. In the extant literature, home visits represent a significant portion of effective CRR strategies, particularly in the case of residential emergency preparedness [8]. Home visits are defined as strategies that focus on public safety officials leveraging face-to-face methods to engage in discussion about risks with citizens. The literature points to the utility of home visits internationally, that is, even outside the United States, home visits account for higher levels of engagement with civilians in the community [8]. Along these lines, studies in rural communities indicate that exposure to emergency preparedness materials and campaigns led to greater awareness of hazards and enhanced preparedness practices [9].

Wildland Urban Interface (WUI). Perhaps one of the richest areas that focus on citizen and community involvement in risk reduction efforts in the area of wildland firefighting. This literature is often described in terms of community involvement due to the serious nature of risk assessment and its impact on individual stakeholders [10–13]. More importantly, the risk to the community more broadly emphasizes the importance of sharing information between the public and the agencies serving them in times of crisis.

For example, the design of applications such as Wildfire Analyst supports wildland fire operations by allowing firefighters to dynamically assess fire behavior using real-time 3D models [14]. The advent of such mobile applications supports fire operations but typically does not involve end-users other than experienced firefighters who need to build situation awareness of the environment around them. Therefore, the majority of research in this area focuses more on risk communication messages to engage the public and local community in mitigation and preparedness efforts.

Similar to WUI risk, public health is a domain that has received considerable attention in terms of addressing community-wide involvement and mitigating public health crises based on location, vulnerability, and risk assessment. We provide a brief overview of the literature in this space below.

Public Health. In addition to emergency preparedness and hazard mitigation efforts, community engagement may also take the form of public health initiatives. As outlined by Israel et al. [15], the importance of individual risk factors often minimizes some of the barriers to accessibility of treatment and related concerns in managing public health issues. This has led to an emphasis on the idea that individuals are entrenched in social, political, and economic systems that are directly linked to maintaining health. Meaning that obstacles or barriers to accessing resources can negatively influence health outcomes. Consequently, there have been movements to address these barriers through community-based health initiatives. These initiatives focus on engaging citizens to participate directly in partnerships that contribute to understanding these barriers in a way that addresses inequity [15]. For example, this has led to programs that focus not only on integrating citizens into public health initiatives, but also focus on how to self-evaluate and measure the impact of these initiatives in terms that health organizations can leverage [16]. The design of such an assessment allows for organizations to monitor the efficacy in community involvement, ultimately leading to better outcomes for all stakeholders involved, including healthcare providers, patients, and communities.

Volunteered Geographic Information (VGI). The majority of research in stakeholder engagement beyond agency specific CRR efforts such as smoke detector initiatives, has focused on understanding the impact of involving citizens in the collection of GIS data, sometimes referred to as volunteered geographic information (VGI) [17]. This information is prevalent within the fields of GIS and geography and is gaining traction as a way for the government to gather large amounts of data. However, the quality and credibility of this information has been scrutinized for decades [18–20]. Due to the interdisciplinary nature of VGI and quality control challenges, **there currently is no existing integrative framework to interpret or apply stakeholder perceptions of security and privacy in the context of volunteered information for CRR efforts.** Moreover, there is little attention given to conceptualizing the structure of these information systems or mobile applications as *intentional communication, or dialogue,* between first responders and the citizens they serve.

We contend that these issues in crowdsourced information might hinder the creation of more comprehensive applications, as there is no current theoretical framework to paint a whole picture of how these findings fit together and how widely they can be applied. Consequently, it is critical to understand the ways to support both citizens and emergency responders in the context of these current and future data applications to better support all stakeholders involved in the process of managing hazard-related data. In subsequent sections of this paper, we draw from literature in multiple disciplines to better understand the impact of sociotechnical dimensions on community engagement in hazard mitigation.

2.2 The Changing Landscape of Emergency Response

Increasingly, new demands have been placed on first responders. As fire-based emergency medical services (EMS) have expanded, the demands and needs of emergency medical providers have shifted [21]. These new demands require a more comprehensive analysis of the information systems EMS providers rely upon to gather information about their communities and related risks. Additionally, this changing landscape requires expansion of the data management frameworks and approaches leveraged by first responders. The introduction of mobile applications to self-report medical history affords an opportunity for emergency medical providers to treat patients more effectively, but this data comes with a cost.

Additionally, this changing dynamic is impacted by the availability of information. Pre-incident plans are documents, paper or electronic, that provide essential information about a facility and its associated hazards to first responders in the event of an emergency [22]. Typically, firefighters and other first responders do not have access to pre-incident planning information for single-family homes and other residential structures outside of apartment complexes or long-term care facilities [23]. Efforts have been made to make pre-planning residential structures a higher priority, but these efforts are largely unique to each department and their responding areas [24]. Consequently, some departments do have the time or resources to manage residential structure data in addition to their existing pre-plan program. Recent studies have demonstrated the utility of such information in the context of residential fires [23, 24].

More importantly, firefighters also face hazard risks that they may not be adequately trained or equipped to understand, such as hoarding behaviors and vacant structures [25, 26]. These hazards increase the likelihood of injuries or fatalities on the fireground, which warrants closer consideration. The availability of data associated with these hazards could potentially reduce risk of injury or fatality, but this information is difficult to obtain, and civilians may be reluctant to report these types of hazards due to broader social and ethical barriers. Care must be taken when eliciting this information from socially vulnerable populations as well to ensure sound ethical guidelines are followed.

3 Method

We conducted a scoping review to map the landscape of the existing literature to better understand how different disciplines have addressed related concerns in CRR efforts. The purpose of this review was to identify work that has focused on stakeholder perceptions of self-reported hazards in the context of CRR efforts. More specifically, we were interested in examining the existing landscape with regard to the utility and availability of self-reported hazard data from the perspective of multiple stakeholders. These stakeholders would include the civilians uploading the information, the first responders leveraging the information on the scene of an emergency, and government agencies or other agencies that may play a role in emergency preparedness efforts or data management.

The process involved three iterations and was conducted between November 2020 and January 2021. We conducted our search via the ISI Web of Knowledge, EBSCO, and Science Direct. The search terms were derived from key words used in combination such as: "self-report and hazards," "self-reported hazards," "citizen engagement and risk reduction," "civic engagement and disaster response," "citizen involvement," "citizen participation," and "vulnerability assessment."

For the purposes of our literature review, articles must have met two criteria to warrant inclusion:

1. Peer reviewed and published work
2. Involved discussion of risk assessment or community risk reduction in the context of citizen participation or engagement

We excluded articles and works that covered topics outside the scope of citizen engagement, such as epidemiology. Our search terms identified over 500 papers that were initially reviewed for relevance based on the criteria above. Of the remaining articles, all were reviewed for relevancy and duplicates. A total of 37 papers were included in this review. We aggregated findings to communicate general trends related to sociotechnical dimensions of citizen engagement in CRR efforts to guide the broader discussion on how to enhance communication between the community and first responders in the context of self-reported hazards.

4   Results

This section outlines findings from our review of the literature. First, we provide a general overview of the articles. In the following sections, we identify the emergent themes gathered from the articles reviewed. We discuss some of the challenges and opportunities associated with maintaining citizen engagement and participation, as well as some of the more practical challenges associated with data management policies and processes. Then we leverage the framework initially proposed by Barnes [29] to map the existing landscape of participation and to provide guidance to agencies interested in exploring and evaluating dimensions of public participation in the context of self-reported hazards.

4.1   Thematic Analysis

Credibility. For the last decade, VGI credibility is often cited as a concern due to the crowdsourced nature of the information and the lack of experience on the part of involved citizens [18]. However, the increasing availability and involvement of multiple stakeholders is driving change in this area [20]. Although credibility is still a concern, VGI bridges a gap that otherwise may not be addressed due to the complexity and resource-heavy requirements of collecting large amounts of data.

Despite the increase in citizen participation, this still poses challenges due to the nature of the data. In the research context we have identified in this paper, we are examining the impact of self-reported hazards *on the success* of incident management, as represented by a first responder's ability to use this information. This has critical implications due to the dynamic nature of incident response and the importance of understanding how information is leveraged in crisis situations.

If citizens are not engaged in this kind of work, it is plausible that the information submitted may not be optimized for first responder use. In that case, either the agency collecting the information, or the first responder end-users must identify and refine the information for use on the scene of an emergency. This process is resource intensive and requires multiple quality control checks, which may not present a realistic solution for public safety agencies and departments that are already managing with less staff and resources.

Privacy. Dainty et al. [2] collected data on the perception of mobile applications that crowdsourced basic life support (BLS) from civilians for cardiac arrest incidents From their data, respondents indicated that legal and privacy concerns were an important issue. For example, location tracking and misuse of the data were brought up as potential data concerns. Additionally, further work in this space focused on stakeholder perceptions and end-user perceptions of the application [1]. We contend that this dimension of privacy and information security will impact the acceptance of these risk mitigation techniques within the community due to the nature of residential structure data. If participants have previously indicated that they are uncomfortable with the tracking and monitoring capabilities of a mobile application, it will be important to capture this information in order to strategize potential opportunities for technology adoption. Additionally, residential data would allow potential adversaries to gain critical information about community homes, that could lead to potential security breaches or dangerous outcomes. Therefore, data management and security will be of critical importance moving forward.

More specifically, from a first responder perspective, some of the challenge will come from interpreting the information submitted. However, the greater challenge will be maintaining this information and keeping it secure so only authorized personnel can access the data, as outlined in the current (2020) version of the NFPA 1620 standard [22].

Reliability. One of the more critical aspects to consider is the reliability of information provided to first responders. To determine the reliability of information, it would be necessary for civilians to upload multiple versions of their data and for responders to track changes from one version to another. This presents data management challenges as first responders must work quickly and have different needs than civilian users of such a system. According to recent statistics, the average home can become dangerous within five minutes [28, 29]. Therefore, one of the more critical challenges will be presenting and displaying changes in information to first responders in a way that is easily consumed within just a few seconds.

Transparency. Given the information exchange between civilians and responders during the event of an emergency, transparency plays a critical role. As illustrated in previous research, transparency plays a role in ensuring that civilians heed warnings, as well as in practices for sound governance [32].

Trust. Trust in the context of CRR focuses on the interrelationships and connections between civilians, responders, and the public safety agency or government agency involved in risk communication processes. One of the key aspects of trust is this idea that the government or agencies having authority should be able to demonstrate that they have more resources and capabilities for identifying threats than individuals [33]. This relates to the idea of transparency, but even extends beyond that. For individuals and community members to build relationships with public safety agencies, trust is a critical factor [34].

Vulnerability. Vulnerability encompasses assessments that focus not only on physical vulnerability of property, but some of the broader concerns surrounding social vulnerability. Based upon the WUI literature and the extant literature related to citizen risk assessment, vulnerability remains an area that requires further exploration. This is because certain groups or populations may be more vulnerable than others, leading to health disparities or an inability to participate in initiatives designed to engage citizens due to accessibility barriers [35].

We summarize the important dimensions outlined in the review of the literature in the Table 1 below.

Table 1. Thematic analysis of the literature: sociotechnical themes identified

Dimension	Definition
Credibility	The level to which information gathered about hazards is actually representative. This encompasses source, as well as information credibility as well
Privacy	Refers to the general concept that all stakeholders have a right to selectively choose how information is shared about them
Reliability	The extent to which users can rely on the information (e.g., First responders are confident the information is accurate)
Transparency	Availability of information about how and why decisions are made
Trust	Belief that the intentions and behaviors of an agency or individual are inherently in the best interest of involved stakeholders
Vulnerability	The extent to which there is a possibility for harm

4.2 Framework for Public Participation

Seminal work in defining public participation focused on adopting a framework that clearly identified the key dimensions to analyze public participation. Although this paper serves as a review of the literature, it is important to identify how and why participation is required. To better understand how this applies to our work, we leverage Barnes' model to identify the key aspects of participation and to scope the problem space in terms of risk reduction efforts [29].

Whose Participation Is Being Sought. In the context of this paper, we are seeking to understand how the community or stakeholders located in a specific region, municipality, or county engage with public safety agencies in terms of data management practices. As mentioned by Barnes, it is important to distinguish **whether the public or the user** is the sample of interest. However, we contend that in this particular case, the users are the community or public we are referring to. This is because there are multiple stakeholders using systems designed for sharing this information across and between agencies and individuals. Therefore, *we define the users as civilians, business owners, community officials, as well as the first responders, incident commanders, federal, state, and local agencies that have access to, collect, and manage such data sources.*

Type of Knowledge Accessed Through Participation.
Perhaps most important in this framework is the type of knowledge accessed through participation. In the case of submitting information about residential structures, the type of knowledge accessed during participation is both *explicit and tacit.* We define these types of knowledge in greater detail.

Explicit knowledge is shared through recorded mediums [36]. In the case of self-reported hazard data, this information would be shared through a database or mobile application. It is recorded in the form of images, blueprints, descriptive text, and data that can be captured as artifacts for later use.

Tacit knowledge is more abstract than explicit knowledge [36]. Tacit knowledge is accessed through the ability of community members to share their experiences and through the willingness of first responders to understand and derive meaning from community member experience. For instance, studies demonstrate that tacit knowledge sharing is more likely to develop from relationship building and affect-based trust [37]. A form of tacit knowledge could be an understanding that a particular building in an area represents a community hub or area of value to that community. This could mean that in efforts to save life and property, this property is valued as central and meaningful to the community members. The ability to recognize this building as a value of the local community represents one example of how tacit knowledge could be shared between community members and first responders. This contrasts with the idea that the use or willingness to leverage tacit knowledge is grounded in cognition-based trust.

Location of Participation
Community members participate in their respective locations. Typically, this would mean the community they reside in, but in the case of some stakeholders, such as business owners, this community may be different from their residential areas. The location of public safety agencies and their jurisdictions will drive participation of these groups.

Objective and Purposes of Participation
For the sake of simplifying the objectives and purpose of this data, participation is driven by a need for more effective emergency response operations [5]. This focuses on both the civilian and first responder sides of the coin. By providing more accurate and timely information, more lives and property can potentially be saved. Therefore, the goal of participation is to enhance the ability for community members to recognize the value of this information and for first responders to build relationships with their communities, to enhance trust and transparency, and to potentially increase the ability for tacit knowledge transfer.

The Degree of Power Sharing Implied
In the context of this research, we acknowledge that civilians must understand how and when their data is being used. More importantly, there is a dynamic of power between the individuals sharing information and the agencies entrusted to store this information for use in the event of an emergency. Therefore, it would be advantageous to map the extant landscape with regard to civilian perceptions. For example, as identified by Haworth, often in emergency management, the power is perceived to be conceptualized in terms of the agencies having jurisdiction or authority over communities due to their role in managing disaster scenarios [38]. To better support the public and the end-users of these systems, we must clearly research the methods for sharing power between civilians and the responding agencies.

The Scope of Participation and the Level at Which Change is Achieved.
In the context of this work, we propose the idea that the scope of participation is limited to the extent that the sociotechnical dimensions discussed in the above sections are factored into the conversation. Participation remains limited to the willingness of the community to volunteer information, and the willingness of agencies to demonstrate sound practices for obtaining, storing, and managing the data with an emphasis on privacy and security.

5 Discussion

In this paper, we present an integrative framework that draws on previous research by classifying and synthesizing the opportunities and challenges associated with citizen engagement for self-reported residential hazards and information. We argue that such a framework is an organizing and unifying structure that accounts for enhanced communication and thus, better opportunities for more successful CRR efforts. Such an integrative framework is timely because, within the emergency response field, there exists no single theoretical perspective that can support a common communication platform. This platform would need to incentivize citizens to provide this information and would need to further evaluate the level to which law enforcement, firefighters, and emergency medical providers can rely upon this information. Initial analysis of the literature did not find evidence suggesting that a common set of terminology exists to describe community engagement. We hypothesize that a set of dimensions for classifying and understanding the user experience of multiple stakeholders could lay the groundwork for explicitly consolidating extant literature. Without further analysis it is difficult to understand what self-reporting implies for citizens, much less the challenges and opportunities for technology designers to assist in enhancing user experience. In contrast, with a framework to refer to, technology designers, engineers, citizens, and public safety agencies can easily understand how these components play a role in the success of these mobile applications and information systems.

5.1 Practical Implications

In terms of addressing some of the problems associated with collecting, managing, retrieving, and storing residential data, one of the major areas for concern that we identified was the credibility of the information. As previously outlined by Flanagin and Metzger [18], volunteered information presents challenges due to the nature of the work. The individuals volunteering the information typically do not receive adequate training and may not be interested in some of the more practical aspects of learning about the science of fire behavior. Consequently, some information may be misrepresented. Meldrum et al. [10] highlighted similar concerns in their study on assessing property risk. This was due to individual property owners' lack of understanding surrounding wildland fire behavior. Thus, this review demonstrates the importance of considering how training for civilians could and should be implemented to better support public safety agencies.

However, this also poses practical challenges for public safety agencies who need to secure funding for training, allocate staff to run the training, and find methods for providing the training across the community, to reach multiple groups of stakeholders. A seemingly straightforward concern can quickly morph into a barrier for some departments and agencies already struggling to obtain adequate funding and resources to develop more effective programs. Despite these challenges, there are also benefits and opportunities that we have captured in the section below to demonstrate the potential positive impact of these programs.

5.2 Theoretical Implications

Community building and relationship building remain important factors that drive the success of emergency response agencies [34]. By identifying the sociotechnical dimensions inherent in self-reported hazard communication, it is possible to enhance the channels through which emergency response operations are managed. Although we mentioned some of the more practical challenges in the above section, it is also valid that through this framework, there is a potential to change public perceptions of public safety agencies to facilitate more effective communication, particularly in the context of emergency preparedness and hazard mitigation efforts. However, this framework has not been experimentally tested and therefore, empirical analysis is necessary to validate this framework.

5.3 Conclusion

We emphasized aspects of sociotechnical systems that are important for identifying ways first responders and citizens can communicate with one another through self-reporting hazard applications. We identified some of the dimensions that would prevent citizen engagement in reporting self-hazards, and we described how these dimensions, if addressed in information systems, can facilitate two-way communication. We outlined the advantages of citizen engagement, with a focus on the contribution of such an approach to our understanding of risk reduction, grounded in two-way communication between first responders and the citizen they serve. Then, we presented a brief overview of the user experience framework and discuss its dimensions. These dimensions are described in terms that can be measured and evaluated in empirical studies. Thus, the combination of dimensions used to construct the framework provides movement towards a clearer definition for effective two-way communication, which in turn is expected to predict the actual degree of citizen engagement and emergency response agency engagement. More importantly, *this framework can be used to define the development of mobile applications, tools, and other related information systems in which multiple stakeholders are sharing information.* Without a detailed description of the constructs that underpin communication between civilians and first responders, it would be difficult to design systems that facilitate this relationship. On the other hand, with a set of definitions, more informed decisions and recommendations can easily be made during the creation of these tools, therefore enhancing the perception of the multiple stakeholders utilizing these tools for CRR. This paper presents a research plan with an overarching goal to help ensure that community risk reduction software and mobile applications for emergency response are developed systematically with scientific validation principles grounded in HCI best practices. The result of this plan and future work will be a set of best practices to improve communication between first responders and community stakeholders.

Acknowledgments. The authors would like to thank all the firefighters who sacrificed so much last wildland fire season. Thank you for answering the call and selflessly serving. This paper is dedicated to the memory of Dustin Schieber.

References

1. Welhausen, C.A., Bivens, K.M.: Using content analysis to explore users' perceptions and experiences using a novel citizen first responder app. In: SIGDOC 2019 - Proceedings of 37th ACM International Conference on Design of Communication (2019). https://doi.org/10.1145/3328020.3353953
2. Dainty, K.N., Vaid, H., Brooks, S.C.: North American public opinion survey on the acceptability of crowdsourcing basic life support for out-of-hospital cardiac arrest with the pulsepoint mobile phone app. JMIR MHealth UHealth 5, 1–11 (2017). https://doi.org/10.2196/mhealth.6926
3. Tan, M.L., Prasanna, R., Stock, K., Hudson-Doyle, E., Leonard, G., Johnston, D.: Mobile applications in crisis informatics literature: A systematic review. Int. J. Disaster Risk Red. 24, 297–311 (2017). https://doi.org/10.1016/j.ijdrr.2017.06.009
4. Ahrens, M.B.: Evarts, Fire Loss in the United States During 2019 (2020)
5. Grant, C., Hamins, A., Bryner, N., Jones, A., Koepke, G.: Resea (2015)
6. Kafle, S.K.: Integrated community based risk reduction: an approach to building disaster resilient communities. Ann. Int. Work. Expo Sumatra Tsunami Disaster Recover, 1–20 (2010)
7. Madaio, M., et al.: Firebird: predicting fire risk and prioritizing fire inspections in Atlanta. In: Proceedings of ACM SIGKDD International Conference on Knowledge Discovery and Data Mining, pp. 185–194, 13–17 August (2016). https://doi.org/10.1145/2939672.2939682
8. Clare, J., Garis, L., Plecas, D., Jennings, C.: Reduced frequency and severity of residential fires following delivery of fire prevention education by on-duty fire fighters: Cluster randomized controlled study. J. Saf. Res. 43, 123–128 (2012). https://doi.org/10.1016/j.jsr.2012.03.003
9. McNeill, C.C., Alfred, D., Mastel-Smith, B., Fountain, R., MacClements, J.: Changes in self-reported household preparedness levels among a rural population after exposure to emergency preparedness campaign materials. J. Homel. Secur. Emerg. Manag. 13, 113–135 (2016). https://doi.org/10.1515/jhsem-2014-0096
10. Meldrum, J.R., Champ, P.A., Brenkert-smith, H., Warziniack, T., Barth, C.M., Falk, L.C.: Understanding gaps between the risk perceptions of wildland – urban interface (WUI) residents and wildfire Professionals (2015). https://doi.org/10.1111/risa.12370
11. McCaffrey, S., Toman, E., Stidham, M., Shindler, B.: Social science research related to wildfire management: an overview of recent findings and future research needs. Int. J. Wildl. Fire. 22, 15–24 (2013)
12. Toman, E., Shindler, B.: Communicating the wildland fire message : influences on knowledge and attitude change in two case studies related research, USDA For. Serv. Proc. RMRS-P-41, pp. 715–728 (2006)
13. Shindler, B.A., Toman, E., McCaffrey, S.M.: Public perspectives of fire, fuels and the forest service in the great lakes region: a survey of citizen agency communication and trust. Int. J. Wildl. Fire. 18, 157–164 (2009). https://doi.org/10.1071/WF07135
14. Monedero, S., Ramirez, J., Cardil, A.: Predicting fire spread and behaviour on the fireline. Wildfire analyst pocket: a mobile app for wildland fire prediction. Ecol. Modell. 392, 103–107 (2019). https://doi.org/10.1016/j.ecolmodel.2018.11.016
15. Israel, B.A., Schulz, A.J., Parker, E.A., Becker, A.B.: Review of community-based research: Assessing partnership approaches to improve public health. Ann. Rev. Public Health 19, 173–202 (1998). https://doi.org/10.1146/annurev.publhealth.19.1.173
16. South, J., Fairfax, P., Green, E.: Developing an assessment tool for evaluating community involvement. Heal. Expect. 8, 64–73 (2005). https://doi.org/10.1111/j.1369-7625.2004.00313.x
17. Goodchild, M.F.: Citizens as sensors: the world of volunteered geography. GeoJournal 69, 211–221 (2007). https://doi.org/10.1007/s10708-007-9111-y

18. Flanagin, A.J., Metzger, M.J.: The credibility of volunteered geographic information. GeoJournal **72**, 137–148 (2008). https://doi.org/10.1007/s10708-008-9188-y
19. Goodchild, M.F.: Assuring the quality of volunteered geographic information (n.d.), pp. 1–21 (2012)
20. Yan, Y., Feng, C.C., Huang, W., Fan, H., Wang, Y.C., Zipf, A.: Volunteered geographic information research in the first decade: a narrative review of selected journal articles in GIScience. Int. J. Geogr. Inf. Sci. **34**, 1765–1791 (2020). https://doi.org/10.1080/13658816.2020.1730848
21. Breyer, T.: An analysis of rules, regulations, and policies to identify opportunities and limitations for fire-based ems systems to integrate into healthcare using a community paramedic model, p. 9 (2015)
22. National Fire Protection Association (NFPA), 1620: standard for pre-incident planning, (2020). https://www.nfpa.org/codes-and-standards/all-codes-and-standards/list-of-codes-and-standards/detail?code=1620
23. Kapalo, K.A., LaViola, J.J.: Failing to plan is planning to fail: capturing the pre-incident planning needs of firefighters. Proc. Hum. Factors Ergon. Soc. Ann. Meet. **63**, 612–616 (2019). https://doi.org/10.1177/1071181319631113
24. Wiley, R.: Pre-planning residential fire operations, FireRescue1.Com (2012)
25. Weidinger, J., Robel, M., Schlauderer, S., Overhage, S.: Analyzing the potential of graphical building information for emergency responses: research in progress. In: Twenty-Sixth European Conference on Information Systems, pp. 1–10 (2018)
26. Weidinger, J., Schlauderer, S., Overhage, S.: Analyzing the potential of graphical building information for fire emergency responses: findings from a controlled experiment. In: Wirtschaftsinformatik, pp. 1085–1098 (2019)
27. Dozier, M., Porter, B.: Prevalence of probable hoarding and associated consequences at the scene of mississippi fires, 2009–2019. J. Public Heal. Deep South **1** (2020)
28. Kwok, N., Bratiotis, C., Luu, M., Lauster, N., Kysow, K., Woody, S.R.: Examining the role of fire prevention on hoarding response teams: vancouver fire and rescue services as a case study. Fire Technol. **54**, 57–73 (2018). https://doi.org/10.1007/s10694-017-0672-0
29. Barnes, M.: Researching public participation. Local Gov. Stud. **25**, 60–75 (1999). https://doi.org/10.1080/03003939908433967
30. Traina, N., Kerber, S., Kyritsis, D.C., Horn, G.P.: Occupant tenability in single family homes: part i — impact of structure type fire location and interior doors prior to fire department arrival. Fire Technol. **53**, 1589–1610 (2017). https://doi.org/10.1007/s10694-017-0651-5
31. Kerber, S.: Analysis of changing residential fire dynamics and its implications on firefighter operational timeframes. Fire Technol. **48**, 865–891 (2012). https://doi.org/10.1007/s10694-011-0249-2
32. Ahrens, J., Rudolph, P.M.: The importance of governance in risk reduction and disaster management. J. Contingencies Cris. Manag. **14**, 207–220 (2006). https://doi.org/10.1111/j.1468-5973.2006.00497.x
33. Oulasvirta, A., Suomalainen, T., Hamari, J., Lampinen, A., Karvonen, K.: Transparency of intentions decreases privacy concerns in ubiquitous surveillance, Cyberpsychology. Behav. Soc. Netw. **17**, 1–6 (2014). https://doi.org/10.1089/cyber.2013.0585
34. Van de Walle, S., Bouckaert, G.: Public service performance and trust in government: the problem of causality. Int. J. Public Adm. **29**, 891–913 (2003)
35. Newport, J.K., Jawahar, G.G.P.: Community participation and public awareness in disaster mitigation. Disaster Prev. Manag. **12**, 33–36 (2001). https://doi.org/10.1108/09653560310463838
36. Wong, W.L.P., Radcliffe, D.F.: The tacit nature of design knowledge. Technol. Anal. Strateg. Manag. **12**, 493–512 (2000). https://doi.org/10.1080/713698497

37. Holste, J.S., Fields, D.: Trust and tacit knowledge sharing and use. J. Knowl. Manag. **14**, 128–140 (2010). https://doi.org/10.1108/13673271011015615
38. Haworth, B.: Emergency management perspectives on volunteered geographic information: opportunities, challenges and change. Comput. Environ. Urban Syst. **57**, 189–198 (2016). https://doi.org/10.1016/j.compenvurbsys.2016.02.009

Global Challenges of Mobile Communication

Taowen Le[(✉)]

Weber State University, Ogden, USA
Let@weber.edu

Abstract. Mobile communication has been deployed as an important form of communication by transnational businesses as well as by individuals throughout the world. While it has performed wonders for individuals, societies, and nations worldwide, it has also created numerous challenges or issues. This paper surveyed and discussed six of such challenges or issues: interruption of traditional business models, threats to privacy, cyberbullying, unethical behavior in the workplace, undesirable impact of texting, and online piracy.

Keywords: Mobile communication · Mobile impact · Digital privacy · Cyberbullying · Workplace behavior · Texting · Online piracy

1   Introduction

Owing to continuing advancements in information technology, mobile communication has become not only a significant form of communication, but also a critical part of everyday life for people across the world. Aided by cloud computing, mobile communication connects people throughout the world digitally and instantly. It has brought enormous changes to public domains such as business, education, healthcare, and government. It has also fundamentally changed the way people socialize.

Business – Aside from the many newly-emerged businesses providing hardware, software, and database services in support of mobile communication, mobile communication has also brought forth new business models such as mobile commerce or E-commerce (Hayden and Webster 2014; Ahokangas et al. 2018). Mobile payments have enabled small businesses across the world to thrive and to enhance the quality of their services (Mbogo 2010).

Education – With the design of EdNet (Education Networks), Internet-based distant education first became available in countries such as the United States in the 1990s. Interactive courses taught on one campus could be attended by students at various satellite campuses. Online education programs have benefited students of every level throughout the world. Virtual course delivery through software programs such as Zoom and Conference have not only enabled universities and K-12 schools to survive the COVID-19 pandemic, but also changed education as a whole.

Healthcare – Mobile communication technologies have enabled medical personnel to provide patients with accurate diagnoses and effective treatments remotely.

© Springer Nature Switzerland AG 2021
G. Salvendy and J. Wei (Eds.): HCII 2021, LNCS 12796, pp. 243–253, 2021.
https://doi.org/10.1007/978-3-030-77025-9_21

Government – Mobile government (or e-government) has enabled governments throughout the world to provide more convenient and effective services to citizens and residents. Hundreds of services which traditionally require physical presence of people are now available to people without geographical or time constraints (Wang and Thompson 2020).

Socialization – Mobile-communication technologies have made socialization easier, cheaper, and more instant. Video conferencing has provided a very convenient platform for people across the global to meet "face-to-face." Popular social networking sites such as Facebook, Twitter, WeChat, LinkedIn, Google+, YouTube, Instagram, Pinterest, Tumblr, Snapchat, Reddit, Flickr, Swarm by Foursquare, Kik, and Shots have enabled families, communities, and people throughout the world to stay connected.

Indeed, mobile-communication technologies have enabled the entire world to stay digitally connected. Some might question whether a digitally-connected world is necessarily a better place. While few would want to revert to a world without all the convenience and benefits provided by mobile-communication technologies, many would agree that mobile-communication technologies have also created numerous challenges or issues worldwide.

This paper surveys and discusses six such challenges or issues.

2   Interruption of Traditional Business Models

A company's business model is defined by its revenue source, products or services to offer, pricing strategies, and targeted customer groups. Prior to the diffusion of mobile-communication technologies, businesses throughout the world basically followed the model of direct sales of products or services, revenues were typically generated from these products or services, and business competitions were usually more recognizable and manageable because they were typically local.

The diffusion of mobile-communication technologies brought forth the era of mobile-commerce or E-commerce. Mobile-commerce offers many great advantages to businesses and customers. Businesses enjoy lower operational costs and a virtually-unlimited customer base. Physical company set-ups are no longer mandatory, and it is much easier to start and manage a business. Customers could now easily locate, compare, and acquire products without having to travel from store to store. They are no longer constrained by geographical or time limitations.

However, there are serious trade-offs with mobile-commerce. Businesses now face much wider and greater competitions. Competitions are no longer local or within the country, but global. The greater availability of similar products or services combined with limited face-to-face interactions between businesses and customers result in lesser customer loyalty. Moreover, many hackers target at businesses, and information security becomes a serious challenge for many businesses. For customers, there is little guarantee of product quality, and since it is easier to start a business, many not-so-great businesses have emerged to mislead customers and swallowed up customers' savings. Online registration and online payment processes present equally-challenging security risks for customers.

3 Threats to Privacy

To many people, security and privacy seem to go hand in hand. Better-protected privacy means greater personal security. However, security and privacy could also become a paradox. As the world becomes more turbulent and chaotic, citizens and residents desire greater protection or security from their governments. To provide greater public security, governments collect more private and sensitive data from citizens and residents. In a digital world where information security is constantly threatened, government databases that stores vast amounts of citizen and resident information remain popular targets for hackers throughout the world.

In addition to government organizations, business organizations such as utility companies and healthcare providers also collect and maintain great volumes of information about their customers. Prior to the digital age, the physical nature of customer information files and the limited potential for information spreading did not cause too many people to worry. However, diffusions of mobile-communication technologies are eliminating barriers that used to protect customers' information and privacy. With the availability of mobile-communication technologies, customer data now becomes much more vulnerable to security breaches, and any security leakage could lead to immediate and unlimited information spreading.

Of particular concerns are the many information service providers such as Google, Baidu, and Youtube. They provide seemingly free services to customers such as website searching or video uploading and downloading, yet they not only electronically track and record every action users perform while using their services, but also install software such as cookies to user devices to track user behaviors on the network. As people walk on a dirt road leaving footsteps, their online activities including searching, purchases, reading, watching, writing, and communication leave digital traces which are targets of collection, storage, analyses, and manipulation by these companies.

Social media websites such as Facebook have also caused privacy concerns. As described by Tom Simonite, Facebook has implemented numerous technologies to capture everyone's every relationship with objects, organizations, and each other. Facebook not only gathers data from user profiles which contain age, gender, e-mail address, relationship status, mobile telephone numbers, historical information such as places users have lived and worked, but also collect user photos shared on the site as they are often tagged with a precise location. Facebook also tracks user activity elsewhere on the Internet, using the "Like" button. The button appears on apps and websites outside Facebook and allures people to reveal their interests in brands, products, or digital contents with a simple click. Moreover, Facebook also automatically collects data on users' online lives outside Facebook's borders: in certain apps or websites, when users listen to a song or read an article, the information is passed along to Facebook, even though the user does not click "Like." Combining such information with a map of social connections users make on Facebook website, Facebook has an incredibly rich record of users' lives and interactions (Simonite 2012).

Concerned customers and users naturally turn to the government for remedies. They pressure their governments to enact more and tighter laws and regulations to protect their privacy. However, two potential problems exist.

First, the world consists of many countries, and each country is deeply influenced by a unique set of cultures and beliefs. Government regulations in one country might not be applicable to others. Take Google for example, Google is a U.S.-based company whose primary service to the public is free website searching. In the United States, freedom of speech is so highly valued that it seems to surpass both rights to privacy and societal harmony. Thus, no filtering or censorship exists with Google in the U.S. However, Google faced difficulties both in China and Europe a few years ago. China, with a recorded history of five thousand years, highly values societal harmony. In the Chinese culture, people value societal harmony more than personal freedom, and they are willing to sacrifice certain personal freedom for the greater good of societal peace and harmony. Therefore, when China's national government demanded Google in China to place certain filters against search results that would likely cause social disturbances or challenge moral standards in China, people in China supported the government with great understanding.

In Europe, people seem to value privacy more than freedom of speech. For Europeans, privacy is a fundamental right to all residents, according to Article 8 of the European Convention of Human Rights, in which it states: "Everyone has the right to respect for his private and family life, his home and his correspondence." In January 2011, the European Commission made a legislative proposal on the "right to be forgotten," empowering every European resident the right to force Web companies as well as offline firms to delete or remove their data to preserve their privacy (Whittaker 2013).

Secondly, even in one single country, government regulations might not be the ultimate solution. As Nicholas Thompson of the U.S. observed, "Congress has been debating privacy forever and doing nothing, ... laws tend to pass slowly, technology moves quickly" (Thompson 2012).

Realistically, the best privacy protection governments could provide for citizens and residents might be (1) educating users about the risks of the digital world, (2) encouraging users to exercise self-control in the digital world, and (3) requiring service providers to provide explanation of how they utilize user information.

Regardless of what governments throughout the world would do, privacy will remain a vital concern.

4   Cyberbullying

Mobile-communication technologies have fundamentally changed the way people interact or relate with each other. Along with this change emerges the unfortunate issue of cyberbullying. While bullying has never been extinct from the world, the virtual digital space afforded by mobile-communication technologies seems to have added an additional dimension to bullying, which may be referred to as cyberbullying. As more and more younger people become users of modern mobile devices such as iPhones or smart phones, cyberbullying is becoming an increasingly serious challenge for nations worldwide.

For the purpose of this paper, cyberbullying refers to bullying behavior carried out through Internet service such as e-mails, chat rooms, discussion groups, online social networking, instant messaging, or web pages. Cyberbullying behaviors include but are not limited to sending malicious emails and texts, spreading rumors via email or social media sites, posting defamatory comments, photos, or videos online, setting up fake profiles to launch cyberattacks on others, and other harassment offenses (NoBullying.com 2017).

The following statistics about cyberbullying in the U.S. as reported by the National Crime Prevention Center, i-SAFE inc., the Cyberbullying Research Center, knowthenet.org.uk, the Hartford County Examiner, Cyberbulling.us, the American Osteopathic Association, Ipsos (the global research association for Reuters) News, Bitdefender and Covenant Eyes help portray the seriousness of cyberbullying in the world today (GuardChild.com 2017):

- Over 50% of adolescents and teens have been cyberbullied; about the same percentage have engaged in cyberbullying acts
- Over 25% of adolescents and teens have been cyberbullied repeatedly through their cell phones or the Internet
- 88% of teens using social media have seen others cyberbullied on a social media site
- The most common type of cyberbullying is mean, hurtful comments and rumor spreading
- Of those cyberbullied, 87% reported occurrence on Facebook, 19% on Twitter, and 13% on BlackBerry messenger
- The most frequent locations where cyberbullying occurs are chat rooms, social media sites, email, and instant messaging
- All races are impacted by cyberbullying

Damages from cyberbullying are more real and profound than many might realize. The vicious nature of cyberbullying and its extensive reach make it much more treacherous than bullying in person. While seasoned adults are more capable of withstanding cyberbullying, younger people are particularly vulnerable and susceptible to psychological and physical damages of cyberbullying. These damages include not only embarrassments and depression, but also losses of interest in school, changes of life course, and even suicides.

It is possible that cyberbullying might occur more frequently in the U.S. than in some other countries because the U.S. culture deeply roots itself in freedom of speech, and some might mistake such freedom as saying whatever they want. However, cyberbullying is a wide-spread problem throughout the world and is causing damages worldwide. How might such damages be minimized if not altogether eliminated? While different people might suggest different preventive measures, two are particularly attention-worthy: (1) timely reporting to proper authorities or sharing with family members or friends, and (2) timely giving appropriate guidance to students, children, or friends who have experienced cyberbullying.

It has been reported that the in the U.S., only a small percentage of cyberbullying victims would reveal to proper authorities or share with others, and considering that over 50% of adolescents and teens have experienced cyberbullying, a much smaller percentage of parents are aware that their children have been cyberbullied (GuardChild.com 2017):

- Only 16% parents know their child has been cyberbullied
- Only 12% parents say their child has experienced cyberbullying
- Over 50% of young people do not tell their parents about their being cyberbullied
- Only 10% of cyberbullied kids tell parents about the incident
- 60% of teens never reported the problem to relevant social media website
- Less than 20% of cyberbullying incidents were reported to law enforcement
- Only 1% of teenagers would consider telling a teacher as their first response to cyberbullying

It is not difficult to imagine that if people are not reporting cyberbullying sufficiently in the U.S. where people are generally outspoken, the percentage of incident reporting would be even lower in countries where people are generally more conservative and timid.

While prevention and management efforts might be necessary at multiple levels involving adolescents, parents, teachers, and health care professionals, parents play a particularly important role. Experts believe that parents should not only monitor their children's activities online and on social media, but also ask pressing questions about how things are going at school and with friends (Dotinga 2015).

Equally important is proper education. Parents and teachers need to communicate to young people that they genuinely care about them and stand ready to support them. To encourage victim reporting, Internet service providers should not only implement and enforce rules governing the use of their services, but should also provide easy, friendly, and encouraging reporting mechanisms for potential victims to report their incidents.

Upon learning about cyberbullying incidents, parents and teachers should offer victims timely and appropriate counsel and guidance on how to cope with the incidents. Internet service providers could also offer easy-to-notice and easy-to-access counsel and guidance to potential victims of cyberbullying.

5   Unethical Behavior in the Workplace

Unethical behaviors in the workplace have always existed. According to a report by the Ethics Resource Center (ERC) in the U.S., each day roughly 120 million people walk into a workplace somewhere in the United States, and almost half of them personally witnessed some form of ethical misconduct during a one-year time period. The five types of most frequently observed unethical behaviors in the U.S. workplace are (1) misusing company time, (2) abusive behavior, (3) employee theft, (4) lying to employees, and (5) violating company Internet policies (Schwartz 2015).

Although these behaviors are nothing new, mobile-communication technologies have made them more complicated and more difficult to control.

Misusing Company Time: Companies pay employees to do companies' work. Typical traditional violations might include lengthy work-irrelevant conversations with fellow employees, making personal phone calls during work hours, and running personal errands on company time. Such violations are generally noticeable and easy to catch and control. However, with mobile communication, personal messaging (email or instant messaging) could be easily covered, surfing the web for personal reasons could be easily disguised, and personal errands could be easily conducted online during work hours.

Abusive Behavior: Traditionally, certain employees might abuse their position and power to mistreat others through unkind or improper words or deeds. However, the abused employees would know who the abusers are, and the abusers might feel the pressure of potential lawsuits. With mobile communication, however, certain abuses could be easily committed anonymously. Some people might argue that the awareness that all digital behaviors leave traces may cause abusers to think twice before committing abuses, the fact that few have been actually caught encourages abusive behavior in the workplace as well.

Employee Theft: Traditionally, employee thefts would occur in the form of shoplifting, check tampering, hiding sales in order to skim, or manipulating expense reimbursements. Although the problems might be serious, the good-and-old practice of segregation of duties (with duty to authorize, duty to keep physical goods, and duty to keep records respectively resting on different individuals) makes employee thefts relatively easy to detect. However, in a mobile-communication-supported digital world, any employee who obtains certain "inside" information could invade the company's information systems and "exercise" the power of all three duties, authorizing the transferring of company goods or resources and forging transaction records difficult to track.

Lying to Employees: Traditionally, employers might lie to employees about earning expectations, personnel changes, competitions, salaries, or certain transactions. However, most of such lies could be discovered by employees afterwards. In a mobile-communication-supported digital world, employers could easily gather enough "supporting" evidences from the practically unlimited resources of data and information available from the Internet and patch up "truthful" lies. Employers could also easily manipulate or mislead public opinions about certain issues, products, or policies.

Violating Company Internet Policies: Nearly all companies in the U.S. and many companies worldwide provide Internet access in the workplace. However, Internet access is provided for the benefit of company work, not personal enjoyment or fulfillment. Yet the digital world is a tempting place; it is full of websites to browse, movies to watch, and games to play. Mobile communication technologies make it much easier for employees to engage in activities unrelated to company work.

In addition to the above five types of unethical workplace behaviors, the following types of unethical workplace behaviors are also intensified by mobile communication:

Disclosing Confidential Information: Keeping business secretes such as funding strategies, pricing models, design specifications, or product formulas is extremely important for companies as they strive to survive and thrive in a world of competition. It is unethical for employees to disadvantage their companies by disclosing their companies' confidential information. However, mobile-communication technologies make it extremely easy to disclose confidential information anonymously and make such disclosures very difficult to track or prosecute.

Stealing Others' Work: The World Wide Web is a giant sea of knowledge and carries the work of millions of authors, scientists, engineers, and other intellectual contributors. Search engines such as Google and Bing empower Internet users with the capability to find and tap into such tremendous resources in a matter of seconds. Mobile-communication technologies, together with word processing and imaging tools, make it extremely easy for people to steal others' ideas, thoughts, and work.

6 Undesirable Impact of Texting

Texting has significantly changed the way of communication, especially among those of the younger generations. While teenagers were the first to embrace texting, texting has also established popularity among adults and elementary school children, who are texting much more frequently than before. Texting offers numerous advantages compared with traditional ways of communication, including more concise communication, less disturbance to people around, quicker turnaround, higher response rate, easier ice-breaking, easier record keeping, and cleaner communication.

Despite the many advantages texting offers, its undesirable impact should not be ignored. The following are just a few identifications of such impact:

Development of Discomfort with Face-to-Face Communication: Longtime users who depend on texting as primary means of communication may become uncomfortable with face-to-face communication. This could be particularly true for younger people since they have not established or solidified their face-to-face communication skills. The reason that young people are often found texting to each other in the same room may very well be that they are uncomfortable with face-to-face communication.

Easy Misunderstanding: Unlike in-person communication, texting does not offer the benefit of facial expressions, speech tongues, voice volumes, and body gestures. Even though there are smiley faces to aid the texting process, the accuracy of communication in texting is not comparable to that in face-to-face communication, and texting could easily result in misunderstanding.

Increased Distraction from Work: Texting seems so brief and harmless that people text each other without much consideration of where the recipients might be or what they might be doing. As a result, people receive more text messages than they used to receive telephone calls. Driven by a natural urge to read and respond, people at work and students in the classroom become more easily and more frequently distracted from work on hand.

Difficult In-Depth Communication: Texting can be ineffective or awkward when complex or technical issues are discussed or when discussion requires high frequencies of interactive diagnoses or analyses. Short bursts of phrases common in texting encourage superficial conversations, but are insufficient for in-depth communication.

Limited Message Size: Texting programs typically impose a size limit on messages, and longer messages usually result in confirmation procedures which require senders to approve the splitting of the message into multiple smaller messages. Consequently, most texting users choose writing shorter and less descriptive messages instead of longer and more expressive messages.

Deterioration of Proper Language Usages: Most people do not follow proper grammar or practice proper language usage while texting. Longtime texting will likely develop and fortify incorrect language usage habits. Some people might argue that language is a means of communication; just as language usages of one hundred years ago replaced certain language usages of one thousand years ago, why should not popular language usages today replace some languages usages of yesterday?

Development of Impatience: People might be slow to respond to a telephone call or email message, but they seem more responsive to text messages. Overtime, such immediate texting turnarounds could develop greater impatience in people and promote people's expectation of immediate gratification of their requests or desires. This could result in serious challenges for societies and for the world, as impulsive and impatient members of the world are causing increasingly greater damages to societies and the world already.

Uninterrupted Intrusion: With traditional means of communication, there is a possible hideout for people. In the absence of emergency, telephone callers usually restrain from telephoning after certain hours, and people traveling could setup message systems to handle incoming phone calls. However, texting can be so brief and quiet that people feel no geographical or time constraints sending texts.

Disastrous Driving: Numberless tragedies involving texting while driving have been reported by television stations, newspapers, news websites, or Internet in general. Drivers might think reading or sending a text message takes only a brief moment; however, too many variables and unknowns exist on the road to allow distractions from the road, even just a brief moment.

7   Online Piracy

Online piracy refers to any unauthorized reproduction or use via Internet technologies of copyrighted books, recordings, television programs, patented invention, trademarked product, or other forms of protected intellectual property.

Piracy existed long before digital media became prominent; however, it had relatively limited impact for several reasons: (1) the associated risk was high compared to the financial benefits, (2) pirating goods was often difficult and required technical expertise, (3) the quality of pirated products were usually inferior compared to the originals. However, with mobile-communication technologies, these limiting factors quickly disappeared. For example, an identical quality copy can be easily manufactured and costs very little. A digital download or copy can be made instantly and costs nothing financially. Consequently, online piracy has become a very serious global issue worldwide, and developers and distributors of various types of media are increasingly focused on combating piracy and the loss of potential profits it represents (Harenber 2011).

Many developers and distributors seek solutions from technology itself. They place various digital controls such as registration procedures or authorization mechanisms over downloading, copying, or using of digital materials. However, technical measures alone have proven insufficient.

Relevant industries have placed great pressures on legislative bodies throughout the world to establish and enforce more up-to-date and more effective laws to safe-guard their interests. However, because of the many potential parties and interest groups involved, law making remains a lengthy process in almost all countries while technologies continue emerging at high speed and change cultures and societies along the way. Laws and regulations simply cannot keep up with technologies, and an effective worldwide anti-online-piracy agreement or legal measure would be very difficult to achieve. Yet anything less than a unified global system of protection would be ineffective in combating online piracy. Therefore, online piracy will remain a challenging global issue for years to come.

8   Conclusion

In his address to the New Tech'98 Conference, Neil Postman shared five ideas about new technologies: (1) All technological change is a trade-off; there are pros and cons with every new technology. (2) The advantages and disadvantages of new technologies are never distributed evenly among the population. (3) Embedded in every technology there is a powerful idea, sometimes two or three powerful ideas. (4) Technological change is not additive but ecological. New technologies are not simple additions to what is already there; they change the world. (5) People often become mythic about diffused technologies; they tend to think of technological creations as a part of the natural order of things instead of thinking of them as strange intruders whose capacity for good or evil rests on human awareness of what they do for us and to us (Postman 1998).

As discussed in this paper, mobile-communication technologies have been deployed as a key competitive advantage by multinational and transnational businesses throughout the world. They have performed wonders for individuals, societies, and nations world-wide. Nevertheless, they have also generated numerous global challenges or issues. This paper briefly sampled and discussed six of these challenges or issues.

We could ask ourselves: What tradeoffs do mobile-communication technologies present? Who are the winners and losers as these technologies are diffused into regular use? What countries are most likely positively impacted and what countries most likely negatively impacted by these technologies? What grand idea(s) underline(s) these new technologies and how the idea(s) might impact the economic, social, cultural, and political institutions? How might the diffusion of these technologies changing structures, patterns, or norms in the world?

Asking and answering these questions would help us realize that humans desire productivity, efficiency, comfort, convenience, freedom, good health, peace, safety, and happiness. Theses desires will never end and will continue to drive discoveries and inventions of new technologies. As new technologies emerge, there will be new issues to face and new challenges to overcome.

However, to humans, challenges and issues are opportunities for enhancements and improvements. They motivate people to search for better solutions, and they drive newer technology innovations. So has human history evolved, and so will it continue to move forward.

References

Ahokangas, P., et al.: Business models for local 5G micro operators. In: IEEE International Symposium on Dynamic Spectrum Access Networks, 22–25 October 2018, Soul, South Korea, pp. 1–11 (2018)

Dotinga, R.: One in Five Teens May Be Bullied on Social Media. HealthDay News, 22 June 2015. https://health.usnews.com/health-news/articles/2015/06/22/1-in-5-teens-may-be-bullied-on-social-media. Accessed 5 Mar 2021

GuardChild.com: Cyber Bullying Statistics (2017). https://www.guardchild.com/cyber-bullying-statistics/. Accessed 5 March 2021

Harenber: Online Piracy (2011). https://piracy.web.unc.edu/brief-history-of-online-piracy/. Accessed 31 July 2017

Hayden, T., Webster, T.: The Mobile Commerce Revolution: Business Success in a Wireless World. Que Publishing, 208 p. (2014)

Mbogo, M.: The impact of mobile payments on the success and growth of micro-business: the case of M-Pesa in Kenya. Afr. j. Online 2(1), 182–203 (2010)

NoBullying.com: A Comprehensive View of Cyberbullying in the USA (2017). https://nobullying.com/cyberbullying-in-usa/. Accessed 28 July 2017

Postman, N.: Five things we need to know about technological change. In: Address to New Tech 1998 Conference, Denver, CO, March 1998

Schwartz, A.: The 5 Most Common Unethical Behaviors in the Workplace (2015). https://www.bizjournals.com/philadelphia/blog/guest-comment/2015/01/most-common-unethical-behaviors-in-the.html. Accessed 5 Mar 2021

Somonite, T.: What Facebook knows. Technol. Rev. (2012). https://www.technologyreview.com/s/428150/what-facebook-knows/. Accessed 5 Mar 2021

Thompson, N.: How to get privacy right. New Yorker Mag. (2012). https://www.newyorker.com/culture/culture-desk/how-to-get-privacy-right/. Accessed 5 Mar 2021

Wang, C., Thompson, S.H.T.:. Online service quality and perceived value in mobile government success: an empirical study of mobile police in China. Int. J. Inf. Manage. 52(C) (2020). https://doi.org/10.1016/j.ijinfomgt.2020.102076. Accessed 5 Mar 2021

Whittaker, Z.: Google's European Conundrum: When Does Privacy Mean Censorship? (2013). https://www.cnet.com/news/googles-european-conundrum-when-does-privacy-mean-censorship/. Accessed 5 Mar 2021

The Impact of Mobile IT on the Service Innovation Performance of Manufacturing

Caihong Liu[1(✉)], Hannah Ji[2], and June Wei[3]

[1] Department of Business, Jiaxing University, Jiaxing 314001, China
[2] Carey Business School, Johns Hopkins University, Baltimore, MD 20723, USA
[3] College of Business, University of West Florida, Pensacola, FL 32514, USA

Abstract. Facing the service transformation of China's manufacturing industry and the in-depth application of mobile information technology in the manufacturing industry, based on the relevant literature and theoretical analysis, this paper establishes a theoretical model of the impact of T on enterprise innovation service performance. The model structure reveals the mediating role of enterprise innovation service capability, and puts forward the corresponding research hypotheses. Then, taking some Chinese manufacturing enterprises as the research object, through the statistical analysis of the questionnaire data, it is concluded that the variable setting is reasonable and effective. On this basis, this paper studies the influence of manufacturing enterprises' MIT capability on service innovation performance, and tests its influence path and influencing factors. This paper argues that it is an effective way to improve the service capability of enterprises through MIT, and then indirectly affect the service innovation performance of enterprises.

Keywords: Mobile information technology · Service innovation · Manufacturing enterprise

1 Introduction

With the development of production service industry, the service is gradually diversified. The new service or new business model formed around product related services, entering various types of service markets, and expanding relationship based or process centered services, accepting and managing end-user business operations are typical representatives [1]. However, service innovation must be driven by IT or new IT. As the IT based on mobile devices, MIT, thanks to its characteristics [2] of mobile convenience, real-time interaction, mobile device ubiquity, information service personalization and information service content enrichment, should change the internal and external environment of enterprises, and changed the competition rules of products, processes and even industries [3]. Based on MIT, the service function and the service channels for enterprises can be expanded, so as to shorten the process of enterprise innovation, improve the accuracy and efficiency of enterprise innovation, reduce the cost of enterprise innovation, and then enhance the value of enterprise innovation [4, 5].

© Springer Nature Switzerland AG 2021
G. Salvendy and J. Wei (Eds.): HCII 2021, LNCS 12796, pp. 254–262, 2021.
https://doi.org/10.1007/978-3-030-77025-9_22

Hence, from the perspective of technology resources, in this paper, the influence structure among MIT capability, the service innovation capability of enterprise and the service innovation performance of enterprise has been given, so as trying to deepen and expand the relevant research from these aspects of testing the constituent factors and revealing the influence path by empirical data. The purpose of this study is not only to deepen the research framework of MIT, but also to provide a reference for enterprises to effectively improve their service innovation capabilities and enhance their market competitiveness through appropriate adopting and deployment the MIT.

2 Theory and Hypotheses

2.1 MIT

MIT, as an embodiment of advanced IT equipment and advanced IT means, has more outstanding advantages than conventional ones in terms of information accessibility, accuracy, information transparency and decision support. MIT enables enterprises to use advanced information technologies such as big data and cloud computing to obtain valuable external information [6]. It can also facilitate the rapid and effective transmission and sharing of information within the enterprise through teleconferencing and other forms [7]. In addition, the employees' sense of belonging and innovation enthusiasm could be improved by optimizing appropriate performance evaluation methods and tools, and the data and information for effective decision-making can also be accumulated quickly by combining with databases and other ways [8]. Generally, MIT has attracted the attention of enterprise innovation. Generally, MIT, is the integrated information technology of the application of wireless information identification, wireless information processing and transmission, IT service and information data management decision, such as BIM technology, Web technology, GIS technology, RFID technology, and other emerging information technologies [9, 10]. Considering that the service innovation of service-oriented manufacturing enterprises is an innovation activity around the change of service content in the whole product life cycle, which is embodied in the innovation of service concept, service submission system, service submission interface and service support technology. As it happens, the technical characteristics of MIT can better meet these service innovation needs [11]. With the continuous integration of information technology and manufacturing technology, managers' perceptions and thinking about MIT are advancing with the times.

2.2 Research on the Impact of IT Capabilityon the Service Innovation Performance of Enterprise

There are many studies on the impact of it on enterprise performance at home and abroad. With the research being deepened, the relevant research has been extended from a local perspective (such as the impact of IT on the financial performance of an enterprise) to the overall performance of an enterprise.

IT with acquiring, transmitting, and using information has penetrated into economic activities fields such as research and development, manufacturing, and sales, has become a sharp tool for enterprise innovation management [12, 13]. Based on enterprise resource theory and enterprise capability theory, the concept of "IT capability" is put forward by scholars [14]. According to resource-based theory, IT capability can be regarded as a kind of enterprise resource, which can be integrated with other resources, management systems and business processes [15]. IT capability refers to obtain, analyze and interpret information, control related costs and achieve organizational goals through the effective use of IT tools and resources [16]. However, IT itself cannot bring profits to enterprises in technological innovation. Only when it is organically combined with the unique resources, organizational flexibility, organizational culture and other characteristics of enterprises to form a certain technical ability, can it create better innovation performance [17, 18]. At present, the performance management of most companies does not match their own development strategy. With the increasingly significant role of IT and management information system, more and more scholars have analyzed the relationship between the IT based management information system and enterprise performance according to the actual situation of enterprises [19]. The use of IT has a statistically significant positive impact on the profit performance of enterprises [20]. IT can significantly affect enterprise sales, labor demand, turnover rate of current assets and accounts receivable [21]. IT can influence innovation performance by changing the way of acquiring and processing knowledge resources and improving the process of innovation [22]. However, this influence is not direct, which needs to form a complex chain of assets and capabilities through the influence of IT on the competitive activities of enterprises, and finally bring a continuous competitive advantage to enterprises [23]. Generally speaking, the role of IT capabilities is more recognized. But, the research of IT capability on service innovation performance is still less. In particular, the empirical research on the performance of MIT capability enterprises is rare. IT capability can improve the service capability of the supply chain by transforming the information architecture of the supply chain and enhancing the link and responsiveness between the supply chain nodes, so as to achieve higher supply chain performance.

On the basis of the above research, from the view of technological resources theory and the knowledge innovation driven by IT, this paper will analyze the effect path of MIT capability to the service innovation performance of manufacturing enterprises, which should to be carried out through the structural equation model and the questionnaire data. So the following hypothesizes are put forward:

H1: MIT capability with three factors (MIT infrastructure, the technical advantages of MIT and Quality of MIT' technician) are directly and positively correlated with firm innovation performance.

The research hypothesis H2 is proposed: MIT has a strong positive influence on SI. This is the key intermediary for MIT.

At the same time, the research hypothesizes of H3 can be set that SI has a direct positive impact on SP.

3   Theoretical Model

Information technology capabilities can bring intangible resources to the supply chain, such as improving service quality, reducing costs, improving customer satisfaction, and increasing enterprise innovation capabilities, which have a positive effect on supply chain performance. Based on the above analysis, taking the Service strategy as the moderating variable, the theoretical model shown in Fig. 1 is proposed.

Fig. 1. Theoretical model of MIT influencing on the service innovation performance of manufacturing enterprise

Ravarini (2010) proposed that information technology capability is the basis to improve the communication and sharing ability of logistics, business flow and information flow of each node in the supply chain, and resource sharing is based on the integration of the supply chain [24]. Kelle and akbulut (2005) information technology can drive supply chain integration because it can obtain the key information inside and outside the supply chain [25]. Turulja (2015) believes that for companies that rely heavily on information technology (IT), information security management (ISM) has become a major challenge for corporate sustainable management through the three sustainable IT capabilities, namely, IT infrastructure, IT business development capabilities and IT forward-looking attitude [26]. Ni Wenbin (2010) believes that supply chain integration can connect all the node enterprises in the supply chain, and make the means of production reach consumers quickly through production, processing and sales [27]. Chen et al. (2006) found that through supply chain integration, supply chain performance shows the following management advantages: improve transaction speed, reduce costs (including procurement costs, inventory costs, etc.); reduce inventory, improve the turnover rate of goods; It can reduce the bullwhip effect, reduce the adverse impact of market uncertainty, improve the reaction rate and shorten the product cycle [28].

To this end, this article uses MIT facilities (MIT1), MIT's information collection capabilities (MIT2), and MIT's ease of use (MIT3) to measure MIT capabilities. Supply chain integration (SI1) and information sharing (SI2) and service innovation (SI3) are three indicators to measure SI. The service cost of the supply chain (SP1), service added value (SP2) and customer satisfaction (SP3) are used to measure SP.

4 Reliability and Validity of Questionnaire Data

4.1 Study Design

The selection of questionnaire indicators has been shown in Fig. 1, and the question items corresponding to these indicators are summarized in Table 2 mainly through literature reading methods. To test the theoretical model proposed, questionnaire survey were conducted with 160 manufacturing companies in China as the research objects, excluding invalid questionnaires, and finally 146 valid questionnaire data were formed. Most of the variables involved in this study are difficult to quantify. The Likert seven-point scale was used to measure the variables. The score of each measurable item is measured on five levels of 5, 4, 3, 2, 1 points respectively. The larger the number is, the higher the score of the item is. Then, survey data based, SPSS19.0 software will be used to analyze the survey results.

4.2 Descriptive Analysis

In this paper, spss22 software was used for statistical analysis (Table 1).

Table 1. Reliability analysis.

Variable	Correction item total correlation (CITC)	Alpha after item deleted	Cronbach's alpha
MIT1	0.664	0.895	0.905
MIT2	0.595	0.9	
MIT3	0.648	0.896	
SI1	0.63	0.899	
SI2	0.731	0.891	
SI3	0.731	0.89	
SP1	0.618	0.899	
SP2	0.748	0.889	
SP3	0.769	0.887	

It can be seen from the above table that the value of the reliability coefficient is 0.908, which is greater than 0.9, which indicates that the reliability quality of the research data is very high. For the "deleted α coefficient", after any item is deleted, the reliability coefficient will not increase obviously, so it shows that the item should not be deleted.

And, the CITC values of the analysis items are all greater than 0.4, showing that there is a good correlation between the analysis items, and that the level of reliability is good. In conclusion, the research data reliability is of high quality and can be used for further analysis.

At the same time, in order to analyze the rationality of the scale item, the results of validity analysis are shown in Table 2.

It is obvious from Table 2 that the KMO value is greater than 0.8, and the validity of the research data is very good.

To test the suitability of the data for structural equation models, it is also necessary to test the internal convergent validity of latent variable, which is shown as Table 3.

CFA analysis was carried out for these 3 factors, as well as 9 analysis items. Table 3 shows that all the AVE values are greater than 0.5, and all the CR values are higher than 0.7, which means that the data of this analysis have good aggregation (convergence) validity. Therefore, a structural equation model can be constructed based on these data.

Table 2. Validity analysis.

KMO and Bartlett's test		
KMO		0.895
Bartlett	Approximate chi-square	795.966
	df	36
	p	0

Table 3. Convergent validity.

Factor	Average variance extraction (AVE)	Combination Reliability (CR)
MIT	0.563	0.794
SI	0.549	0.785
SP	0.574	0.801

5 Hypothesis Testing

5.1 Fitting Analysis of the Model

Based on the survey data, empirical analysis is performed on Fig. 1 and the proposed research hypotheses by SMOSS software. The influence relationship between latent variables in the structural equation model is shown in Table 4.

Table 4. Regression coefficient of model.

X	->	Y	Non standardized path coefficient	z	SE	p	Standardized path coefficient
MIT	->	SI	0.786	6.599	0.119	0	0.804
MIT	->	SP	0.064	0.724	0.089	0.469	0.076
SI	->	SP	0.818	5.625	0.145	0	0.937

As can be seen from the above table, the standardized path coefficient of MIT on SI is $0.804 > 0$, and this path shows a significance level ($z = 6.599$, $p = 0.000 < 0.01$), which indicates that MIT will impact on SI significantly and positively. SI also has a significant positive impact on SP. Moreover, MIT has no direct impact on SP. These also show that the structural relationship assumptions of the model proposed above are valid.

6   Hypothesis Testing

According to the results of paths and model, the research hypotheses are tested as follows.

1. The research hypothesis of H1 is not tenable. However, H3 is working. That is to say, MIT can play a positive effect on SP, but this effect is indirectly exerted through SI.
2. The hypothesis of H2 is established. SI has a strong positive force on SP. Therefore, the innovation service performance of an enterprise depends on its innovation service ability. This also presents that although IT is the most important driving force for service innovation, technology itself cannot create value. The premise of playing MIT utility into the manufacturing enterprise is to make the enterprise have certain technology application ability by embedding MIT into their activities.

In addition, we can see that the technological advantage of MIT is the most critical factor affecting the service innovation ability of enterprises.

7   Conclusion

Compared with traditional IT technology, MIT has the characteristics of anytime and any-where, which improves the availability and timely-ness of information. In addition, MIT integrates information communication channels, monitors business processes anytime, anywhere, and can detect problems in business processes in real time and provide suited information in a timely manner, making business process implementation more efficient and smooth. Based on MIT's information capabilities and the service capabilities of manufacturing enterprises in China, the empirical analysis on the structural model, shows that MIT is an important strategic tool and resource for modern manufacturing enterprises. So, MIT can be an effective auxiliary measure for the service-oriented transformation of Chinese manufacturing enterprises, and it is the key to help enterprises maintain long-term competitive advantages with unique innovative manufacturing services.

Funding.   This research was supported by the Natural Science Foundation of Zhejiang Province in China (Grant No. LY18G010011).

References

1. Zhao, Y., Luo, J., Feng, Q.: Case study on the service innovation ecosystem in equipment manufacturing enterprises. Technoecon. Manage. Res. (5):42–46 (2019). https://doi.org/10.3969/j.issn.1004-292X.2019.05.008
2. Liu, C.: Construction of multi dimensional evaluation system in higher vocational English teaching under the assistance of mobile information technology. J. Baotou Vocat. Tech. Coll. **20**(2), 48–50 (2019). https://doi.org/10.3969/j.issn.1672-0903.2019.02.017
3. Wood, K.R.: Leaders' perceptions of mobile technology in the workplace. ProquestLlc, 196 (2012)
4. Barras, R.: Towards a theory of innovation in services. Res. Pol. **15**(4), 161–173 (1986). https://doi.org/10.1016/0048-7333(86)90012-0

5. Grnroos, C.: Service Management and Marketing: A Customer Relationship Management Approach, 2nd edn. John Wiley & Sons Ltd., Hoboken (2020). ISBN: 0-471-72034-8

6. Bharadwaj, A.S.: A resource-based perspective on information technology capability and firm performance: an empirical investigation. MIS Q. **24**(1), 169–196 (2000). https://doi.org/10.2307/3250983

7. Chen, Y., Wang, Y., Nevo, S., Benitez-Amado, J., Kou, G.: It capabilities and product innovation performance: the roles of corporate entrepreneurship and competitive intensity. Inf. Manage. **52**(6), 643–657 (2015). https://doi.org/10.1016/j.im.2015.05.003

8. Xie, W., Cheng, M., et al.: Influence mechanism of IT capability on the enterprise's absorptive capacity—based on the perspective of IT governance. R & D Manage. **27**(6), 124–134 (2015). https://doi.org/10.3969/j.issn.1004-8308.2015.06.014

9. Zhang, X.: Research on construction project progress information management system based on mobile IT. Master's thesis of Harbin Institute of Technology (2017)

10. Zhu, J., Huang, S., Luo, F.: Research and implementation of mobile application based on IT operation and maintenance data monitoring management. Telecom Power Technol. **36**(8), 10–13 (2019). https://doi.org/10.19399/j.cnki.tpt.2019.08.004

11. Zhao, Y., Chen, J., et al.: Research on function paths of IT capability on service innovation performance of manufacturing enterprises. Stat. Inf. Forum **30**(7), 101–106 (2015). https://doi.org/10.3969/j.issn.1007-3116.2015.07.016

12. Shao, Y., Pang, B., Fang, J.: Research on inner-enterprise synergy and innovation performance from the perspective of IT capability. Manage. Rev. **30**(6), 70–80. CNKI:SUN:ZWGD.0.2018-06-006

13. Zhang, T., Zhuang, G.: It capability, channel relationship governance behavior and channel satisfaction: the contingent influence of the speculative atmosphere of distributors. Manage. Rev. **27**(7), 116–126 (2015)

14. Kießling, M., Marrone, M., Kolbe, L.M.: Influence of IT service management on innovation management: first insights from exploratory studies. Management of the interconnected world. Physica-Verlag HD (2010). https://doi.org/10.1007/978-3-7908-2404-9_16

15. Mishra, S., Modi, S.B., Animesh, A.: The relationship between information technology capability, inventory efficiency, and shareholder wealth: a firm-level empirical analysis. J. Oper. Manage. **31**(6), 298–312 (2013). https://doi.org/10.1016/j.jom.2013.07.006

16. Ross, J.W., Beath, C.M., Goodhue, D.: Develop long-term competitiveness through IT assets. Sloan Manage. Rev. **38**, 31–45 (1996)

17. Chae, H.C., Koh, C.E., Prybutok, V.R.: Information technology capability and firm performance: contradictory findings and their possible causes. Soc. Inf. Manage. Manage. Inf. Syst. Res. Center **38**(1), 305–326 (2014). https://doi.org/10.1080/17517575.2012.688541

18. ZengFu'e, Z., Xue, L.: A research on the relationship between IT capability and sustainability performance from the perspective of business process agility. Sci. Res. Manage. **39**(4), 92–101 (2018). https://doi.org/10.19571/j.cnki.1000-2995.2018.04.010

19. Haitao, C., Xuemei, Z.: Research on Relationship between flexible IT infrastructure and firm performance. Sci. Technol. Manage. Res. **38**(14), 140–146 (2018). https://doi.org/10.3969/j.issn.1000-7695.2018.14.022

20. Lou, R.P., XueSh, G.: ERP and corporate profit performance: empirical evidence from listed companies in Shanghai and Shenzhen. Syst. Eng. Theory Pract. **31**(08), 1460–1469 (2011)

21. Yang, H.D., Kang, H.R., Mason, R.M.: An exploratory study on meta skills in software development teams: antecedent cooperation skills and personality for shared mental models. Eur. J. Inf. Syst. **17**(1), 47–61 (2008). https://doi.org/10.1057/palgrave.ejis.3000730

22. Ravichandran, T., Lertwongsatien, C., Lertwongsatien, C.: Impact of information systems resources and capabilities on firm performance: a resource-based perspective. In: Proceedings of the International Conference on Information Systems, ICIS 2002, Barcelona, Spain, 15–18 December 2002, DBLP (2002). https://doi.org/10.1057/palgrave.jibs.8400130

23. Wade, M.R., Hulland, J.: The resource-based view and information systems research: review, extension, and suggestions for future research. MIS Q. **28**(1), 107–142 (2004). https://doi.org/10.2307/25148626

24. Ravarini, A.: Information technology capability within small-medium enterprises. J. Digit. Imaging **23**(2), 133–141 (2010). https://doi.org/10.1007/s10278-008-9167-3

25. Kelle, P, Akbulut, A.: The role of ERP tools in supply chain information sharing, cooperation, and cost optimization. Int. J. Prod. Econ. 93–94, 41–52 (2005). https://doi.org/10.1016/j.ijpe.2004.06.004

26. Turulja, L., Bajgorić, N.: Information technology capability and its impact on firms performance. Social Science Electronic Publishing (2015). https://doi.org/10.2139/ssrn.3280270

27. Ni, W., Zhang, H.: Review of supply chain integration. Bus. Econ. (20), 68–70 (2010). https://doi.org/10.3969/j.issn.1009-6043.2010.20.031

28. Chen, J., Ma, S.: Implementable mechanisms and technical solution for supply chain integration management. Ind. Eng. Manage. **11**(1), 23–31 (2006). https://doi.org/10.3969/j.issn.1007-5429.2006.01.006

User Co-creation Value of Short-Video Platform from the Perspective of Interactivity: The Mediating Role of Psychological Attachment

Yumei Luo[1], Dongyan Li[2], and Qiongwei Ye[3]($\boxtimes$)

[1] Yunnan University, Kunming 650021, China
[2] Southwestern University of Finance and Economics, Chengdu 610074, China
[3] Yunnan University of Finance and Economics, Kunming 650500, China

Abstract. This paper's purpose is to explore how psychological attachment impacts users' value co-creation on short-video platforms and its mediating role between interactivity and value co-creation. A conceptual model is proposed whereby interactivity (user–machine, user–user and user–celebrity interactivity) impacts the value co-creation of users (sponsored co-creation and autonomous co-creation) through psychological attachments (internalisation and identification). The proposed research model was empirically evaluated using 248 users on the Tik Tok short-video platform and examined using PLS. The findings revealed that users' psychological attachment differed across types of value co-creation. Psychological attachment was also found to have an underlying mediating role in the relationship between interactivity and value co-creation. In particular, the internalisation psychology attachment and identification psychology attachment completely mediated the impact of user–machine interactivity and user–user inter-activity on value co-creation, respectively. This study indicated that user–celebrity interactivity had a greater effect on value co-creation behaviour, either directly or indirectly. This study provides a useful insight into user value co-creation by drawing from psychological attachment on short-video platforms, and it explains the mechanism behind the effects of interactivity to value co-creation by revealing the mediating influences of psychological attachment.

Keywords: Value co-creation · Short-video platform · Interactivity · Psychological attachment

1 Introduction

The short video—a new communication mode of online communities—refers to videos with a playtime of fewer than 5 min and concise content [1]. With technological progress increasing the pace of life, short-video platforms have appeared to meet the needs of users who want to record short, fragmentary videos. Despite the importance and success of some high-profile online short-video platforms, many others have faltered. As the data of iiMedia Research showed in China, the user scales of Tik Tok and Kuaishou are approximately 477.32 million and 370.84 million users, respectively, by 2020, while the

© Springer Nature Switzerland AG 2021
G. Salvendy and J. Wei (Eds.): HCII 2021, LNCS 12796, pp. 263–283, 2021.
https://doi.org/10.1007/978-3-030-77025-9_23

number of users on other platforms (e.g. Xigua, huoshan and Meipai) is less than 100 million [2].

The literature on short-video platforms suggests that short videos are usually generated by platform users [4]; this suggests that user-generated content, which is a form of user value co-creation (UVCC), is crucial for short-video platforms, which has led to a burst of interest of scholars and practitioners. Short-video platforms enable users to create and upload videos to be shared online, and then users' active participation keeps the online platforms alive [5]. Zwass [6] anticipates two types of co-creation activities based on different initiators: sponsored value co-creation (SVC) and autonomous value co-creation (AVC). These activities deploy users as a co-creator of value and then utilises the users as an operant resource in the short-video platforms, making use of their skills, knowledge and creativity [7].

A review of emerging literature shows that the majority of research has focused on the nature of consumer value co-creation [7]. What is absent in the debate is a thorough examination of why users engage in value co-creation activities with enterprises and, in turn, what factors motivate users to engage in such activities. Responding to this research challenge is important because understanding what motivates users to engage in value co-creation might enable enterprises to strategically manage their interactions with users in a way that creates superior value for the users and for the enterprises themselves. Literature on online communities suggests that user engagement and retention depend on users' psychological attachment [3]. Psychological attachment refers to users' affective connection to and care for an online short-video platform in which they become involved. Users who have a strong psychological attachment to their online short-video platform are crucial to its success. Other studies reveal the role emotions play in stimulating consumer involvement in the co-creation of valuable innovations, as well as the product-service [8], community and medium-related benefits that consumers realize by participating in new product development [9]. Despite these studies, it is unclear if consumers' psychological attachment differs across types of UVCC, whether they are creating directly or contributing to the creation activities of enterprises or communities.

Other studies on the value co-creation of consumers in virtual communities have shown that online communities provide opportunities for users to share and exchange information as well as to communicate, enabling them participate actively in value co-creation [10–13]. This interactivity, based on interaction objects, could generally be classified into user–machine interactivity and user–user interactivity [14]. Ren [3] suggests that different interactive functions provided by online communities would build different attachments: group-level interaction to build identity-based attachment and interpersonal interaction to build bond-based attachment. These studies tell us that psychological attachment differs by interactivity across areas of co-creation, but these differences remain unclear. Our study attempts to address these gaps in our knowledge of UVCC in short-video platforms. Three research questions are answered. First, how does users' psychological attachment differ across types of UVCC (i.e. SVC and AVC). Second, how does value co-creation differ by interactivity? Third, how does interactivity impact UVCC through psychological attachment and why?

In the following, we firstly present different forms of UVCC, psychological attachment and interactivity. Second, to foreshadow the mediating role of psychological attachment, theories of internalisation attachment point to interactivity functions that build attachment by focusing users' attention on the values of a platform, resulting in more SVC; whereas theories of identification attachment point to interactivity functions that build attachment by focusing users' attention on other users, resulting in more AVC.

2 Theoretical Background

2.1 User Value Co-creation

The early idea of value co-creation stemmed from co-production. At present, the research on value co-creation mainly includes value connotation [13, 15], subjects and their interrelationship of value co-creation [11, 16] and motivations and process of value co-creation [12, 17]. With the rapid development of Internet technology and information technology, especially in the mobile field, the online platform can provide more opportunities for interactivity than offline platforms. Value co-creation has expanded into virtual cyberspace, and virtual value co-creation has gradually become a universal phenomenon [6]. Madupu and Cooley [5] propose that value co-creation in the virtual community refers to the behaviour of members to maintain the vitality of the community by actively participating in community interactivity. Zwass [6] suggests that the short-video community connects different people, things and objects through a series of interesting short videos, creating a typical virtual community platform for value co-creation. Users can participate in value co-creation in the short-video community through creatively designing and shooting short videos. Therefore, this research defines 'value co-creation' as the active participation of users with the short-video community platform and other users in the design, shooting and production of short videos.

Since consumers can adopt various ways to participate in the value co-creation process of enterprises or virtual communities, scholars have also classified value co-creation and studied value co-creation under different scenarios. Zwass [6] believes that the value co-creation activity in the virtual community could be initiated by enterprises or users and divides value co-creation into SVC and AVC based on different initiators. Therefore, based on the recommendation of Zwass [6], this study also divides the value co-creation of users in the short-video community into SVC initiated by community platforms or enterprises and AVC initiated by users. To be more specific, SVC refers to the participation of users in the design and production activity of new videos initiated by enterprises or community platforms, such as the topic shooting in community platforms and the video collection activity initiated by enterprises; AVC refers to the voluntary shooting and sharing of short videos by users, such as recording and sharing their lives and initiating challenge topics using the short-video community.

So far, some scholars have studied the motivations and factors of customers' participation in value co-creation. To obtain consumption experience, consumers participate in value co-creation through interactivity with enterprises to achieve service exchange and resource integration. Thus, they emphasise that interactivity, service and experience enable the value co-creation of users [5]; Grönroos and Voima [17] also reveal that direct or indirect interactivity between customers and enterprises leads to different forms of value co-creation. These studies point out that interactivity enables consumers' participation in value co-creation, but there is no specific research studying how interactivity leads to value co-creation behaviour.

2.2 Psychological Attachment

Psychological attachment refers to the psychological and emotional bond of individuals to an organisation [18]. Ball and Tasaki [19] believe that the formation of psychological attachment depends on the one hand on the type of items and intensity of the individuals' ownership of the item and, on the other hand, on the social identity and emotional meaning of the item or organisation for individuals. Burris, Detert, and Chiaburu [20] point out that psychological attachment will generate a positive emotional response and supportive attitude and behaviour, such as active participation in organisational activities and obedience to organisational behaviours [18]. Therefore, psychological attachment is directly used as a variable for predicting behaviours [21]. However, few researches have applied psychosocial attachment to the short-video community platform.

Many researchers believe that psychological attachment should be multidimensional [22, 23]. In the virtual community, there is a certain emotional connection among different members of the community and between members and the community. This emotional connection can be divided into the emotion for the whole community and the emotion for other members of the community [24]. According to the basis of psychological attachment, O'Reilly and Chatman [18] propose that psychological attachment contains three constructs, namely, internalization, identification and compliance. However, this study focuses on different object of users' attachment, that is, users' attachment to the platform or other users. Therefore, this research only adopts internalization and identification psychological attachment. The internalisation psychological attachment refers to attachment to the platform because the goals and values of users are consistent with the community platform. For identification psychological attachment, users pay more attention to attachment to establish and maintain connections with other users, and they only regard the platform as a communication medium. In other words, without the platform, users can generate this kind of attachment between users.

2.3 Interactivity

Interactivity is a core function of the short-video community and a key feature of new media when compared to traditional media. In many studies, interactivity has also been classified into different forms. Hoffman and Novak [14] classify interactivity into human–human and user–machine interactivity. It can be seen that interactivity can be roughly classified into two categories: user–machine and interpersonal interactivity [25–29]. In this study, user–machine interactivity is defined as control over the content, time and order of short videos perceived by users in the short-video community platform; the degree of response of the community platform to users' input; and the degree of two-way communication [14], which includes three characteristics: controllability, synchronicity and bidirectionality [30].

Interpersonal interactivity is defined as the communication among users in the community with the short-video community platform as the interactive medium [14]. At the same time, there is a remarkable feature in the short-video community that celebrities as one kind of user are invited to the platform due to the 'celebrity effect'. This effect is fully utilised to obtain a large number of fans, achieve a large number of users and realise good communication effect. Customer loyalty can be enhanced with the high-quality short videos produced by them [31]. H. Li [32] and B. Liu [33] also point out that the transmission of short videos relies on the 'celebrity effect' of online celebrities. With the participation of stars and online celebrities, the short-video community can continue to heat up, and the number of users increases continuously. Therefore, in the short-video community, interpersonal interactivity involves user–user interactivity and user–celebrity interactivity, where the user refers to common users compared to the online celebrity.

In the virtual community platform, a certain amount of literature focuses on interactive behaviour in value co-creation. The interactivity among customers in the virtual community is an important means for customers to create and obtain value [34]. The interactivity between customers and enterprises drives value co-creation, which can bring about better experiences for users through increasing their sincerity and trust [10, 12]. The interactivity among customers is also a typical form of value co-creation, and this form of interactivity has become an emerging, independent and promising research theme in marketing academics [35], which enables customers to obtain a better service experience in the service process and influences their satisfaction and loyalty to the enterprise [36–38]. However, there is a lack of research exploring the shift from interactivity to value co-creation.

3 Research Model and Hypothesis

3.1 Psychological Attachment and Value Co-creation

Ball and Tasaki [19] propose that psychological attachment be often accompanied by a positive emotional response and lead to a supportive attitude and behaviour, which could be used to predict customer behaviour. In other words, positive emotional perception promotes the active contribution behaviour of individuals [39]. Users generate psychological emotions for the short-video community, thereby generating the motivation to maintain this psychological attachment. This motivation will prompt users to enact behaviours that are beneficial for the community platform and other users in the platform—that is, they will be more effectively and actively engaged in sponsored and autonomous co-creation. We thus posit that increased attachment in an online community, whatever the source of that attachment, will lead to a set of visible behaviours such as more active participation.

H1: Psychological attachment has positive impacts on UVCC.

In addition to these general effects of attachment, the literature also suggests that internalisation and identification attachment may have some different consequences, especially in relation to members' attitudes towards the community or individuals to whom they have become attached [40]. In the context of participating in community-sponsored activities, users' sense of internalisation to the community will assume more significance than their sense of identification with other users. Internalisation attachment reflects users' perceptions of the overlap of their own values with the core or defining characteristics of the community—characteristics that are central to the short-video platform, that distinguish it from other platforms and that are relatively enduring over time. A user who internalises with a short-video platform regards the community as a whole; perceives a sense of obligation or commitment to the community; becomes a champion of the community; and is more likely to share their knowledge, make helpful contributions and engage in favourable, community-related behaviours. Hence, we propose that:

H2a: Psychological internalisation attachment of users to the short-video community has a stronger impact on SVC than on AVC.

By contrast, in the context of participating in autonomous-sponsored activities, users' sense of identification with other users will assume more significance than their sense of internalisation to the community. Based on social identity theory, user' identification attachment emphasises the extent to which a user identifies with other users in the online short-video community, rather than the community as a whole. Identification attachment should cause users to focus on individual relationships with one another, which will in turn increase their willingness to exert effort to help individuals [3]. Users who perceive that they share similarities with other users are more likely to relate to or perceive 'kinship' with the other users of the short-video community with users' contributions so as to actively initiate short-video designing, creation and sharing activities. Hence, we propose that:

H2b: Psychological identification attachment of users to the short-video community has a stronger impact on AVC than on SVC.

3.2 Interactivity and Value Co-creation

Interactivity is a core function of the short-video community platform, and shooting, uploading, commenting and forwarding videos are basic means for the interactivity among users of the short-video community platform. In existing studies, many scholars have confirmed that interactivity increases users' participation in value co-creation behaviour [11, 41, 42].

On the short-video community platform, user–machine interactivity is mainly interactivity between users and the platform, which is reflected by the perception of users for the controllability, synchronicity and bidirectionality of the content and function of the platform. When users can completely control and obtain the videos they want to watch and upload and share videos simply and effectively, the self-efficacy of users of using these functions will improve. That is, users believe that they are fully capable of using the functions provided by this community platform to participate, create and share videos [43], thereby facilitating the active participation of users in value co-creation. In addition, when users can effectively obtain feedback from the platform, the predictability for the performance of value co-creation activity can be enhanced. The predictability of result/performance will effectively promote the adoption behaviour of users. At the same time, the degree of bidirectionality means users can freely communicate and share and even help each other. The autonomy of users can effectively promote individual innovation [44]. Therefore, the controllability, synchronicity and bidirectionality of users to platform will also promote users to actively participate in the value co-creation activity initiated by enterprises/platforms or themselves. Therefore,

H3a: User–machine interactivity positively influences users' participation in SVC behaviour.

H3b: User–machine interactivity positively influences users' participation in AVC behaviour.

User–user interactivity has a positive impact on users' willingness of value co-creation. Yi and Gong [45], Baumann and Meunier-FitzHugh [46] verified that the interactivity between customers and salespersons plays an important role in value co-creation. Interactivity among users was conducive to users to gain valuable knowledge and resources, such as information, problem-solving methods, ideas, creativity and support [47], and mutual help and encouragement among users are also beneficial for users to gain confidence, reduce anxiety and risk [48] and reduce the cost of value co-creation activities [49]. Therefore, the degree of interactivity among users is beneficial to users in obtaining information, users are more likely to get opportunities to participate short videos creation activities initiated by relevant platforms or enterprises, as well as be influenced by other users, thereby promoting the participation of users in co-creation activities initiated by platforms or enterprises. Hence, we propose that:

H4a: On the short-video community platform, user–user interactivity positively influences the SVC behaviour of users.

In addition, for autonomous co-creation short videos, users will face greater uncertainty and risks. In this case, the user-user interactivity is conducive to users to obtain support and help from other users, so as to promote them to actively initiate video co-creation activities. Hence, we propose that:

H4b: On the short-video community platform, user–user interactivity positively influences the AVC behaviour of users.

In the virtual community platform, it is easier to highlight the 'celebrity effect' of introduced online celebrities. In the virtual community platform, the celebrity effect plays an important role in attracting users' attention, guiding public opinions and promoting the continuous participation and interactivity of users [50]. On the short-video community platform, communication and interactivity between users and online celebrities enable users to be more susceptible to the celebrity effect. Under the promotion and support of online celebrities, users will be more actively engaged in value co-creation activity initiated by the platform; at the same time, users can often interact with online celebrities, and their interactivity can be shared with other users. In this way, users will receive more attention from other users so that they obtain more support for their activities on the platform, thereby further promoting the AVC of users.

H5a: On the short-video community platform, user–celebrity interactivity positively influences the SVC behaviour of users.

H5b: On the short-video community platform, user–celebrity interactivity positively influences the AVC behaviour of users.

3.3 Mediating Role of Psychological Attachment

Ren et al. [3] observed that interactive contact with a group contributes to attachment to the group, while contact among individual members can increase interpersonal attachment, and thus that it contributes to the active role of users in participation co-creation. Thus, we intended to test for the mediating effect of attachment between interactivity and

UVCC. Firstly, in the user–machine interactivity process, users perceive the community platform as a whole. The trust and emotional dependence of the community platform of users will be enhanced through good interactivity with the community platform [51]. The enrichment and appeal of the interactive scenario are also conducive to users to form good emotional connections and share their views of the platform [52]. Thus, when the platform provides professional and high-quality interactive functions, users will trust the platform more and perceive a higher value of the platform, thus generating psychological attachment to the platform.

H6: Internalisation psychological attachment of users to the short-video community plays a mediating role between user–machine interactivity and the value co-creation of users.

H6a: Internalisation psychological attachment mediates the relationship between user–machine interactivity and SVC.

H6b: Internalisation psychological attachment mediates the relationship between user–machine interactivity and AVC.

Secondly, user–user interactivity helps users gain social support, self-esteem and a sense of belonging [47]. McGrath and Otnes [53] believe that interactivity among consumers is conducive to establishing and maintaining close relationships with acquaintances, building relationships with people who were not familiar before and forming a sense of self-identity and social belonging. Therefore, in the short-video community, user–user interactivity drives users to develop interpersonal attraction. The frequency of user–user communication determines the extent to which people can build relationships. The relationship promotes users to perceive a sense of belonging with one other, thus forming their identification psychological attachment to other users.

H7: Identification psychological attachment of users to the short-video community plays a mediating role between user–user interactivity and value co-creation.

H7a: Identification psychological attachment mediates the relationship between user–user interactivity and SVC.

H7b: Identification psychological attachment mediates the relationship between user–user interactivity and AVC.

Finally, on the short-video community platform, the opportunity to interact with online celebrities greatly attracts users' attention [32]. As a special type of user on the short-video platform, online celebrities not only have individual characteristics but also represent the platform to some extent. On the short-video community platform, the content and activities that users use to interact with online celebrities can be presented to all fans in real time, which further promotes users to establish relationships with other users and gain a sense of social belonging. Thus, users who interact with online celebrities will generate two types of psychological attachment at the same time, namely internalised psychological attachment to the platform and identification psychological attachment to other users.

H8: Psychological attachment of users to the short-video community plays a mediating role between user–celebrity interactivity and the value co-creation of users.

H8a: Internalisation psychological attachment mediates the relationship between user–celebrity interactivity and SVC.

H8b: Internalisation psychological attachment mediates the relationship between user–celebrity interactivity and AVC.

H8c: Identification psychological attachment mediates the relationship between user–celebrity interactivity and SVC.

H8d: Identification psychological attachment mediates the relationship between user–celebrity interactivity and AVC.

Based on the discussion above, the a model is proposed, as shown in Fig. 1.

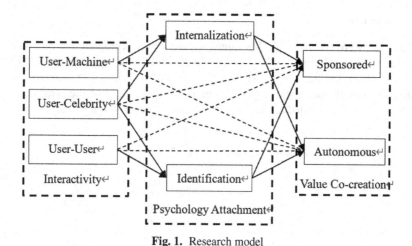

Fig. 1. Research model

4   Research Method

4.1   Data Collection

By the end of 2019, China had more than 24 short-video platforms. Furthermore, the number of short-video users has increased sharply in recent years; the number is expected to reach 630 million users [54]. The present study collected data from a short-video platform in China, namely Tik Tok, which has become the short-video platform with the largest number of users in China [55]. A convenience sampling strategy involving an online questionnaire was adopted to collect primary data from users of the Tik Tok short-video application. To identify target participants, we asked users the following screening question: 'Have you ever used Tik Tok to shoot and upload videos?' Respondents who fulfilled the criteria (answered 'yes' to the question) were the target participants of this study. The questionnaire was issued from May to July 2019. After exclusion of incomplete responses, 248 eligible samples were collected for analysis.

4.2   Instrument

The present study adopted well-established measures from prior studies. As mentioned, user–machine interactivity was defined as the information transmission ability between users and the medium itself and was measured using a three-item, 7-point scale concerning controllability, synchronicity and bidirectionality developed by Yoo et al. [30]. User–user and user–celebrity interactivity were measured using three-item, 7-point scale modified by Paechter, Maier, and Macher [56]. Internalisation and identification psychological attachment were measured through a three-item, 7-point scale developed by O'Reilly and Chatman [18]. Finally, the two constructs about UVCC, namely SVC and AVC, were measured using a three-item, 7-point scale modified by Zwass [6].

4.3 Sample Profile

After the data were screened, all 248 samples were used to complete the data analysis (see Table 1). QuestMobile (2019) show that in 2019 the ratio of male to female of Tik Tok user in China is about 4.9:5.2, with nearly 76.1% of users under 35 years old, which suggests that the characteristics of gender and age distribution of the samples in the study basically corresponded to the basic characteristics of Tik Tok users.

Table 1. Sample profile (N = 248)

Description profile		Frequency	Percentage (%)
Gender	Male	105	42.3
	Female	143	57.7
Age	Below 20	5	2.0
	20–35	203	81.9
	36–50	37	14.9
	Above 50	3	1.2
Education background	High school or below	3	1.2
	Undergraduate	227	91.5
	Postgraduate and above	18	7.3

4.4 Results

We chose partial least squares (PLS) because PLS's ability to assess the measurement model within the context of its theoretical mediated model makes it superior to multiple regression. PLS employs component-based estimation [57], thereby maximising the variance explained in the dependent variable. It does not require the data to have multivariate normality [58]. For the aforementioned reasons, SmartPLS 3.0 [59] was applied to the data analysis.

Measurement Model. To validate the measurement model, we assessed the reliability, convergent validity and discriminant validity of all constructs assessed for the samples. To measure scale reliability, we computed composite reliability (CR) values and the recommended a threshold of 0.70 [60]. Table 2 shows that all CR values exceeded 0.70 and fell between 0.856 and 0.881, indicating acceptable reliability [61].

Table 2. Results of confirmatory factor analysis

Constructs		Items	Loading	CR	AVE
Interactivity	User–Machine	UMI1	0.832	0.856	0.665
		UMI2	0.809		
		UMI3	0.805		
	User–User	UUI1	0.715	0.869	0.692
		UUI2	0.850		
		UUI3	0.917		
	User–Celebrity	UCI1	0.811	0.861	0.673
		UCI2	0.836		
		UCI3	0.814		
Psychology attachment	Internalisation	IntPA1	0.856	0.881	0.707
		IntPA2	0.827		
		IntPA3	0.848		
	Identification	IdPA1	0.880	0.878	0.711
		IdPA2	0.823		
		IdPA3	0.817		
Value Co-creation	Sponsored	SVC1	0.871	0.873	0.697
		SVC2	0.816		
		SVC3	0.817		
	Autonomous	AVC1	0.831	0.860	0.672
		AVC2	0.755		
		AVC3	0.869		

Convergent validity was evaluated through the significance of all item loadings exceeding 0.70 [62] and the construct's estimated average variance extracted (AVE) being above 0.50. As shown in Table 2, the value of factor loadings exceeded 0.617, and all the construct AVE estimates were over 0.50, which confirmed the convergent validity. According to Fornell and Larcker [62], for the construct to demonstrate discriminant validity, all construct AVE should be larger than the corresponding squared inter-construct correlation estimates. Table 3 shows that all constructs passed the criteria.

Structural Model. The path coefficients and explained variances for the conceptual model in this study are shown in Table 4. A bootstrapping procedure with replacement

Table 3. Correlations of latent variables and square roots of AVE

Variable	Mean	S.D	Gender	Age	Education	UMI	UUI	UCI	IntPA	IdPA	SVC	AVC
Gender	1.580	0.495	–									
Age	2.150	0.442	−0.146	–								
Education	2.060	0.285	−0.162	0.151	–							
UMI	4.093	0.658	0.076	0.151	0.020	**0.815**						
UUI	4.031	0.633	−0.122	0.066	0.015	0.300	**0.832**					
UCI	3.320	0.762	−0.122	0.060	0.108	0.286	0.285	**0.820**				
IntPA	3.343	0.819	−0.160	0.093	−0.112	0.298	0.188	0.376	**0.844**			
IdPA	3.700	0.799	−0.093	0.153	−0.101	0.302	0.361	0.394	0.609	**0.841**		
SVC	3.456	0.777	−0.143	0.155	−0.049	0.310	0.296	0.332	0.602	0.556	**0.835**	
AVC	3.427	0.773	−0.118	0.036	−0.117	0.223	0.238	0.420	0.620	0.657	0.611	**0.820**

1. Square roots of AVE appear in bold font
2. UMI: User–Machine Interactivity; UUI: User–User Interactivity; UCI: User–Celebrity Interactivity; IntPA: Internalisation Psychology Attachment; IdPA: Identification Psychology Attachment; SVC: Sponsored Value Co-creation; AVC: Autonomous Value Co-creation

Table 4. Results of hypotheses testing

Dependent variables								
Variables	SVC	AVC	SVC	AVC	IntPA	IdPA	SVC	AVC
	Model1a	Model1b	Model2a	Model2b	Model3a	Model3b	Model4a	Model4b
Control variables								
Age	0.064	−0.067	0.099	0.003	0.046	0.138*	0.056	−0.059
Gender	−0.038	−0.035	−0.116	−0.100	−0.161**	−0.028	−0.041	−0.026
Education	0.011	−0.028	−0.117	−0.177**	−0.183**	−0.166**	−0.004	−0.051
Independent variables								
UMI			0.199**	0.095	0.220**		0.080	−0.026
UUI			0.154*	0.099		0.259***	0.096	−0.006
UCI			0.229**	0.369***	0.311***	0.326***	0. 035	0.153**
IntPA	0.413***	0.342***					0.394***	0.313***
IdPA	0.293***	0.453***					0.231**	0.418***
R2	0.427	0.514	0.223	0.232	0.233	0.262	0.446	0.532

Notes: *p < 0.05, **p < 0.01, ***p < 0.001. Standardised path coefficients.
UMI: User–Machine Interactivity; UUI: User–User Interactivity; UCI: User–Celebrity Interactivity; IntPA: Internal-isation Psychology Attachment; IdPA: Identification Psychology Attachment; SVC: Sponsored Value Co-creation; AVC: Autonomous Value Co-creation

using 2,000 subsamples was used to estimate the statistical significance of the parameter estimates. The structural model was examined, and the effects among those latent constructs were also tested.

Regarding the effect of psychological attachment on UVCC, Table 4 shows the direct and indirect effects from all of the antecedents in the conceptual frame-work. Regarding the direct effect of psychological attachment on UVCC, Model1a and Model1b in Table 4 show that IntPA exhibited a positive effect on SVC ($\beta = 0.413$, $p < 0.001$) and AVC ($\beta = 0.342$, $p < 0.001$), and IdPA also showed a positive effect on SVC ($\beta = 0.293$, $p < 0.01$) and AVC ($\beta = 0.453$, $p < 0.001$), supporting H1. The results also show that the standardised path coefficients of IntPA on SVC ($\beta = 0.413$) were greater than those on AVC ($\beta = 0.342$), supporting H2a; the standardised path coefficients of IdPA on SVC ($\beta = 0.293$) were greater than those on AVC ($\beta = 0.453$), supporting H2b.

Model2a and Model2b show the results about the direct effect of the interactivity on UVCC. UMI was positively related with SVA ($\beta = 0.199$, $p < 0.01$), but it exhibited no significant influence on AVC ($\beta = 0.095$, n.s.). UUI had a positive and significant effect on SVC ($\beta = 0.154$, $p < 0.05$), while it had a non-significant effect on AVC ($\beta = 0.099$, n.s.), and UCI had a positive and significant effect on both SVC ($\beta = 0.229$, $p < 0.01$) and AVC ($\beta = 0.369$, $p < 0.001$). Hence, H3a, H4a, H5a and H5b were supported, whereas H3b and H4b were not.

To test whether the effects of interactivity on value co-creation were mediated by psychology attachment, we followed the mediation tests suggested by Baron and Harris [48] and used the bootstrapping method to assess the significance of mediating effects (see Table 5).

Table 5. Results of indirect effects

Indirect Effect	Indirect Effect Coefficients	95% Bias-corrected Confidence Intervals
UMI→IntPA→SVC	0.086	[0.024, 0.149]
UMI→IntPA→AVC	0.069	[0.019, 0.118]
UUI→IdPA→SVC	0.060	[0.017, 0.102]
UUI→IdPA→AVC	0.108	[0.046, 0.170]
UCI→IntPA→SVC	0.122	[0.057, 0.188]
UCI→IntPA→AVC	0.097	[0.044, 0.150]
UCI→IdPA→SVC	0.075	[0.024, 0.127]
UCI→IdPA→AVC	0.136	[0.079, 0.193]

First, for H6a and H6b, UMI had a positive and significant effect on IntPA ($\beta = 0.220$, $p < 0.01$, see Model3a). In the presence of IntPA (see Model4a), the effects of UMI on SVC and AVC were not significant ($\beta = 0.080$, n.s.; $\beta = -0.026$, n.s., respectively). According to the results in Table 5, the bootstrap results of the indirect effects of UMI on SVC and AVC through IntPA revealed bias-corrected 95% confidence intervals that did not involve zero ($\beta = 0.086$, BCCI [0.024, 0.149] for UMI to SVC; $\beta = 0.069$, BCCI [0.019, 0.118] for UMI to AVC), thereby illustrating that IntPA completely mediated the relationship between UMI and value co-creation (i.e. SVC and AVC). The results provide support for H6a and H6b.

Second, as shown in Model3b, UUI had a positive and significant effect on IdPA ($\beta = 0.259$, $p < 0.001$). In Model4a and Model4b, the effect of UUI on SVC became not significant ($\beta = 0.096$, n.s.), and on AVC it was not significant ($\beta = -0.006$, n.s.).

According to the results in Table 5, the bootstrap results of the indirect effect of UUI on SVC and AVC through IdPA reveal bias-corrected 95% confidence intervals that did not involve zero ($\beta = 0.060$, BCCI [0.017, 0.102] for UUI to SVC; $\beta = 0.108$, BCCI [0.046, 0.170] for UUI to AVC), thereby illustrating that IdPA mediated the relationship between UUI and value co-creation (i.e. SVC and AVC), supporting H7a and H7b.

Third, Model3a and Model3b show that UCI had a positive and significant effect on IntPA ($\beta = 0.311$, $p < 0.001$) and on IdPA ($\beta = 0.326$, $p < 0.001$). In the presence of the mediator, IntPA and IdPA, the effect of UCI on SVC became not significant ($\beta = 0.035$, n.s.), and on AVC it became less significant ($\beta = 0.153$, $p < 0.01$) (see Model4a and Model4b). According to the results in Table 5, the boot-strap results of the indirect effect of UCI on SVC and AVC through IntPA revealed bias-corrected 95% confidence intervals that did not involve zero ($\beta = 0.122$, BCCI [0.057, 0.188] for UCI to SVC; $\beta = 0.097$, BCCI [0.044, 0.150] for UCI to AVC). IdPA revealed bias-corrected 95% confidence intervals that also did not involve zero ($\beta = 0.075$, BCCI [0.024, 0.127] for UCI to SVC; $\beta = 0.136$, BCCI [0.079, 0.193] for UCI to AVC). These results suggested that IntPA and IdPA completely mediated the effect of UCI on SVC and partially mediated the effect of UCI on AVC. H8 (H8a–H8d) is supported. Table 6 summarises the results of the hypotheses testing.

Table 6. Summary of hypotheses testing

Hypothesis	Path	Result
	Direct effects	
H1	IntPA→SVC	Supported
	IntPA→AVC	
	IdPA→SVC	
	IdPA→AVC	
H2a	IntPA→SVC > IntPA→AVC	Supported
H2b	IdPA→AVC > IdPA→SVC	Supported
H3a	UMI→SVC	Supported
H3b	UMI→AVC	Not Supported
H4a	UUI→SVC	Supported
H4b	UUI→AVC	Not Supported
H5a	UCI→SVC	Supported
H5b	UCI→AVC	Supported
	Indirect effects	
H6a	UMI→IntPA→SVC	Supported
H6b	UMI→IntPA→AVC	Supported
H7a	UUI→IdPA→SVC	Supported
H7b	UUI→IdPA→AVC	Supported
H8a	UCI→IntPA→SVC	Supported
H8b	UCI→IntPA→AVC	Supported
H8c	UCI→IdPA→SVC	Supported
H8c	UCI→IdPA→AVC	Supported

5 Discussion and Conclusion

5.1 Discussion

The objective of this study was to examine the impacts of interactivity and psychological attachment on UVCC in the emerging context of the short-video community. Overall, the empirical results supported most of our hypotheses, except for two path relationship (H3b and H4b).

First, this study found that psychological attachment promotes UVCC (H1). More significantly, the study revealed that users' psychological attachment differs across types of value co-creation (H2a and H2b). These findings are consistent with those of previous studies that have asserted that different types of psychological attachment are related to different behaviours [18]. Second, the study revealed that the direct effect of the interactivity on UVCC was not completely supported. In particular, user–machine interactivity and user–user interactivity only significantly promote SVC but have no impact on AVC, while user–celebrity interactivity significantly promotes both SVC and AVC. Third, the study observed the underlying mediating role of psychological attachment for the relationship between interactivity and value co-creation. Users' internalisation psychological attachment completely mediates the relationship between user–machine interactivity and value co-creation (H6a and H6b), and identification psychological attachment also completely mediates the relationship between user–machine interactivity and value co-creation (H7a and H7b). However, the shift from user–celebrity interactivity to value co-creation is through generating psychological attachment to both the whole platform and other users on the platform.

5.2 Implications for Theory

First, this study offers a fresh perspective on UVCC by drawing from psychological attachment [18] to develop a research model. This research extends psychological attachment theory in terms of organisational behaviour and marketing. Second, this research explains the mechanism behind the effects of interactivity to value co-creation and extends the literature by revealing the mediating influences of psychological attachment on the relationship between interactivity and value co-creation. Additionally, the findings of the present study complement those of Ren et al. [3] by revealing that psychological attachment stems from different interactivity and differs by the type of interactivity. Moreover, the present research offers further elucidation by regarding psychological attachment as having a mediating role that can reveal the mechanism about the shift from interactivity to value co-creation. Third, this research advances understanding of the effects of different interactivity by showing the direct and indirect effects of interactivity on value co-creation. This study revealed that user–celebrity interactivity had a stronger effect on value co-creation than user–user or user–machine interactivity. This research offers a more fine-grained perspective for understanding the influence of interactivity on value co-creation.

5.3 Implications for Practice

This research is pertinent for the short-video platform industry. The findings offer managerial guidelines for marketers in this industry to balance their effort and resources in marketing activities to promote effectiveness.

Firstly, in the virtual community platform, how to promote the value co-creation of users has become a focus for enterprises across the globe. Users in the virtual community have shown different value co-creation behaviours, so enterprises should fully recognise the pattern of manifestation of these value co-creation behaviours. Secondly, psychological attachment is the most significant element in facilitating users' value co-creation behaviour. Managers should consider psychological attachment to promote users' participation of shooting, uploading and sharing videos. Moreover, the different effect of psychological attachment on different value co-creation behaviours suggests that managers should change their marketing strategies to provide programmes to promote psychological attachment for different value co-creation activities. Thirdly, the virtual community platform strives to provide various forms of interaction. These interactions not only satisfy different demands of users but play different roles as well. Therefore, managers of the platform or enterprise should clearly recognise the mechanism of different interactivity and provide better interactive services in a targeted manner so that they can continuously increase the number of users, user engagement and user activity on the platform. Fourthly, on the short-video community platform, the introduction and training of online celebrities are also keys to continuous survival of the platform. Therefore, administrators of the platform should effectively introduce online celebrities or cultivate online celebrities on the platform, thus generating the celebrity effect.

5.4 Limitations

This study has several limitations. First, psychological attachment can be classified based on different dimensions, while this study only considers two dimensions, namely internalisation and identification. In future studies, more dimensions can be taken into consideration so as to cover more psychological factors that affect the value co-creation behaviour of users; second, the sample was taken from a short-video platform, namely Tik Tok, and thus, different characteristics of different short-video community platforms were not considered. Future studies should consider adopting a random sampling strategy to collect data while guaranteeing sample representativeness to further expand the applicability to all short-video platforms.

Appendix

Table 7. Survey measurement scales

Variables		Item		References
Interactivity	User–Machine	UMI1	When using Tik Tok, I can choose the content that I want to watch	Yoo et al. [30]
		UMI2	When using Tik Tok, I can obtain the information that I want in a timely manner	
		UMI3	Tik Tok provides a communication channel for users	
	User–User	UUI1	In Tik Tok, I can establish a connection with other common users	Paechter et al. [56]
		UUI2	In Tik Tok, I can interact with other common users in various ways (comment, private message etc.)	
		UUI3	In Tik Tok, I can communicate with other common uses easily	
	User–Celebrity	UCI1	In Tik Tok, I can receive a reply from online celebrities quickly	Paechter et al. [56]
		UCI2	In Tik Tok, I can establish a connection with online celebrities	
		UCI3	In Tik Tok, I can consult online celebrities for knowledge and problem-solving methods	

(*continued*)

Table 7. (*continued*)

Variables		Item		References
Psychological attachment	Internalisation	IntPA1	My values are similar to the values of Tik Tok	O'Reilly and Chatman [18]
		IntPA2	I like Tik Tok because it represents my values	
		IntPA3	After using Tik Tok, my values become more similar to the values of Tik Tok	
	Identification	IdPA1	I will tell others that I use Tik Tok with pride	
		IdPA2	I would like to recommend Tik Tok to others	
		IdPA3	I have a sense of belonging to Tik Tok because I am not only a user	
Value co-creation	Sponsored	SVC1	I often participate in video shooting activities initiated by Tik Tok	Zwass [6]
		SVC2	I often participate in creativity collection and evaluation activities initiated by Tik Tok	
		SVC3	I often participate in Tik Tok short video collection activities initiated by enterprises or organisations	
	Autonomous	AVC1	I will use Tik Tok to share my life with others	
		AVC2	I often initiate challenge topics on Tik Tok	
		AVC3	I often actively respond to topics or videos initiated by other users on Tik Tok	

References

1. Qiu, Y., Zheng, J.: Research on the current situation and development trend of short video App from the perspective of demand. China Market (10), 125–126 (2019)
2. iiresearch.cn: Research Report on the Competition of China Micro-Video Head Market (2020). https://report.iimedia.cn/repo13-0/39194.html
3. Ren, Y., Harper, F.M., Drenner, S., Terveen, L., Kiesler, S.: Building member attachment in online communities: applying theories of group identity and interpersonal bonds. MIS Q. **36**(3), 841–864 (2012)
4. Xie, X.-Z., Tsai, N.-C., Xu, S.-Q., Zhang, B.-Y.: Does customer co-creation value lead to electronic word-of-mouth? An empirical study on the short-video platform industry. Soc. Sci. J. **56**(3), 401–416 (2019)
5. Madupu, V., Cooley, D.O.: Antecedents and consequences of online brand community participation: a conceptual framework. J. Internet Commer. **9**(2), 127–147 (2010)
6. Zwass, V.: Co-creation: toward a taxonomy and an integrated research perspective. Int. J. Electron. Commer. **15**(1), 11–48 (2010)
7. Roberts, D., Hughes, M., Kertbo, K.: Exploring consumers' motivations to engage in innovation through co-creation activities. Eur. J. Market. **48**(1/2), 147–169 (2014)
8. Fuller, J., Matzler, K., Hoppe, M.: Brand community members as a source of innovation. J. Prod. Innov. Manage. **25**(6), 608–609 (2008)
9. Namibisan, S.: Designing virtual customer environments for new product development: towards a theory. Acad. Manage. Rev. **27**(3), 392–413 (2002)
10. Lanier, C., Hampton, R.: Consumer participation and experiential marketing: understanding the relationship between co-creation and the fantasy life cycle. Adv. Consum. Res. **35**(1), 44–48 (2008)
11. Prahalad, C.K., Ramaswamy, V.: Co-creation experiences: the next practice in value creation. J. Interact. Market. **18**(3), 5–14 (2004)
12. Prahalad, C.K., Ramaswamy, V.: The Future of Competition: Co-Creating Unique Value with Customers. Harvard Business Press (2004)
13. Vargo, S.L., Maglio, P.P., Akaka, M.A.: On value and value co-creation: a service systems and service logic perspective. Eur. Manage. J. **26**(3), 145–152 (2008)
14. Hoffman, D.L., Novak, T.P.: Marketing in hypermedia computer-mediated environments: conceptual foundations. J. Market. **60**(3), 50–68 (1996)
15. Akaka, M.A., Vargo, S.L., Lusch, R.F.: The complexity of context: a service ecosystems approach for international marketing. J. Int. Market. **21**(4), 1–20 (2013)
16. Vargo, S.L., Lusch, R.F.: Service-dominant logic: continuing the evolution. J. Acad. Market. Sci. **36**(1), 1–10 (2008)
17. Grönroos, C., Voima, P.: Critical service logic: making sense of value creation and co-creation. J. Acad. Market. Sci. **41**(2), 133–150 (2013)
18. O'Reilly, C., Chatman, J.: Organizational commitment and psychological attachment: the effects of compliance, identification, and internalization on prosocial behavior. J. Appl. Psychol. **71**(3), 492–499 (1986)
19. Ball, D., Tasaki, L.H.: The role and measurement of attachment in consumer behavior. J. Consum. Psychol. **1**(2), 155–172 (1992)
20. Burris, E.R., Detert, J.R., Chiaburu, D.S.: Quitting before leaving: the mediating effects of psychological attachment and detachment on voice. J. Appl. Psychol. **93**(4), 912–922 (2008)
21. Glasman, L.R., Albarracin, D.: Forming attitudes that predict future behavior: a meta-analysis of the attitude-behavior relation. Psychol. Bull. **132**(5), 778 (2006)
22. Riketta, M., Dick, R.V.: Foci of attachment in organizations: a meta-analytic comparison of the strength and correlates of workgroup versus organizational identification and commitment ☆. J. Vocat. Behav. **67**(3), 490–510 (2005)

23. Lavelle, J.J., et al.: Commitment, procedural fairness, and organizational citizenship behavior: a multifoci analysis. J. Organ. Behav. **30**(3), 337–357 (2010)
24. Prentice, D.A., Miller, D.T., Lightdale, J.R.: Asymmetries in attachments to groups and to their members: distinguishing between common-identity and common-bond groups. Pers. Soc. Psychol. Bull. **20**(5), 484–493 (1994)
25. Coyle, J.R., Thorson, E.: The effects of progressive levels of interactivity and vividness in web marketing sites. J. Adv. **30**(3), 65–77 (2001)
26. Ha, L., James, E.L.: Interactivity reexamined: a baseline analysis of early business web sites. J. Broadcast. Electron. Media **42**(4), 457–474 (1998)
27. Stromer-Galley, J.: On-line interaction and why candidates avoid it. J. Commun. **50**(4), 111–132 (2006)
28. Liu, C.-C.: A model for exploring players flow experience in online games. Inf. Technol. People **30**(1), 139–162 (2017)
29. Cheng, Y.M.: Exploring the roles of interaction and flow in explaining nurses' e-learning acceptance. Nurse Educ. Today **33**(1), 73–80 (2013)
30. Yoo, W.-S., Lee, Y., Park, J.: The role of interactivity in e-tailing: creating value and increasing satisfaction. J. Retail. Consum. Serv. **17**(2), 89–96 (2010)
31. Yang, X., Lan, B., Sun, F.: How brand microblogging attract fans interaction?—An empirical study based on CMC theory. Manage. Rev. **27**(1), 158–168 (2015)
32. Li, H.: Research on the communication dependence of Douyin APP. China Newspaper Ind. (02), 45–46 (2018)
33. Liu, B.: Exploration on the communication capability of short video social platform-take Tik Tok as an example. Media (19), 53–54 (2018)
34. Wang, Y.: The key drivers of customer interactions and their effects on customer satisfaction: an empirical study in the context of virtual brand community. Chin. J. Manage. **10**(9), 1375 (2013)
35. Li, Z.: A literature review of customer-to-customer interaction and prospect. Foreign Econ. Manage. **37**(12), 73–85 (2015)
36. Yang, J., Zheng, R., Zhao, L., Gupta, S.: Enhancing customer brand experience and loyalty through enterprise microblogs: empirical evidence from a communication framework perspective. Inf. Technol. People **30**(3), 580–601 (2017)
37. Prahalad, C.K., Ramaswamy, V.: Co-opting customer competence. Harvard Bus. Rev. **78**(1), 79–90 (2000)
38. Langeard, E., Bateson, J., Lovelock, C.H., Eiglier, P.: Marketing of services: new insights from consumers and managers. Market Science Institute, Cambridge, MA, pp. 81–104 (1981)
39. Zhang, D., Lin, M., Chen, C., Liu, S.: Do emotions and relationships in brand community inspire recommendations? Research on the influence of customer psychological attachment on their recommendation intentions. Manage. Rev. **31**(2), 155–168 (2019)
40. Ren, Y., Kraut, R.E., Kiesler, S.: Applying common identity and bond theory to design of online communities. Organ. Stud. **28**(3), 377–408 (2007)
41. Gummesson, E., Mele, C.: Marketing as value co-creation through network interaction and resource integration. J. Bus. Market Manage. **4**(4), 181–198 (2010)
42. Grönroos, C.: Adopting a service business logic in relational business-to-business marketing: value creation, interaction and joint value co-creation. Paper Presented at the Otago Forum (2008)
43. Compeau, D.R., Higgins, C.A.: Computer self-efficacy: development of a measure and initial test. MIS Q. **19**(2), 189–211 (1995)
44. Ahuja, M.K., Thatcher, J.B.: Moving beyond intentions and toward the theory of trying: effects of work environment and gender on post-adoption information technology use. MIS Q. **29**(3), 427–459 (2005)

45. Yi, Y., Gong, T.: Customer value co-creation behavior: scale development and validation. J. Bus. Res. **66**(9), 1279–1284 (2013)
46. Baumann, J., Meunier-FitzHugh, K.L.: Trust as a facilitator of co-creation in customer-salesperson interaction–an imperative for the realization of episodic and relational value? AMS Rev. **4**(1–2), 5–20 (2014)
47. Bruhn, M., Schnebelen, S., Schäfer, D.: Antecedents and consequences of the quality of e-customer-to-customer interactions in B2B brand communities. Ind. Market. Manage. **43**(1), 164–176 (2014)
48. Baron, S., Harris, K.: Toward an understanding of consumer perspectives on experiences. J. Serv. Market. **24**(24), 518–531 (2010)
49. Libai, B., Bolton, R., Bugel, M.S., Ruyter, K.D., Gotz, O., Risselada, H., Stephen, A.T.: Customer-to-customer interactions: broadening the scope of word of mouth research. J. Serv. Res. **13**(3), 267–282 (2010)
50. Guo, Y., He, Y.: Study on the celebrity users' characteristics mining and the effects of Sina micro-blog. J. Intell. **32**(2), 112–116 (2013)
51. Ridings, C., Gefen, D., Arinze, B.: Psychological barriers: lurker and poster motivation and behavior in online communities. Commun. Assoc. Inf. Syst. **18**(1), 16 (2006)
52. Guo, Q., & Meng, Q.: Interaction ritual chains of Tik Tok and value creation. Chin. Editorials (09), 70–75 (2018)
53. McGrath, M.A., Otnes, C.: Unacquainted influencers: when strangers interact in the retail setting. J. Bus. Res. **32**(3), 261–272 (1995)
54. iiresearch.cn.: 2018–2019 China Short Video Industry Special Survey and Analysis Report (2019). https://www.iimedia.cn/c400/63582.html
55. iiresearch.cn: 2019 China short video electronic commerce industry and benchmarking case analysis report (2019). https://report.iimedia.cn/repo1-0/38839.html
56. Paechter, M., Maier, B., Macher, D.: Students' expectations of, and experiences in e-learning: their relation to learning achievements and course satisfaction (2010)
57. Lohmoller, J.B.: The PLS program system: latent variables path analysis with partial least squares estimation. Multivar. Behav. Res. **23**(1), 125 (1988)
58. Gefen, D., Straub, D., Rigdon, E.: An update and extension to SEM guidelines for admnistrative and social science research. MIS Q. **35**(2), iii–xiv (2011)
59. Ringle, C. M., Wende, S., Will, A.: Finite mixture partial least squares analysis: methodology and numerical examples. In: Handbook of Partial Least Squares, pp. 195–218 (2010)
60. Werts, C.E., Linn, R.L., Jöreskog, K.G.: Intraclass reliability estimates: testing structural assumptions. Educ. Psychol. Meas. **34**(1), 25–33 (1974)
61. Gefen, D., Straub, D.W., Boudreau, M.C.: Structural equation modeling and regression: guidelines for research practice (2000)
62. Fornell, C., Larcker, D.F.: Evaluating structural equation models with unobservable variables and measurement error. J. Market. Res. **18**(1), 39–50 (1981)

Bibliometric Structured Review of Mobile Information Systems

Sunday Adewale Olaleye[1], Ismaila Temitayo Sanusi[2(✉)],
and Oluwaseun Alexander Dada[3]

[1] University of Oulu, Oulu, Finland
sunday.olaleye@oulu.fi
[2] University of Eastern Finland, Joensuu, Finland
ismails@uef.fi
[3] University of Helsinki, Helsinki, Finland
alexander.dada@helsinki.fi

Abstract. This study attempts to fill the identified research gap in the existing literature through a bibliometric analysis and discovered 20 highly global cited papers with 1376 citations and yielded eight (8) core categories of knowledge in MobIS: (1) Information Systems, (2) Adoption, (3) Acceptance, (4) Satisfaction, (5) Information Systems Success and (6) Information Systems continuance. The results show that the distribution of the annual papers flows along the downslope. It was a bit stable in 2016 and since then descend from 2017 to 2020. As a young discipline, there is a need for more productivity, impact, and collaboration in the field of MobIS.

Keywords: Mobile information systems · Bibliometric · Structured review · MobIS

1 Introduction

Mobile information systems (MobIS) is a growing trend in the industry because of its potential to enhance the business processes and performance. Ubiquitous MobIS allows interaction of mobile devices and other systems with impact on the society, economy, governance, education, commerce, healthcare [1], and industry [2]. This MobIS has been extremely useful during the ongoing pandemic (COVID-19). For instance, recent study of Drew [3] reported the rapid implementation of mobile technology for real-time epidemiology of COVID-19. According to the authors this real-time information systems has potential to showcase data on predictive symptoms, risk factors, clinical outcomes, and geographical hotspots and so far, has generated above 2.8 million users. The use of MobIS is relevant in different fields and in academia its research is ongoing because (MobIS) is an evolving discipline.

This study discovered a gap in the study of Shiau, Yan and Lin [4] and this study intend to fill this gap and expand the work of [4]. For instance, the intellectual structure composition of MobIS is subject to change from time-to-time and [4] extracted data from

© Springer Nature Switzerland AG 2021
G. Salvendy and J. Wei (Eds.): HCII 2021, LNCS 12796, pp. 284–297, 2021.
https://doi.org/10.1007/978-3-030-77025-9_24

the Web of Science from 1996–2015 and this study follow up their study by extracting data from the Web of Science from 2016–2020. Due to the gap in the existing literature, this study proposed the following research questions: (1) Why is important to explore the trend of the core knowledge and the intellectual structure of the MobIS in detail? Why is TCCM framework relevant to the discipline of MobIS?

MobIS is diffusing across the continents and a recent study investigates the use of interaction design patterns in Brazil with focus on government mobile information systems and discovered that in Brazil, the government's mobile information systems is at the low level of employing the interaction design patterns. This paper could be a panacea for the Brazilian to use governmental services in mobile systems efficiently [5]. Further, Saeed and Xu [6] extended the Bass model to information system-based services and discovered the effect of dis-adoption and re-adoption in innovation diffusion process. Besides, [7] proposed a MobIS framework for Bangladeshi ready-made garments (RMG) and showcase the relevance of MobIS for empowerment process. The study of He, Nazir and Hussain [8] emphasised the importance of literature review and mentioned that it will help to understand the researchers and other academic stakeholder's productivity levels, relevant theories and methods that works best in different situations.

The introduction to MobIS precedes the synopsis of MobIS, then followed by methodology section and results section. Also, with discussion, conclusion and finally, the recommendations for the future research.

2 Synopsis of Mobile Information Systems

Combination of mobile technology and information systems evolved as the discipline of mobile information systems. Mobile technology use and advancement is expanding globally and contributes to the ubiquitous of information systems. Information systems has metamorphized over years from traditional record keeping to the present cloud storage system. Mobile information systems is an "information systems in which access to information resources and services is gained through end-user terminals that are easily movable in space, operable no matter what the location, and, typically, provided with wireless connection" [9]. This definition indicate accessibility, technology, operability, and connectivity. MobIS will continue to be relevant to the academic community and the industry because it can provide future new value-added services in different context of use [9]. MobIS addresses a wider user group and pose new challenges such as privacy, users' orientation, poor quality of network connection and use high distraction. Model-based approach and Task-Technology Fit was proposed for the development of MobIS [10, 11]. A recent study also contribute to the literature of MobIS and explored the key content of the MobIS field and identified the intellectual structure of MobIS [4]. The existing studies motivates this bibliometric review and TCCM analysis.

3 Bibliometric Methodology

There are different types of literature review, approaches, techniques, and tools (He et al. 2021) [8]. The earlier studies have employed the traditional method and software to explain different kinds of phenomenon in conjunction with academic community productivity. One of such review is bibliometric method. Bibliometric method focus on bibliographic data analysis based on published literature to give insights of the body of knowledge for a specific or combined field of inquiry [12, 13]. This study adopts bibliometric method to explain the phenomenon of mobile information systems. The study utilised relevant literature from leading global database (ISI Web of Knowledge database) and extracted 1074 from 2016–2020 with 37814 references, 3980 author's keywords (Table 1) with the following search query: ((Abstract-Title-Keyword ("mobile information systems")). The total collected data was 1132 and after language exclusion (Portuguese – 12, Spanish – 9, Russian – 3 and Turkish – 3), the English outlet accounts for 1100 and the inclusion of articles and conference proceedings yield 1074. A full record information from Web of Science database with focus on bibliographical information, citation information, abstract, keywords and other relevant information was exported in BibTeX file format. Because of the limitation of 500 dataset per download, the study employed Texmaker (a free cross-platform latex editor) to merge the files. This study utilised bibliometrix R package (R studio) for the data analysis because of its dynamic statistical algorithm and integrated data visualization features [14]. The study combined the bibliometric and TCCM framework to get a better understanding of mobile information systems impact.

Table 1. Demographic information

Description	Result
Main information data	
Timespan	2016–2020
Sources (Journals, Books, and others)	682
Documents	1074
Average years from publication	3.18
Average citations per documents	5.101
Average citations per year per doc	1.183
References	37814
Document types	
Article	674
Article; early access	28
Article; proceedings paper	6
Proceedings paper	366
Document contents	
Keywords Plus	1671
Author's Keywords	3980

(continued)

Table 1. (*continued*)

Description	Result
Main information data	
Authors	
Authors	3221
Author Appearances	3609
Authors of single-authored documents	87
Authors of multi-authored documents	3134
Authors collaboration	
Single-authored documents	95
Documents per Author	0.333
Authors per Document	3
Co-Authors per Documents	3.36
Collaboration Index	3.2

4 Analysis

4.1 Trends of MobIS Research

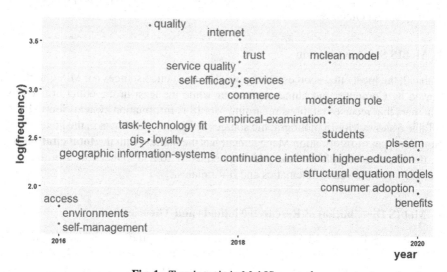

Fig. 1. Trends topic in MobIS research

Shown in Fig. 1 are trend topics in MobIS research. Among the top 24 most trend topics, quality has the highest frequency followed closely by internet and trust. The least trending topic is self-management.

4.2 Yearly Articles vs Citation

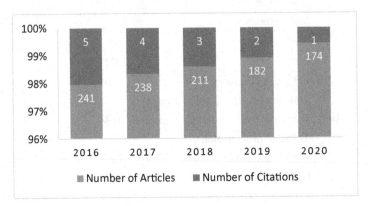

Fig. 2. Yearly articles vs citation

Figure 2 shows the number of articles and citation garnered yearly from 2016 to 2010. There is decline in article production from 2016 to 2020. Despite that MobIS is a growing trend, it is unexpected that the rate of publication will keep decreasing yearly. With this constant decline for over four years, there is possibility of further decline in coming years. It can also be seen in Fig. 2 that the number of citations increase by the year the highest articles are published. This trend shows that the more articles are produced, the more they attract citations.

4.3 MobIS Sources Citation

In Table 2, the most cited sources are shown. The most cited sources are MIS Quarterly followed by Computer and human behaviour while the least in the outlet utilized by researchers that receives citations regarding MobIS is Information systems journal.

Table 3 shows MobIS bibliographic sources of articles. As shown in the table, International Journal of Information Management has the highest with the **total citations** of 350, the **number of publications** which amounts to 20 and h_index of 9 in the year 2016. Closely followed is Telematics and Informatics.

4.4 MobIS Distribution of Research Methods and Theories

Table 4 evinces the methodological approach utilized in producing scientific articles. The research methods adopted in the publications include mixed methodology, quantitative methods, qualitative method, constructive learning methods, interpolation methods and IDEF0, IDEF3. Such methodologies as IDEF0 and IDEF3 were implemented for business processes description.

The theories utilized in MobIS literatures are shown in Table 5. The theories are categorized into three namely, information systems theory, psychology cognitive theory and others. According to [15], effective application of theory is critical to the development of

Table 2. MobIS most cited sources

Sources	Citations
Mis Quart	1615
Comput Hum Behav	1116
Inform Syst Res	670
Inform Manage-Amster	643
Decis Support Syst	498
Int J Inform Manage	458
J Marketing Res	343
Manage Sci	328
J Manage Inform Syst	323
Eur J Inform Syst	300
J Marketing	296
J Bus Res	286
Lect Notes Comput Sc	284
Comput Educ	268
Internet Res	264
Int J Med Inform	247
Telemat Inform	237
J Assoc Inf Syst	227
Electron Commer R A	224
Inform Syst J	217

new knowledge in information systems (IS) research. As shown in the table, psychology theories emerge in MobIS literatures. This is consistent with the study of [15] which states that IS research draws from a diverse set of disciplines, with Psychology emerging as a consistently dominant source of theories for IS.

4.5 Authors Productivity Over Time

Regarding authors' production over time, we investigated the top six authors and our findings showed that the majority of those top authors were already publishing articles on MobIS by the year 2016. As seen in Table 6, the author Li Y. has the highest publication over time having had several articles published yearly consistently since 2016 till 2020.

As shown in Table 7, among the top 20 most cited authors, only two have received ≥ 100 citations, three have been cited ≥ 80 times, and five have not reached 10 citations. Overall, those authors who had the largest number of citations also had the highest h-index (i.e., h-index > 4). However, Li Y. who has been cited a total of 27 times had a h-index of 4 while Liu, Y. with 140 citations had a h-index of 3. According to [16] a bigger

Table 3. MobIS publication outlets impact

Bibliographic Source	h_index	TC	NP	PY
International Journal of Information Management	9	350	20	2016
Electronic Journal of Information Systems In Developing Countries	2	12	12	2016
JMIR mHealth and uHealth	5	51	12	2016
IEEE Access	4	33	11	2017
Telematics and Informatics	6	256	11	2016
AMCIS 2017 Proceedings	0	0	10	2017
Internet Research	6	168	10	2016
IET Intelligent Transport Systems	4	24	9	2016
Information Systems Frontiers	5	127	9	2017
International Journal of Mobile Communications	2	34	9	2016
Centeris 2018 - International Conference on Enterprise Information Systems/Projman 2018 - International Conference on Project Management/Hcist 2018 - International Conference On Health And Social Care Information Systems And Technologies, Centeri	2	12	7	2018
Industrial Management & Data Systems	3	97	7	2016
International Journal of Medical Informatics	6	91	7	2016
ISPRS International Journal of Geo-Information	3	29	7	2016
Journal of Computer Information Systems	2	27	7	2017
Sustainability	2	15	7	2017
AMCIS 2016 Proceedings	0	0	6	2016
Computers in Human Behavior	4	158	6	2016
Information Technology & People	4	37	6	2017
JMIR Medical Informatics	2	15	6	2016
International Journal of Information Management	9	350	20	2016
Electronic Journal of Information Systems In Developing Countries	2	12	12	2016
JMIR mHealth and uHealth	5	51	12	2016

number of publications was an indicative of a higher author's scientific productivity as measured by the h-index and/or the g-index, but for Li Y. (h-index = 4, g-index = 4) that has the highest publications (10) and only received 27 citations so far. Considering the length of academic career, the m-index showed that Oliveira T., (0.67), and Kim J., (0.60), Sharma S.K. (0.60), were the authors who had higher growth in their scientific productivity.

Table 4. Research methods utilized in MobIS studies

Utilized methods
Mixed methodology
Quantitative methodology
Qualitative method
IDEF0
IDEF3
Constructive learning methods
Interpolation methods

Table 5. MobIS distribution of theories

Information systems theory, psychology cognitive theory and others		
Design theory	Motivation theory	Boulder model
Innovation diffusion-theory	Shafer evidence theory	Conceptual-model
Technology acceptance model		Dual-model
UTAUT model		Effects models
Cognitive theory		Evaluation model
Social cognitive theory		Expectation confirmation model
Management theory		Hegadas model
Complexity theory		Hierarchical model
Structuration theory		Hofstedes model
Self-determination theory		Integrated model
Protection motivation theory		McLean IS success model
Prospect-theory		Success model
The unified theory of acceptance and use of technology (UTAUT)		Theoretical-model

4.6 MobIS Relevant Keywords

The analyses of the 10 most frequently used terms included in all the retrieved documents using the author keywords and the keyword plus terms (i.e., keywords associated to the manuscript by Thomson Reuters' Institute for Scientific Information (ISI) WOS databases) are shown in Fig. 3. A total of 3980 author keywords were retrieved. Based on the higher frequency of keywords Information systems is most used and relevant keyword followed by mobile and systems. The least amongst them is health and continuance intention.

Table 6. Authors yearly production and citations

Author	Year	freq	TC	TCpY
Defranco A	2016	1	27	4.5
Defranco A	2017	1	11	2.2
Defranco A	2019	2	1	0.3
Ferreira M.J.	2016	2	0	0.0
Ferreira M.J.	2017	2	6	1.2
Ginige A	2017	1	4	0.8
Ginige A	2018	1	0	0.0
Ginige A	2019	3	0	0.0
Ginige A	2020	1	0	0.0
Kazimierski W	2016	3	40	6.7
Kazimierski W	2019	1	0	0.0
Kim J	2016	1	1	0.2
Kim J	2017	4	20	4.0
Kim J	2018	1	52	13.0
Kim J	2019	2	2	0.7
Li Y	2016	3	11	1.8
Li Y	2017	3	9	1.8
Li Y	2018	1	4	1.0
Li Y	2019	1	3	1.0
Li Y	2020	1	0	0.0

4.7 MobIS TCCM Analysis

Using a simple framework of TCCM, in which T stands for theory, C for context, C for characteristics and M for methodology: accordingly, the following section deals with analysis of the findings in relation to theory development, context, characteristics and methodology of MobIS as revealed in the bibliometric analysis based on the data generated from WoS databases from 2016–2020.

Theory Development (T)
In this review, several theories were adopted and as expected in the realm of information systems since our focus is on mobile information systems. However, few theories utilized are from the psychology field to explain the concepts of mobIS. As revealed in Table 5, several models were also used in the mobIS research. According to [15], effective application of theory is critical to the development of new knowledge in information systems (IS) research. With the emergence of psychology theories in MobIS literatures, this study is consistent with [15] research which founds that IS research draws from a diverse set of disciplines, with psychology emerging as a consistently dominant source

Table 7. Authors research impact and metrics

Author	h_index	g_index	m_index	TC	NP	PY_start
Li Y	4	4	–	27	10	2016
Zhang X	1	2	0.17	8	8	2016
Liu Y	3	7	0.50	140	7	2016
Ginige A	1	2	0.20	4	6	2017
Oliveira T	4	6	0.67	156	6	2016
Al-Emran M	2	4	–	25	4	2018
Defranco A	2	4	0.33	39	4	2016
Ferreira M.J.	1	2	0.17	6	4	2016
Kazimierski W	3	4	0.50	40	4	2016
Kim J	3	4	0.60	18	4	2017
Liu J	2	4	0.33	81	4	2016
Moreira F	1	2	0.17	6	4	2016
Morosan C	2	4	0.33	39	4	2016
O'Connor Y	2	3	0.33	13	4	2016
Schmidt R	1	2	0.25	6	4	2018
Sharma S.K.	3	4	0.60	84	4	2017
Wang J	3	4	0.50	90	4	2016
Wlodarczyk-Sielicka M	2	4	0.33	30	4	2016
Zhang F	3	4	0.50	21	4	2016
Zhang M	2	4	0.50	22	4	2018

*TC: total citations; NP: number of publications; PY: publication year first indexed

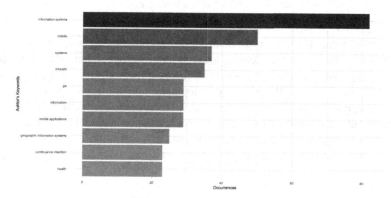

Fig. 3. Relevant keywords

of theories for IS. New theoretical lenses that could explain uncovered areas in mobIS is needed as driving empirical studies with theories is necessary. Earlier studies suggested [17] that without a close interaction between theoretical development and empirical reality, mobIS could become merely an area of application for applied concepts from other disciplines. Arising from this, the need for new theoretical frameworks and models to explain the link among the concepts related to mobIS is recommended.

Context (C)

Research in the field of mobIS has advanced our knowledge on interaction design patterns [5], relevance for empowerment process [7] and its potential to enhance the business processes and performance. As revealed in the analysis, the context at which the mobIS research are carried out include largely Information systems, Mobile health, Mobile application, social apps. More research context is required and should also be extended to developing countries as the developed context presently dominates the research space.

Characteristics (C)

This study examined the characteristics of the selected articles to explore the research directions further [21]. The topic dendrogram shows two dinstict clusters and the first cluster showcase Delone and McLean IS success model. The model shows the direct relationship of information quality, system quality and service quality to usage intentions while system quality and service quality predicts user satisfaction. On the other hand, user satisfaction predicts usage intentions and system use relates with user satisfaction. Three dependent variables (net benefits, intention to use and user satisfaction characterize this model. This model is applicable to both user of IS and the organization. This model has widely used in the context of information systems, but it will be more relevant for the growing discipline of mobile information systems in the future. The second clusters introduce integrated theories of intrinsic motivation, technology acceptance, unified theory of acceptance and use of technology, innovation, users experience. All these featured under mobile technology, information technology, information systems, Internet, services, performance with moderators. Due to the dynamic landscape of mobile information systems, in the future more there will more emerging theories, methodologies, mobile information systems intelligence.

Methodology (M)

As reported in Table 4, different methodological approaches are widely used in this area of research. However, the methods used in mobIS research have become sophisticated spanning from geometric constructive learning methods, interpolation methods and IDEF0, IDEF3. The challenge is to develop more mixed-method approaches when studying concepts in relation to mobIS research. To improve the methodological rigor of mobIS research, the use of more diverse analytical techniques and methods, such as content analysis, qualitative research, meta-analysis and multi-level methodologies is recommended since survey, descriptive and mixed method are mostly used in prior research in the area.

5   MobIS Results, Discussion and Conclusion

The current study aimed to assess the scientific literature on MobIS from 2016–2020. By using the TCCM framework, we were able to uncover some significant theoretical and contextual insights.

Theoretical Insights
Looking from a theoretical standpoint, we observed a need for further development and use of more psychological-related theories. As noted in Fig. 1, we found that there were limited psychological cognitive theories. These theories focus on human's ability to problem-solve, make decisions, learn, and collaborate among others [18]. Since mobIS have unique capabilities to support the ever-increasing mobile technology users and processes [11], psychological cognitive theories should be developed.

Contextual Insights
Contextually, the TCCM framework shows a gap in the context already covered in the field of mobIS. So far, the contextual coverage of the literature, especially between 2016 and 2020, have already touched on some relevant research areas (as depicted in Fig. 1 and Table 7) such as geographic information systems, mobile computing, service quality, mobile adoption, cloud computing and commerce. We noticed that more attention is yet to be expended on mobile-data research [19]. The rapid growth of mobIS, over the years, with it, brought opportunities and challenges of mobile data from sundry standpoints [20].

To summarise, a total of 1040 documents were produced between 2016 and 2020 - considering only journal articles and conference proceedings. Out of the 1040 documents, 95 were single authored. The average authors per document was 3 and the collaboration index was 3.2. The most productive author was Kim J (citation: 75, documents: 8). On the average, about 3 publications were made per year and an average citations per document. The most cited source was the Mis Quarterly (1615 citations). The bibliographic source with the highest impact score was International Journal of Information Management (impact score: 9).

5.1   Managerial Implications and Direction for Future Studies

MobIS research and technological advancements go hand-in-hand. Thus, the persistent decline in mobIS research productivity should be addressed urgently. The cause of the decline is yet to be ascertained, at this point. We recommend that studies should be conducted to investigate this issue. Empirical work should be conducted with goals of developing cognitive theories to support mobIS. In the same vein, future researchers should also explore mobile data from various perspectives such as security, privacy, monitoring.

5.2   Study Limitations

One of the main limitations we experienced was our inability to extract more than 1040 documents (journal articles and conference proceedings) due to the limited timespan of four years (that is, 2016 to 2020).

References

1. Ammenwerth, E., Buchauer, A., Bludau, B., Haux, R.: Mobile information and communication tools in the hospital. Int. J. Med. Inform. **57**(1), 21–40 (2000)
2. Olaleye, S.A., Oyelere, S.S., Sanusi, I.T., Agbo, F.J.: Experience of ubiquitous computing technology driven mobile commerce in Africa: impact of usability, privacy, trust, and reputation concern (2018)
3. Drew, D.A., et al.: Rapid implementation of mobile technology for real-time epidemiology of COVID-19. Science **368**(6497), 1362–1367 (2020)
4. Shiau, W.L., Yan, C.M., Lin, B.W.: Exploration into the intellectual structure of mobile information systems. Int. J. Inf. Manage. **47**, 241–251 (2019)
5. da Silva, L.F., Freire, A.P.: An investigation on the use of interaction design patterns in Brazilian government mobile information systems. In: XVI Brazilian Symposium on Information Systems, pp. 1–8 (2020)
6. Saeed, K.A., Xu, J.D.: Understanding diffusion of information systems-based services: evidence from mobile banking services. Int. Res. **30**(4), 1281–1304 (2020)
7. Ahad, T., Busch, P., Blount, Y., Picoto, W.: Mobile phone-based information systems for empowerment: opportunities for ready-made garment industries. J. Glob. Inf. Technol. Manage. **24**(1), 57–85 (2021). https://doi.org/10.1080/1097198X.2020.1866896
8. He, W., Nazir, S., Hussain, Z.: Big data insights and comprehensions in industrial healthcare: an overview. Mob. Inf. Syst. 1–11 (2021)
9. Pernici, B.: Mobile Information Systems. Springer, Heidelberg (2006). https://doi.org/10.1007/3-540-31008-8
10. Krogstie, J., Lyytinen, K., Opdahl, A.L., Pernici, B., Siau, K., Smolander, K.: Research areas and challenges for mobile information systems. Int. J. Mob. Commun. **2**(3), 220–234 (2004)
11. Gebauer, J., Shaw, M.J., Gribbins, M.L.: Task-technology fit for mobile information systems. J. Inf. Technol. **25**(3), 259–272 (2010)
12. Liu, Z., Yin, Y., Liu, W., Dunford, M.: Visualizing the intellectual structure and evolution of innovation systems research: a bibliometric analysis. Scientometrics **103**(1), 135–158 (2015). https://doi.org/10.1007/s11192-014-1517-y
13. Olaleye, S.A.: Visualizing cultural emotional intelligence literature: a bibliometric review 2001–2020. In: Laine, P., Némethová, I., Wiwczaroski, T. (eds.) Intercultural Competence at Work. Seinäjoki: Seinäjoen ammattikorkeakoulu. Publications of Seinäjoki University of Applied Sciences B. Reports 160, 142–156 (2020). https://urn.fi/URN:NBN:fi-fe20201215100768.
14. Aria, M., Cuccurullo, C.: bibliometrix: an R-tool for comprehensive science mapping analysis, J. Inform. **11**(4), 959–975 (2017). https://doi.org/10.1016/j.joi.2017.08.007
15. Lim, S., Saldanha, T.J., Malladi, S., Melville, N.P.: Theories used in information systems research: Insights from complex network analysis. JITTA J. Inf. Technol. Theory Appl. **14**(2), 5 (2013)
16. Valera-Gran, D., Prieto-Botella, D., Peral-Gómez, P., Hurtado-Pomares, M., Sánchez-Pérez, A., Navarrete-Muñoz, E.M.: Bibliometric analysis of research on telomere length in children: a review of scientific literature. Int. J. Environ. Res. Public Health **17**(12), 4593 (2020)
17. Paul, J., Rosado-Serrano, A.: Gradual internationalization vs born-global/international new venture models: a review and research agenda. Int. Market. Rev. **36**(6), 830–858 (2019)
18. Palich, L.E., Bagby, D.R.: Using cognitive theory to explain entrepreneurial risk-taking: challenging conventional wisdom. J. Bus. Ventur. **10**(6), 425–438 (1995)
19. Hong, S.J., Thong, J.Y., Moon, J.Y., Tam, K.Y.: Understanding the behavior of mobile data services consumers. Inf. Syst. Front. **10**(4), 431–445 (2008)

20. Laurila, J.K., et al.: From big smartphone data to worldwide research: the mobile data challenge. Pervasive Mob. Comput. **9**(6), 752–771 (2013)
21. Srivastava, S., Singh, S., Dhir, S.: Culture and international business research: a review and research agenda. Int. Bus. Rev. **29**, 101709 1–15 (2020)

Analysis of Malaria Information on a Social Media Platform

Benjamin Omwando[✉] and Jin Zhang

School of Information Studies, University of Wisconsin, Milwaukee, WI 53201, USA
{bomwando,jzhang}@uwm.edu

Abstract. This study explores malaria-related YouTube posts in Africa to identify patterns, themes and terms related to malaria.

Mixed method research was used where both qualitative and quantitative research paradigms were employed. Subject analysis method and Multidimensional scaling (MDS) technique were adapted in this study to discover themes and visualize related terms. Visual analyses were conducted at two levels: subject analysis within categories and category analysis among the categories in a malaria related schema. There were four resultant categories (Causes and facilitators of malaria pandemic, Methods of prevention and treatment of malaria, Effects of malaria, and Vulnerable population) from the subject analysis. The subject hierarchy and subcategories of the schema are associated with a group of relevant terms related to malaria in Africa.

The findings of this research study shed light on understanding malaria related information from the social media perspective, help users seek more relevant information on malaria, enrich existing thesaurus or subject headings by adding new terms related to malaria, and create a more user-oriented subject directory for malaria related portals or websites.

Keywords: Malaria · Africa · YouTube · Visualization · Schema

1 Introduction

According to the CDC (2020) and Mayo (2018), malaria is a dangerous disease caused by a parasitic infection on a certain type of mosquito which feeds on humans through biting. Once a human is infected with the disease, he/she portrays symptoms such as high fevers, shaking chills, and flu-like illness.

African countries are mostly affected, and other countries that lie in tropical areas such as the Asian subcontinent, Haiti, and Dominican Republic (Mayo 2018). Unfortunately, in 2018 approximately 228 million cases of malaria were reported, and the deaths were estimated to be 405,000 globally as the world keep fighting against malaria (Nghochuzie et al. 2020; World Health Organization 2019).

Social media platforms such as YouTube have been used globally to create awareness and fight malaria pandemic. YouTube as one of the social media platforms is widely used to host videos. Most of the videos contain information ranging from healthcare, sports, academia, repairing, troubleshooting, cooking, and others (Esen et al. 2018).

© Springer Nature Switzerland AG 2021
G. Salvendy and J. Wei (Eds.): HCII 2021, LNCS 12796, pp. 298–316, 2021.
https://doi.org/10.1007/978-3-030-77025-9_25

Subject analysis and visualization technique are popular means to effectively analyze and reveal subject themes of a dataset and discover relationships and connections of related terms in the dataset. These method and techniques were adapted in this study.

The primary research aims are to investigate malaria related videos on YouTube, reveal subject themes hidden in the video based on the corresponding transcripts, and analyze the trend and patterns of malaria related information on YouTube by using mixed subject analysis and information visualization methods.

The findings of this research study shed light on understanding malaria related information from the social media perspective, help users seek more relevant information on malaria, enrich existing thesaurus or subject headings by adding new terms related to malaria, and create a more user-oriented subject directory for malaria related portals or websites.

2 Literature Review

2.1 Malaria in Africa

An article by Mouchet et al. (1998) examined evolution of malaria in Africa for a period of 40 years. Mouchet et al. (1998) notes that because of cultivation and heavy rains in the countries along the equator more cases of malaria were emerging. In 1984–85 and 1987–88 in Swaziland and Madagascar respectively malaria cases increased due to cessation of malaria control programs (Mouchet et al. 1998). In a study by Snow et al. (2003) proclaimed that the accurate number of fatal deaths due to malarial infections may not be known.

Weiss et al. (2020) employed spatiotemporal Bayesian geostatistical models to establish an estimated malaria anticipation in absence of Covid-19 and found out that there could be an increase in cases. In a pessimistic conclusion Weiss et al. (2020) concluded that with Covid-19 disruptions, malaria could potentially double in 2020 and the subsequent year(s) if not keen measures are put in place.

2.2 Health Information Seeking Online, Social Media, and YouTube

When it comes to health information seeking online different studies have published a variety of topics related to the subject. In those studies, they have discussed different diseases, benefits verses disadvantage of online information seeking as well given recommendations on what needs to be improved for quality and trustworthy information. Zhao and Zhang (2017) found out that health information seekers' needs vary with their health status of a family member, relative or friends. Zhao and Zhang further argue that the information gap is filled with the experience of similar cases, questions and answer posted on the social networks, and the emotional and cohort support offered in the networks.

Deng and Liu (2017) did a survey to understand the seeking behavior of online information consumers from risk perception attitude and social support. They found out that health risk and healthy self-efficacy could significantly influence how consumers search for information online.

A survey on consumer health information seeking on social media discovered that while previous studies have stated that social media is becoming more trustworthy and could significantly affect the healthcare outcomes (Lin et al. 2016; Wu et al. 2018).

Social media, recognized as Web 2.0, is a set of Internet-based applications that build on the ideological and technological foundations of participative and social Web that emphasizes user-generated content; usability; collaboration; and cultural diversity of products, systems, devices and services (Lober and Flowers 2011; Kaplan and Haenlein 2010; Kietzmann et al. 2011; Zhang et al. 2020).

Lober and Flowers (2011) argue that social media is a vital platform for "consumer empowerment in health". Consumers can get desired information by communicating with providers, peers, family members and friends, which leads to better shared understanding and decision-making process. Lober and Flowers outlines that health care organizations have shown with other businesses in reaching out to consumers through blogs, social networking sites, Twitter feeds, YouTube posts, and location-based services to empower consumers. Java et al. (2007) also argue that users mostly embrace using social media with intentions of chatting regularly, receiving, and reporting news, and sharing information.

With the increased availability of the Internet, social media is a popular platform to disseminate information (Keir et al. 2019; Zhang et al. 2020). For, example due to the recent outbreak of Covid-19 healthcare institutions were using social media to disseminate infographics within the departments and beyond through Twitter and WeChat (Chan et al. 2020).

YouTube is one of the popular social media platforms where users can easily post, watch, and share video clips via the internet (Freeman and Chapman 2007; YouTube 2011). It is considered as a search engine that catalogues videos while allowing the users to have control of managing different features such as allowing or disabling comments, keeping track of who has commented, how many replies, likes, dislike (Freeman and Chapman 2007; Smith et al. 2012; YouTube 2011).

Gul and Diri (2019) found out that YouTube is a good source of data about management of premature ejaculation. In their analysis they discovered that videos with trustworthy information outnumbered the one with untrustworthy information. Thus, they recommended that healthcare providers should be encouraged to post more information on social media to reach the ever-growing population of consumers.

2.3 MDS/Information Visualization

Multidimensional scaling (MDS) is an exploratory and multivariate data analysis technique used to represent the higher dimensional data into lower space (Saeed et al. 2018; Zhang et al. 2020; Zhang and Zhao 2013). MDS analysis technique employs dissimilarity or similarity of objects being observed, resulting in spatial maps—where the dissimilar objects tend to be far apart while similar ones are closer to each other (Saeed et al. 2018; Schiffman et al. 1981; Young and Hamer 1987; Zhang et al. 2020). MDS is applied to data mining, pattern recognition, information theory, psychometry, ecology, and marketing (Priyantha et al. 2003; Saeed et al. 2018; Zhang 2008; Zhang et al. 2020). The roles of MDS in data analysis include scientific visualization, psychological structure, data exploration, testing structural hypothesis, pattern recognition and ordination of ecology

(Buja et al. 2008; Hansen and Johnson 2005; Jaworska and Chupetlovska-Anastasova, 2009; Lopes et al. 2014; Saeed et al. 2018; Webb and Copsey 2011; Zhang 2008; Zhang and Zhao 2013).

Saeed et al. (2018) states that MDS has some advantage over other traditional methods such as factor analysis. MDS and factor analysis are similar techniques but MDS is preferred over factor analysis because MDS does not depend on most common assumptions like linearity and normality (Lopes et al. 2014; Saeed et al. 2018; Webb and Copsey 2011; Zhang 2008 Zhang and Zhao 2013).

MDS is an exceptionally accommodating technique that is not restricted by numerous assumptions associated with general linear models. It has capability to model non-linear relationships using multiple proximity matrices, which can be derived from individual or subgroups (Saeed et al. 2018; Jaworska and Chupetlovska-Anastasova, 2009; Zhang and Zhao 2013).

2.4   Data Mining on Social Media for Other Diseases and Especially for Malaria

Since the late 1980s data mining has become an established discipline within the scope of computer science and information retrieval (Coenen 2011).

Clifton (2017) defines data mining as "the process of discovering interesting and useful patterns and relationships in large volumes of data" (para. 1). It is a field that brings together different statistical tools and techniques (such as neural networks and machine learning) with database management to analyze data sets. Coenen further states that data mining techniques can be classified as pattern extraction/identification, data clustering or classification/categorization.

In healthcare, data mining is increasingly becoming intensely and extensively applicable (Kaur and Wasan 2006; Koh and Tan 2011; Tomar and Agarwal 2013; Yoo et al. 2012). Researchers argue that several factors have motivated the application of data mining in healthcare. They include existence of medical insurance fraud and data due to digitization of healthcare system and complex heterogeneous data from social media; and the realization that data mining can generate information that is very useful to all parties involved in the healthcare industry. The parties involved are healthcare insurers, healthcare providers like hospitals, clinics and physicians, and patients.

Data in social media may also lack vocabulary control and this becomes tedious when mining, cleaning, and analyzing data (Tomar and Agarwal 2013). To mine such data users should have knowledge in the field of study as well as data mining methodologies, technologies and tools used, and techniques applied in the process. Without a collective possession of domain knowledge; statistical and research expertise; and IT and data mining knowledge and skills, data mining would not be effective.

Most of the studies on health information on YouTube have focused more on quality, advantages, false, or misleading, seeking behavior among other aspects regarding to health-related information online about different diseases such as diabetes, cancer, among others (Langford and Loeb 2019; Zhao and Zhang 2017). Weiss et al. (2020) employed spatiotemporal Bayesian geostatistical models to establish an estimated malaria anticipation in absence of Covid-19. In another recent study by Zhang et al. (2020) also did a study on zika-related virus and used Yahoo! Answers as the platform but did not use YouTube either. But none or a few if any have done a study on information visualization of YouTube content about malaria in Africa. Thus, more research is needed to be carried out on how to improve the quality and authority of information posted in YouTube.

3 Research Method

This research study focuses on investigating transcripts of YouTube posts on malaria in Africa and discovering the hidden subjects in YouTube content. The population was YouTube posts focusing on malaria in Africa.

Three widely used methodologies include: quantitative, qualitative, and mixed methods. These methods include components such as research design, sampling methods, data collection methods, and data analysis techniques (Creswell and Creswell 2017; Creswell 2013; Zhang et al. 2020). A mixed method research including subject analysis method, and information visualization method was used in this study.

3.1 Data Collection

YouTube is an information repository that is different from the traditional media like television. It has more flexibility and a two-way communication between its viewers and creators. It encompasses detailed transaction logs recording publisher name, date of publication, comments, dislike, likes, share, and transcript section of a content posted.

To date, much of datasets from social media data are accessible for researchers (Paltoglou 2014). However, the level of access to social media content in the future is not known with the allegation on user's data privacy breaches, for example, Facebook's continual user privacy breach (McNamee and Parakilas 2018; Steel and Fowler 2010). YouTube data sets on malaria in Africa were used in this study because they are publicly available.

A group of searches were conducted to collect data on YouTube. The keywords used were "malaria", "malaria Africa", "plasmodium falciparum", "malaria southern Africa", "malaria northern Africa", "malaria western Africa", and "malaria eastern Africa". The data collected covered from April 17th, 2008 to September 4th, 2019. Videos in English but without transcripts were excluded. Other clips in French, Swahili, Arabic, and other languages were also discarded during the initial data collection. As a result 100 valid video clips from YouTube were collected and selected for data analysis.

A record has a complete information about a clip/video on YouTube and it consists of its title, transcript, likes, dislikes, comments, share, publish name, posting time, duration, and ID. Each collected clip had to be converted into a complete record for further analysis.

3.2 Cleansing Collected Videos

The collected data from YouTube posts were cleansed using free online text analyzer and normalized to produce a word list. From the transcripts two categories of words were identified. The first set consist of functional and grammatical words such as "a", "an", "or", "and", "if", "the", "in", "of", "up", "how", "then", "otherwise", "again", "could", "can", and others. Then normalization of the terms was performed, where one term/word was chosen to represent its synonyms. For example, ill and sick were normalized to sick; kid, infant, toddler, and child were normalized to child. The second set consist of words with low frequencies. When clustering keywords, the words with low frequencies make little contribution to it. Because of it a cut-off threshold was set for each category to eliminate the words, ranging from 2 to 9 points as shown in Table 6.

3.3 Subject Analysis

During data extraction, YouTube posts' transcripts and titles were extracted. They were used for subject analysis and visualization analysis. The subject coding analysis method, and multidimensional scaling (MDS) visualization analysis method was employed in three phases. In the first phase, data mining technique was used to extract transcripts and titles. Raw texts were parsed, terms in a text were extracted, and frequency of a term was tallied to determine the association between the term and a record. In the second phase coding analysis was employed to categorize and classify the initial set of the records into categories. Content of the title and transcript of each record was analyzed by the researchers. Then the record was classified into a proper category. This stage produced a schema related to malaria in Africa. In the next stage, proximities between terms were calculated and related matrices were generated, then the MDS technique was utilized for visual analysis, where clusters were created and sub-categories were formed based on related terms in each of different categories (Zhang and Zhao 2013; Zhang et al. 2020).

3.4 Data Organization

A video clip/document on YouTube consists a group of attributes or terms for analysis. To discover hidden meaning from these terms the documents were organized in a vector space, where a matrix is formed. The matrix consists of rows that are documents/videos (clips), and the columns are the terms extracted. Then, the remaining term-document matrix was converted to a term-term proximity matrix-based on the cosine similarity measure. The term-term matrix was finally projected onto the visual space for data analysis using SPSS to create clusters.

3.5 MDS Analysis

The MDS analysis yielded clustering result, the RSQ (R^2) and stress value. Zhang and Wolfram (2009) notes that "stress values below 0.10 and R^2 values above 0.90 are considered sound and satisfactory, indicating that each outcome is acceptable for interpretation." These parameters were used to judge the quality of the MDS analysis results.

4 Results and Discussion

4.1 Summary of Collected Data/Descriptive Data Analysis

In this study the sample was YouTube posts related to malaria in Africa. The sample size of 100 video clips was used to mine the transcript content. Only video clips in English with transcripts were picked and analyzed as explained earlier in the data collection section.

4.2 Creation of Schema

Subject analysis resulted in a schema of 4 categories related to malaria. The result is shown in Table 1. The categories of the schema were used for further MDS analysis to generate more sub-categories in each category.

Table 1. Summary of the schema

Category 1	Category 2	Category 3	Category 4
Causes and facilitators of malaria pandemic	Methods of prevention and treatment of malaria	Effects of malaria	Vulnerable population
No. of records = 12	No. of records = 55	No. of records = 22	No. of records = 11

4.3 Visualization Analysis

The MDS technique was used in this study because it has capability to model non-linear relationships among terms using a term-term proximity matrix. Another vital advantage of MDS is the ability to represent an intuitive display of clusters during analysis. The visual analysis for each category was conducted and the results are shown in Fig. 1 through Fig. 4.

Causes and Facilitators of Malaria Pandemic

This category has a total of 79 keywords with three explicit clusters. The clusters contain 31, 21, and 27 keywords, respectively. The stress value was equal to 0.000 and the RSQ was equal to 1.000 as shown in Tables 6. The keywords of each cluster are shown in Table 2. The visual display of the resultant MDS analysis for this category is showed in Fig. 1.

Cluster 1 (C1) is the largest cluster with 31 keywords, and it was situated in the middle of the MDS space. The keywords revealed that African countries are struggling with the negative effects associated with the deadly and infectious disease. The disease is transmitted by anopheles' mosquitos. For instance, the female anopheles' mosquito transmits malaria through infecting human cells. Here the parasite which causes malaria is transferred from the mosquito while sucking blood. Mosquitos and human blood are examples of facilitators and the parasite is the cause of malaria in humans.

In Cluster 2 (C2) keywords reflected that malaria takes around a week or more for the symptoms to appear. If not treated malaria could easily lead to death. From the cluster we have keywords need, doctor, drug, treat, severe, malaria, case and help grouped together. This indicated that severe cases of malaria can be prevented with the help of doctor's drug prescriptions depending on the severity of symptoms displayed upon diagnosis. For instance, distribution of anti-malaria drugs in African countries is used as a long-term approach to effectively deal with malaria.

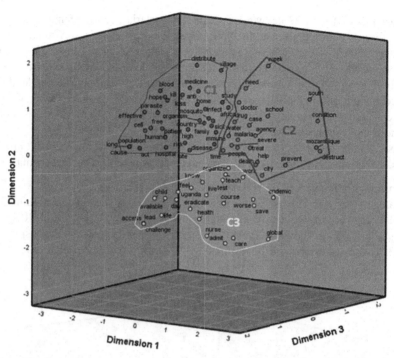

Fig. 1. MDS Visual display of Cause and facilitation of malaria pandemic

Table 2. Result of Cause and facilitation of malaria pandemic.

Cluster	Number of keywords	Keywords
C1	31	cause, long, act, population, hospital, human, cell, effective, free, patient, high, risk, disease, family, immune, sick, infect, parasite, Africa, country, mosquito, home, loss, anti, kill, hope, blood, medicine, distribute, village, study
C2	21	time, week, need, doctor, drug, case, treat, malaria, severe, water, people, death, city, help, prevent, agency, school, south, condition, Mozambique, destruct
C3	27	child, available, access, lead, challenge, life, day, feel, know, Uganda, eradicate, health, Uganda, live, test, organize, teach, test, work, course, worse, save, endemic, global, care, admit, nurse

Cluster 3 (C3) with 27 keywords reveals that malaria is an epidemic that is chal-lenging lives of children all over the globe. Uganda being one of the African countries affected with the disease, efforts to eradicate malaria are underway via tests, providing healthcare access to young children and teaching the community. Nurses are involved not only in treating but in organizing and teaching the public about the pandemic. For instance, populations in the village or country sides of Africa are more at risk of getting infected with malaria parasite due to lack of hospital facilities and medical suppliers. They need more support.

Based on the keywords in the clusters, the sub-categories were produced: infection factors, symptoms, and support. These subcategories were added to the schema.

Prevention and Treatment of Malaria

This category has four clusters with a total of 81 keywords. The cluster contain 13, 27, 16, and 25 keywords, respectively. The stress value was equal to 0.000 and the RSQ value was equal to 1.000 as shown in Table 6. The keywords of each cluster are displayed in Table 3. The visual display of the resultant MDS analysis for this category is shown in Fig. 2.

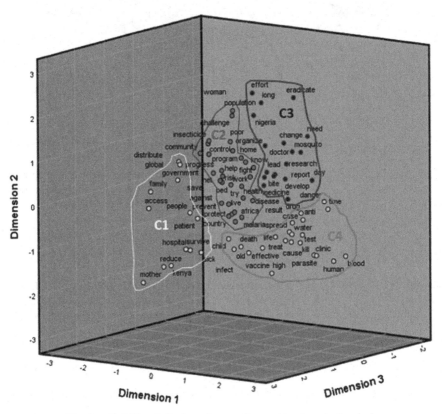

Fig. 2. MDS Visual display of prevention and treatment of malaria

Table 3. Results of prevention and treatment of malaria.

Cluster	Number of keywords	Results
C1	13	mother, reduce, Kenya, hospital, survive, patient, people, access, family, government, progress, global, distribute
C2	27	woman, population, challenge, poor, organize, insecticide, community, control, program, help, fight, know, risk, net, work, bed, try, health, disease, save, against, prevent, protect, country, malaria, Africa, live
C3	16	effort, eradicate, long, Nigeria, need, change, mosquito, doctor, lead, research, day, develop, bite, medicine, danger, home
C4	25	sick, child, infect, death, old, vaccine, effective, high, cause, parasite, treat, malaria, spread, life, result, drug, anti, time, case, water, test, kill, clinic, human, blood

Cluster 1 (C1) primarily demonstrated that mothers and patients who have access to hospitals in Kenya and globally are more likely to survive after getting the malaria infection. That is, if governments increase the access to hospitals and distribution of drugs, people will survive, and malaria would be reduced globally. Especially when it comes to access of bed nets, making sure the sick is taken care of, mothers play a critical role in most families.

Cluster 2 (C2) had the largest pool of keywords. This cluster suggested that women from poor communities are involved in the fight against malaria. Different methods are employed to prevent the spread of malaria. They include use of insecticide, bed nets, and community programs to sensitize populations within the countries in Africa. Therefore, it would be more prudent if more help is directed towards empowering women since they are more involved in the family settings than men. This is a clear indication that, men need to be more enlightened about the effects of malaria and what role they need to play in the fight against the disease.

The keywords in Cluster 3 (C3) illustrated that in Nigeria doctors are leading in the research studies to develop medicine to eradicate malaria. This is a positive change taken by African countries in leading research and development of a long-term solution towards eradicating this dangerous disease.

Cluster 4 (C4) denotes that children and the old populations are the most affected by the disease, and they are likely to die within a short time after infection. This is attributed to the fact that their immunities are weak in terms of the disease prevention and treatment. Testing, use of anti-malaria drugs and vaccine are employed as some of the effective means of prevention and treatment.

Based on the keywords in the four clusters, the sub-categories were produced: globe, prevention methods, local effort, and children and old people. These subcategories were added to the schema.

Effects of Malaria

In this category there were a total of 83 keywords with four clusters. The clusters have 30, 24, 19, and 10 keywords, respectively. The stress value was equal to 0.000 and the RSQ value was equal to 1.000 as shown in Table 6. The keywords of each cluster are displayed in Table 4. The visual display of the resultant MDS analysis for this category is shown in Fig. 3.

Cluster 1 (C1) disclosed that as a result of the global malaria pandemic, the countries have embarked in fighting the spread of the disease by employing different intervention methods such as using insecticides, bed nets, tests, and teaching communities the effects of malaria. For example, Nigeria is using community groups and health centers to target women, children, and pregnant women in testing, diagnosing, treating, and teaching the effects of the disease.

In Cluster 2 (C2), it appeared that female anopheles mosquitoes spread the parasitic infection from an infected person through biting. The time for signs of the malaria infection varies from a few days to a week. If not diagnosed, tested, and treated, the infected person gets cerebral malaria or die. This has prompted African countries to use anti-malaria drugs to protect the public.

Cluster 3 C3) shows that sick people due to malaria infections undergo a painful or severe fever. Because of the fever, neither sick people can go to work nor sick children go to school. Therefore, governments need to come up with a system to ensure the sick have access to doctors and medicine.

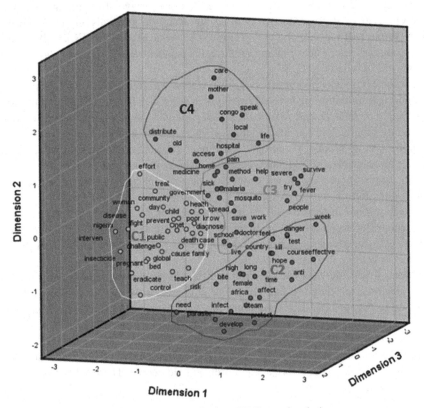

Fig. 3. MDS Visual display of Effects of malaria

Table 4. Results of Effects of malaria

Cluster	Number of keywords	Results
C1	30	effort, treat, community, woman, day, child, health, spread, know, poor, prevent, net, fight, disease, Nigeria, intervene, insecticide, pregnant, eradicate, control, teach, bed, global, challenge, public, death, case, cause, family, diagnose
C2	24	develop, protect, parasite, need, infect, team, affect, Africa, risk, bite, high, long, female, time, country, kill, hope, anti, course, effective, test, danger, feel, week
C3	19	pain, method, help, severe, survive, fever, try, people, sick, malaria, government, mosquito, save, work, doctor, school, live, home, medicine
C4	10	care, mother, Congo, speak, local, life, distribute, old, access, hospital

Keywords in Cluster 4 (C4) suggested that old people and mothers at the local level (countryside) need care and access to hospitals to survive from malaria. Infrastructural systems at the local level need improvement to facilitate seamless distribution of medical supplies and services to the vulnerable and marginalized populations.

Based on the keywords in the four clusters, the sub-categories were produced: intervention methods, protection, government involvement, and access to facilities.

Vulnerable Population

The Vulnerable population category has a total of 56 keywords with four clusters. The clusters contained 13, 13, 19, and 11 keywords, respectively. The stress value was equal to 0.000 and the RSQ value was equal to 1.000 as shown in Table 6. The keywords of each cluster are displayed in Table 5. The visual display of the resultant MDS analysis for this category is shown in Fig. 4.

Cluster 1 (C1) grouped the following words together (need, blood, develop, research, try, against, long, save, live, hope, work, lead, community). It is evident that in order to save the most vulnerable people in a community from the disease, there is desperate need for related research and vaccine trials.

Cluster 2 (C2) tied with Cluster 1 in terms of the number of keywords. From the cluster it is apparent that the old people face the danger and challenges associated with the malaria. The old people are more likely to get infected with malaria and it is one of the causes of the high mortality rate amongst old people in Africa.

Cluster 3 (C3) portrays that there is a global effort to eradicate malaria in Africa. This is evident that the African countries are in the partnership from the USA to fight malaria. For example, during President Bush's era, White House started the President's initiative spending of $1.2 billion over five years to eradicate malaria in Africa. This initiative targeted the most vulnerable populations such as women, elderly folks, and children.

The fourth cluster (C4) suggested that in order to assist the vulnerable communities in fighting malaria, the government of Congo was distributing bed nets to the sick people as well as making sure that they can access medication via hospitals.

Based on the keywords in the four clusters, the sub-categories were produced: research, challenge, partnership, and local government.

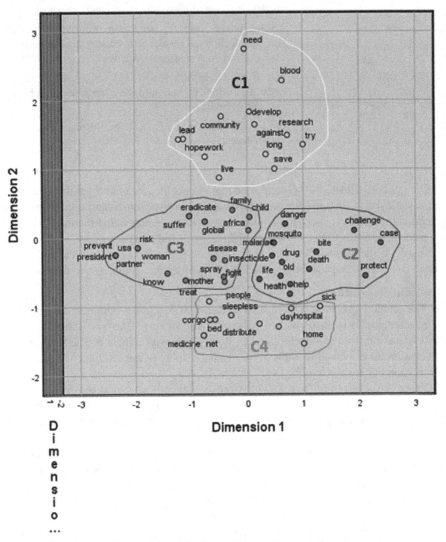

Fig. 4. Visual display of Vulnerable population

Table 5. Vulnerable population

Cluster	Number of keywords	Keywords
C1	13	need, blood, develop, research, try, against, long, save, live, hope, work, lead, community
C2	13	danger, challenge, case, mosquito, malaria, drug, bite, death, protect, help, health, life, old
C3	19	prevent, president, USA, partner, risk, woman, know, suffer, eradicate, global, Africa, family, child, disease, insecticide, fight, spray, mother, treat
C4	11	people, sleepless, Congo, medicine, bed, net, distribute, day, hospital, home, sick

A summary of all MDS analysis results including the RSQ (R^2) values, stress value, similarity measures used for matrix conversion, and the cutoff points for the keyword elimination are demonstrated in Table 6. From Table 6, the R^2 values for all the all MDS analyses were equal to 1.000 and the corresponding stress values were equal to 0.000, which was a clear indication of satisfactory outcomes of the MDS results.

Table 6. Summary of MDS results

Category	Cutoff point	Number of words	Similarity	Stress value	R^2
1. Causes and facilitators of malaria pandemic	2	79	Cosine	0.000	1.0000
2. Methods of prevention and treatment of malaria	9	81	Cosine	0.000	1.0000
3. Effects of Malaria	4	83	Cosine	0.000	1.0000
4. Vulnerable population	2	56	Cosine	0.000	1.0000

Based on the first content analysis and visualization analysis two more layers were emerged with different sub-categories. The finalized detailed schema is showed in Fig. 5.

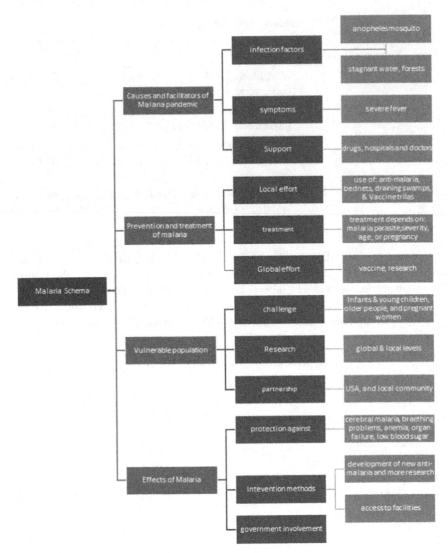

Fig. 5. Finalized malaria related Schema.

4.4 Discussion

The results can be compared with other similar research findings on social media.

Zhang and Zhao (2013) discovered themes about diabetes from the Yahoo! questions and answer (Q&A) forum. The revealed themes are Cause & Pathophysiology, Sign & Symptom, Diagnosis & Test, Organ & Body Part, Complication & Related Disease, Medication, Treatment, Education & Info Resource, Affect, Social & Culture, Lifestyle, and Nutrient. The shared themes among this study and other related studies are causes, symptoms, prevention, and treatment (Bowler et al. 2012; 2012; Rutten et al. 2005; Zhang and Zhao 2013; Zhang et al. 2020).

As Zhang et al. (2020) stated that health-related subjects may have their unique focus. For instance, unique theme(s) identified in this study is Vulnerable population. Under the vulnerable population subthemes identified include challenges, research, partnership, and local government. Zhang et al. (2020) discovered protection and surveillance, activities and responses, and social events and travel sub-themes under the theme social impact of Zika virus. However, for this study intervention methods, protection, government involvement, and access to facilities are subthemes under the theme Effects of malaria. It is evident that from both the studies different terms can be used to suit a particular group or community and the disease.

Unique themes in other related studies include family medical history, acceptance, unprotected sex, smoking/alcohol (Oh et al. 2012). Confession, deep talk, reflection, and manuscript ideas were specified as the unique themes in eating disorder (Bowler et al. 2012) study. Rutten et al. (2005) had cancer-specific, and medical system as their unique themes.

There is a clear affirmation that a disease in health-related subjects may have its unique focus. There is need to conduct research studies on terms related to a particular disease topic in healthcare and update the controlled vocabularies, thesaurus, and subject headings.

MDS has gained popularity especially in content analysis and subject analysis. Zhang and Wolfram (2009) used the MDS technique to visualize health-subjects based on query term cooccurrences and discovered that terms in medical subjects can be categorized into 2–4 clusters. Similarly, in this research study 3–4 clusters were identified from different subject categories. The clusters and sub-categories emerged can help enrich and revise the National Library of Medicine's controlled vocabulary thesaurus and Medical Subject Headings (MeSH).

5 Conclusion

This research study investigated malaria related information in Africa related on YouTube. It revealed subject themes hidden in the corresponding transcripts and analyzed the trends and patterns of malaria related keywords on YouTube by using mixed subject analysis and information visualization methods.

The research study produced a user-oriented malaria schema. Each subcategory of the schema is associated with a group of relevant terms. The research method can be applied to investigations of other similar diseases like Covid-19 on social media platforms such as Instagram, Facebook, and Twitter.

The findings of this research study shed light on understanding malaria related information from the social media perspective, help users seek more relevant information on malaria, enrich existing thesaurus by adding new terms related to malaria, and create a more user-oriented subject directory for malaria related portals or websites.

The sample size of this study was relatively small, and the sample was limited to clips in English. Other languages like Swahili, Portuguese, French, Zulu, and Africana were not covered. Also, video posts in English without transcripts were not included.

References

Bowler, L., Oh, J.S., He, D., Mattern, E., Jeng, W.: Eating disorder questions in Yahoo! answers: information, conversation, or reflection. Proc. Am. Soc. Inf. Sci. Technol. **49**(1), 1–11 (2012)

Buja, A., Swayne, D., Littman, M., Dean, N., Hofmann, H., Chen, L.: Data visualization with multidimensional scaling. J. Comput. Graph. Stat. **17**(2), 444–472 (2008)

CDC - Malaria - About Malaria (2020). https://www.cdc.gov/malaria/about/. Accessed 22 Sept 2020

Chan, A.K., Nickson, C.P., Rudolph, J.W., Lee, A., Joynt, G.M.: Social media for rapid knowledge dissemination: early experience from the COVID-19 pandemic. Anaesthesia **75**, 1579–1582 (2020)

Clifton, C.: Data mining. Encyclopedia Britanica, 26 September 2017. https://www.britannica.com/technology/data-mining. Accessed 14 Aug 2018

Coenen, F.: Data mining: past, present and future. Knowl. Eng. Rev. **26**(1), 25–29 (2011)

Creswell, J.W.: Qualitative Inquiry and Research Design: Choosing among Five Approaches, 3rd edn. Sage Publications, Thousand Oaks (2013)

Creswell, J.W., Creswell, J.D.: Research design: Qualitative, Quantitative, and Mixed Methods Approaches. Sage Publications, Thousand Oaks (2017)

Deng, Z., Liu, S.: Understanding consumer health information-seeking behavior from the perspective of the risk perception attitude framework and social support in mobile social media websites. Int. J. Med. Inf. **105**, 98–109 (2017)

Esen, E., Aslan, M., Sonbahar, B., Kerimoğlu, R.: YouTube English videos as a source of information on breast self-examination. Breast Cancer Res. Treat. **173**(3), 629–635 (2018). https://doi.org/10.1007/s10549-018-5044-z

Freeman, B., Chapman, S.: Is "YouTube" telling or selling you something? Tobacco content on the YouTube video-sharing website. Tobacco Control **16**(3), 207–210 (2007)

Gul, M., Diri, M.A.: YouTube as a source of information about premature ejaculation treatment. J. Sex. Med. **16**(11), 1734–1740 (2019)

Hansen, C., Johnson, Chris R.: The Visualization Handbook. Elsevier Butterworth-Heinemann, Burlington (2005)

Java, A., Song, X., Finin, T., Tseng, B.: Why we twitter: understanding microblogging usage and communities. In: Proceedings of the 9th WebKDD and 1st SNA-KDD 2007 Workshop on Web Mining and Social Network Analysis, pp. 56–65. ACM (2007)

Jaworska, N., Chupetlovska-Anastasova, A.: A review of multidimensional scaling (MDS) and its utility in various psychological domains. Tutorials in Quant. Methods Psychol. **5**(1), 1–10 (2009)

Kaplan, A.M., Haenlein, M.: Users of the world, unite! The challenges and opportunities of social media. Bus. Horiz. **53**(1), 59–68 (2010)

Kaur, H., Wasan, S.K.: Empirical study on applications of data mining techniques in healthcare. J. Comput. Sci. **2**(2), 194–200 (2006)

Keir, A., Bamat, N., Patel, R.M., Elkhateeb, O., Roland, D.: Utilising social media to educate and inform healthcare professionals, policy-makers and the broader community in evidence-based healthcare. BMJ Evid. Based Med. **24**(3), 87–89 (2019)

Kietzmann, J.H., Hermkens, K., McCarthy, I.P., Silvestre, B.S.: Social media? Get serious! Understanding the functional building blocks of social media. Bus. Horiz. **54**(3), 241–251 (2011)

Koh, H.C., Tan, G.: Data mining applications in healthcare. J. Healthc. Inf. Manage. **19**(2), 65 (2011)

Langford, A., Loeb, S.: Perceived patient-provider communication quality and sociodemographic factors associated with watching health-related videos on YouTube: a cross-sectional analysis. J. Med. Internet Res. **21**(5), e13512 (2019)

Lin, W.Y., Zhang, X., Song, H., Omori, K.: Health information seeking in the Web 2.0 age: trust in social media, uncertainty reduction, and self-disclosure. Comput. Hum. Behav. **56**, 289–294 (2016)

Lober, W.B., Flowers, J.L.: Consumer empowerment in health care amid the internet and social media. In: Seminars in Oncology Nursing, vol. 27, no. 3, pp. 169–182. WB Saunders (2011)

Lopes, A., Machado, J., Pinto, C.M.A., Galhano, A.M.S.F.: Multidimensional scaling visualization of earthquake phenomena. J. Seismol. **18**(1), 163–179 (2014). https://doi.org/10.1007/s10950-013-9409-9

Mayo. Malaria (2018). https://www.mayoclinic.org/diseases-conditions/malaria/symptoms-cau ses/syc-20351184. Accessed 30 Sept 2020

McNamee, R., Parakilas, S.: The Facebook breach makes it clear: data must be regulated, The Guardian, 19 March 2018. https://theguardian.com/commentisfree/2018/mar/19/facebook-data-cambridge-analytica-privacy-breach. Accessed 21 Sept 2020

Mouchet, J.E.A.N., et al.: Evolution of malaria in Africa for the past 40 years: impact of climatic and human factors. J. Am. Mosq. Control Assoc. **14**(2), 121 (1998)

Nghochuzie, N.N., Olwal, C.O., Udoakang, A.J., Amenga-Etego, L.N.K., Amambua-Ngwa, A.: Pausing the Fight against malaria to combat the COVID-19 pandemic in Africa: is the future of malaria bleak? Front. Microbiol. **11**, 1476 (2020)

Oh, S., Zhang, Y., Park, M.: Health information needs on diseases: a coding schema development for analyzing health questions in social Q&A. In: Proceedings of the 75th Annual Conference of the American Society for Information Science & Technology, vol. 49, no. 1, pp. 1–4 (2012)

Paltoglou, G.: Sentiment analysis in social media. In: Agarwal, N., Lim, M., Wigand, R. (eds.) Online Collective Action. Lecture Notes in Social Networks. Springer, Vienna (2014). https://doi.org/10.1007/978-3-7091-1340-0_1

Priyantha, N.B., Balakrishnan, H., Demaine, E., Teller, S.: Anchor-free distributed localization in sensor networks. In: Proceedings of the 1st International Conference on Embedded Networked Sensor Systems, pp. 340–341. ACM (2003)

Rutten, L.J.F., Arora, N.K., Bakos, A.D., Aziz, N., Rowland, J.: Information needs and sources of information among cancer patients: a systematic review of research (1980–2003). Patient Educ. Counsel. **57**(3), 250–261 (2005)

Saeed, N., Nam, H., Haq, M.I.U., Muhammad Saqib, D.B.: A survey on multidimensional scaling. ACM Comput. Surv. (CSUR) **51**(3), 47 (2018)

Schiffman, S.S., Reynolds, M.L., Young, F.W.: Introduction to Multidimensional Scaling, pp. 74–82. Academic Press, New York (1981)

Smith, A.N., Fischer, E., Yongjian, C.: How does brand-related user-generated content differ across YouTube, Facebook, and Twitter? J. Interact. Market. **26**(2), 102–113 (2012)

Snow, R.W., Craig, M.H., Newton, C.R.J.C., Steketee, R.W.: The public health burden of Plasmodium falciparum malaria in Africa. Working Paper 11. Disease Control Priorities Project. Fogarty International Center, National Institutes of Health, Bethesda, Maryland, USA (2003)

Steel, E., Fowler, G.A.: Facebook in Privacy Breach. Wall Street J., 18 October (2010). https://www.wsj.com/articles/SB10001424052702304772804575558484075236968. Accessed 04 Sept 2020

Tomar, D., Agarwal, S.: A survey on data mining approaches for healthcare. Int. J. Bio-Sci. Bio-Technol. **5**(5), 241–266 (2013)

Webb, A.R., Copsey, K.D.: Introduction to statistical pattern recognition. In: Statistical Pattern Recognition, pp. 433–500. Wiley, Chichester (2011)

Weiss, D.J., et al.: Indirect effects of the COVID-19 pandemic on malaria intervention coverage, morbidity, and mortality in Africa: a geospatial modelling analysis. Lancet Infect. Dis. **21**, 59–69 (2020)

World Health Organization: World Malaria Report 2019 (2019). https://www.who.int/malaria/pub lications/world-malaria-report-2019/en/. Accessed 03 Oct 2020

Wu, T., Deng, Z., Zhang, D., Buchanan, P.R., Zha, D., Wang, R.: Seeking and using intention of health information from doctors in social media: the effect of doctor-consumer interaction. Int. J. Med. Inf. **115**, 106–113 (2018)

Yoo, I., et al.: Data mining in healthcare and biomedicine: a survey of the literature. J. Med. Syst. **36**(4), 2431–2448 (2012). https://doi.org/10.1007/s10916-011-9710-5

Young, F.W., Hamer, R.M.: Multidimensional Scaling: History Theory and Applications. Erlbaum, New York (1987)

YouTube, L. L. C.: YouTube (2011). https://www.YouTube.com/. Accessed 25 Sept 2020

Zhang, J.: Visualization for Information Retrieval. Springer, Heidelberg (2008). https://doi.org/10.1007/978-3-540-75148-9. Zhang, J., foreword by Edie Rasmussen (Information retrieval series)

Zhang, J., Chen, Y., Zhao, Y., Wolfram, D., Ma, F.: Public health and social media: a study of Zika virus-related posts on Yahoo! Answers. J. Assoc. Inf. Sci. Technol. **71**(3), 282–299 (2020)

Zhang, J., Zhao, Y.: A user term visualization analysis based on a social question and answer log. Inf. Process. Manage. **49**(5), 1019–1048 (2013)

Zhang, J., Wolfram, D.: Visual analysis of obesity-related query terms on HealthLink. Online Information Review (2009).

Zhao, Y., Zhang, J.: Consumer health information seeking in social media: a literature review. Health Inf. Libr. J. **34**(4), 268–283 (2017)

The Influence and Prospect of Mobile Communication Technology on Advanced Manufacturing Industry

Mei Shao[1,2][✉], Miao Zhang[1], and Yue Jiang[1]

[1] Zhejiang University of Finance and Economics, Hangzhou, Zhejiang, China
[2] Jiaxing University, Jiaxing, Zhejiang, China

Abstract. The arrival of 5G era has brought the development of mobile communication technology to a new historical period. Based on the summary of mobile communication technology from four aspects of the influence of the advanced manufacturing industries, on the basis of prospects the future Internet of things era, the advanced manufacturing industry based on mobile communication technology will form (1) the pattern of automated production. (2) Resource sharing has become a "platform", especially to the development of the "Shared machine platform". (3) Provide more personalized and customized services. We will make the advantages of advanced manufacturing more prominent and inject new vitality and lasting vitality into it.

Keywords: Mobile communication technology · Advanced manufacturing · Internet of things · Resource-sharing "platform" · Sharing machine platform · Customized services

1 Introduction

In 2020, "vigorously promote modern service industry and advanced manufacturing fusion (originally recorded)", advanced manufacturing industries Jiang Yuelong mentioned is compared with the traditional manufacturing industry, traditional manufacturing absorbs the high-tech achievements, such as information technology, informatization, automation, intelligence, flexibility and ecological production, which evolved into advanced manufacturing industry. As a high-tech industry, advanced manufacturing industry should be the sail to promote the development of Industry 4.0. In the process of promoting the growth of Industry 4.0, advanced manufacturing industry must closely rely on mobile communication, Internet of Things, cloud manufacturing and other advanced technologies, keep up with the trend of The Times, rely on advanced technology industries, and become the pioneer to explore industrial technological transformation.

Nowadays, the integrated development of mobile communication technology and advanced manufacturing industry is accelerating the reform of advanced manufacturing industry in research and development, design, manufacturing, industrial form, business model, supply mechanism and other aspects in all corners of the world, and the continuous innovation ability of science and technology has become the main driving force for

G. Salvendy and J. Wei (Eds.): HCII 2021, LNCS 12796, pp. 317–328, 2021.
https://doi.org/10.1007/978-3-030-77025-9_26

the development of advanced manufacturing industry. Some advanced manufacturing enterprises are catching up with the pace of The Times, using mobile communication technology and other cutting-edge technologies, to produce industrial robots, remote operation, automation, industrial automation, etc.

In the future, mobile communication technology will develop to a relatively optimal state. The delay will be further reduced to a negligible level and its mass will thus peak. Finally, advanced manufacturing industries can take advantage of its advanced technology and machinery and put advanced technology and machinery equipment on a shared "platform" to gain more advantages. Mobile communication technology will inject new vitality into the production automation of advanced manufacturing enterprises, the "platformization" of resources (among which the most advantageous is the construction of "machine equipment sharing platform"), and the customization of goods or services.

2 The Research Background

2.1 The History of Mobile Communication Technology

The definition of mobile communication is very broad. In my opinion, the author Wang Yuduo pointed out in "Communication Engineering and Its Development Prospect" in 2013 that mobile communication refers to the information exchange and transmission between people or between people and nature through certain behaviors or media [24], which is most appropriate.

In 2020, Liu Haipeng introduced the development course of mobile communication technology in the "Research on the Impact of Mobile Communication Technology Development on Production Safety" [11]. I looked up further information and learned about the antecedent cause of the development of mobile communication technology: 1G system was introduced in the late 1970s and early 1980s due to the problem of system capacity. 2G systems were introduced in the late 1980s and early 1990s due to roaming problems. In the late 1990s, the 3G system came into being because of the transmission problems of multimedia services. At the beginning of the 21st century, due to the transmission problem of high-quality multimedia services, 4G system came into being.

In the late 1910s, 5G systems came into being, featuring enhanced mobile broadband, large connection Internet of Things, low latency, and ultra-reliable communications. In 2019, Chai Yuelin "5G mobile communication technology development and research in the new period" of low latency of mobile communication technology and the characteristics of high reliability application in the practical life way [2]. Summarize his point of view, I think, among them, the mobile communication technology for virtual reality, video broadcast and resource sharing, and other large cloud access broadband application provides support. In 2017, Miao Hui can be in "introduction to 5G and the development outlook" mentioned in the application of mobile communication technology to the Internet of things, and the ways to other areas [14]. Summarizes her point of view, I think the low latency and high reliability of mobile communication technology for intelligent manufacturing, remote monitoring, remote control, automatic driving machinery, such as the low latency services provides a strong support.

2.2 The History of Advanced Manufacturing Industry

Qi Guotang in 2012, in "the basic approach of developing advanced manufacturing industries research" in advanced manufacturing industries is defined as: absorption of electronic information, computer, machinery, manufacturing materials and high-tech achievements of modern management technology, and integrated application of advanced technology manufacturing products research and development design, production, testing, network marketing services and whole process management and realize high quality, high efficiency, low consumption, clean, flexible production, has obtained the good economic benefit and effect of manufacturing market [16]. In my opinion, Guotang's definition of advanced manufacturing industry is actually relative to traditional manufacturing industry. Moreover, mobile communication technology is a high-tech achievement, and its application to advanced manufacturing industry will further promote the development of advanced manufacturing industry.

Since the 1980s, Europe, the United States, Japan and other developed industrial countries have exhausted all human resources, money and other resources to make themselves the leader of the world's manufacturing industry and promote "intelligent manufacturing".

At the beginning of the 21st century, China began to attach importance to the development of advanced manufacturing industries and vigorously promoted the innovation and informatization of manufacturing. China's manufacturing industry actively responded to the call of the state, China's manufacturing industry officially entered a new round of rapid development period.

2.3 The Influence of Mobile Communication Technology on Advanced Manufacturing Industry

The impact of mobile communications technology on advanced manufacturing industries can be seen in every aspect of its production, supervision and distribution. It has played an important role in the development of advanced manufacturing industries. Here are seven aspects of these impacts:

First, as stated by Cheng Feng in 2020, 5G provides support for automation [3]. In my opinion, 5G mobile communication technology provides technical support for automated production in advanced manufacturing industry, which is mainly reflected in real-time transmission of workshop information, tracking of production and distribution process, and remote control of production quality.

Secondly, 5G simplifies the operating system of the manufacturing process and reduces the labor dependency, thus reducing the production cost.

Third, like in 2019, Zhang Sanfeng said that 5G provides technical support for green development [30]. In my opinion, 5G provides technical support for advanced manufacturing industries to achieve efficient production, energy conservation, environmental protection and green development.

Fourth, 5G mobile communication technology can help advanced manufacturing industries update their existing information technology facilities.

Fifth, just like in 2019, Wu Lele said that 5G has promoted the development of the Internet of Things [26]. In my opinion, among the promoting effects of mobile communication technology on advanced manufacturing industry, 5G mobile communication

technology can help advanced manufacturing industry better adapt to its needs of applying the Internet of Things, so as to promote the development of the Internet of Things
and create new business models for advanced manufacturing industry.

Sixth, 5G provides technical support for the digital transformation of advanced manufacturing industry, and provides an opportunity for its deep integration with vertical
industries such as agriculture and transportation. Agricultural producers can to sell the
products to manufacturing industry, manufacturing industry will be obtained from agricultural producers of products produced for higher value products, and the higher value
products sold to transportation and other industries, transportation industry further production, get more value of the final product, make our products improve the value of the
step by step, make manufacturers to obtain the biggest marginal revenue.

Seventh, in 2020, Wang Yueting said that 5G has promoted the application of technology [23]. I think, fundamentally speaking, mobile communication technology provides
a way for advanced manufacturing industries application technology innovation.

3 The Influence Mechanism of 5G on Advanced Manufacturing Industry

The impact of 5G on advanced manufacturing industries is concentrated in many ways.
This paper expounds these influences from four aspects: production process, supply and
demand matching, enterprise cooperation and enterprise competition mode (Fig. 1).

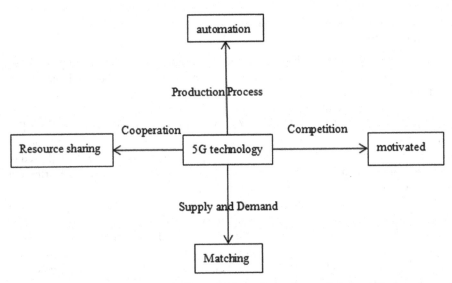

Fig. 1. The influence mechanism of 5G on advanced manufacturing industry

3.1 The Impact of 5G on the Production Process of Advanced Manufacturing Industry

The application of 5G mobile communication technology has made advanced manufacturing industry take a more firm step towards the goal of transforming to automated production and rational use of resources, making it more confident to adhere to the original intention of manufacturing industry in such a turbulent environment. In 2018, in "Wireless Technology Injects New Power into Industrial Internet", 5G has the characteristics of low latency and high reliability [25]. On the production side, 5G technology by shortening the time of computer aided design, computer aided process planning, the use of information equipment, improve the production efficiency of advanced manufacturing, computer-aided manufacturing and computer-aided manufacturing engineering department in the monitoring and maintenance of production line and production equipment, the use of 5G mobile communication technology, production process automation, Automation provides new ideas for advanced manufacturing and timeliness, which can meet the needs of enterprises to reduce production costs and improve production efficiency. Increase confidence and determination in the use of networked equipment in advanced manufacturing industries. In terms of resource utilization, 5G makes the financial management, production management, human resource management, material management, quality management, sales and distribution management of advanced manufacturing more efficient. In product optimization, the use of 5G technology, the production process of advanced manufacturing industry is more convenient, make product quality inspection and improve more quickly and properly, make the product of the follow-up to ensure leaner, make product performance analysis more scientific, make the product tracking process faster, improve the speed and quality of advanced manufacturing product update.

Advanced manufacturing industries is different from manufacturing industries mainly because of the high efficiency of the production link of advanced manufacturing industries, and the application of 5G promotes this efficiency difference, making the advantages of new manufacturing more prominent.

3.2 The Impact of 5G on the Matching of Supply and Demand in Advanced Manufacturing

5G enables advanced manufacturing industries to forecast consumer demand more reasonably and quickly, and determine production according to demand, which has changed the problem of oversupply or short supply caused by unreasonable production in the past. 5G mobile communication technology enables advanced manufacturing industries to more accurately grasp the relationship between market supply and demand.

In the era of the Internet of Things, enterprises only need to grasp the main line of matching supply and demand to make resources flow in the market as reasonably as possible. At the same time, the use of 5G can promote the customer logistics management system, enterprise portal system, decision support system and other enterprise systems to adapt to supply and demand, so that the quantity, speed and customer stickiness of enterprise supply have been improved to a certain extent.

At the same time, from the perspective of consumers, a more detailed grasp of the needs of consumers by suppliers can save consumers' time and improve the efficiency of consumer selection.

3.3   Impact of 5G on Cooperation Among Advanced Manufacturing Enterprises

5G has made advanced manufacturing industries more closely connected and the division of labor clearer. Through the establishment of enterprise alliance, the upstream and downstream manufacturing industries that are willing to cooperate can realize the sharing of information, equipment, human resources and other resources through machine interconnection, so as to promote the integration and development of manufacturing enterprises. Upstream manufacturers can rely on technological innovation to maintain competitive advantage, at the same time, by relying on my company form of risk investment, incubator, get more new technology from downstream manufacturing companies, supplement existing technology constantly, keep competitive advantage, at the same time, in the absence of its technology to obtain benefits, open up new markets or to explore a new business model, expand its competitive advantage. Upstream and downstream manufacturing can take advantage of its own technological innovation for enterprises to provide funds, technology, services and other resources, thus improve the willingness and ability of enterprise to a higher goal, the rapid growth of small and medium-sized enterprises to outsourcing enterprises, make the threshold of the advanced manufacturing industry is not only reflected in the large resources, on the basis of more embodied in the technology, promote the development of advanced manufacturing enterprises.

5G provides technical support for the deep integration of advanced manufacturing industry with agriculture, transportation and other industries, enabling advanced manufacturing industry to adapt to this changing, uncertain, complex and fuzzy era, seize the opportunity, and build a business ecosystem with strong adaptability. Advanced manufacturing plays a very important role in the business ecosystem. Advanced manufacturing should shoulder the responsibility of making good use of the production fruits of agriculture and other industries to provide raw materials for transportation and other industries. Advanced manufacturing industry should make use of its own advantages, so that the cooperation among various industries is closer, and the cooperation of multiple industries can promote the rapid development of economy.

3.4   The Impact of 5G on the Competitive Mode of Advanced Manufacturing Industry

The application of 5G has formed a trend of win-win cooperation among manufacturing enterprises, weakened the competitive relationship between competitors and enhanced the willingness to cooperate. Isolation seems to be one of the fundamental factors that hastens the demise of low-quality competitors. The reasons for the demise of these isolated competitors are as follows:

First of all, isolation will make the company lose access to resources, resulting in the problem of insufficient supply of resources.

Second, isolation will make the manufacturing enterprises can not get more information, blind collision problems.

Third, isolation will make enterprises fall into the trap of blind confidence, aggravating the crisis of resource recycling.

Finally, isolation will make an advanced manufacturing enterprise fall into one or more technological development traps, leading to the situation that its technological level will decline rather than rise.

Nowadays, the globalization process is accelerating, and the game of advanced manufacturing industry is no longer limited to a certain country or a certain manufacturing industry. In order to maintain its position, the advanced manufacturing industry must learn to maintain competition in cooperation, make full use of 5G and its own technological innovation, and form an all-round competitive advantage.

4 Future Outlook of Advanced Manufacturing Industry Closely Dependent on 5G

4.1 Production Automation

The low delay of mobile communication technology enables the machine to receive instructions quickly and respond to instructions in the shortest time, so that advanced manufacturing industry can set a fixed program to produce a certain product, realize production automation, and even get rid of the "pure automated production" of human resources (Fig. 2).

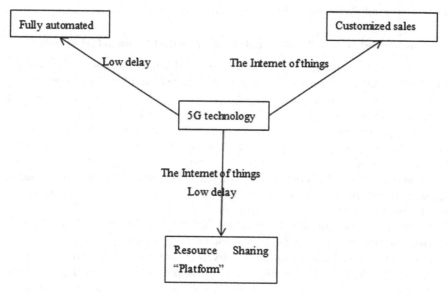

Fig. 2. The prospect of the integration of 5G and advanced manufacturing

Although it is difficult to get rid of the "purely automated production" of human resources, in today's era, science and technology are developing so rapidly that innovation has become a common practice. On the way to the future, we can use our knowledge to plan a better advanced manufacturing industry.

4.2 Resource Sharing "Platform" in the Internet of Things Era

In the current mobile communication technology has entered the 5G era, advanced manufacturing industry can make use of 5G mobile communication technology to create their own unique "platform". On this "platform", manpower, capital, raw materials, products and even machinery and equipment can be used and shared, making the originally fixed "fixed assets" more active and giving full play to their functions. Advanced manufacturing can use this resource-sharing "platform" to obtain resources and sell products.

"The Machine sharing platform". The development of 5G has promoted the supervision and control of machines. As a special shared resource, the machine can enable small and medium-sized enterprises to enjoy the "platform" dividend and reduce the cost of telephone bill caused by the purchase of the machine. At the same time, large enterprises can gain additional machine sharing benefits by sharing machine resources.

In the future, the application of 5G mobile communication technology may bring about earth-shaking changes in the global industrial chain. The application of 5G mobile communication technology has enabled the integrated development of many high-tech technologies, such as artificial intelligence and blockchain, and promoted the wide application of technologies in different fields.

The production mode of advanced manufacturing industries will be more flexible and the production process will be more personalized. Advanced manufacturing industries can make use of the transformed production chain and rely on shared "platforms" to create a more colorful combination of production modes.

4.3 Customized Service Transformation of Advanced Manufacturing Industry

5G has narrowed the distance between advanced manufacturing and consumers, enabling consumers to speak out their needs, enabling advanced manufacturing to produce on demand, reducing resource waste and achieving the highest matching degree between the demand side and the supply side. 5G provides the possibility for real intelligent manufacturing, putting fully automated production on the agenda, which not only liberates the labor force, but also saves a lot of costs, making small-scale customization possible. Advanced manufacturing industry can obtain consumer demand information in the first time, and quickly find the corresponding equipment combination information based on this information, and then realize customized information flow and the acceleration of production process based on this information.

5G offers the possibility of truly smart manufacturing. In 2019, Wu Lele proposed that advanced manufacturing could facilitate cloud ordering. In my opinion, the production equipment of advanced manufacturing industry can be ordered directly through the cloud, and the intelligent production machine can adjust the production mode and raw materials at any time, truly meeting the personalized and customized consumption trend. 5G technology for complementary information of enterprises, and to rely on more convenient logistics resources to act quickly and equipment such as the effective application can use a company's production equipment will be for some semi-finished products, raw materials, production and logistics to another enterprise, and through its complete follow-up production equipment, in order to obtain the finished product in accordance with the needs of the consumers.

5G has fully opened the digital age. 5G underpins the development of the digital age. Big data systems are full of all kinds of information, which can be collected by advanced manufacturing industry to provide consumers with some choice basis, according to which consumers can combine and find the right product.

5 Challenges Faced by Advanced Manufacturing Industries in Utilizing Mobile Communication Technology

5.1 Lack of Innovation and Application Capacity Construction

Increases the complexity of system management. The integration of 5G and advanced manufacturing enables advanced manufacturing industries to be integrated into a variety of other systems, making the whole business system more complex.

Cost. At present, many enterprises have not entered the 5G transition process, mainly because many advanced manufacturing industries have invested heavily in the existing industrial network. If they make the 5G transition, they will face huge cost pressure.

In the application of 5G mobile communication technology, there are great uncertainties. As we all know, the application of 5G mobile communication technology needs the support of many basic technologies and resources. Even if these issues are resolved, there are still significant uncertainties and risks in other areas.

In 2020, Tan Mei mentioned security threats to 5G in her "Overview of 5G Key Technologies and Challenges" [19]. In fact, 5G applications are mainly faced with selfish misconduct, harmful interference, authorized user imitation, authorized user competition and other behaviors.

5.2 Lack of Versatile Talents Who Can Take Advantage of 5G

The application of 5G in advanced manufacturing requires the support of versatile talents, but there is a shortage of talents suitable for this position.

5.3 The Digital Transformation of Advanced Manufacturing Infrastructure Needs to Be Strengthened

The application of 5G in advanced manufacturing industries needs to be premised on the digitization of infrastructure, which is Ren Ren's view in "Technology spillover effects of ICT on Chinese industries" in 2019. In my opinion, although the digital foundation of advanced manufacturing industry is stronger than that of general manufacturing industry, there are still some shortcomings. This is indeed one of the major issues that advanced manufacturing industry must consider.

5.4 The Technology Concentration of Advanced Manufacturing Is Low

With the development of economic globalization, the international division of labor in advanced manufacturing industry is developing from vertical division of labor to horizontal division of labor even network division of labor. The industry chain has been segmented to an unprecedented level. In 2006, Yang Daqing pointed out that self-interest in various industries, especially in the high-tech sector, was spreading technology distribution [27].

6 Advanced Manufacturing Industry Relying on Mobile Communication Technology

6.1 The World Level

The advanced manufacturing industries of all countries should realize information sharing and conduct healthy competition on the basis of mutual cooperation. Only by learning from each other and having their own advantages can we promote the rapid and high-quality development of the industry.

6.2 The National Level

In 2017, Li Yang pointed out that China's advanced technology development should learn from Japan's integration of "industry-university-research officials" and promote the theoretical construction, practical application and policy support of mobile communication technology [13]. Based on Li Yang's point of view, I believe that China's advanced manufacturing industry should keep learning spirit. First, the country should establish a system to promote the use of communication technology in the manufacturing industry; Second, the country should encourage advanced manufacturing and speed up research and development of advanced technologies to support 5G; Finally, the country should promote the theoretical construction of the application of 5G in universities, research institutions and other institutions in the field of advanced manufacturing.

6.3 Industry Level

Manufacturing is one of the main decisive industries in the operation of a country. All businesses in this industry should breathe and stick together. There can be a suitable competition between each other, but absolutely cannot ignore the necessity of cooperation, high status in the industry of the enterprise, should play a leading role, can establish a business platform", "technology alliance", promote the industrial enterprises mutually beneficial and win-win business model, constantly promote the development of high and new technology.

6.4 Corporate Level

Advanced manufacturing industries must speed up access to technological innovation. Advanced manufacturing industries, when they have sufficient resources, can use internal research and development to obtain new technological innovations. In the case of low R&D intensity, advanced manufacturing industry can obtain more technological innovation from external enterprises through venture capital, incubators, accelerators and technology alliances.

References

1. Shathik, F.A.: Future enhancements and propensities in forthcoming communication system – 5G Network Technology. In: International Conference On Computational Physics in Emerging Technologies (ICCPET) (2020)

2. Chai, Y.: Research on the development of 5G mobile communication technology in the new era, in Chinese. Sci. Inform. Technol. **011**(000), 24–24 (2019). (in Chinese)
3. Cheng, F.: Integration of 5G will continue to change society. Commun. Enterp. Manage. **397**(05), 13–17 (2020). (in Chinese)
4. Cheng, J.: Industrial IoT in 5G environment towards smart manufacturing. J. Ind. Inform. Integr. **10**, 10–19 (2018). (in Chinese)
5. Duan, C.: Internet of things era under 5G mobile communication technology. In: 2019 4th International Industrial Informatics and Computer Engineering Conference (IIICEC 2019), pp. 318–322. Francis Academic Press, UK (2019)
6. Fu, X.: 5G+industrial internet enables industrial intelligent manufacturing. China Ind. Inform. Technol. (8), 74 (2020). (in Chinese)
7. Jiang, R.: Technology spillover effect of information and communication technology on Chinese industry. Finance Trade Res. **30**(02), 5–20 (2019). (in Chinese)
8. Vinoy, K.J.: Design of front-end modules for MMwave 5G communication. In: 2020 URSI Regional Conference on Radio Science (URSI-RCRS), (2020)
9. Lan, K.: Application and development prospect of 5G mobile communication technology in the era of big data. China New Commun. **22**(04), 16–16 (2020). (in Chinese)
10. Liang, F.: Research on the development of 5G mobile communication technology under the new era. Hot-Point Perspect. **64**, 19 (2017). (in Chinese)
11. Liu, H.: Research on the impact of mobile communication technology development on safety production. Chin. J. Prod. Saf. Sci. Technol. **16**(08), 163–168 (2020). (in Chinese)
12. Li, R.: Research on mining and acquisition strategy of technology frontier tracking information sources in specific domain–taking 5G as an example. Mod. Intell. (08), 122–128 (2017). (in Chinese)
13. Li, Y.: Enlightenment of Japanese manufacturing innovation system. China Ind. Rev. (10), 42–45 (2017). (in Chinese)
14. Miao, H.: Discussion on 5G and development prospect. Caixun (20), 79–79 (2017). (in Chinese)
15. Puspita, R.H.: Reinforcement learning based 5G enabled cognitive radio networks. In: 2019 International Conference on Information and Communication Technology Convergence (ICTC). IEEE 5G World Forum, USA (2019)
16. Qi, G.: Research on the basic measures of developing advanced manufacturing industry vigorously. Urban Econ. 22–24 (2012). (in Chinese)
17. Rathee, G.: Cognitive automation for smart decision making in industrial internet of things. IEEE Trans. Ind. Inform. **99**, 1 (2020)
18. Silva, R.: Mobility-optimized dynamic content placement for fast vehicles in 5G networks. In: IEEE International Symposium on Personal, Indoor and Mobile Radio Communications. IEEE, USA (2019)
19. Tan, M.: A review of key technologies and challenges of 5G. Satell. TV Broadband Multimedia (1), 1–2 (2020). (in Chinese)
20. Tokody, D.: Digitising the European industry - holonic systems approach. Procedia Manuf. **22**, 1015–1022 (2019)
21. G helps develop smart factories. Smart factory, pp. 28–29 (2019). (in Chinese)
22. Wang, Y.: Characteristics and application scenarios of 5G mobile communication technology. Management & Technology of SME, pp. 164–165 (2020). (in Chinese)
23. Wang, Y.: Industrial structure technology upgrade based on 5G network service and IoT intelligent manufacturing. Microprocess. Microsyst. **14**, 1–6 (2021). (in Chinese)
24. Wang, Y.: Communication engineering and its development prospect. Eng. Technol. **5**(2), 234–234 (2013). (in Chinese)
25. Wireless Technology Injects New Power to Industrial Internet. China Radio (2018). (in Chinese)

26. Wu, L.: Research on the application of 5G mobile communication technology in the Internet of Things. Commun. World **026**(008), 157–158 (2019). (in Chinese)
27. Yang, D.: Development experience of world advanced manufacturing industry and its reference. Northern Econ. **000**(002), 65–66 (2006). (in Chinese)
28. Zhao, J., Li, W., Yang, Y., Meng, H., Huang, W.: Design and realization of information service system of agricultural expert based on wireless mobile communication technology. Computer and Computing Technologies in Agriculture IV—4th IFIP TC 12 Conference (CCTA2010) Part III. Nanchang, Jiangxi, China (2010). (in Chinese)
29. Zhang, P.: Technology prospect of 6G mobile communications. J. Commun. **40**(1), 141–148 (2019). (in Chinese)
30. Zhang, S.: Does information and communication technology reduce enterprise energy consumption? Evidence from survey data of manufacturing enterprises in China. China Ind. Econ. **371**(02), 157–175 (2019). (in Chinese)
31. Zhong, Z.: Intelligent manufacturing promotes the comprehensive upgrading and innovative growth of China's manufacturing industry. China Eng. Sci. **22**(06), 136–142 (2020). (in Chinese)

Learners' Perception on Integration of Human Personality Types on Mobile Learning Platform

Kasthuri Subaramaniam[1,2]([⊠]) and Sellappan Palaniappan[2]

[1] Institute of Computer Science and Digital Innovation, UCSI University,
Kuala Lumpur, Malaysia
`kasthurisuba@ucsiuniversity.edu.my`
[2] School of Information Technology, Malaysia University of Science and Technology (MUST),
Petaling Jaya, Malaysia

Abstract. E-learning has always been a part of higher education learning for several years now. Universities and colleges have all adopted the use of e-learning and mobile learning to perform their teaching and learning to their students. However, even with the convenience that e-learning and mobile learning provides, students nowadays face difficulties in learning productively and efficiently. This issue can further be analysed and investigated by improving the presentation of information of e-learning to students. User interface designs play a vital and important role for the receptivity of information to students. The relationship between user interface designs and different human personality types also have a strong association with each other. This study looks into the different personality types of students and their personality preferences. A survey questionnaire was distributed among students of higher learning to investigate and to see the different user interface designs of their liking. This is to better understand the learners' perception of users on integration of human personality types of the application. The results of the survey were analysed in detail.

Keywords: Human personality types · Mobile learning · MBTI

1 Introduction

Human-computer interaction (HCI) is the study of how people communicate with computers and how computers are or are not equipped to interact effectively with human beings (Dix 2017). In other words, it is the study of the relationship between people, computer and tasks. HCI is mainly concerned with understanding how activities can be carried out interactively by people and computers and how such interactive systems are constructed (Stephanidis et al. 2019). It can also be defined as 'the discipline concerned with the design, evaluation, and implementation of and the analysis of major phenomena involving interactive computer systems for human use.' HCI is a multidisciplinary subject that draws on expertise from the fields of science, engineering and art.

The original version of this chapter was revised: the affiliation of the author Kasthuri Subaramaniam was not complete. This has been corrected. The correction to this chapter is available at
https://doi.org/10.1007/978-3-030-77025-9_28

G. Salvendy and J. Wei (Eds.): HCII 2021, LNCS 12796, pp. 329–343, 2021.
https://doi.org/10.1007/978-3-030-77025-9_27

In information technology, the user interface (UI) is everything designed into an information system through which a human being can communicate. This involves a mouse, keyboard, screen, appearance of a desktop, help messages, special characters and others. Thus, all these invite interaction and response from it. In short, interfaces act as a bridge between the man-machine system (MMS) by facilitating the exchange of information between them (Rouse and Draganova 1984; Lupton and Tanner 1987). The real efficacy of software applications depends not on computer experts, but the end user's acceptance and usability (Vajde and Rozman 1991).

It has become a common recommendation to computer interface designers that they should "Know the user" (Rubinstein and Hersh 1984). The rising number of users with a wide range of ability levels is rapidly increasing, making higher demands on interactive systems in a wide range of contexts. It is important to get a detailed understanding of the users and their tasks for any system development process. Criticism of the design of user interfaces and the functionality incorporated into products has been discussed in several articles in recent years. This is because human factors have taken a back seat, especially the recent rush to 'e-market' due to the rapid growth of web-based applications.

The widespread use of the Internet for education, commerce, entertainment and communication via email has been increasing from year to year (Greenhow and Askari 2017). Apart from that, our smartphones and tablets are with us all the time (Norman 2017). Consequently, the web culture has changed significantly, instigating a need to reconsider the way designers approach web interface design. In other words, systems can be designed easier by analysing the moods, attitudes and motives of users (Rapp et al. 2018). Therefore, the communication between the computer and the user must be simple, precise, versatile, consistent and as fast as possible. Moreover, improving user interfaces in the software that are developed may be the key to expanding the use of computers to a larger portion of the population. In other words, a flexible approach with a new aspect of developing web interfaces must be undertaken.

In view of that, this study presents the findings of a survey relating to the necessity of incorporation of human personality types in the user interface design so that the resulting system is more usable by different types of people. This research incorporates the personality types of human beings in the field of human-computer interaction, in particular, and computer science, in general. This study, too, investigates the various human factors as well as personality types of human beings within the context of interfaces for software applications. Learning styles, for instance, vary between ethnic groups as well as gender. Therefore, by offering users successful interface designs, users with different learning style preferences and skills can have a greater opportunity to explore what best suits their strengths, needs, and limitations (Truong 2016). Therefore, in a software application, a good interface can communicate effectively with the intended users and stimulate their minds to understand the materials or the meaning of the text.

The results of the present study are based on a small sample and are therefore only suggestive. However, the findings indicate that human personality types and user interface preferences are indeed related. Therefore, this study explores the need to develop such user interfaces whereby the information layout is easy to understand with the corresponding features for different personality types of users.

2 Literature Review

2.1 E-Learning

Today, educational institutions have adopted the use of technology. This ranges from kindergartens, primary schools, secondary schools and to tertiary education institutions such as public and private colleges and universities. In the year 2020, technology is seen as a tool that has been ingrained into the minds of everyday humans due to COVID-19 pandemic. The usage of digital devices such as computers, laptops, smartphones and others are no longer an unusual scene.

The incorporation of technology in the classroom has been used not only in developed countries but also in less developed countries like Ghana. It is now a growing trend to include technology in the classroom environment to fulfil the technological expectations of students (Hartshorne and Ajjan 2009). The Internet is a very good example of a technological tool highly used by students and teachers. This is because the Internet is a very important source of information sharing among students and teachers, in the context of education.

2.2 Human-Computer Interaction

A simple definition of HCI is the research of how different users interact with different computer systems. Human-computer interaction consists of three main components that include the user, the computer and the interaction. In other words, it is the study of the interaction between the user and the computer. Its main goals are to achieve good functionality and usability. This in turn will increase the effectiveness of user interaction with the computer system and creates a better user experience (Draganova and Doran 2013).

A designed system is determined by what a system can do. For example, the objective and purpose of a system developed are based on its functions. According to Karray et al. (2008), functionality is defined as the collection of actions or services the system contributes to its users. This functionality can only be measured by its value when a user effectively utilizes the system. In other words. definition of the usability of a system is how user goals are accomplished with the amount of degree of an efficient system is used (Karray et al. 2008). Apart from that, personalisation plays a significant role in the field of human-computer interaction. For example, computer-based interface interaction requires users to exhibit a wide variety of physical and cognitive abilities that vary from person to person (Augstein et al. 2019).

2.3 Graphical User Interface

Faure and Vanderdonckt (2014) have stated that in software systems, user interface accounts for more than 50 percent of the cost and development time. The development of user interface to satisfy diversified users, preferences, and usability is a challenging task for some designers because of complexities of improving multi-cultural, multi-modality, and usability features of a user interface (Faure and Vanderdonckt 2014). The user interface is an interaction between human and computer device (Bouchrika et al.

2014).

User interface execution began with the regular input of device components, such as a keyboard and mouse (Bouchrika et al. 2014).

Alves et al. (2020) depict how designers provide a better user experience by adapting a user interface to specific features. Meanwhile, Breese and Ball (1999) noted that the innovation is embodied in a computer user interface that involves an observer capable of observing user behaviour, an agent capable of conveying emotion and personality by displaying a user's corresponding behaviour and a network that connects user behaviour observed by said observer and emotion and personality conveyed by said agent. Hassan (2020) introduced a visual design approach, which guides researchers to know which part of the interface they need to refine it to meet the users' needs and goals. A study has indicated that learner's personality influences learning strategies and outcomes in real practice (Chen and Lin 2002). Douglas and Riding (1993) have indicated that the physical and material organization of the e-learning parameters such as text size, headings, layout and size of a window affect the e-learning process.

2.4   User Interface in Mobile Applications

One of the reasons why mobile applications are taking over desktop and web applications is because of their user interface design. Due to the size of a mobile device, the user interface designs in a mobile application appear to be more compact and compressed. Thus, information inside in the media elements such as Buttons and TextView (in Android XML) appear summarised and organised.

However, user interface designs sometimes are being neglected because developers tend to focus more on the functions of a mobile application. This has created a major issue as end-users give up in using the mobile application and decide to switch to using a normal desktop application on a PC (Karlson et al. 2010). This further justifies the fact the user interface design is extremely important in maintaining end-users loyalty and acceptance.

Online stores in mobile operating systems for downloading mobile applications such as the Google Play Store in an Android OS and the App Store in Apple iOS contains millions of apps. Not only that, but the online stores have also advanced throughout the years to include other things like renting and buying movies online, renting and buying books, and even subscribing to monthly or yearly paid news subscription using the Newsstand (on Android). Each component of this contains reviews and ratings which can be evaluated by the user post-deployment. Users can express their opinions regarding the application based on their respective usage on the application, such as commenting on the functions of the application or giving suggestions to improve on the application.

The user interface design in every application represents a very important role as it is what the end-users perceive right at the start of the execution of the application. It is a very crucial role indeed in shaping the quality of the mobile application perceived by the user. The quality of the mobile application can also be further reflected based on the number of downloads each application gets every month. Therefore, developers can then assess the quality of their application and gauge if the mobile application that was developed and deployed has met the requirements of the current market (Taba et al. 2017). In his paper, Weichbroth (2020) stated that mobile apps have the potential to communicate with a user with software that emphasises various aspects of his/her skills, such as user values, feelings, desires, expectations, physical and psychological reactions, behaviours and achievements that occur before, during and after application usage.

Therefore, it is considered as a difficult task to reach an exceptional perceived quality for users especially in designing user interface designs in a mobile application. According to a journal article by Karlson et al. (2010), developers find it strenuous and difficult to design mobile application due to the limitations of mobile applications. These limitations can be a hassle because of its screen that is small in size, incompetent hardware and it is more susceptible to have problems with the network since smartphones use a wireless network connection all the time. Consequently, developers should then be more careful when developing designing mobile applications, as more emphasis and focus should be placed in mobile development rather than on desktop. There are many ways and practices to ease the work of the developer. For instance, the adoption of practices can be acquired by developers and designers using other templates that have sets of UI elements that are used by others.

2.5 Personality Types

Personality type is what you want when using your mind or concentrating your attention. Studies and experience have shown that each person has clear patterns. A preference is what you like. You may like or prefer strawberry candy over orange. You may prefer cooking over sewing. This doesn't mean you won't sometimes choose, or be pressured to choose orange candy or sewing. But in general, you will prefer to choose strawberry candy or cooking. There are no right or wrong preferences exist. Each one has its strengths and its issues. Most people can do both, even though they do not like one or the other. Personality preferences are like any other preferences, also known as psychological preferences, (Myers and Briggs Foundation 2020).

Personality has been described as the complex amalgam of an individual's unique behavioural, temperamental, emotional and mental attributes. This fusion of characteristics and functions may be conceptualized as the entire mental organization of a person's circumstances and their physically stable set of individual attributes (Kaushal and Patwardhan 2018). The 2020 Encyclopædia Britannica adds to this definition by referencing how personality may express itself:

Personality embraces moods, attitudes, and opinions and is most clearly expressed in interactions with other people. It includes behavioural characteristics, both inherent and acquired, that distinguish one person from another and that can be observed in people's relations to the environment and the social group (Holzman 2020).

Both definitions of personality are based upon the assumption that personality traits are pre-eminently distinguishable and distinguishing features of personality, yet neither explicitly defines nor enumerates these traits. There are several advantages of knowing your interests, including how they affect you, how they shape your communication style, and how they vary from what other individuals prefer. Preferences allow us to have different desires, different therapeutic approaches, and different ways of seeing the world. While all preferences are equal, there are different strengths and different challenges for each one. Understanding these personality attributes and challenges will help you to understand and appreciate how everybody contributes to a situation, a mission, or the solution to a problem.

The theoretical basis of this work is based on the writings of the founder of analytical psychology, a Swiss psychiatrist known as Carl G. Jung (1875–1961). According to Carl G. Jung's theory of psychological types (Jung 1971), people can be characterized by (a) their general attitude preference - Extraverted (E) vs. Introverted (I), (b) their preference for one of the two perception functions - Sensing (S) vs. Intuition (N), and (c) their preference of one of the two judging functions: Thinking (T) vs. Feeling (F).

Dichotomies are the three areas of preference introduced by Jung (i.e. bipolar dimensions where each pole represents a different preference). Jung also indicated that one of the four functions above is dominant in an individual, either a perception function or a judging function. Isabel Briggs Myers, a Jung theory researcher and practitioner, suggested that the judging-perceiving relationship is a fourth dichotomy governing the Judging (J) vs. Perceiving (P) types (Myers and Myers 1995).

2.6   The Myers- Briggs Type Indicator (MBTI)

The Myers-Briggs Type Indicator (MBTI) is a self-report questionnaire designed to measure personality type based on Jung's theory of psychological types. The results of MBTI identify important distinctions between average, healthy individuals. The authors, Katharine Cook Briggs (1875–1968) and Isabel Briggs Myers (1897–1980), her daughter, were astute observers of the differences between human personalities. They investigated Carl Jung's theories and applied them to human interaction (Myers 1993). The categorisation works on how people relate the world around them. It is also stated that each person is inclined to a preference depending on his or her personality type that works in every functional area.

Based on the journal article by Lindsey (2011), Jung also said that the human mind has four functions that are divided into two opposing functions, that are Thinking or Feeling, and Sensation and Intuition. Since there are opposing functions, which means that Thinking is opposed to Feeling whereas Sensation is opposed to Intuition. Furthermore, people can be divided into two types, where one group prefers an internal world known as Introversion and the other prefers an external world known as Extraversion. In layman terms, Introversion also means an introvert and Extraversion also means an extrovert.

The Myers and Briggs Foundation (2020) website stated that "the MBTI® instrument has been the subject of hundreds of research projects studying the links between personality type and different aspects of life." In the MBTI® theory, the following points are evident: (a) random behavioural variance is quite orderly and consistent and (b) variations are clarified in the way people choose to use their vision and judgement. The Qualifying.org (2008) website further claimed that "the MBTI® tool provides a framework for understanding one's way of both collecting information and making decisions to allow for maximizing personal and interpersonal effectiveness."

2.7 MBTI as a Research Tool

The MBTI is a valuable instrument when used correctly. The instrument is an indicator and not a test. There is no "good" or "bad" type (Mason and Mitroff 1973). The instrument is designed to measure type and not to stereotype any individual. It measures preferences and not the abilities of people. MBTI highlights strengths and not weaknesses. It is based on the premise that we have inborn tendencies that take their form as they are developed (i.e. we have a "true type").

Therefore, this research will use the Jung Typology Test™ which contains 64 brief questions. This free personality test is based on Carl Jung's and Isabel Briggs Myers' personality type theory that classifies personality types. MBTI was chosen as the personality research tool because it has a long history, it is grounded in theory, and it continues to be used worldwide by over 2 million people annually (Stein and Swan 2019). It has been used in studies where researchers are looking for correlations between personality types and academic study choices: for example, Kim and Han's (2014) study which looked at the relationships between MBTI types, academic performance and student satisfaction in nursing students, and the Zarafshani et al. (2011) study which examined the relationships between personality type and the entrepreneurial intentions of Iranian university students completing a course in entrepreneurship. The other researches include the study by Putro and Rosmansyah (2020) on the development of online learning groups based on MBTI learning style and fuzzy algorithm, Kollipara et al. (2019) did research on selecting project team members through MBTI method, and Kruck et al. (2014) research was to find out whether if different students with different personality types can perform differently, be it better or worse on student grades. These are the few studies mentioned here compared to the numerous research done using the MBTI instrument.

In addition, for this analysis, the Jungian paradigm was chosen as it provides the basis for the most enduring definition of cognitive style (Brightman and Shesai 1982). These cognitive modes are directly related to learning styles and are important to the study of information systems, whereby the use of questionnaires can easily identify individuals as opposed to the elaborate assessments needed in other frameworks. The Jungian framework's dimensions are distinct (Carlyn 1977). In addition, it has been widely used and validated in education (DiTiberio 1996, 1998). Other related researches include the decision-science and automation-science (Blaylock and Rees 1984; Alavi and Henderson 1981; Davis and Elnicki 1984; Henderson and Marinko 1981; Henderson and Nutt 1980; Mitroff and Kilmann 1975).

3   Methodology

The proposed research adopted the quantitative and qualitative approaches because the methodology offered participants a sense of freedom to respond or provide views, thoughts and opinions that generate diverse results (Branthwaite and Peterson 2011). The research problem undertaken for this qualitative nature is an exploratory study on how user interface designs can be improved for the different types of users. The exploratory qualitative approach was found to be suitable for this research as it was intended to draw data from intentionally selected participants in semi-structured interviews using open-ended questions. (Creswell and Creswell 2017). The Myers-Briggs Type Indicator was selected as the personality type instrument based on the reasons.

The overall research question can be formulated in the following way: In an electronic learning platform, do students with different personality types learn and gauge better when using a user interface designed to their personality preference?

To determine if students "learn better", tests have conducted that show the degree to which the participants have a better understanding of the material. Interviews and surveys helped to clarify qualitative aspects of this issue, which include the satisfaction or frustration with the user interface used. The qualitative data also helps support the quantitative results.

3.1   Population and Sample

The population in this research study were students of higher institutions of learning in Malaysia who are active users of learning applications. Interviews with students proceeded until data saturation was met. Students with more than 2 yrs of experience and knowledge of user interface elements and diversified backgrounds from different geographical areas in Malaysia were included in the study population. A pilot study with ten participants was performed to determine the reliability of the standardised research instrument (Rubin and Rubin 2011).

3.2   Sampling Procedure

The appropriateness of the sampling method applied to the research was focused on the personal experience of the IT participants, with an emphasis on user interface design and software development. The parameters used to select participants are as follows: (a) participants must be 18 yrs of age or older; (b) participants who are students of institutions of higher learning (c) participants who have 2 yrs of experience and knowledge of user interface elements, (d) participants must have used learning application(s) and (e) participants must be able to be interviewed by following the standardized interview protocol and procedure if requested.

The total number of respondents of the survey to determine their personality types was 468 that came from different students from different study backgrounds. The survey consists of three major sections and one minor section. Before respondents are redirected to the major sections, respondents need to first go through a minor section. The minor section is to ensure that all respondents have done the Myers-Briggs Type Indicator personality test before proceeding to the major sections.

3.3 Instrumentation

The personality test undertaken with the user interface elements survey gave a good insight on how to devise user interfaces for the different personality types. Both questionnaires were the starting point to discover the common elements required for the designs. Apart from that, various literature on learning style preference for the different personality types (Myers et al. 1998; DiTiberio 1996; DiTiberio 1998), were taken into consideration by looking into the common elements in the designs that were important for designers of a personality type. Elements related to colours and appearance were grouped under the visual cues. The navigational elements of the interface were grouped under the navigational cues. Meanwhile, semantic cues relate to the presentation of the contents such as the scope of coverage and the order. The interfaces were designed based on the criteria gathered from the questionnaires and storyboards. Usability tests were conducted to ascertain that the designs of user interface elements were easy to use and practical. This is also to ensure that the human-computer interaction design principles were not violated. The usability study was undertaken by participants by matching the interface design with their personality type. This included the experimental design shown followed by a semi-structured interview.

4 Results and Findings

A section in the survey included the verification of the respondents on their personality type using the Myers-Briggs Type Indicator personality. The demographics of this survey were also analyzed.

■ Have performed the personality test

■ Have never done the personality test

Fig. 1. Users' knowledge of their personality types (Subaramaniam et al. 2020)

This section of the survey is crucial to study the respondent's knowledge of their own personality type. According to the Fig. 1, it can be seen that only 25 respondents out of the total 468 respondents have done the personality test before meanwhile the other respondents did not. The age criterion is made up of different age groups which are i) under 18 yrs old, ii) 18–25 yrs old, iii) 26–30 yrs old and iv) above 30 yrs old. Results show that most of the respondents are from the "18 to 25 yrs old" age group, that is, 310 respondents out of 468 respondents. This is due to as the survey that was conducted was distributed among college and university students in higher education. There was also a total of 129 respondents out of 468 respondents that are from the "26 to 30 yrs old" age group, which is believed and assumed to be final year university students.

The last criterion is gender where it is made up of male, female and option for respondents who prefer not to say. Most of the respondents were males that made up of 226 respondents and the others were all females.

The bar chart below shows the analysis of the results based on the font sizes chosen by respondents based on each font (Fig. 2).

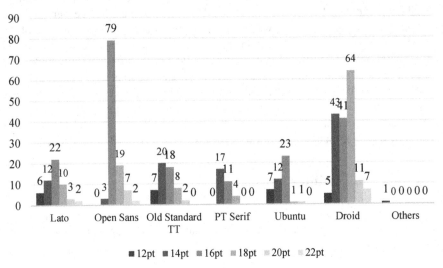

Fig. 2. Users' preference to different font sizes (Subaramaniam et al. 2020)

The bar chart below shows the analysis of the results based on the font colours chosen by respondents based on each font (Fig. 3).

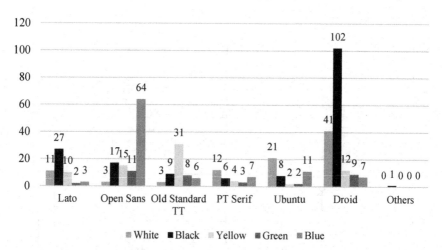

Fig. 3. Users' preference to different font colours (Subaramaniam et al. 2020)

The bar chart below shows the analysis of the results based on the font styles chosen by respondents based on each font (Fig. 4).

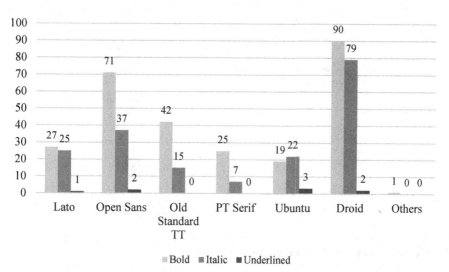

Fig. 4. Users' preference to different font style bar chart (Subaramaniam et al. 2020)

After the analysis of the survey results are being conducted, the results are examined, and a list of functional requirements were identified. The activity diagram below shows the system flow of accessing lecture notes by the user (Fig. 5).

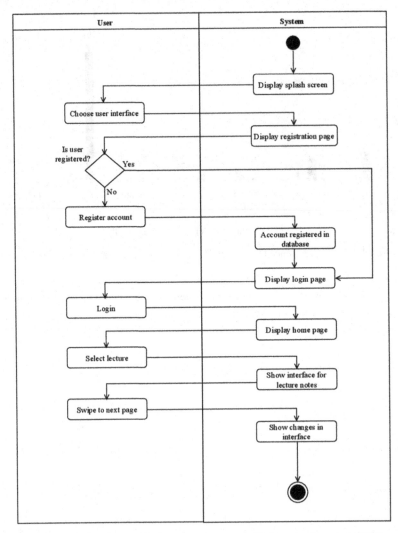

Fig. 5. Activity diagram for lecture notes access (Subaramaniam et al. 2020)

5   Conclusions and Recommendations

The user acceptance test has been undertaken to evaluate the effectiveness of the system that has been developed. The user acceptance testing was conducted through interviews with different human personality categories A list of features of the system were tabulated for the evaluation of the mobile application by the users. The interview conducted are based on 2 phases. Phase One was about how users perceive the system features and Phase Two was about users' own opinions and suggestions for the system. The interviews were conducted with people of different personality types. The names and identities of the users were kept confidential. After the development of the e-learning mobile application and having done the testing, it can be said and deduced that all objectives that were proposed earlier have all been achieved.

This mobile application enables users to be aware of their personality type according to the Myers-Briggs Type Indicator. In the mobile application itself, users can perform the MBTI personality test while at the same time accessing different user interfaces that are based on different personality types. Since the user interface layouts are specifically designed for students with different personality types, it increases students' productivity of learning as they will perceive their learning information difference in accordance to their own personalities. This is how the main aim of the project has been met. In the future, universities and colleges can utilize this research further to cater more designs for other personality types and follow the practice of using personality types as a measure to improve learning productivity and increase learning interest amongst students in higher education. As a result, this can transform e-learning to a different approach and dimension and learning in general will be very different from the present.

References

Alavi, M., Henderson, J.C.: An evolutionary strategy for implementing a decision support system. Manage. Sci. **27**(11), 1309–1323 (1981)

Alves, T., Natálio, J., Henriques-Calado, J., Gama, S.: Incorporating personality in user interface design: a review. Personal. Individ. Differ. **155**, (2020)

Augstein, M., Herder, E., Wörndl, W. (eds.): Personalized Human-Computer Interaction. Walter de Gruyter GmbH & Co KG (2019)

Blaylock, B.K., Rees, L.P.: Cognitive style and the usefulness of information. Decis. Sci. **15**(1), 74–91 (1984)

Bouchrika, T., Zaied, M., Jemai, O., Amar, C.B.: Neural solutions to interact with computers by hand gesture recognition. Multimedia Tools Appl. **72**(3), 2949–2975 (2014)

Branthwaite, A., Patterson, S.: The power of qualitative research in the era of social media. Qual. Market Res.: Int. J. **14**(4), 430–440 (2011)

Breese, J.S., Ball, J.E.: U.S. Patent No. 5,987,415. Washington, DC: U.S. Patent and Trademark Office (1999)

Brightman, H.J., Shesai, E.L.: The Impact of problem generation and solving behaviour and cognitive style on management performance. In: Proceedings of the American Institute for Decision Sciences, vol. 1 (1982)

Carlyn, M.: An assessment of the Myers-Briggs type indicator. J. Personal. Assess. **41**(5), 461–473 (1977)

Chen, N.S., Lin, K.M.: Factors affecting e-learning for achievement. In: IEEE International Conference on Advanced Learning Technologies, pp. 9–12 (2002)

Creswell, J.W., Creswell, J.D.: Research Design: Qualitative, Quantitative, and Mixed Methods Approaches. Sage publications (2017)

Davis, D.L., Elnicki, R.A.: User cognitive types for decision support systems. Omega **12**(6), 601–614 (1984)

DiTiberio, J.: Education, learning styles, and cognitive styles. MBTI applications: A decade of research on the Myers-Briggs Type Indicator, pp. 123–166. Consulting Psychologists Press, AL Hammer. Palo Alto (1996)

DiTiberio, J.: Uses of type in education. In: Myers, I.B., McCaulley, M.H., Quenk, N. (eds.) MBTI Manual: A Guide to the Development and Use of the Myers-Briggs Type Indicator. Consulting Psychologists Press, Palo Alto (1998)

Dix, A.: Human–computer interaction, foundations and new paradigms. J. Vis. Lang. Comput. **42**, 122–134 (2017)

Douglas, G., Riding, R.J.: The effect of pupil cognitive style and position of prose passage title on recall. Educ. Psychol. **13**(3–4), 385–393 (1993)

Draganova, A., Doran, P.: Use of HCI components into IT courses. Int. J. Inform. Educ. Technol. **3**(2), 245 (2013)

Faure, D., Vanderdonckt, J.: User interface standardization. Inter. J. User-Syst. Interact. **7**(2), 89 (2014)

Greenhow, C., Askari, E.: Learning and teaching with social network sites: a decade of research in K-12 related education. Educ. Inform. Technol. **22**(2), 623–645 (2017)

Hartshorne, R., Ajjan, H.: Examining student decisions to adopt Web 2.0 technologies: theory and empirical tests. J. Comput. High. Educ. **21**(3), 183 (2009)

Hassan, I.: The graphical experience: user interface design approach based on user-centered design to support usability. In: Internet of Things—Applications and Future, pp. 377–399. Springer, Singapore (2020)

Henderson, J.C., Martinko, M.J.: Cognitive learning theory and the design of decision support systems. DSS-81 Transactions, pp. 45–50 (1981)

Henderson, J.C., Nutt, P.C.: The influence of decision style on decision making behavior. Manage. Sci. **26**(4), 371–386 (1980)

Holzman, P.S.: Personality. In: Encyclopædia Britannica. Encyclopædia Britannica, Inc. (2020) www.britannica.com/topic/personality

Jung, C.G.: Psychological types (1971) (Collected works of C. G. Jung, volume 6, Chapter X)

Karlson, A.K., Iqbal, S.T., Meyers, B., Ramos, G., Lee, K., Tang, J.C.: Mobile taskflow in context: a screenshot study of smartphone usage. In: Proceedings of the SIGCHI Conference on Human Factors in Computing Systems, pp. 2009–2018 (2010)

Karray, F., Alemzadeh, M., Abou Saleh, J., Arab, M.N.: Human-computer interaction: overview on state of the art. Int. J. Smart Sens. Intell. Syst. **1**(1), 137–159 (2008)

Subaramaniam, K., Ern-Rong, J.L., Palaniappan, S.: Interface designs with MBTI personality types. In: The 7th Mechanical Engineering Research Day 2020, pp. 178–179, 16 December 2020, Melaka, Malaysia (2020)

Kaushal, V., Patwardhan, M.: Emerging trends in personality identification using online social networks—a literature survey. ACM Trans. Knowl. Discov. Data (TKDD) **12**(2), 1–30 (2018)

Kim, M.R., Han, S.J.: Relationships between the Myers-Briggs Type Indicator personality profiling, academic performance and student satisfaction in nursing students. Inter. J. Bio-Science Bio-Technology **6**(6), 1–12 (2014)

Kollipara, P.B., Regalla, L., Ghosh, G., Kasturi, N.: Selecting project team members through MBTI method: an investigation with homophily and behavioural analysis. In: 2019 Second International Conference on Advanced Computational and Communication Paradigms (ICACCP), pp. 1–9. IEEE (2019)

Kruck, S.E., Sendall, P., Ceccucci, W., Peslak, A., Hunsinger, S.: Does personality play a role in computer information systems performance? Issues Inform. Syst. **15**(2), 383 (2014)

Lindsey, W.H.: The Relationship Between Personality Type and Software Usability Using the Myers-Briggs Type Indicator (MBTI®) and the Software Usability Measurement Inventory (SUMI) (2011)

Lupton, T., Tanner, I.: Achieving Change: A Systematic Approach. Gower Publishing Company (1987)

Mason, R.O., Mitroff, I.I.: A program for research on management information systems. Manage. Sci. **19**(5), 475–487 (1973)

Mitroff, I.I., Kilmann, R.H.: Stories managers tell: A new tool for organizational problem solving. Manage. Rev. **64**(7), 18–28 (1975)

Myers and Briggs Foundation. Myers and Briggs Foundation website (2020). https://www.mye rsbriggs.org/my-mbti-personality-type/mbti-basics/preferences.htm

Myers, I.B.: Introduction to Type, 5th edn. Consulting Psychologists Press, Palo Alto (1993)

Myers, I.B., Myers, P.B.: Gifts Differing – Understanding Personality Type, pp. 139–147. Davies-Black Publishing, Palo Alto (1995)

Myers, I.B., McCaulley, M.H., Quenk, N.L., Hammer, A.L.: MBTI manual: a guide to the development and use of the Myers-Briggs Type Indicator. Consulting Psychologists Press, Palo Alto (1998)

Norman, K.L.: Cyberpsychology: An Introduction to Human-Computer Interaction. Cambridge university press, Cambridge (2017)

Putro, B.L., Rosmansyah, Y.: Development of online learning groups based on MBTI learning style and fuzzy algorithm. Telkomnika 18(1), 199–207 (2020)

Qualifying.org. Certification and Advanced Training website (2008). http://qualifying.org/

Rapp, A., Marcengo, A., Buriano, L., Ruffo, G., Lai, M., Cena, F.: Designing a personal informatics system for users without experience in self-tracking: a case study. Behav. Inform. Technol. 37(4), 335–366 (2018)

Rouse, W.B., Draganova, S.H.: Human information seeking and design of information systems. Inform. Process. Manage. 20(1–2), 129–138 (1984)

Rubin, H.J., Rubin, I.S.: Qualitative Interviewing: The Art of Hearing Data. Sage publications (2011)

Rubinstein, R., Hersh, H.M.: Design philosophy. The Human Factor: Designing Computer Systems for People, pp. 12–22 (1984)

Stein, R., Swan, A.B.: Evaluating the validity of Myers-Briggs Type Indicator theory: A teaching tool and window into intuitive psychology. Soc. Pers. Psychol. Compass 13(2), e12434 (2019)

Stephanidis, C., Salvendy, G., Antona, M., Chen, J.Y., Dong, J., Duffy, V.G., Fang, X., Fidopiastis, C., Fragomeni, G., Fu, L.P., Guo, Y.: Seven HCI grand challenges. Int. J. Hum.-Comput. Interact. 35(14), 1229–1269 (2019)

Taba, S.E.S., Keivanloo, I., Zou, Y., Wang, S.: An exploratory study on the usage of common interface elements in android applications. J. Syst. Softw. 131, 491–504 (2017)

Truong, H.M.: Integrating learning styles and adaptive e-learning system: Current developments, problems and opportunities. Comput. Hum. Behav. 55, 1185–1193 (2016)

Vajde, R., Rozman, I.: May. Tools for human-computer interface and dialogue management. In: [1991 Proceedings] 6th Mediterranean Electrotechnical Conference, pp. 1141–1144. IEEE (1991)

Weichbroth, P.: Usability of mobile applications: a systematic literature study. IEEE Access 8, 55563–55577 (2020)

Zarafshani, K., Cano, J., Sharafi, L., Rajabi, S., Sulaimani, A.: Using the Myers-Briggs Type Indicator (MBTI®) in the teaching of entrepreneurial skills at an Iranian University. NACTA J. 55(4), 14 (2011)

Correction to: Learners' Perception on Integration of Human Personality Types on Mobile Learning Platform

Kasthuri Subaramaniam and Sellappan Palaniappan

Correction to:
Chapter "Learners' Perception on Integration of Human Personality Types on Mobile Learning Platform"
in: G. Salvendy and J. Wei (Eds.): *Design, Operation and Evaluation of Mobile Communications*, LNCS 12796,
https://doi.org/10.1007/978-3-030-77025-9_27

In the original version the affiliation of the author Kasthuri Subaramaniam was not complete. This has been corrected.

The updated version of this chapter can be found at
https://doi.org/10.1007/978-3-030-77025-9_27

© Springer Nature Switzerland AG 2021
G. Salvendy and J. Wei (Eds.): HCII 2021, LNCS 12796, p. C1, 2021.
https://doi.org/10.1007/978-3-030-77025-9_28

Author Index

Printed in the United States
by Baker & Taylor Publisher Services